D0945294

Innovation and the Development of Flight

INNOVATION

AND THE

DEVELOPMENT

OF FLIGHT

EDITED BY ROGER D. LAUNIUS

Texas A&M University Press
College Station

The paper used in this book meets the minimum requirements
of the American National Standard for Permanence
of Paper for Printed Library Materials, z39.48-1984.
Binding materials have been chosen for durability.
∞

Library of Congress Cataloging-in-Publication Data

Innovation and the development of flight / edited by Roger D. Launius.
     p.   cm.
   Includes index.
   ISBN 0-89096-876-4 (cloth)
   1. Aeronautics—History.   2. Aeronautics—Technological
innovations—History.   3. Flight—History.   I. Launius, Roger D.
TL515.I49   1999
629.13'09—dc21   98-48723
                                                    CIP

FOR V. L.

Contents

Illustrations

Acknowledgments

The authors and I would like to acknowledge the assistance of several individuals who aided in the preparation of this collection of essays. For their many contributions in completing this project I wish especially to thank Lee D. Saegesser, who helped track down information and correct inconsistencies; J. D. Hunley and Stephen J. Garber, both of whom offered valuable advice; Nadine Andreassen, who helped with proofreading and compilation; the staffs of the NASA Headquarters Library and the Scientific and Technical Information Program, who provided assistance in locating materials; and archivists at various presidential libraries and the National Archives and Records Administration, who aided with research efforts.

Also, I wish to acknowledge the following scholars who aided in a variety of ways: John D. Anderson, Roger E. Bilstein, Rebecca Hancock Cameron, Henry C. Dethloff, Andrew Dunar, Robert H. Ferrell, Michael H. Gorn, Charles J. Gross, R. Cargill Hall, Richard P. Hallion, James R. Hansen, Von Hardesty, Perry D. Jamieson, Richard H. Kohn, Sylvia K. Kraemer, W. Henry Lambright, John M. Logsdon, John L. Loos, Howard E. McCurdy, F. Mark McKiernan, and Stephen P. Waring. All of these people would disagree with some conclusions offered here, but such is both the boon and the bane of historical inquiry.

I also wish to thank the authors of the individual articles for their patience and helpfulness. Finally, I extend my thanks to the staff at Texas A&M University Press for their work on this volume.

Innovation and the Development of Flight

Introduction

Patterns of Innovation in Aeronautical Technology

Roger D. Launius

I nnovation—I like the sound of the word. So do most other Americans, although few other cultures are as intrigued by the concept of change. Innovation has long been one of America's highest aims, summarizing the best that we have to offer. With meanings ranging from novel approaches toward anything to the latest fashions or trivial gadgets, it has always been associated with some good and just development.

No society has been more enamored with machines and what they might do for us—or to us—than modern America.[1] If there is one hallmark of the American people, it is their enthusiasm for technology and what it can help them to accomplish. Historian Perry Miller wrote of the Puritans of New England that they "flung themselves in the technological torrent, how they shouted with glee in the midst of the cataract, and cried to each other as they went headlong down the chute that here was their destiny" as they used technology to transform a wilderness into their "City upon a hill."[2] Since that time the United States has been known as a nation of technological system builders who could use this ability to create great machines of wonder. In twentieth-century America, innovation has entered the lexicon of the success story, especially those stories associated with technology.

Perceptive foreigners might be enamored of American political and social developments, with democracy and pluralism, but they are more taken with U.S. technology. The United States is not just the nation of George Washington, Thomas Jefferson, Abraham Lincoln, Frederick Douglas, and Elizabeth Cady Stanton, but also of Thomas Edison, Henry Ford, the Wright brothers, the Tennessee Valley Authority, the Manhattan Project, and Steve Jobs and Apple computers. These innovators reinforced the belief throughout the world that the United States was *the* technological giant among all nations. Until the loss of the *Challenger* space shuttle and a few other embarrassing missteps, NASA and its accomplishments symbolized, more than any other institution, America's technological creativity. That symbolism, misplaced as it might have been all along, accounts more than any other for the difficulties the space agency has felt in the recent past. Every NASA failure raises the question of U.S. technological virtuosity in the world, and because questioning of much American capability in so many other areas is already underway, setbacks in this one are all the more damaging to the American image. American self-doubt has increased with every perceived failure in the space program.[3]

THE POSSIBILITY OF INNOVATION IN AVIATION

For the twentieth century no set of technological innovations is more intriguing than that associated with aviation. The compelling nature of flight and the activities that it has engendered on the part of many peoples and governments make the development of aviation technology an important area of investigation. Perhaps no technological development in this century has more fundamentally transformed human life than the airplane, coupled with its ground support apparatus and infrastructure. The capability for rapid transportation to anyplace in the globe made possible by the airplane brought a see change in the collective mind-set. Flight represented the triumph of humanity over its environment and a triumph over modern machinery which threatened to dictate to Americans their lifestyles. John William Ward, in analyzing the significance of Charles Lindbergh's 1927 solo Atlantic crossing, made a vital point which is applicable here. The ability to fly celebrated "the complex institutions which made modern society possible," the technology and organization then emerging, and reaffirmed an "escape from institutions, from forms of society, and from limitations put upon the free individual."[4] Accordingly, there are many avenues of historical exploration at this juncture. Why did aeronautical technology take the shape it did; which individuals and organizations were involved in driving it; what factors influenced particular choices of scientific objectives and technologies to be used; and what were the political, economic, managerial, international, and cultural contexts in which the events of the aeronautical age have unfolded?

More importantly, how has innovation affected this technology? If there is a folklore in the public mind about the history of aeronautical engineering, it is the story of genius and its role in innovation. Americans love the idea of the lone inventor, especially if that inventor strives against odds to develop some revolutionary piece of technology in a basement or garage. There have been enough instances of this in U.S. history to feed this folklore and allow it to persist. The "Renaissance man" with a broad background who can build a technological system from the ground up permeates this ideal.

Individualism and versatility have characterized this concept of engineering. Its quintessential expression was the Italian painter, sculptor, architect, and engineer Leonardo da Vinci (1452–1519), the leading figure in the technology of his time. It has also been more recently expressed in the work of the American inventor Thomas A. Edison (1847–1931), whose many accomplishments in technology have been seminal for modern life. These same virtuoso expressions of engineering mastery have also been recognized in the work of U.S. aeronautics and rocket pioneers Wilbur and Orville Wright (1871–1948 and 1867–1912, respectively) and Robert H. Goddard (1882–1945), who spent most of their careers as lone researchers. The Wrights secretively developed their flying machine in their native Dayton, Ohio, and tested it on the dunes at Kitty Hawk, North Carolina. Goddard designed and tested ever more sophisticated rockets on a parcel of isolated land near Roswell, New Mexico. Neither sought outside assistance nor welcomed colleagues. Theirs were solitary accomplishments.

Despite these examples that stick in our minds, the "Renaissance man" has never been very common in the history of science and technology, and certainly not in the rise of aeronautics. The kind of lone wolves that make up the folklore, reinforced by the reality of a few bona fide geniuses, are rare indeed. In twentieth-century aeronautical engineering the increasing depth of information in the individual disciplines ensures that no one person can now master the multifarious skills necessary in the research, design, development, and building of a piece of aerospace hardware.

In the latter nineteenth century, leading American engineering educators made a conscious decision to emphasize theoretical engineering issues. Then they had to reintegrate the discipline so that new engineering accomplishments could be realized. The discussion that follows describes this evolutionary process. It is a process that has affected major aspects of public policy ever since, changing fundamentally how individuals perceive "big government" and its management of issues ranging from medicine to nuclear power.[5]

There were two central reasons for this change. The first is relatively easy to comprehend, and it has already been hinted at here: the development of something as complex as an aircraft capable of operating in three dimensions is too large for any one individual to oversee, regardless of how much mastery of however large a body of knowledge might exist in one expert's mind. The breadth and depth of engineering and scientific information is simply too large for any one person to comprehend fully. It must be parceled out and managed through a team approach.

The second reason is more complex, and ultimately more interesting. Before the Second World War, by all accounts, engineering education in the United States was overwhelmingly oriented toward training young engineers in a very practical "shop culture." The orientation of instructors in engineering was not directed toward research and theory, but toward practical application. Where research was conducted, it usually emerged naturally from consulting projects, and focused on the narrow questions informing the consulting work.[6]

This began to change in the first part of the twentieth century as an influx of European engineers came to the United States and brought their educational ethos to the nation's academies. In the aerospace engineering community these included such men as Theodore von Kármán, the brilliant Hungarian aerodynamicist and one of the founders of the Jet Propulsion Laboratory (JPL), who came to the California Institute of Technology in the 1930s. Von Kármán was not only a hard-edged aeronautical engineer, but also a leading theorist who contributed important concepts to aerodynamics.[7] At the same time, the requirements of complex high-technology artifacts required for war prompted the United States to expend for the first time massive amounts of government funding for technology projects. Those with broad-based theoretical implications were most readily funded.[8]

By the end of World War II, however, most engineering in the United States had become so theoretical that much of its practical application was lost on working technicians. Increasingly, it became difficult to distinguish between engineering projects and purely scientific explorations without immediately practical application.[9] The reasons for this change were soon visible in the engineering discipline. American engineering faculty were no longer necessarily experienced in industry's practical needs and had instead made their careers as theoretically oriented researchers who published scholarly papers in journals but did not design and build machines for public use. Two subcultures emerged that were sometimes contradictory and often combative.[10]

The more complex the theoretical foundations, the more complex the components and the less likely that a single individual, or a single genius with some assistants, could carry to successful completion pathbreaking development. Certainly, this was true in aerospace technology, which has since World War II of necessity been a group effort, with various individuals in charge of certain segments of the work under some overall management to keep the effort on track. There might be an overall project manager, but the demands of the project always forced more breadth and depth of knowledge than even geniuses like da Vinci or the Wrights or Goddard could master. Indeed, it might be that the "Renaissance man" was an illusion all along, for complete success was always beyond even the most creative genius's grasp.

For the successful accomplishment of major aeronautical endeavors, engineers have adopted a systems management and integration approach. Each government laboratory, university, and corporate research facility has had differing perspectives on how to go about the tasks of accomplishing these endeavors, but all have parceled work among teams of engineers and scientists.[11] One of the fundamental tenets of the program management concept was that three critical factors—cost, schedule, and reliability—were interrelated, and had to be managed as a group. Many also recognized these factors' constancy; if program managers held cost to a specific level, then one of the other two factors, or both of them to a somewhat lesser degree, would be adversely affected. The schedules, dictated by industrial or political requirements, were often firm. Since aircraft had to accomplish practical tasks, program managers always placed a heavy emphasis on reliability so that failures would be both predictable and minor. The significance of both of these factors has often forced the third factor, cost, much higher than might have otherwise been the case.[12]

To reign in these elements, aeronautical design organizations increasingly became complex bureaucracies exercising centralized authority over design, engineering, procurement, testing, construction, manufacturing, spare parts, logistics, training, and operations. Understanding the management of complex structures for the successful completion of a multifarious task was an important outgrowth of these efforts. Getting all of the personnel elements to work together has always challenged program managers, regardless of whether or not they were civil service, industry, or university personnel.

At the same time, as aircraft became more costly to develop and organizations became more complex to manage the aircraft system—establishing structures to ensure control over the effort—they set up boundaries often impassable for individual innovation. An irony of the first magnitude is that aviation, one of the most technologically driven industries in the United States—one built on a series of pathbreaking innovations—has become so expensive to participate in that firms involved in it can hardly afford to support potentially excellent but perhaps risky ideas and see them to completion. Innovation is difficult in such settings. This has been partially mitigated by efforts in government laboratories and in universities, but too often radical innovations do not find easy acceptance. Not because of a basic aversion but because the risk to cost, schedule, or reliability might be too great.[13]

To be successful in aircraft design, with its rapidly evolving technologies, an organization must be able to stimulate and simulate change, gamble on the future, have a vision that is multifaceted as well as clear as to objectives, and be able to allocate limited resources and to make external allies. It must reward or tolerate risk taking and expect some failures. This is a very tall order when dealing with a system as complex and expensive as aviation, where an airframe manufacturer literally bets the company on any new design that it offers. Caution tends to rule in that very dizzying environment.[14]

The logical outgrowth of this has been a search for what amounts to "command innovation." Can a firm, a government, a university, a research facility, or a person arrange for innovation that will solve some great problem in aeronautical technology? Guaranteeing innovation accounts for not an insignificant quantity of effort in the field. But there seems not to be a formula for such developments, and a guarantee for any research project cannot be assured. History suggests that those who contend otherwise are fools or charlatans or both.

THE INCONSISTENCY OF INNOVATION

The central ingredient of the innovative process in aviation is the set of interrelationships that make up the aeronautical enterprise. Since human beings are at the core of this enterprise, the complexity expands to include chance and nonlinear factors endemic to the real world of people. The challenge for the historian interested in the development of aeronautical innovation is that these complexities make analysis difficult and explanation virtually impossible to understand except for the most probing specialist. The relationships between technological innovation; various aeronautical institutions; innovative concepts, practices, or organizations; and the people associated with each are intrinsically complex. Essentially nonlinear, these relationships allow innovation to take place, no doubt, but there does not seem to be a way to guarantee it. Those who seek to command innovation find that changes in inputs to various aspects of the systems, themselves designed to yield innovative alterations, do not necessarily ensure proportionate positive developments in output. It is nonlinearity writ large.[15]

This did not become apparent to even those involved in directing the aeronautical enterprise until at least World War II. Since then, research fields as diverse as meteorology, the earth sciences, physics, aerodynamics, space sciences, biology, and mathematics have come forward with confirmation of a position first taken by Albert Einstein more than half a century earlier, that the universe was a relative place. Whereas dynamic and exceptionally small systems might have been considered deterministic in orientation beforehand, now they began to be seen as much more complex and virtually unpredictable in their long-term behavior. The rise of "chaos" theory to help explain this unpredictability has fundamentally reshaped the nature of science and engineering in the latter twentieth century. Seemingly unrelated phenomena—the rise and fall of animal species, the origin and mutation of viruses and bacteria, the behavior of the human heart, the dripping of a water faucet, the performance of a superconductor, and a host of other observable occurrences—all bespeak a fundamental unpredictability, or "chaos," in their performance. This nonlinearity seems to be the norm, for as scientists John Briggs and F. David Peat have concluded, predictable dynamics "are in fact exceptions in nature rather than the rule."[16]

Historians interested in innovation in aviation have much to learn from the sciences and their development of chaos theory. First developed as an identifiable unit of scientific theory in the mid-1970s, chaos theory asserts that the universe cannot be understood using standard approaches but only with the acceptance of "nonrandom complicated motions that exhibit a very rapid growth of errors that, despite perfect determinism, inhibits any pragmatic ability to render long-term predictions."[17] The implications of these scientific theories offer profound opportunities for historians by suggesting that the world does not work in a deterministic, automatic fashion. They suggest that to all of the other factors that account for change in history that the discipline has been wrestling with since the beginning of the study of human affairs, we must add literally thousands of other independent variables not previously considered. Accepting that their pursuit is an art, not a science, historians wishing to come to grips with aeronautical innovation must understand and explain the complex interrelationships of institutions and cultures, myriad actions and agendas, technologies and their evolution, the uncertainties of conflict and cooperation in human relations, and the inexactitude of possibilities. This is a task not without difficulties.

THE INNOVATION PROCESS

Notwithstanding the complexity of the innovation process and the inexact and nonlinear nature of it, both those engaged in seeking it and those recording it tend to seek order, clarity, and linearity. This is ultimately a foolhardy goal, and the essays in this volume help to overcome this tendency by embracing the complexity and noting that even the actors in the innovation dramas depicted sometimes did not understand the process. A certain opaqueness of the entire process often seems to be its most salient feature.

Even so, there are important forces acting upon innovation that guide its course and inform its adoption, and these can be approximated, even if they are largely beyond the control of ordinary organizations. One of the most obvious for aeronautics in the United States, although it was also true to a certain extent elsewhere, is geography.[18] The wide expanse of the North American continent necessitated the development of aircraft that could fly higher (safely transiting over great mountain ranges) and farther (coast to coast) and faster (reducing the time required for continental travel) than were required in other parts of the world. The same realities of geography also helped foster a variety of innovations in the support infrastructure, such as more sophisticated navigation equipment, the air traffic control system, and the siting of airfields. Such considerations of geography prompted the early development of rental car agencies as a routine component of the support services provided at U.S. airports. Without them, passengers had no way to complete their journeys. In Europe, where the populations were more tightly compressed and airfields located closer to major urban areas, other methods of transportation, such as trains, were routinely available for the use of disembarking passengers, and the innovation of rental cars came more slowly.

Nowhere did geography play a more important role in shaping the direction of aeronautical innovation than in the American West. The modern West's oases of large urban centers scattered across the vastness of a largely unpopulated land prompted an early embracing of aviation as an efficient means of travel around the region and to the outside. Regional aeronautics contributed to the expansion of vital industrial enterprises, to an infrastructure for air support activities, to significant federal involvement in military and civil air endeavors, and to other air ventures directly affecting the West. Aviation was also politically significant for the West; business and government leaders at every level jockeyed for a piece of the aeronautics pie. Rivalries between cities, between states, and on the national level were important attributes of the development of western aviation.[19]

The geography of the American West, as an especially representative example, shaped the approach toward aeronautical innovation as a social device. For instance, the pioneering heritage of the region ensured that the early western airmail pilots had more of a kinship with Pony Express riders than most have recognized. At the same time aviation contributed significantly to changes in western society. It helped foster urbanization and economic diversification, bringing with it changing social ideas. Aviation moved people into and out of the West more quickly and easily than ever before, in the process exposing the region to new and different influences.[20]

Aeronautical innovation takes place at all levels, at all times, and in all circumstances. Those that have the greatest influence change the context within which flight takes place. By pursuing ever more efficient fuels, the increasing sophistication of airfields, or the development of the jet engine, those involved in aeronautics reshaped the nature of flight and opened new possibilities for the future of the airplane and its support infrastructure. This type of aeronautical innovation, therefore, is more than the incorporation of new equipment and technical know-how into the existing system; it is the fundamental reshaping of the enterprise.

This type of innovation, revolutionary and fundamental as it is, appears to require the vision of one or more aggressive leaders who see a better way and press its implementation. In every instance in this book, innovation required the insistence on its adoption by forceful leaders. Whether it was General H. H. Arnold compelling American industry to develop on a crash basis a jet engine or the Wright brothers teaching the world to fly, revolutionary aeronautical innovation required leadership that could navigate the channels of the complex systems in place throughout the enterprise. Those systems have been largely resistant to revolutionary innovation and suspicious of even incremental change.

Not all revolutionary innovations achieve adoption. Eugene L. Vidal's visionary plan for making aircraft as generally available in America as automobiles in the 1930s fell to pieces amid political and technological and personality-driven crises. Likewise, Samuel Langley's reputation was destroyed by his very public failure to achieve the revolutionary innovation of flight in 1903 despite both his best efforts and his other contributions to the advancement of science. Other revolutionary innovations were successful to the extent that they were demonstrable, but the leadership did not exist to win their acceptance by the enterprise. For instance, Ernst Heinkel's rocket-powered aircraft in the 1930s was decidedly revolutionary and might have altered the course of World War II in Germany's favor had it been embraced by the Luftwaffe. Vidal, Langley, and Heinkel had the vision but not the leadership or technical or creative skills necessary to ensure the adoption of their revolutionary ideas.

Most innovation, at least in aeronautics, is not revolutionary. Instead it necessitates a complex process in which the idea moves from conceptualization through development and testing to gradual implementation. Every step of the way, those advocating adoption negotiate the hazards of organizational cultures, strategic requirements, political priorities, and competing positions. This type of evolutionary innovation takes place over a much more gradual period during which equipment, ideas, and approaches to problems change. Examples of this include Graham Edgar of the Ethyl Gasoline Corporation, working on a standardized rating system for aviation fuel, the routine development of airfields, and how they operated and the services they provided; and Frederick Rentschler at Pratt & Whitney, methodically improving the performance of reciprocating engines over the course of two decades. These innovations do not necessarily look like innovations at all, but year by year they pile up so that cumulatively they achieve dramatic proportions for the progress of aviation.

Whether innovation in aviation was revolutionary or evolutionary, and this book includes examples of both, several ingredients seem to have been present in the process. One of these is a specificity to a problem requiring solution that would afford significant advantages to aviation in general and to the person or institution solving it in particular. Nothing is more important than having a concrete problem to work on; its presence ensures innovation. Lack of understanding of a problem to solve ensures wasted energy. The National Advisory Committee for Aeronautics' (NACA) routine involvement of the aircraft manufacturers in helping to define its research and development agenda, as described in Deborah Douglas's essay in this volume, cinched the NACA's grasp of practical problems deserving its attention, which helped to make the agency into one of the most valuable engines of innovation on the American aviation scene in the first half of the twentieth century.[21] One precondition for significant aeronautical innovation, therefore, is the recognition by aeronautical institutions of tangible problems requiring timely solutions.

Another critical factor in successful aeronautical innovation is the institutional culture in which the innovation is hatched and promulgated. Every human institution has a culture, best characterized as the intellectual, professional, and traditional values of its members. This culture has its share of positives and negatives and acts as both blinders and spectacles in dealing with any problem. The complexity of institutions has caused them to be little understood, even by those who are a part of them. Indeed, outsiders sometimes are more capable of deciphering the nuances of institutional culture than those living in the midst of it, but even for them difficulties remain.[22]

Organizations tend to value certain ideas and approaches that become steeped over time in tradition and ritual. Pratt & Whitney emphasized propeller research and development through World War II, pooh-poohing the possibilities of jet engines, because of its tradition of excellence in reciprocating engine technology. Only in crisis did it abandon its traditional approach and pursue jet engine innovation. The same largely held true for the National Advisory Committee for Aeronautics, whose research in aerodynamics before World War II had been pathbreaking but whose interest in propulsion was at best sporadic and its involvement in jet engines almost nonexistent. Boeing's attempt to hang on to stick and wood construction materials for aircraft may have been acceptable from a technological perspective, but the company's culture demanded it despite the fact that the technology in the 1920s had moved to other materials. Eventually Boeing had to do so as well.[23]

To some extent, adhering to traditional methods and ideas is understandable. It is the real-life equivalent of "dancing with the one that brought you," that is, staying with practices that brought success before and perhaps sustained the institution in others times of crisis. But without the ability to innovate, eventual failure of the entire institution will be assured as well. This seems to be where leadership comes in, and its vision can turn around institutions and reform them for new realities.[24]

AIRCRAFT TECHNOLOGY AND INNOVATION

Aviation technology has long provided ample promise for innovation, but at no time has it determined the process of change. At every step of the way options presented themselves to those involved in developing new technology. The choice of options helped to shape the course of aeronautics, along with thousands of other choices made by designers at other locations. Gradually a consensus emerged to move in a certain direction with the technology. It did not emerge without complex interactions carried out, differing ideas expressed, mutually exclusive models built, and minority positions eventually destroyed. Such processes are at the heart of what Walter Vincenti called the "variation-selection model" of technological change, as several possible answers to aeronautical problems are shaped by a host of technical and nontechnical considerations.[25]

The adoption of retractable landing gear is a case in point. Seemingly in retrospect so logical an innovation to be incorporated into aircraft, its virtues were not nearly so self-evident to engineers working on the problem of streamlining aircraft in the 1930s. There were genuine trade-offs between safety and reliability of retractable landing gear versus the drag produced by fixed gear. Manufacturers dealt with the problem in a variety of ways. Some skirted the gear to reduce drag. Others built systems that retracted the gear partially. Still others constructed elaborate retractable systems. The industry's standard fix for this problem emerged only after intense competition and remarkable machinations.[26]

To a very real extent, aeronautical innovation is an example of heterogeneous engineering, which recognizes that technological issues are simultaneously organizational, economic, social, cultural, political, and on occasion irrational. Various interests often clash in the decision-making process as difficult calculations have to be made. A complex web or system of ties between various people, institutions, and interests shaped aircraft and its support apparatus as they eventually evolved.[27] When these came together they made it possible to develop aircraft that satisfied the majority of the priorities brought into the process of development by the various parties concerned with the issue, but they always left some concerns untamed.

AN OVERVIEW OF THIS VOLUME

The essays in this collection survey twelve major areas in the development of aviation and describe the process of innovation, broadly construed. They include discussions of innovation on command and as serendipity, innovation in aircraft and their systems, innovation in support structures, and innovation in aeronautical policy processes and ideology. As such they provide a useful collection of case studies in aeronautical innovation that will provide the foundations for continued exploration of this field.

In some respects this volume represents an attempt to coalesce a "New Aviation History." Like the "New Western History" or the "New Social History," this approach represents a significant transformation that has been taking place in the field. Specifically, this "New Aviation History" is committed to relating the subject to the larger issues of society, politics, and culture, taking a more sophisticated view of the technology than historians previously held. In the past, many writers on aviation history expressed a fascination with the machinery, which has been largely anthropomorphized and often seen as "magical."[28]

This "New Aviation History" moves beyond a fetish for the artifact to emphasize the broader role of the airplane and, more importantly, the whole technological system, including not just the vehicle but also the other components that make up the aviation climate, as an integral part of the human experience. This is not to be understood as lacking an interest in the artifact, being artifactless, or going beyond the artifact. Rather, it is an affirmation that one moves through reason and study to a larger understanding. It suggests that many unanswered questions concerning the development of modern aviation remain, and that inquisitive individuals seek to know that which they do not understand. This assumption arises in the work of historians and is based on their understanding of humans, for technological systems are constructions of the human mind (or minds).

Critiques of the reification of the artifact in aviation history have largely fallen on deaf ears in the past. Perhaps the influence of buffs is too strong; perhaps some extraordinary features of the technology seduce staid historians so that they "go native" and lose perspective on the human and social forces that are the true essence of technology. Perhaps because of this, most of the sophisticated work done in aviation history to date has come from outside of aviation history. The one part of aviation history that has received sustained, repeated, high-quality treatment from trained, professional historians—the political causes and effects of strategic bombing—has been addressed by military historians. And in the more restricted topic of the history of aviation technology, much of the strongest theoretically motivated work is by more general historians of technology dabbling in aviation.[29]

This "New Aviation History" emphasizes, therefore, research in aviation and aerospace topics that are no longer limited to the vehicle-centered, internalist style of aviation history. Many of the recommendations that historian James R. Hansen suggested in a historiographical article in *Technology and Culture* are beginning to come to fruition; this work is tangible evidence of the changes being made on the technology side of the proverbial aviation history "house."[30]

The dozen chapters that follow relate directly to this development in aviation history by exploring specific elements of the innovation question. A major theme in the essays is the innovative process not only in the development of aircraft components and systems but also in the formation of aviation's invisible infrastructure and its relationships to the aircraft. Several of the contributions, for instance, concentrate on the support system that surrounds the aircraft and emphasize linkages between the technological system that flies in the air and the infrastructure left on the ground that makes it possible to fly in the air. Innovation took place, the writers of these essays remind us, not merely in the visible progress of aerodynamics, engines, fuels, other components, and reliability of aircraft but also in a hidden infrastructure ranging from metallurgy and testing to operational support. They assert that the revolutionary rate of innovation in aircraft would not have been possible without the invisible infrastructure that enabled innovation to be converted into functional reality.

Taken altogether, this collection presents the first tentative explorations of major themes in innovative aviation technology. As such it builds on much effort that has gone before.

NOTES

1. This is the theme of the seminal study by Thomas P. Hughes, *American Genesis: A Century of Invention and Technological Enthusiasm, 1870–1970* (New York: Viking, 1989). For a broader perspective, see Lewis Mumford, *The Myth of the Machine*, 3 vols. (New York: Harcourt Brace Jovanovich, 1967–70).

2. Perry Miller, "The Responsibility of a Mind in a Civilization of Machines," *The American Scholar* 31 (Winter 1961–62): 51–69.

3. Hughes, *American Genesis*, p. 2.

4. John William Ward, "The Meaning of Lindbergh's Flight," *American Quarterly* 10 (Spring 1958): 3–16, quotation from p. 15.

5. Malcolm L. Goggin, ed., *Governing Science and Technology in a Democracy* (Knoxville: University of Tennessee Press, 1986); Manfred Stanley, *The Technological Conscience: Survival and Dignity in an Age of Expertise* (New York: Free Press, 1978); Sylvia Doughty Fries, "Expertise against Politics: Technology as Ideology on Capitol Hill, 1966–1972," *Science, Technology, & Human Values* 8 (Spring

1983): 6–15; David McKay, *Domestic Policy and Ideology: Presidents and the American State, 1964–1987* (Cambridge, Eng.: Cambridge University Press, 1989).

6. See Monte Calvert, *The Mechanical Engineer in America, 1830–1910: Professional Cultures in Conflict* (Baltimore, Md.: Johns Hopkins University Press, 1967).

7. On von Kármán's life see Theodore von Kármán, with Lee Edson, *The Wind and Beyond: Theodore von Kármán, Pioneer in Aviation and Pathfinder in Space* (Boston: Little, Brown, 1967); and Michael H. Gorn, *The Universal Man: Theodore von Kármán's Life in Aeronautics* (Washington, D.C.: Smithsonian Institution Press, 1992).

8. See Paul L. Hanle, *Bringing Aerodynamics to America* (Cambridge, Mass.: MIT Press, 1982).

9. This is the thesis of the important article by Bruce Seely, "Research, Engineering, and Science in American Engineering Colleges, 1900–1960," *Technology and Culture* 34 (Apr. 1993): 344–86.

10. See Terry Reynolds, *Seventy-Five Years of Progress: A History of the American Institute of Chemical Engineers* (New York: American Institute of Chemical Engineers, 1983), pp. 62–63.

11. For examples of how this worked in three aeronautical examples, see F. Robert van der Linden, *The Boeing 247: The First Modern Airliner* (Seattle: University of Washington Press, 1991); Clive Irving, *Wide-body: The Triumph of the 747* (New York: William Morrow, 1993); Karl Sabbagh, *Twenty-First Jet: The Making and Marketing of the Boeing 777* (New York: Scribners, 1996).

12. Aaron Cohen, "Project Management: JSC's Heritage and Challenge," *Issues in NASA Program and Project Management* (Washington, D.C.: NASA SP-6101, 1989), pp. 7–16; C. Thomas Newman, "Controlling Resources in the Apollo Program," *Issues in NASA Program and Project Management* (Washington, D.C.: NASA SP-6101, 1989), pp. 23–26; Eberhard Rees, "Project and Systems Management in the Apollo Program," *Issues in NASA Program and Project Management* (Washington, D.C.: NASA SP-6101 [02], 1989), pp. 24–34.

13. This was certainly the case with the revolution in flight deck displays of the 1970s and 1980s. Although it was demonstrated in NASA research laboratories, American firms balked at exploiting the new technology until Airbus adopted it for its airliners. See Lane E. Wallace, *Airborne Trailblazer: Two Decades with NASA Langley's 737 Flying Laboratory* (Washington, D.C.: NASA SP-4216, 1994), pp. 25–39.

14. The complexity of this business climate is explored in detail, and with real ingenuity, in John Newhouse, *The Sporty Game* (New York: Alfred A. Knopf, 1983).

15. The complexity of nonlinearity in historical study has been discussed in its larger context in Bryan D. Palmer, *Descent into Discourse: The Reification of Language and the Writing of Social History* (Philadelphia, Pa.: Temple University Press, 1990), pp. 188–206; Brook Thomas, *The New Historicism, and Other Old-Fashioned Topics* (Princeton, N.J.: Princeton University Press, 1991), pp. 24–50; Peter Novick, *The Noble Dream: The "Objectivity Question" and the American Historical Profession* (New York: Cambridge University Press, 1988), pp. 415–628, passim.

16. John Briggs and F. David Peat, *Turbulent Mirror: An Illustrated Guide to Chaos Theory and the Science of Wholeness* (New York: Random House, 1989), p. 110.

17. Mitchell J. Feigenbaum, in Heinz-Otto Peitgen, Hartmut Jürgens, and Dietmar Saupe, eds., *Chaos and Fractals: New Frontiers of Science* (New York: Springer Verlag, 1992), p. 6.

18. This has also been observed in the area of military technology. See the pathbreaking work by Williamson Murray, "Innovation: Past and Future," in Williamson Murray and Allan R. Millett, eds., *Military Innovation in the Interwar Period* (Cambridge, Eng.: Cambridge University Press, 1996), pp. 304–305.

19. Jessie L. Embry and I have argued these points in a series of articles. See "Fledgling Wings: Aviation Comes to the Southwest, 1910–1930," *New Mexico Historical Review* 70 (Jan. 1995): 1–27; "A Transforming Force: Military Aviation and Utah in World War II," *Utah Historical Review* 63 (Summer 1995): 222–40; "The 1910 Los Angeles Airshow: The Beginnings of Air Awareness in the West," *Southern California Quarterly* 77 (Winter 1996): 329–46; "Cheyenne versus Denver: City Rivalry and

the Quest for Transcontinental Air Routes," *Annals of Wyoming: The Wyoming History Journal* 68 (Summer 1996): 8–23.

20. John Keegan, *Fields of Battle: The Wars for North America* (New York: Alfred A. Knopf, 1995), pp. 315–34.

21. See Roger D. Launius, "'Never Was Life More Interesting': The National Advisory Committee for Aeronautics, 1936–1945," *Prologue: Quarterly of the National Archives* 24 (Winter 1992): 361–73.

22. Case studies of various institutional cultures can be found in Samuel P. Huntington, *The Soldier and the State: The Theory and Politics of Civil-Military Relations* (Cambridge, Mass.: Harvard University Press, 1957); Herbert Kaufman, *The Forest Ranger* (Baltimore, Md.: Johns Hopkins University Press, 1960); Anthony Downs, *Inside Bureaucracy* (Boston: Little, Brown, 1967); Edgar H. Schein, ed., *Organizational Culture and Leadership* (San Francisco, Calif.: Jossey-Bass, 1985); J. Stephen Ott, *The Organizational Culture Imperative* (Chicago: Dorsey, 1989); Herbert Kaufman, *Times, Chance, and Organization: Natural Selection in a Perilous Environment* (Chatham, N.J.: Chatham House, 1991 ed.).

23. Virginia P. Dawson, "The American Turbojet Industry and British Competition: The Mediating Influence of Government Research," in William M. Leary, ed., *From Airships to Airbus: The History of Civil and Commercial Aviation*, vol. 1, *Infrastructure and Environment* (Washington, D.C.: Smithsonian Institution Press, 1995), pp. 127–50; Launius, "'Never Was Life More Interesting,'" pp. 369–70; Charles D. Bright, "Machine Tools and the Aircraft Industry: The Boeing Case," *Journal of the West* 30 (Jan. 1991): 50–57; Eric M. Schatzberg, "Ideology and Technical Choice: The Decline of the Wooden Airplane in the United States, 1920–1945," *Technology and Culture* 35 (Jan. 1994): 34–69.

24. This is never easily accomplished, however. Throughout the 1980s American businesses sought to change the way in which they conducted their work and viewed their responsibilities. Some were successful, others failed, most accommodated to a greater or lesser degree. All tried to deal with the institutional culture of their organizations, a task that always proved difficult. As a result management consultants took center stage as never before and a succession of corporate reform handbooks and seminars circulated through the business world.

25. Walter G. Vincenti, *What Engineers Know and How They Know It: Analytical Studies from Aeronautical History* (Baltimore, Md.: Johns Hopkins University Press, 1990), chapter 8.

26. Walter G. Vincenti, "The Retractable Airplane Landing Gear and the Northrop 'Anomaly': Variation-Election and the Shaping of Technology," *Technology and Culture* 35 (Jan. 1994): 1–33.

27. John Law, "Technology and Heterogeneous Engineering: The Case of Portuguese Expansion," pp. 111–34, and Donald MacKenzie, "Missile Accuracy: A Case Study in the Social Processes of Technological Change," pp. 195–222, both in Wiebe E. Bijker, Thomas P. Hughes, and Trevor J. Pinch, eds., *The Social Construction of Technological Systems: New Directions in the Sociology and History of Technology* (Cambridge, Mass.: MIT Press, 1987).

28. This still seems very much the case, in spite of a concerted effort by professional historians to move in a more scholarly direction. For instance, the only journal in the United States dedicated exclusively to aviation history, the *American Aviation Historical Society Journal*, for all of its very positive attributes, is focused almost totally on the evolution of the artifact.

29. I do not want to make too much of this point and must note that there are some first-class earlier studies that prove the exception to the rule. For instance, Roger E. Bilstein's dissertation from the mid-1960s was published as the seminal *Flight Patterns: Trends of Aeronautical Development in the United States, 1918–1929* (Athens: University of Georgia Press, 1983). In it Bilstein wrestled with the meaning of aviation in the decade and set a standard for later historians to emulate. This work might be appropriately considered one of the pioneers of the "New Aviation History."

30. James R. Hansen, "Aviation History in the Wider Context," *Technology and Culture* 30 (Fall 1989): 643–49.

CHAPTER 1

The Langley and Wright Aero Accidents

Two Responses to Early Aeronautical Innovation and Government Patronage

NORRISS S. HETHERINGTON

I n the crisis of confidence following the grounding of the space shuttle and the discovery that the space telescope was flawed, a modicum of historical perspective on the nature of technological innovation would have provided valuable understanding to the American public and helped in the forging of public policy. A particularly useful case study contrasts responses to the Langley and Wright aero accidents nearly a century ago, illuminating the trials and tribulations inherent in early aeronautical innovation and the attendant problem of government patronage for scientific and technological research in a democracy.

Samuel Pierpont Langley's failed effort saw the government's investment in aeronautical innovation repaid many times over in public ridicule. On 8 December 1903 his aerodrome plunged into the Potomac River, unleashing upon the hapless inventor the wrath of both the press and politicians. Although the War Department had excellent reasons to hope for eventual success, in the wake of congressional criticism the department prudently decided not to provide additional funding for Langley's experiment. Less than five years later, on 17 September 1908, a trial flight by Orville Wright at Fort Myer, outside Washington, D.C., ended in a bloody disaster: the machine was a total wreck, the passenger never regained consciousness, and Orville was in serious condition but expected to live. Less had ruined Langley. This time, however, influential publications called for patience and urged — successfully — that the War Department extend the time for the Wrights' trial flights. Much had changed in only a handful of years, and in that change is a lesson for our current generation.

LANGLEY'S EXPERIMENTAL AERODROME

Langley, secretary of the Smithsonian Institution, was one of America's most respected scientists. His experiments to determine what amount of mechanical power was needed to sustain a given weight in the air and make it advance at a given speed "gave the sanction of high scientific authority to a line of investigation theretofore despised and left to 'cranks.'"[1] The *New York Times* noted that "the question [of manned flight] is passing from the domain of visionary inventions into the field of realities — we really seem to be on the verge of one of the greatest discoveries. It would be a glory to our century if the true principles were put in action before A.D. 1900."[2]

Langley had models with engines by March 1893, and in November and December he made several attempts to launch one of these machines, all without success. In 1894 a new launching device put the machine into the air, only to reveal that it was too unbalanced to fly. Adjustments followed, but to little immediate effect. Langley persevered into 1895, when model number 5, with a wingspan of thirteen feet, remained in the air for 7.2 seconds and advanced a distance of 123 feet. Real success, however, came only after yet further modifications and another year of experimenting. On 6 May 1896, model number 5 flew for 120 seconds, traveling approximately 3,300 feet in a spiral path, completing two turns and starting a third. It had climbed steadily, to a height estimated at between 70 and a 100 feet.[3] Alexander Graham Bell, famous for the invention of the telephone, witnessed the flight and corroborated Langley's report to the scientific world.[4]

Langley and the War Department

By 1897 Langley had successfully flown small models nearly a mile. But now, in his sixties, he was ready to pass on to others the task of building and flying a full-scale, manned aerodrome. The next step most likely would have to come without assistance from the federal government. Beginning as early as 1822 with a petition requesting a monopoly on the right to fly in the atmosphere pressing on the United States, Congress had considered various petitions and bills calling for appropriations to enable inventors to carry on experiments and to construct flying machines. Few of the bills were voted upon, and none were enacted.[5] Langley's model aerodrome flights in 1896 heightened public enthusiasm for aviation, but Congress declined to enact a bill granting him aid for further experiments on aerial navigation. The aging Langley, advised by his physician that resumption of concentrated thought and vigorous endeavor would materially shorten his life, had little hope of financial aid from Congress, and his retirement from aeronautics was imminent.

Fig. 1.1. Samuel Pierpont Langley, secretary of the Smithsonian Institution and internationally renowned scientist. His work on flight was pathbreaking, but he failed to complete a controlled powered flight. Courtesy NASA

Langley's retirement from aeronautics, if indeed he did retire, was brief. In less than a year, circumstances related to the Spanish-American War led Langley to attempt the construction of a flying machine of such power that it would carry a man. On 25 March 1898, Langley's assistant secretary at the Smithsonian Institution and eventually his successor, Charles D. Walcott, met with Theodore Roosevelt, then assistant secretary of the navy.[6] It is not known at whose initiative the meeting was held, or if Langley was aware of the meeting. Walcott described to Roosevelt Langley's aerodrome, weighing thirty pounds, with a thirteen-foot wingspan and a tiny steam-driven engine. Two years earlier the model had flown for a minute and a half, covering a distance of over half a mile.

The result of the meeting was a memorandum from Roosevelt to the secretary of the navy pointing out that "the machine has worked. It seems to me worthwhile for this government to try whether it will not work on a large enough scale to be of use in the event of war." War was close. Two weeks earlier, with military preparations already underway, Congress had voted $50 million for national defense; a month later, Congress declared war on Spain. Roosevelt proposed a board composed of naval officers of scientific attainments, army representatives, and civilian authorities to make recommendations as to the practicability of constructing a flying machine and — anticipating a positive answer — to submit estimates of the cost. It was, Roosevelt wrote, "well worth doing."[7]

The board agreed. They found "reasonable ground" for believing that a full-size machine could be built capable of carrying a man for several hours and also light explosives to drop on an enemy's camp or fleet. An airplane could be used for reconnaissance, for communication, and as an engine of offense. By now Langley was actively involved in the discussions and had furnished an estimate of $50,000 for experiments. The board, realizing that Langley's machine would not immediately be a complete success and that modifications and improvements would be necessary, found his estimate reasonable. The secretary of the navy added his comments on what European nations were doing in aviation and sent the recommendation on to the Board of Construction. There it died. The reason given was that such an apparatus pertained strictly to the land service and not to the navy.

The army was not so constrained by this qualification, and the Board of Ordnance and Fortification of the U.S. Army gave Langley $25,000 for research in November, after the end of hostilities but before the peace treaty officially ending the war with Spain. The army gave Langley the other half of the required $50,000 the next year, after the navy had withdrawn. It was a large amount for aeronautical research, but only one tenth of one percent of the congressional authorization for national defense on 9 March 1898, preceding the outbreak of war, and a mere two one-hundredths of one percent of the estimated $250 million total cost of the war with Spain.[8]

Government patronage for aeronautical research, from the Board of Ordnance and Fortifications and without direct congressional authorization, coincided with a peak of public optimism regarding the possibility of heavier-than-air flight and a sense of urgency driven by war. The war quickly ended, however, and optimism faded as the new century dawned with heavier-than-air flight seemingly no closer to realization. The *New York Times*, which earlier had anticipated manned heavier-than-air flight as the crowning glory of the nineteenth century, greeted the twentieth century in a less optimistic mood. Man dreamed of flight, but "everything thus far attempted in the way of aerial navigation has assumed a mathematical impossibility as its starting point and a mechanical paradox as its objective."[9]

Aviation was leading to jokes, and satire can be the most devastating of criticisms. The humor magazine *Puck*, read widely in the United States as well as in Great Britain, had an individual asking a friend when he would fly. "Just as soon as I can get the laws of gravitation repealed," was the answer.[10] Langley's progress with War Department money, insufficient to restore lost optimism, furnished material for more jokes. A newspaper headline on 9 August 1903 reported "Airship as a Submarine."

A quarter-size model with wings nearly six feet long had flown without a human pilot for 27 seconds, for a distance of about 1,000 feet — generously reported in the press as 1,500 feet — before a steering gear defect and engine trouble (the latter problem unknown to the press) sent the machine into the Potomac River. Charles Manly, Langley's assistant, insisted that the experiment was entirely successful: all the data sought were obtained and no essential parts injured. In fact, Manly had wanted to make another test flight immediately after the ducking, but had not been able to get the engine to work properly before a strong wind sprang up.[11]

However favorable the gloss, or spin, that Manly attempted to place on the August flight in his statement to newspaper reporters, the public was not satisfied, and Langley felt obliged to make a statement. He regretted the publicity for this initial experiment. On previous trials, success had been reached only after initial failures. "The fullest publicity," he promised, "consistent with the National interest (since these recent experiments have for their object the development of a machine for war purposes) will be given to this work when it reaches a stage which warrants publication."[12]

A defender of Langley accused the newspapers of pouring vials of their wrath on Langley for not letting reporters photograph ("kodak") the machine (a soldier from the War Department had tried to cover the wreck with cloth when it was pulled from the Potomac) and for not satisfying the newspapers' impertinent curiosity. Langley was not a mere scientist, but a government agent, supplied with government money for the purpose of perfecting a machine which the government might use as a substitute for its present armaments.[13]

Money was running out. Langley had gone through the original $50,000 from the War Department and more from a special fund of the Smithsonian Institution. He also may have obtained additional assistance from the War De-

Fig. 1.2. The Langley Aerodrome "A" on the houseboat in the Potomac River just prior to being unsuccessfully launched on 7 October 1903. Courtesy NASA

partment, though the record is not clear on this point. In the Fortification Act of 6 June 1902, Congress had appropriated $100,000 for tests of the most effective guns and other implements and engines of war, and the War Department may have stretched the latter category to include Langley's flying machine.

Repeated and discouraging failures during the summer of 1903 raised doubts over the propriety of spending more money on Langley's experiments. In September he asked for more money. He explained his ideas fully and convincingly. Newspapers, still generally favorable to his efforts, thought that the Board of Ordnance probably would accede to Langley's request.[14]

On 7 October 1903, all was ready for the great test of the full-size man-carrying flyer. Manly started the engine, gradually raised its speed to maximum, took a last survey of the machine, and gave the order to release. The machine rushed down its track—impressively and majestically, according to witnesses. But on reaching the end of the launch track, it plunged sharply downward, demolishing the front wings as it struck the water. Manly grasped the main guy-wires above his head, pulled himself through the narrow space between them, freeing himself from the machine, and swam upward as rapidly as possible. The first thing he saw was a newspaper reporter, his boatman exerting every effort to be the first to reach the wreck.

Manly did not want to make any statement until a complete examination determined the cause of the crash and the extent of the damage, but the press representatives threatened to write their own conclusions if Manly didn't give them a statement. He asked for understanding that the test was entirely an experiment and the first of its kind ever made. The balancing, based upon tests of models, had proved to be incorrect, but only an actual trial of the full-size machine itself could determine this. Manly remained confident of the future success of the work. Any further information must await a formal report to Langley.[15]

Newspapers reported a "Flying Machine Fiasco." The experiment, carefully planned and delayed for months, was a complete failure. The airship had been carried a hundred yards by its own momentum before falling into the river, a total wreck. At no time was there any semblance of flight. Manly escaped with only a ducking. An official statement, asserting confidence in ultimate success, admitted that the experiment had been unsuccessful.[16] The *Washington Post* report was especially caustic, noting that Langley's costly contrivance was unable to take wing, and that "the 'flying-machine' over which a force of government-paid scientists has been working for ten years—was as incapable of flight as a dancing-pavilion floor. Confronted by a defeat so evident, the experts did not attempt to explain away their failure. They just threw up their hands. The once pretty and artistic-looking airship was little more than a bedraggled pile of torn rags and kindling-wood, with an apparent value of a dollar. Its ruination was complete."[17] Newspapers had turned hostile—some with a measured tone of regret, others gleefully.

The unsuccessful outcome of Langley's experiment probably was the major reason for the changed attitude, though newspapers also may have become prejudiced against Langley because of the expense of maintaining special correspondents at inconvenient places on the Potomac River and because of Langley's greater anxiety for the outcome of his experiments than for the comfort of the correspondents.[18] Langley's focus on results was admirable, but his disdain for public relations was myopic. In the absence of immediate and stunning technological success, unlikely in such a venture and certainly unanticipated by Langley after so many years of trial flights, favorable public perception of the endeavor and its eventual prospects was crucial.

After recovering and examining the aerodrome, Manly and Langley were convinced that the accident had been caused by a fault in the launching gear, which had drawn the aerodrome abruptly downward at the moment of release and cast it into the water. The machine was little damaged, and it might be possible to attempt another flight before the onset of bad weather. The aerodrome was repaired by the middle of November. Finally the wind quieted down, on 8 December 1903, making possible a second attempt at flight, even though the river was full of large blocks of floating ice. It was now or never. Langley had exhausted his War Department funds and had used as much Smithsonian money as he felt he could. There was nothing left to meet continuing expenses if the test were postponed.

Once again Manly started the engine, brought it to full speed, and gave the signal to release. The aerodrome started down the track. Something seemed to happen to the machine just before it reached the end of the launching track. A photographer for the *Washington Star* caught the aerodrome just after launch in a vertical position. It had shot upward, perhaps because the rudder had become entangled in the launching track. Then the aerodrome fell backward. Manly swung himself around and hung by his arms, so that in striking the water with the machine on top of him he would land feet first. The floor of the aviator's car pressing on his head prevented him from surfacing, and his cork-lined jacket, caught on the fittings of the framework, preventing him from diving downward. He managed to rip the jacket in two, dive under the machine, and swim some distance away under water, only to come up under a block of ice. Another dive got Manly free of the ice, but now directly in the path of the houseboat that served as the launching platform. Manly, with the assistance of a rowboat, reached the houseboat, where he was pulled from the water and helped into warm, dry clothing.[19]

The second attempt and second failure, on 8 December 1903, further eroded public confidence. The fruit of months of study, labor, and a great expenditure of money again disappeared beneath the water. Army support wavered. Newspapers reported that U.S. Army officers were saying that Langley's aerodrome was not properly planned for flight; the officers judged the propeller too small and faulted the lack of controls for the wings. Continuation of support from the fund for miscellaneous encouragement of defensive inventions would depend on the success of a third test.[20]

The Political Cost of Failure

Langley, however, was not to make another test. Damage from the December failure was complete—to the plane, to Langley's hopes, and to his reputation. The *New York Times* concluded that Langley was not a mechanic and his mathematics was better adapted to astronomy than to calculating the strength of materials and mechanical stresses. The editors hoped "that Prof. Langley will not put his substantial greatness as a scientist further in peril by continuing to waste his time, and the money involved, in further wasting experiments." Other papers were less restrained. One suggested that if only Langley had launched his airship bottom-side up, it would have gone into the air instead of down into the water. Another newspaper, hitting the downed Langley and the soaring cost of living with one stone, lamented, "If Professor Langley had only thought to hitch his airship to the price of beef!" Ambrose Bierce, soon to publish his pessimistic and satirical *The Cynic's Word Book*, later retitled *The Devil's Dictionary*, wrote: "I don't know how much larger Professor Langley's machine is than its flying model was—about large enough, I think, to require an atmosphere a little denser than the intelligence of one scientist and not quite so dense as that of two." The *Washington Post* continued to express its concern over the waste of public funds and called for a withdrawal of the government from all further participation in the financial and scientific calamities of the Langley flying machine. Perhaps most devastating to Langley's reputation was a satirical cartoon in the *Post* showing Langley's aerodrome rescued from the water by mariners, and the pilot, Manly, in diving gear. Langley, the professor standing alongside, was wearing a top hat, his head turned and eyes covered to avoid the sad sight. He had studied buzzards in flight to help design the aerodrome, and so it was depicted in the cartoon, draped over a barrel with water pouring from its mouth.[21]

Congressman Robinson of Indiana on 24 January 1904 charged that "Here is $100,000 of the people's money wasted on this scientific aerial navigation experiment because some man, perchance a professor wandering in his dreams, was able to impress the [military] officers that his aerial scheme had some utility." The military had twisted the construction of the congressional appropriation; it was a system of enlargement running wild. The other topic of house censorship that day was the waste of War Department money on French novels and books of no value.[22]

The War Department report on Langley's trials, dated 6 January 1904, shortly before the congressional criticism, concluded that unfortunate accidents had prevented any test of the apparatus in free flight. The claim that an engine-driven, man-carrying aerodrome had been constructed still lacked the proof of actual flight. It seemed desirable to obtain conclusive proof of the possibility of free flight, and there were excellent reasons to hope for success. Even after a successful test, though, years of constant work and the expenditure of thousands of dollars would be necessary to produce an apparatus of practical utility. On 3 March 1904, after the outburst of congressional criticism, the Board of Ordnance and Fortification decided that it was "not prepared to make an additional allotment at this time." Years later, in 1908, the board would report to the secretary of war that "Doctor Langley considered it desirable to continue the experiments, but the Board deemed it advisable, largely in view of the adverse opinions expressed in Congress and elsewhere, to suspend operations in this direction."[23] Had the board not suspended its aeronautical operations, now under congressional attack, its yearly appropriation for general experimental work might have been curtailed.

In the aftermath of the Langley fiasco there was no public clamor to devote more government money in the uncertain quest for elusive innovation. Nor was any government agency eager to begin a new project that might recall to mind the previous waste. Langley's laboratory, now closed down, stood as "a silent monument to the political hazards of aeronautical research." The ghost of Langley reminded men in Washington of the uncertain outcome of research aimed at innovation and the political vulnerability of government patronage for such research. For years after Langley's death in 1906, whenever aeronautics was mentioned in Congress, "some gray-haired Senator would whisper 'Remember Langley,' and that ended the talk about all things aerial at the Capitol."[24]

Enthusiastic expectations for aeronautical progress at the end of the nineteenth century, coupled with Langley's initial achievements in powered flight and the outbreak of war, had created a brief window of opportunity. Through this window had slipped a favorable decision for government funding of scientific research. Langley's grant from the Board of Ordnance and Fortifications was not a direct, explicit congressional appropriation or authorization, but it was government money. Langley's research constituted a potential turning point in the relationship between science and the federal government. Had his manned aerodrome soared into the sky rather than plummeted into the Potomac, both the aerodrome and Langley's laboratory might well have become beacons illuminating innovation and monuments to the benefit of government patronage for scientific research. The public and the press would have clamored for more, with politicians not far behind them. But instead of triumph, Langley's experiments ended in ignominy. They were ended prematurely by lack of public sympathy and understanding of the uncertain nature of research aimed at innovation, by impatience on the part of the press and politicians, and perhaps as well by Langley's inept handling of public relations. An attempt at innovation had fallen short of its goal, and government patronage for scientific research had proven politically sensitive and politically vulnerable.

THE WRIGHT BROTHERS

Beginnings

Just nine days after the second plunge into the Potomac by Langley's aerodrome, Wilbur and Orville Wright made their first successful piloted flight at Kitty Hawk, North Carolina, on 17 December 1903. Their interest in aviation had been sparked in 1895, when they first read about the German Otto Lilienthal and his glider experiments. After his death a year later, in a glider accident, the Wrights wondered if they might go on from where Lilienthal had left off.

The Wrights were not theoreticians; neither obtained even a high school diploma. The lack of scientific credentials would not help in winning public support. In their work on airplanes, however, the Wrights systematically tested various elements, including wing shapes, more thoroughly than had famous scientists, and with more accurate results. Judged by their procedures and by their results, the Wrights were outstanding scientists. They were also persistent experimenters—improving, and then improving some more—until their invention worked, and then worked better. This was the paradigm for successful innovation in early aeronautics.

The brothers' formula for success exemplified the best in engineering science. They thought through their invention process, controlling their experiments and changing only one variable each attempt. This allowed them to make an accurate evaluation of success or failure. By contrast, Langley altered many parameters from one trial to the next, so he never could accurately assess the success or failure of one or another of the variables. In essence, the Wrights bespoke a certain technological innovation, lifestyle of progress, and sense of muscular entrepreneurship. Before entering the field of aeronautics, they had published a newspaper, designed an improved press, and managed a bicycle sales and repair business. They even produced their own bicycle, the Wright Special. They were neither wealthy nor socially prominent, but they were successful inventors and entrepreneurs.[25]

After the Wright brothers read everything on flight they could find, Wilbur wrote to the Smithsonian Institution in May 1899 for help. He was convinced that human flight was possible and practical. It was only a question of knowledge and skill, as in all acrobatic feats. He was about "to begin a systematic study of the subject in preparation for practical work to which I expect to devote what time I can spare from my regular business." Knowing of Langley's work, Wright wanted papers published by the Smithsonian on flight and, if possible, a list of other works in English. "I am an enthusiast, but not a crank in the sense that I have some pet theories as to the proper construction of a flying machine. I wish to avail myself of all that is already known and then if possible add my mite to help the future worker who will attain final success."[26]

The Smithsonian sent pamphlets and a list of titles. The Wrights "were astonished to learn what an immense amount of time and money had been expended in futile attempts to solve the problem of human flight." Men of the very highest standing, from Leonardo da Vinci to Langley and Bell, had attempted the problem. But the Wrights were not discouraged: "in studying their failures we found many points of interest to us."[27]

The Wrights also received encouragement from Octave Chanute, a Chicago construction engineer who had built the Kansas City bridge and the Chicago stockyards. Chanute's 1894 book *Progress in Flying Machines* was on the list sent by the Smithsonian Institution to the Wrights. Wilbur wrote to Chanute, in-forming him that "for some years I have been afflicted with the belief that flight is possible to man. My disease has increased in severity and I feel that it will soon cost me an increased amount of money if not my life. I have been trying to arrange my affairs in such a way that I can devote my entire time for a few months to experiment in this field." His time for experiment was limited by his bicycle shop business to the months between September and January. Wright believed that what was chiefly necessary was skill, not machinery. Lilienthal had spent only about five hours total in the air in five years of effort; even the sim-plest intellectual or acrobatic feat could not be learned with so little practice.[28]

A letter to the Weather Bureau in Washington obtained for the Wrights cop-ies of the *Monthly Weather Review*, with tables of average hourly wind velocities at all Weather Bureau stations. Kitty Hawk, North Carolina, an isolated strip of beach separating the Atlantic Ocean from Albemarle, Pamlico, and Roanoke Sounds, appeared to have steady winds of ten to twenty miles per hour, winds that would support a glider without movement relative to the ground. (The Wrights would find the winds not as steady, though, as they hoped.) And it was cheaper, Wilbur reasoned, to go to a distant point where he could practice every day than to go to a closer point where fickle winds might cause to be wasted three days out of four. Furthermore, Kitty Hawk had a mile-wide beach extending for nearly sixty miles, clear of trees and high hills — so the Wrights learned in re-sponse to a letter to the weather station at Kitty Hawk; nothing would break the wind into eddies and sudden gusts. (In this expectation, too, the Wrights were overly optimistic.) There wasn't a house for rent at Kitty Hawk, and the Wrights were advised to bring tents. Board could be obtained from a private family, pro-vided there were not too many in the Wrights' party. A mail boat from the Island of Manteo in Albemarle Sound, twelve miles away, provided transporta-tion on Monday, Wednesday, and Friday. The nearest railroad station was Eliza-beth City, North Carolina, nearly forty miles away.[29]

The Wrights' first glider, assembled at a cost of about fifteen dollars, weighed 52 pounds and had a wingspan of 17 feet. Wilbur wrote to his father in Septem-ber 1900 that he was going to the coast of North Carolina "for the purpose of making some experiments with a flying machine. It is my belief that flight is possible and, while I am taking up the investigation for pleasure rather than profit, I think there is a slight possibility of achieving fame and fortune from it." He was certain that he could advance beyond the point reached by others in the field, "even if complete success is not attained just at present. At any rate, I shall have an outing of several weeks and see a part of the world I have never before visited." He intended merely to experiment and practice, hoping to solve the problem of equilibrium. Without a motor, it would not be flight in any true sense. But once the machine were under control, the motor problem could be quickly solved.[30]

The experiments in 1900 consisted of flying the glider as a kite, manipulating it by pulling strings attached to a horizontal rudder. The hunting and fishing were better than the flying, since most of the latter activity consisted of repairing wrecks after crashes. Instead of hours of practice, the Wrights had about ten minutes total. They had borrowed a sewing machine from Mrs. Tate, a local woman, to make repairs; when they left, abandoning the glider, Mrs. Tate used its sateen wing fabric to make dresses for her two daughters. On their return to Dayton, Ohio, after more than a month at Kitty Hawk, the Wrights wrote to Chanute that although the short time at their disposal had prevented thorough tests, the results were favorable and they would continue the experiments in the next year.[31]

In July 1901 the Wrights were back, their arrival delayed by the worst storm ever recorded at Kitty Hawk. The Wright party was now doubled in strength from the previous year. The third member was a young man with medical training and also interested in aeronautics. He was recommended by Chanute, who paid his traveling expenses while the Wrights gave him board. The fourth member of the party was a technical man then building and testing a glider for Chanute. Chanute himself was also briefly a guest at the camp. The men were a bit crowded, and Wilbur asked Chanute to send another tent, if convenient. The mosquitoes were so bad that summer that Orville often thought if he could just survive until morning he would pack up and return home.

The experiments went badly. The Wrights had built a glider with the wing shape recommended by Lilienthal, only to find that the lift was less than that indicated in Lilienthal's tables. The glider could not be kept aloft and tested without considerable motion relative to the ground. The Wrights had to carry their machine four miles south, to Kill Devil Hill, a large sand dune down which they could start the glider. Near Kill Devil Hill they built a rough frame shed to house the machine. Five minutes of free flight a day was the best they attained. Wilbur thought that man wouldn't fly in a thousand years. Orville, however, thought it encouraging that earlier work was not reliable; it meant that more knowledge was needed, not that flight was necessarily impossible.[32]

The next experiments were made at home, first with a curved surface, or wing, attached to a rotating bicycle wheel turned over so that its axis was vertical. Next the Wrights mounted the wing on a spar projecting in front of a bicycle and rode the bicycle. Soon they had a wind tunnel, of sorts, an open-ended wooden box with a fan driven by a one-cylinder gas engine at one end. Each curved surface tested was balanced against the pressure on a square plane. The wind tunnel experiments, a turning point in aeronautical history, occurred after

Wilbur in a public speech had criticized contemporary knowledge and Orville had decided that Wilbur's assertion required further confirmation. Chanute was impressed by the Wrights' progress, and he offered to write to Andrew Carnegie to try to obtain $10,000 per year for the Wrights to continue their work. Wilbur thought Carnegie too hardheaded a businessman to be interested in such a visionary pursuit as flying. It would be folly to back flying attempts as a business proposition. Men of wealth should view the flying problem as similar to that of North Pole hunting. Although Wilbur believed that constant systematic effort could produce a flying machine in a few years, he could not honestly appeal to a rich man on a business basis because of the universal failures of the past.[33]

In August 1902 the Wright brothers made a third trip to Kitty Hawk. They first flew their new machine with a tail as a kite, with good results. Then Orville flew it. On his third or fourth glide, he twisted a control the wrong way and the next thing he knew he was in the center of a heap of cloth and sticks. Orville escaped without a bruise or scratch, and in three days the machine was repaired. Soon the Wrights were making glides of over five hundred feet from the top of the hill, and far flatter glides than before; this meant that in a powered machine they would be able to fly with much less propulsion.

By October 1902 the Wrights had largely solved the basic problem of stability and control that had so vexed earlier experimenters in flight. Stability rested on the use of the canter and extent of surfaces under which the air passed, and a bracing tail section worked to keep the aircraft level. That much was known. Control could be achieved by shifting the center of gravity of the aircraft, and Lilienthal had sought to accomplish it very simply by throwing his body from side to side to control his gliders, but this was a very imprecise form of control and led to instability problems. Lilienthal had died in a glider crash when his attempt to control the craft in this manner caused stability problems. Another method, adopted by the Wrights, provided for manipulating the wings in certain ways to assure control. They developed a technique of wing warping to ensure control, revolutionary in character in itself, but when the Wrights thought to connect the mechanisms controlling the wing warping and the tail operation, they for the first time had a fully controllable flying machine that had the potential to conquer the air.[34]

In September 1903 the Wrights again set out for Kitty Hawk. There they heard the news of the first dive of Langley's full-size, manned aerodrome into the Potomac River, on 7 October. The Wrights were making successful flights in the glider, but the first test flight with a motor twisted a propeller shaft. Both shafts were sent back to the bicycle shop in Dayton for strengthening, putting off the trial flight the Wrights had hoped to make in early November.[35]

There were sharp ups and downs in the Wrights' expectations that autumn at Kitty Hawk. The characteristic gyrations of the stock market furnished an apt figure of speech for the brothers' correspondence, even if their airplane was still far from a business proposition, and they fortunately were insulated from unrealistic expectations. In October Orville wrote from Kitty Hawk to Charles Taylor, the chief mechanic of the Wrights' bicycle shop in Dayton, to inform him that the "flying machine market has been very unsteady the past two days. Opened yesterday morning at about 208 (100% means even chances of success) but by noon had dropped to 110. These fluctuations would have produced a panic, I think in Wall Street, but in this quiet place it only put us to thinking and figuring a little. It gradually improved during the rest of yesterday and today and is now almost back to its old mark."[36]

In contrast to the Wright brothers and their imaginary stock market panic, which little disturbed the tranquillity of Kitty Hawk, Langley had been forced by circumstances to forgo quiet contemplation and isolation from the fluctuations of public opinion. Nor had Langley enjoyed the opportunity to correct inevitable mistakes and try again, and again, and again, before panic in Congress over public opinion and panic in the army over congressional opinion had ended his experiments. Much of the Wrights' freedom from fickle and fluctuating public perception was due to their self-reliance, which in turn was largely the result of cost effectiveness. The track for starting their machine cost all of four dollars, compared to the tens of thousands of dollars that Langley was reported to have spent to launch his aerodrome. And the Wrights' first powered plane, including trips back to Dayton to repair the propeller shafts, cost less than a thousand dollars. These modest costs were met from the profits of their bicycle business, although the profit never exceeded $3,000 in any one year. Neither limited funds nor brief panics of pessimism would end the Wrights' quest for aeronautical innovation.

After three days of effort, the weather was unfavorable on 17 December 1903, with a cold gusty north wind blowing almost a gale. But the Wrights were determined to spend Christmas at home, and they went ahead. Orville managed a flight of 12 seconds, covering about 100 feet, before difficulty with the front rudder caused the machine to dart for the ground, cracking the skid under the rudder. After repairs, Wilbur made the second trial, flying about 175 feet. Then Orville came back for a third trial that day, which was ended by a strong gust of wind. Wilbur took his turn for the fourth and last trip of the day, traveling 852 feet in 59 seconds before the machine began pitching and suddenly darted into the ground, breaking up the front rudder frame.[37]

The Wrights had flown, but the final result was a wreck about as bad as Langley's. This detour on the path toward innovation was a private wreck, however, not a public fiasco. The Wright brothers silently tore down what remained

Fig. 1.3. Perhaps the most recognizable photo in the world, this depicts the first flight of the Wright brothers on 17 December 1903. Courtesy NASA

of their machine, packed it up, and returned home, with most of the world none the wiser nor further disillusioned regarding the prospects of manned heavier-than-air flight.

Fighting Langley's Ghost

The Wright brothers' first flight was reported, but uncertainly and by few newspapers. Orville telegraphed home: "Success four flights Thursday morning all against twenty-one-mile wind started from level with engine power alone average speed through air thirty-one miles longest 59 seconds inform press home Christmas." The telegraph message was taken to the office of the Dayton *Journal*. The city editor, also the local Associated Press representative, didn't think a flight of less than a minute worth a news item. He seemed annoyed at being bothered with such nonsense. Another newspaperman, however, did find the flight worth a story. An employee of the business office of the *Virginian-Pilot* in Norfolk, Virginia, heard from a friend in the railroad freight office that a barrel of oysters had been shipped to "Wright" at Kitty Hawk. He also remembered stories a year earlier about the Wrights flying a box-shaped kite at Kitty Hawk. Putting the two items together, he told his managing editor that there might be a story here. The editor checked with telegraph operators and learned that a message had passed through Norfolk from Kitty Hawk to Dayton announcing successful manned flights. This was enough for a front-page story in the

Virginian-Pilot, topped by a seven-column headline and making up in pictur-
esqueness what it lacked in accurate detail. The story was telegraphed to other
papers, raking in some $175 for its authors. Of twenty-one papers offered the
story, however, only five took it. And of those five, only two, the New York
American and the Cincinnati *Enquirer,* printed the story the next morning. A
few other papers eventually printed the story inconspicuously, not as front-page
news but as fifth-page fantasy from an out-of-the-way place.[38]

The *New York Times,* printing all the news that's fit to print, or at least all
that would fit, ignored the improbable tale lacking a witness. The *Times* did be-
latedly acknowledge the Wrights' initial flight, but only after receiving additional confirmation that the airplane existed and really did fly, at least sort of.
In a page 1 article in May 1904 the *Times* reported that the Wrights had built
a new machine and arranged to test it at a field eight miles east of Dayton. The
headline was: "Fall Wrecks Airship. On Trial Trip It Went Thirty Feet and
Dropped—Inventors Satisfied, Though." The Wright flying machine, "which
made a successful flight at Kitty Hawk, N.C. last December had another trial
near this city [Dayton, Ohio] today [26 May 1904]; which the brothers say
was successful. Great secrecy was maintained about the test, and but few witnessed it."[39]

The Wrights did not seek publicity. After successfully circumnavigating the
field outside Dayton late in 1904, however, they wrote to their congressman to
ascertain if the government had any interest in their flying machine. The Board
of Ordnance and Fortification was not interested, so soon after the Langley episode, in venturing further money on research until the device was brought to a
stage of practical operation without expense to the United States.[40]

The Wrights had not asked for an appropriation; they had offered to produce an actual machine of "agreed specifications, at a contract price." Thus they
interpreted the government reply as a "flat turn down" and reluctantly prepared
to turn to potential buyers abroad.[41]

The Langley legacy remained strong in official Washington. Eventually it
would be overcome; eventually the War Department would undertake to purchase an airplane meeting strict specifications, if not to advance public funds
toward uncertain scientific research. But the Wrights, having developed a heavier-than-air machine that could fly, would also have to win public recognition
for their accomplishment sufficient to overcome the considerable caution of
public officials still haunted by Langley's ghost.

Public Recognition
Because the Wrights had barred newspaper and magazine reporters from their
flights, the results of their investigations initially were little known or appreci-

ated. This situation changed in 1906, when the Aero Club in New York exhibited a model of the Wrights' flying machine. The *New York Times*'s Sunday magazine carried five columns topped by the headline: "Another Attempt to Solve Aerial Navigation Problem. Flying Machine Invented by the Wright Brothers Sails through the Air without Aid of Balloon or Gas Bag—Working On It in Secret for Years." The *Times*'s somewhat unusual source for a straightforward description of a twenty-four-mile flight lasting thirty-eight minutes and reaching a speed of nearly thirty-eight miles per hour was a Medina, Ohio, apiculturist, whose reports had first been published in his own journal, *Gleanings in Bee Culture*. The reports were endorsed by members of the New York Aero Club.[42]

Europeans also heard about the Wright brothers, and perhaps news reports in the United States of negotiations with other governments spurred the Board of Ordnance and Fortification to consider more favorably propositions for the construction of flying machines.[43] The Wrights repeated their offer to sell flying machines, with the United States to pay only after the machine completed an acceptable trial flight before government witnesses. This time the Board of Ordnance and Fortification replied that it was interested in witnessing tests if the Wrights had a machine that could make flights. No specifications had been formulated; the Wrights were asked to specify the conditions their machine could meet.[44]

The Wrights had at least one enthusiast in the military, in the person of Lieutenant Frank P. Lahm of the Signal Corps, stationed in Washington, D.C. Lahm's father, an American businessman in Paris, had obtained a report on the Wrights for the French Aero Club. The younger Lahm had met the Wrights in Paris in the summer of 1907 and had confidence in them. He also was talking to the American press. A half-page article in the *New York Times* in September discussed interesting experiments in aeronautics and possibilities of future military efficiency, though primarily in the context of balloons rather than heavier-than-air machines. Somewhat behind European nations in tackling the problem of military aeronautics, the U.S. Army was now working overtime in its effort to excel in this most modern branch of warfare. Congress would soon be called upon to increase appropriations. One obstacle was the disposition of the public, which knew very little about the matter, to question the practicability of military aeronautics. Lahm, interviewed in Paris, stated that "we should not fail to appreciate the necessity for preparedness for war above the earth as well as on the earth, and when our next war comes we should not be found wanting in this particular branch of military service."[45]

Secretary of War William Howard Taft was expected to ask Congress to make the United States Signal Corps as proficient as were the aerial aspects of the armies of France, Germany, and Great Britain. The government was "really

the only interest capable of putting in money enough and furnishing at the outset a genuine necessity for such a sky ship."[46]

Langley's ghost, however, still haunted Congress and the War Department.
The *New York Times* faced the problem head-on, reminding readers that "the
last efforts of the War Department to conquer the air were under the tutelage of
Prof. Langley, who thought he had worked out this problem of flight by means
of the airplane, but in the final test five years ago his contrivance came to grief
in the tawny waters of the Potomac. The experiments made at that time cost
more than $60,000, and for them the Government has nothing to show to-day
but a pretty little engine of aluminum, which it is asserted can develop ten horse
power and weighs but 100 pounds." Now, however, the situation was changed.
"The science of aeronavigation has been almost wholly developed since the
death of Prof. Langley, and now it will be purely a business matter for the Government to advertise for bids and get its wants in the shape of a skyship."[47]

Lahm, too, thought that memories of Langley were holding back progress.
"Almost everywhere I have been I have asked about the Wright brothers. A
pretty universal impression seems to exist in Europe that they are sheer adver-
tisers without any real merit back of their mystifying unwillingness to show
what they have got; but I have said to everybody that the Wright aeroplane can
undoubtedly accomplish all claimed for it and that the chief reason our government has not acquired the machine is probably that Prof. Langley's costly experiments have prejudiced us against flying machines for some time to come."[48]

Government Flight Tests

The army had not "about concluded" negotiations with the Wrights, as some
newspapers reported, but the U.S. War Department finally did advertise at the
end of 1907 for bids for an airplane.[49] The specifications of the advertisement for
bids were written in consultation with Wilbur Wright; in this sense, the Wrights
were negotiating with the War Department.

There was no danger of wasting public money, since none would be paid out
until the requirements laid down were met by a satisfactory test at Fort Myer,
Virginia, before a government board of experts. The test, the American public
was assured, would be more severe than any ever required in any country, more
exacting even than that governing the Deutsch prize of 100,000 francs, outstanding in Paris for more than a year without takers. It was even doubtful that
the War Department would get a machine meeting all the conditions. Nor,
thus, would the government be required to pay out any money. Nonetheless,
the test flights would help in developing airplanes. The *American Magazine of
Aeronautics* criticized the whole procedure, noting that there was "not a known
flying-machine in the world which could fulfill these specifications at the pres-

ent moment. 'Had an inventor such a machine as required would he not be in a position to ask almost any reasonable sum from the government for its use? Would not the government, instead of the inventor, be a bidder?' We doubt very much if the government receives any bids at all possible to be accepted." [50]

The criticism was valid, but it missed the point. In the aftermath of the Langley fiasco, the government's major concern, and the major concern raised by newspapers, was not to advance aeronautical innovation or even to obtain an airplane, but to avoid the embarrassment of being accused of wasting government money on uncertain aeronautical research. The Wrights' triumph would be not merely to fly, but in flying, to reverse a peevish, perverse, and petulant priority; their unstated task was to exorcise Langley's ghost.

Forty-one bids were received by the War Department, thirty-eight of them criticizing the stringent requirements. Only three bidders put up the required 10 percent of the proposed purchase price. The Wrights offered to produce a machine for $25,000. Because of competition, they had cut their price in half; also, they knew that only $25,000 had been allocated. A patriotic J. F. Scott of Chicago was willing to sell his plane for $1,000, the estimated cost of materials. He was soon to drop out, asking for the return of his 10 percent deposit. A. M. Herring of New York wanted $20,000; he may have intended to subcontract the actual work to the Wrights.

The three bids presented the Signal Corps with a problem. Only the Wrights were thought to have any chance of meeting the requirements, but the government was obligated to accept the lowest bid. Secretary of War Taft suggested that all bids be accepted, an illegal act unless money were available to pay for all the bids. President Theodore Roosevelt guaranteed payment out of an emergency fund at his disposal, should more than one bidder meet the test. The Wrights' bid was accepted on 8 February 1908, and they began preparations for trial flights in August. [51]

They modified their 1905 airplane, adding a passenger seat, changing the control levers so they could be operated from a sitting position rather than prone, and installing an improved engine. In April the Wrights took their airplane to Kitty Hawk. Controlling the machine in flight was their major problem; it was to be solved by repeated practice.

The practice flights were discovered by Bruce Salley, a freelance reporter whose beat stretched south a hundred miles from Norfolk, Virginia, into North Carolina. Roving the coast for maritime news, Salley heard about the Wrights from local people helping them. He surreptitiously approached the Wrights' camp, climbed a tree, and watched through field glasses. Several times Salley observed the Wrights start their machine down a large sand dune, rise into the air, circle about, and land. He telegraphed several newspapers that the Wright brothers had flown almost a thousand feet in a flying machine without a balloon attachment. The Cleveland *Leader* indignantly refused to pay the telegraph tolls and wired Salley to "cut out the wild-cat stuff." The less skeptical New York *Herald* printed the story and sent its own reporter south, accompanied by staff correspondents from the New York *American*, the London *Daily Mail*, and *Collier's* magazine.

This contingent of reporters joined Salley two days later in Elizabeth City, North Carolina. From there they went by motorboat around the Dismal Swamp and through Pamlico, Albemarle, and Roanoke Sounds to the hamlet of Manteo on Roanoke Island, where Sir Walter Raleigh's colony had disappeared in 1586. The reporters now were ten miles from the Wrights' camp, still a boat trip and several hours of walking away. A scout sent out to arrange for the reporters to view the airplane in flight reported back that upon his approach the Wrights had drawn their flying machine into a shed, locked the door, and announced that no one other than their assistants could view the experiments.

Next morning at daybreak the intrepid reporters left the little inn on Manteo, crossed the sound in an open launch, and trudged the weary miles through sand dunes, ponds, and scrub to within sight of the Wrights' camp. There, flat on their stomachs in a clump of bushes, so they reported, they watched through field glasses. A photograph taken on the occasion, however, reveals a good-size picnic basket in the background and the men sitting comfortably, attired in white shirts and ties.

By the third morning the vigil had become irksome and the reporters debated whether to withdraw and denounce the Wrights as frauds. But then it happened. First with a sound like the clacking of a grain reaper, and then a sharper staccato, the Wight's machine rose majestically, its white wings flashing in the morning sun, flew toward a dune, turned in a graceful curve, and then passed almost directly over the reporters, one of whom had the presence of mind to open the shutter of his camera and take a photograph of the airplane in flight.

The news almost didn't reach American readers. The London *Daily Mail* reporter dashed off a few hundred words during the boat trip back to Manteo and immediately filed his story at the little weather bureau office. Then, to keep the wire open for further reports of his own, he marked a page in a magazine and asked that it be sent. His companions were not pleased; indeed, someone might have been hurt had they been at a commercial telegraph company obligated to send the copy. But they were at a government office, and the telegraph operator was able to settle matters amicably, allotting thirty minutes to each reporter. The New York *Herald* reported that the Wrights and flown over two miles, "the distance being computed by the telegraph poles of the U. S. Weather Bureau."[52]

A day later more correspondents arrived. More flights followed, and *Collier's* confirmed with pictures and text "that it was all right, the rumors true. There was no doubt that a man could fly." The *New York Times* also followed closely the flights at Kitty Hawk, beginning with Salley's initial report that the Wrights had flown a thousand feet and "apparently could have flown much further as easily as not." Two days later there were ten flights to report. "With their new airplane under perfect control, the Wright brothers to-day soared over the sand dunes at Kill Devil Hill with perfect ease." A few days later, the Wright airplane flew three miles with Orville at the controls and Charles Furnas, a mechanic from Dayton, in the passenger seat. "They [newspapers mistakenly thought both Wrights were in the plane] were unmistakably seen in it as the machine soared by a group of responsible observers and then were seen to step from the machine when it halted. The performances of the Wrights here, especially that of to-day, have greatly impressed those who have watched them. They have made no statements on what they have accomplished, and seem to regard their flights as mere tests."[53]

The first flights were so impressive that the inevitable crash, after a flight of over eight miles ended when the rudder was turned the wrong way, did little to dampen the enthusiasm and the high expectations of newspaper and magazine reporters in attendance. The disaster was the cause of regret to the Signal Corps, but more than three months remained to construct and deliver a machine, and there was no reason why the task could not be accomplished. The Wrights had produced a machine that would fly and was capable of being controlled. "These reticent and intensely absorbed Westerners, the Wright brothers of Dayton, Ohio, appear to have at last conquered the element which had so long baffled the ingenuity of man, and aerial navigation, so long regarded as a fascinating absurdity, now seems to be very much of a practical reality."[54] If the Wrights' conquest of the air was not yet complete, their conquest of the nation's press was. The test of the Wrights' machine before the War Department was yet to be made, but the outcome already was being judged favorably by newspapers and magazines.

The ghost of Langley still hovered over American aeronautics, but no longer with entirely negative effect. The *New York Times* reviewed the history of the approaching tests:[55]

The way the United States Government came to embark in the flying machine business is an interesting story, and if the Fort Myer trials produce good results several men in Washington will come in for conspicuous credit. Others will nurse regrets. The story began a dozen years back with the "successful failure" of Prof. Langley's first power driven flying machine. Through an unfortunate blunder it was pitched headlong into the Potomac River, but not until the possibility of sustained mechanical flight had been demonstrated. Congress had appropriated $100,000 to carry on the experiments, but when the machine tumbled into the river, Congress, like the public and the newspapers, saw nothing but that part of the thing, and shame-facedly washed its hands of aeronautics for good and all. . . .

Then the aeronautical appropriations bill was introduced in Congress. Gen. Allen and his friends had high hopes of its speedy passage, but before the reading of the title was finished, a patriarchal statesman whispered, "Remember Langley," and down went the bill into the Fortifications Committee, where it will probably remain entombed for all time. But Gen. Allen was not disheartened. After several conferences with the President and Secretary Taft, he announced the Signal Corps would go ahead with its aerial pursuits.

The phrase "Remember Langley" first was raised and then twice repeated in this article, as if chanting it three times were enough to exorcise this ghost.[56]

FORT MYER: 1908

The trial flights of the Wright brothers' flying machine at Fort Myer were expected to be difficult. The famous French aviator Henri Farman thought the conditions—flying for an hour at forty miles per hour with a passenger and enough fuel to fly 125 miles—were too severe, the requirements five years in advance of present developments. The conditions presupposed the existence of a perfect motor-driven heavier-than-air machine.[57]

The Wrights, though, soon proved that they had such a machine. Still pursuing foreign sales, Wilbur made flights at the racetrack at Le Mans, west of Paris, in August 1908. He had spent much of June assembling his flying machine, after French customs agents had uncrated the parts and damaged some of them. And he had spent much of July recovering from a burn caused when a rubber water tube came loose while the motor was being testing, releasing scalding steam. Now in August Wilbur flew around the course at Le Mans, making a figure eight and landing at the starting point. It was a short flight, of just a few minutes, but the French press went wild. According to Le Figaro, the flight was not just a success but a triumph, a decisive victory creating a revolution in the scientific world. L'Intransigeant concluded sadly that French aviators were but debutantes compared with the Wrights. The reaction of the French press quickly was noted in America.[58]

Orville Wright made the long-looked-for public exhibition at Fort Myer, outside the nation's capital, on 4 September 1908, before a crowd grown somewhat skeptical because of numerous postponements. He was flying a new ma-

Fig. 1.4. This Wright Flyer photograph was taken during the U.S. Army trials at Fort Myer, Virginia, on 4 September 1908. Courtesy NASA

chine, in which the pilot sat upright. On his second lap around the parade ground, Orville turned one of the control levers the wrong way and was forced to land to avoid hitting a shed. The next day, though, Orville flew for over four minutes, going around the parade ground five and a half times and providing the army officers with "the most wonderful exhibit of its kind they had ever seen." It was his intent to fly a bit longer each time, and the next day he flew for nearly twenty minutes—coming within a minute of Farman's record for the longest public official flight—and traveling about fifteen miles.

On the strength of these initial flights the Wrights' agent was negotiating with military nations convinced by the Fort Myer and Le Mans flights, so he asserted, that the airplane would eventually be of great military value.[59] This statement obviously was self-serving, and thus is suspect, but the optimism was not completely without foundation. Even if the airplane had yet to satisfy the trial requirements, already it had won a positive place for itself in American newspapers.

On 8 September 1908 Orville flew only 24 seconds before a defect in a con-trol lever brought him down. The next day's flights were more promising, with flights of 7 and 11 minutes duration. The support for Orville's feet was too slip-pery, and he stopped to change it. The machine was working perfectly, and in the opinion of the army board, "Wright could have broken the French record to smithereens under the conditions to-day."

Orville did break the record the very next day. On the morning of 10 September he flew for over fifty-seven minutes, nearly doubling the previous endurance record. Then Orville came back in the afternoon, in front of the secretary of war and the secretary of the navy, to fly for sixty-two minutes. A third flight, with Lieutenant Lahm as a passenger, lasted for six minutes, more than double the former record for such a flight. In three flights Orville Wright had broken three records and wrested from France for America the laurels of the air. America ruled in aviation. Another record was achieved the very next day, with Orville flying for sixty-five minutes in a brisk breeze. There was not the slightest doubt that he could have remained up much longer.

The *New York Times* commented that the government's requirement of an hour of continuous flight with a passenger was so severe that some people had thought it more likely to discourage than to encourage efforts of American inventors, and that the requirement had been seen as intended to suppress anyone threatening to disturb established methods and habits. Maybe so, when only vague rumors of what the Wrights had done justified any expectation of even approaching the government requirements. But now the situation was changed. "There is no doubt at all that, with any sort of luck with his machine and the weather, the standards of achievement set by the government will be far surpassed. The practical uses of the aeroplane, many prophets to the contrary notwithstanding, remain to be discovered, but actual flight, at last attained after centuries and centuries of vain endeavor, ranks among humanity's most remarkable achievements. There need be no fear that the uses will not be promptly found, though probably, most of them and the most important, are still unthought of."[60]

The following day Wright set another record, staying up for over seventy minutes. He could have stayed up another hour, and was only brought down by oncoming dusk. More importantly, his speed was 39.55 miles per hour with the motor at only three-fourths power. Clearly, the requirement of a speed of forty miles per hour was within reach. The next day saw yet another record endurance flight, this time for seventy-four minutes. Experts saw the Fort Myer performances as marking the definite conquest of the air by man. But Wright recognized that the efforts were experimental and should be treated as hazardous.[61]

Wright was all too prescient. On 17 September, with Lieutenant Selfridge a passenger, Orville went up for what now seemed a routine flight. After only three or four minutes in the air, however, he heard or felt a light tapping in the rear of his machine. (Later examination would show that a propeller blade was hitting a wire that had come loose.) Orville decided to shut off the motor and descend. Then two big thumps (as the propeller blade broke) suddenly shook the airplane violently and it swerved, heading for a dangerous gully beyond the field. Orville pulled on the controls, but the tail was inoperative. Twisting the wings, he managed to point the plane toward the field, and he descended about twenty-five feet. Orville then tried to straighten the wing tips; the machine, instead of leveling off, plunged straight down for fifty feet. About twenty-five feet from the ground the machine began to right itself. But Orville needed another ten to twenty feet for a safe landing; his recovery of control had come too late. The machine was a total wreck, and both aviators were removed covered with blood. Selfridge, with a fractured skull, never regained consciousness. Orville, with a fractured left thigh and several ribs, was in serious condition but expected to live.[62]

A lesser disaster had ruined Langley. The Wrights, however, were carried inexorably on a flood tide of favorable opinion. Also, the American press displayed a new maturity and a more sympathetic understanding of the inevitable setbacks in the course of aeronautical innovation. *Collier's* weekly magazine, which a week before had heralded in text and photographs Orville Wright's record-breaking continuous flight in a heavier-than-air machine at Fort Myer as the result of patience, self-control, and methodical, continuous experimentation for six or seven years, resulting in "an achievement of which every American may justly be proud,"[63] now reminded its readers of that long development and well-earned triumph, and at the same time made little of the inevitable accident:

> Rarely, indeed, has the perversity of inanimate things brought about a
> more dramatic and painful tragedy. The smallness and unimportance
> of the immediate cause made the result seem all the more deplorable.
> The accident resulted from no miscalculation, nor did it have anything
> to do with the general principle embodied in the Wright machine,
> which had already brilliantly established its ability to navigate the air.
> It was one of those unforeseen and probably unpreventable things, like
> the breaking of a tire or the spreading of rails, and this apparently trifl-
> ing accident resulted in the destruction of the Wright aeroplane, just
> as it was about, with every apparent chance of success, to undertake
> the tests prescribed by the War Department, in the maiming of one
> of its inventors, and in the death of one of the most promising young
> men in the army.[64]

Journalists, too, had learned patience, at least temporarily. Langley, under pressure from newspapers, had risked all on a premature attempt at flight, only to fail. The Wrights, working without government aid, were less subject to such importunities. Nevertheless, there had been, after the flights in May 1908, a constant clamor from newspapers and magazines for demonstrations and results, a pressure which the Wrights had systematically and ostentatiously resisted. In the end, their attitude prevailed. Now they were applauded for their patient, methodical progress, in which accidents and other setbacks were inevitable and were inevitably overcome. Seemingly no single calamity, no matter how severe, could now turn opinion against the Wright brothers and the inherently uncertain course of aeronautical innovation.

The secretary of the Aero Club of America stated that it was "not likely that the accident, deplorable as it is, will have any serious effect in retarding the work of progress that has been so pronounced within the last few weeks."[65] The *New York Times* commented:

> The human mind reacts upon misfortune. Since the discovery of the potentialities of radium nothing has so stirred the thoughts of man as the practical application of the principles of aerial flight. The long voyages of Count Zeppelin's rigid and dirigible balloon airship caused universal wonder, but the triumph of his idea was not assured until tempest and fire had engulfed its first embodiment. Then the German Nation rose and provided the aeronaut with the means to build a fleet of airships. The fatal plunge of the Wright aeroplane at Fort Myer may not have precisely this result, nevertheless it is the shock and challenge of nature not to desist, but to carry the struggle to the point of conquest. . . . The triumphs and accidents of the present experimenters are also of significance, though only as they have evoked and set in motion forces the inertia of which must insure, and at no distant date, secure success. It is saddening that Lieut. Selfridge may not be the last martyr to the cause.[66]

The War Department was expected—indeed, it was urged by newspapers—to extend the time for the Wrights' trial flights. "The Government is practically satisfied that the Wright aeroplane has solved the problem of aerial flight, and it is not disposed to embarrass the aviator because of an unfortunate accident. It is recognized that the mishap was similar to an accident that might wreck a locomotive when it leaves the track or an automobile when its steering apparatus goes wrong." A few days later the secretary of war agreed that there was "no doubt that the American people would applaud a generous, rather than a strictly technical attitude on the part of the government toward Orville Wright." The secretary cautiously added that "Mr. Wright's achievements won the admiration and his misfortune the sympathy of the whole country, but until the War Department has some recommendation to act upon, I cannot say what course will be followed."[67]

An act of Congress would be necessary for full or partial payment. The

Wrights, though, wanted to satisfy the requirements, and it was clear that they could. Wilbur was still flying at Le Mans, where he set a new world record with a flight of nearly ninety-two minutes. Ten thousand frantic spectators were prevented by the French cavalry from bearing the aeronaut off in triumph. A few days later Wilbur set a new record carrying a passenger, staying aloft more than nine minutes. He surpassed his own record three days later with another flight with a passenger, this one lasting over eleven minutes. The American ambassador commented that if Germany could honor Count Zeppelin, the American people should present a testimonial to the Wrights.[68]

The Wrights applied for a nine-month extension of their flight trials, and the very next day the secretary of war granted the requested extension. The Aero Clubs of France and the United Kingdom honored the Wrights, and the Aero Club of America planned a similar reception. President Roosevelt declined an invitation to the dinner in New York, asking instead that the planned reception for the Wrights be held at the White House. Congress and the Smithsonian Institution awarded medals to the Wrights.[69]

FORT MYER: 1909

The 1909 trials of the Wright airplane at Fort Myer, though ending in successful flights and government purchase of the airplane, were not the complete public relations success that the U.S. Signal Corps had hoped to stage. Anticipating a quick triumph, the corps invited congressional observers. The Wrights, however, experimenting with a new and faster machine (the government purchase price would be higher if they flew faster), approached the trials methodically and patiently. They would not risk all on a premature attempt, no matter who the audience.

The U.S. Senate adjourned to witness the flights. Members of the House of Representatives, army officers, scientists, and diplomats also attended, as did the press. The Signal Corps hoped to make a good impression. The Wrights, however, at the last minute judged the weather too windy for flight. More questionable was their refusal to meet the attending congressmen. Some of the statesmen, already irritated because they had missed a baseball game to attend the test flight, announced that they would not attend any more Signal Corps parties in honor of the Wright brothers. Press reaction was mixed. Considerable goodwill toward the Wright brothers was somewhat diminished because of their lack of diplomacy and the inability of their airplane to fly in all kinds of weather.[70]

The next day was scarcely better in terms of public relations. After struggles with the motor for two hours, the airplane managed a flight of less than a minute. The pattern of balky motor and brief flight was repeated on the last day of June. There followed three good flights on the first day of July. The next day the engine failed in flight and the airplane, hitting a bush on landing, was wrecked. Wilbur vented his anger on a photographer.[71]

Signal Corps officers also were finding the proceedings trying. Their equilibrium was not helped by amusement in army and navy circles over the ludicrous blunder of inviting congressmen to the flight trials. Nor did the Signal Corps appreciate the leisurely unconcern expressed by the Wright brothers toward Congress and its power to make appropriations. The Wrights, on the other hand, did not regard themselves as circus performers; they were their own masters.[72]

Bad luck persisted through much of July, and congressmen frowned at the mishaps. The Wrights had not explained that they were experimenting with a new machine. False start after false start and three accidents were difficult to understand. The successes of the previous year faded from the minds of congressmen. In their opinion, the machine was not practical and its purchase would be a waste of public money. A worried Signal Corps now saw little prospect of getting any money.[73]

At the height of congressional pessimism, Orville Wright on 20 July flew for eighty minutes, setting a new American record. Newspaper headlines noted that he could have crossed the English Channel. A day before, the French aviator Hubert Latham had fallen short in his attempt to fly the English Channel and had been rescued by his military escort ship. Five days later, on 25 July, Louis Bleriot set out in a monoplane, also from near Calais, and landed at Dover. He won fame comparable to that accorded eighteen years later to Charles Lindbergh for his solo crossing of the Atlantic, and furnished dramatic proof of the potential of the airplane.[74]

The Wrights completed their trial flights at Fort Myer on 31 July 1909 by flying a distance of ten miles with a passenger. The average speed was forty-two miles per hour, surpassing the required forty miles per hour and winning for the Wright brothers a bonus of $5,000 ($2,500 for each mile over forty miles per hour). The army purchased the airplane for $30,000. The secretary of the navy had been among the enthusiastic spectators at Fort Myer, and the navy was expected soon to issue bids for two airplanes. It was far from a finished instrument of war, but the navy wanted to experiment. Eager navy aeronauts, however, would have to wait for the secretary to return from his vacation.[75] In fact, they would wait far longer.

Limited Acceptance

The U.S. government formally accepted the Wrights' airplane on 2 August 1909. It was the first airplane purchased and put into service by any government.[76] Already acclaimed by newspapers and magazines, an airplane finally was purchased by the War Department.

It was one thing to purchase a single copy of a product so thoroughly tested and proven in public trials that no one could criticize the decision. It would be a very different proposition to provide government patronage for scientific research, as had been done with such unfortunate results in the case of Langley and his aerodrome. Even in the midst of enthusiasm for the Wright brothers, the U.S. House of Representatives voted 161 to 90 against an amendment to appropriate $500,000 for the purchase and development of flying machines.[77] With the exception of Langley, and most notably with the Wrights, early attempts at aeronautical innovation in the United States were carried forward without government patronage.

Well into the twentieth century there was in the United States little appreciation of scientific research and even less inclination to allocate government funding for such an uncertain activity. Only with World War II and the ensuing Cold War did the federal government become a major patron of science. It is said that those who do not learn the lessons of history are doomed to repeat it. Historians looking back a century from now may recognize the second half of the twentieth century as an aberration, possibly even followed by a return to the sort of fear and paralysis regarding innovation once raised in American political ideology by Langley's ghost.

Reports of the Wrights' adventures in aeronautical innovation helped build sympathy and understanding for the experimental process with its inevitable accidents and setbacks. Little of the sarcastic criticism and political cowardice that played a major role in Langley's destruction repeated its ugly and blighting effect on the Wrights. But how much of this hard-won knowledge has the American public, the American press, and the American political body retained today? With the grounding of the space shuttle and the discovery that the space telescope was flawed, news media shifted into high gear to pursue and purvey entertainment rather than understanding, and politicians with reelection foremost in mind clamored to investigate NASA. It looked like a replay of the Langley witch hunt: "déjà vu all over again." Scientific and technological innovation is too essential and integral a part of our civilization for the nation to be without a consistent policy capable of withstanding transient winds of emotion fanned by inevitable mechanical accidents and human errors. Historical examples might provide perspective and contribute to the formulation of policy, if only historians were as entertaining as the morning newspaper and the nightly newscast.

NOTES

1. Octave Chanute, "Langley's Contribution to Aërial Navigation," in "Samuel Pierpont Langley Memorial Meeting," *Smithsonian Miscellaneous Collections*, vol. 49 (Washington, D.C.: Smithsonian Institution, 1907), pp. 30–35. See also "Portraits of Celebrities at Different Times of Their Lives: Samuel Pierpont Langley, Ph.D., LL.D. Born 1834," *Strand Magazine* 13 (June 1897): 705, and

Charles D. Walcott, "Samuel Pierpont Langley and Modern Aviation," *Proceedings of the American Philosophical Society* 65 (1926): 79–82. Langley's major publication on aeronautics was *Experiments in Aerodynamics* (Washington, D.C.: Smithsonian Institution, 1891; Publication 801, *Smithsonian Contributions to Knowledge* 27: 1). The Langley story has been told in Norriss S. Hetherington, "Langley's Aerodrome," *World War I Aero* 131 (Feb. 1991): 3–16, and in "The National Advisory Committee for Aeronautics: A Forerunner of Federal Governmental Support for Scientific Research," *Minerva* 28 (1990): 59–80. On early American aeronautics see Jeremiah Milbank, Jr., *The First Century of Flight in America* (Princeton, N.J.: Princeton University Press, 1943), and Tom D. Crouch, *A Dream of Wings: Americans and the Airplane 1875–1905* (New York: W. W. Norton, 1981).

2. "Balloon Inventions," *New York Times*, 3 Jan. 1892, p. 4.

3. S. P. Langley, *Langley Memoir on Mechanical Flight*, part 1, *1887 to 1896*, edited by Charles M. Manly (Washington, D.C.: Smithsonian Institution, 1911; Publication 1948, *Smithsonian Contributions to Knowledge* 27: 3).

4. S. P. Langley, "A Successful Trial of the Aerodrome," *Science* (new series) 3 (22 May 1896): 753–54; followed by a letter to the editor from Alexander Graham Bell, dated 12 May 1896. See also *Nature* 54 (28 May 1896): 80. The extract of Langley's communication to the French Academy of Sciences is translated and reprinted in *Langley Memoir*, pp. 3–4.

5. N. H. Randers-Pehrson and A. G. Renstrom, "Aeronautics in Congress Before 1900," in Randers-Pehrson and Renstrom, *Aeronautic Americana: A Bibliography of Books and Pamphlets on Aeronautics Published in America Before 1900* (New York: Institute of the Aeronautical Sciences, 1943).

6. Charles M. Manly, *Langley Memoir on Mechanical Flight*, part 2, *1897 to 1903* (Washington, D.C.: Smithsonian Institution, 1911; Publication 1948, *Smithsonian Contributions to Knowledge* 27: 3), p. 123.

7. Ibid.

8. Archibald D. Turnbull and Clifford L. Lord, *History of United States Naval Aviation* (New Haven, Conn.: Yale University Press, 1949), pp. 1–3.

9. "Dream of Aerial Flight," *New York Times*, 4 Sep. 1901, p. 6.

10. Quoted in Mark Sullivan, *Our Times: The United States 1900–1925*, vol. 2, *America Finding Herself* (New York: Charles Scribner's Sons, 1929), pp. 562–63.

11. "Airship as a Submarine," *New York Times*, 9 Aug. 1903, p. 11.

12. "Professor Langley's Experiments," *New York Times*, 20 Aug. 1903, p. 8.

13. Letter to the editor, *New York Times*, 30 Aug. 1903, p. 9.

14. "Langley Wants More Money," *New York Times*, 20 Sep. 1903, p. 10.

15. Manly, *Langley Memoir*, part 2, pp. 265–66.

16. "Flying Machine Fiasco," *New York Times*, 8 Oct. 1903, p. 1.

17. Quoted in Sullivan, *Our Times*, pp. 562–63.

18. Andrew Dixon White, "Samuel Pierpont Langley," in "Samuel Pierpont Langley Memorial Meeting," p. 7–24.

19. Manly, *Langley Memoir*, part 2, pp. 271–74.

20. "Airship Breaks in Two," *New York Times*, 9 Dec. 1903, p. 1.

21. Editorial, *New York Times*, 10 Dec. 1903, p. 13; quoted in Sullivan, *Our Times*, pp. 565–66.

22. Sullivan, *Our Times*, pp. 565–67; "House Stirred over Novels and Airship," *New York Times*, 24 Jan. 1904, p. 9; see also letter to the editor, *New York Times*, p. 22.

23. Report submitted by Major M. M. Macomb to the Board of Ordnance and Fortification, 6 Jan. 1905; reprinted in Manly, *Langley Memoir*, part 2, pp. 277–78; Report of the Board of Ordnance and Fortification to the Secretary of War, 6 Oct. 1904; reprinted in ibid., pp. 278–79; Report of the Board of Ordnance and Fortification to the Secretary of War, 14 Nov. 1908; reprinted in ibid., pp. 279–80.

24. Alex Roland, *Model Research: The National Advisory Committee for Aeronautics 1915–1958*, vol. 1 (Washington, D.C.: National Aeronautics and Space Administration, 1985), p. 2; "Aeroplanes to Be Put to a Government Test," *New York Times*, 28 June 1908, part 5, p. 8.

25. Fred C. Kelly, *The Wright Brothers* (New York: Harcourt, Brace, 1943). See also Arthur G. Renstrom, *Wilbur and Orville Wright: A Chronology* (Washington, D.C.: Library of Congress, 1975), and Tom D. Crouch, *The Bishop's Boys: A Life of Wilbur and Orville Wright* (New York: W. W. Norton, 1989). On links between the bicycle and the airplane, see Peter L. Jakab, *Visions of a Flying Machine: The Wright Brothers and the Process of Invention* (Washington, D.C.: Smithsonian Institution Press, 1990), p. 9. Jakab's main thesis, that the Wrights had an extraordinary gift for visualizing abstraction, complements rather than contradicts the theme that refinements finally resulting in a practical flying machine were largely trial and error (p. 217).

26. Wilbur Wright to the Smithsonian Institution, 30 May 1899, quoted in Fred C. Kelly, ed., *Miracle at Kitty Hawk: The Letters of Wilbur and Orville Wright* (New York: Farrar, Straus and Young, 1951), pp. 15–16; hereafter cited as *Letters*.

27. Wilbur Wright, deposition before the U.S. Court of Appeals, in *Letters*, pp. 16–17.

28. Wilbur Wright to Octave Chanute, 13 May 1900, in *Letters*, pp, 22–23. On Chanute, see Crouch, *Dream of Wings*, pp. 61–126.

29. Willis L. Moore, Chief of Weather Bureau, to Wright Cycle Co., 4 Dec. 1899; Joseph J. Dosher, weather station, Kitty Hawk, to Wilbur Wright, 16 Aug. 1900; William J. Tate, Kitty Hawk, to Wilbur Wright, 18 Aug. 1900; in *Letters*, pp. 24–26.

30. Wilbur Wright to his father, 3 and 23 Sep. 1900, in *Letters*, pp. 27, 30–31.

31. Orville Wright to his sister, 14 and 18 Oct. 1900; Wilbur Wright to Octave Chanute, 16 Nov. 1900; both in *Letters*, pp. 32–35, 38. See also Kelly, *Wright Brothers*, pp. 58–66.

32. Wilbur Wright to Octave Chanute, 26 July 1901; Wilbur Wright, diary, 30 July 1901; both in *Letters*, pp. 40–42. See also Kelly, *Wright Brothers*, 67–72.

33. Wilbur Wright to Octave Chanute, 6 Oct., 22 Nov., 19 and 23 Dec. 1901, 5 and 19 Jan. 1902, in *Letters*, pp. 51–58.

34. *Letters*, pp. 70–86.

35. *Letters*, pp. 103–12.

36. Orville Wright to Charles Taylor, 20 Oct. 1903, in *Letters*, p. 105.

37. Wilbur Wright to Octave Chanute, 28 Dec. 1903, in *Letters*, pp. 121–22; Orville Wright, diary, 17 Dec. 1903, in *Letters*, pp. 114–16.

38. *Letters*, p. 118; Sullivan, *Our Times*, pp. 592–94; Kelly, *Wright Brothers*, pp. 102–109.

39. "Fall Wrecks Airship," *New York Times*, 27 May 1904, p. 1.

40. Wilbur and Orville Wright to Congressman Robert M. Nevin, 18 Jan. 1905, in *Letters*, pp. 135–36; Major General G. L. Gillespie to Congressman Nevin, in *Letters*, pp. 136–37.

41. Wilbur Wright to Octave Chanute, 1 June 1905, in *Letters*, pp. 142–43.

42. "Another Attempt to Solve Aerial Navigation Problem," *New York Times Sunday Magazine*, 7 Jan. 1906, p. 2. See also "The Aero Club of America's Exhibition of Aeronautical Apparatus," *Scientific American* 94 (22 Jan. 1906): 93–94; *Letters*, p. 153; Roger E. Bilstein, "Popular Attitudes towards Aviation, 1900–1925," in Richard P. Hallion, ed., *The Wright Brothers: Heirs of Prometheus* (Washington, D.C.: Smithsonian Institution Press, 1978), pp. 39–51; Marvin W. McFarland, "When the Airplane Was a Military Secret: A Study of National Attitudes before 1914," *U.S. Air Services* 39 (Sep. 1954): 11–16, and 39 (Oct. 1954): 18–22.

43. On the Wrights and Great Britain, see Wilbur Wright to Octave Chanute, 2 Jan. 1906, in *Letters*, pp. 163–64; Kelly, *Wright Brothers*, pp. 186–87; "English Aeronaut Sees the Wright Brothers," *New York Times*, 9 Dec. 1906, p. 14. On the Wrights and Germany, see "Germany Wants Airship. Wrights' Invention Soon to Have an Official Test," *New York Times*, 28 Apr. 1907, part 3, p. 3; "Germany to Get Wrights' Airship," 1 May 1907, p. 4; "Wrights Sell Airship," 6 June 1907, p. 1; "Wilbur Wright Won't Reply," 4 July 1907, p. 4; *Letters*, pp. 230–37; "The Wrights in Germany," 19 Oct. 1907, p. 1; and Wilbur Wright to Octave Chanute, 9 Dec. 1907, in *Letters*, pp. 242–45. On the Wrights and France, see Wilbur Wright to Octave Chanute, 6 May 1905, and Wilbur Wright to the French Ambas-

sador, 28 Nov. 1905, both in *Letters,* pp. 140–41 and 159–60; Kelly, *Wright Brothers,* pp. 174–75 and 186–87; Sullivan, *Our Times,* pp. 597–98; Wilbur Wright to Octave Chanute, 2 Jan. 1906, in *Letters,* pp. 163–64; "The New Flying Machine," *New York Times,* 2 Mar. 1906, p. 8, and "Aero Club Honors the Wright Brothers," 18 Mar. 1906, p. 8; Wilbur Wright to Orville Wright, 25 June 1907, in *Letters,* p. 220; and "Wilbur Wright Won't Reply," *New York Times,* 4 July 1907, p. 4. The *New York Times* apparently confused francs with dollars and thus exaggerated the amount of the French payment for the Wrights' secret formulas by a factor of five. After France settled its dispute with Germany over Morocco in Apr. 1906, fears of war faded and the French interest in the Wrights' airplane waned as well.

44. *Letters,* pp. 203–15.

45. "Interesting Experiments in Aeronautics Conducted in Washington," *New York Times,* 29 Sep. 1907, part 5, p. 10.

46. "May Ask Congress for Army Airship," *New York Times,* 11 Nov. 1907, p. 16.

47. "To Spend $25,000 for Army Airship," *New York Times,* 20 Nov. 1907, p. 8.

48. "Our Army to Have an Airship Fleet," *New York Times,* 15 Dec. 1907, part 3, p. 3.

49. "Army to Buy Aeroplane," *New York Times,* 26 Nov. 1907, p. 5.

50. Kelly, *Wright Brothers,* pp. 210–11; "Government Asks Bids for Airship," *New York Times,* 24 Dec. 1907, p. 1.

51. *Letters,* pp. 225; "Bids for Army Airships," *New York Times,* 2 Feb. 1908, part 3, p. 3; "Three Aeroplanes for Signal Corps," 9 Feb. 1908, part 2, p. 5; Kelly, *Wright Brothers,* pp. 211–12.

52. Sullivan, *Our Times,* pp. 602–13.

53. Arthur Ruhl, "History at Kill Devil Hill," *Collier's* 41 (30 May 1908): 18–19; "The Wrights Fly 1,000 Feet," *New York Times,* 7 May 1908, p. 1; "Aeroplane's Ten Flights," 9 May 1908, p. 1; "Wright Aeroplane Tests," 10 May 1908, part 3, p. 1; "Good Flights by Wrights," 12 May 1908, p. 1; "Wright Aeroplane Goes Three Miles," 14 May 1908, p. 1; "Aeroplane Crushed after Long Flight," 15 May 1908, p. 1; "Wright Brothers Not Discouraged," 16 May 1908, p. 8.

54. "Two Brothers' Efforts to Master the Air," *New York Times,* 17 May 1908, part 5, p. 17.

55. "Aeroplanes to Be Put to a Government Test," *New York Times,* 28 June 1908, part 5, p. 8.

56. "Air Warships Soon, Chanute Predicts," *New York Times,* 1 July 1908, p. 16.

57. "Farman Doesn't Think Trials at Fort Myer to Result in Much," *New York Times,* 30 July 1908, p. 3.

58. "French Praise Wrights," *New York Times,* 10 Aug. 1908, p. 2; Letters, 265–95; "The Wright Aeroplane in France," *Collier's* 41 (29 Aug. 1908): 4; "The Wright Aeroplane at Close Range at Le Mans, France," *New York Times,* 41 (5 Sep. 1908): 9.

59. "Wright Aeroplane Flies at Capitol," *New York Times,* 4 Sep. 1908, p. 1; "Wright Flies Again," 5 Sep. 1908, p. 1; "Wright Aeroplane Flies 19 Minutes," 6 Sep. 1908, p. 1; "Want Military Aeroplanes," 7 Sep. 1908, p. 1.

60. "Wright Gets More Time," *New York Times,* 30 Sep. 1908, p. 1.

61. "Wright Ship Up Over 70 Minutes," *New York Times,* 12 Sep. 1908, pp. 1, 2; "Experts on Wright's Work," 12 Sep. 1908, p. 2; "Wright Breaks His Airship Record," 13 Sep. 1908, part 3, pp. 1, 3; "President May Go Up in Wright Airship," *New York Times,* 15 Sep. 1908, p. 8.

62. *Letters,* pp. 313–15; "Fatal Fall of Wright Airship," *New York Times,* 18 Sep. 1908, pp. 1, 2.

63. "Skyscraping at Fort Myer," *Collier's* 42 (26 Sep. 1908): 11.

64. "The Tragic Flight at Fort Myer," *Collier's* 42 (3 Oct. 1908): 11.

65. "Fatal Fall of Wright Airship," *New York Times,* 18 Sep. 1908, pp. 1, 2.

66. "The Fall of the Airship," *New York Times,* 19 Sep. 1908, p. 6.

67. "Wright in His Cot Finds Why He Fell," *New York Times,* 19 Sep. 1908, pp. 1–3; "Orville Wright Is Not So Well," 20 Sep. 1908, part 2, p. 6.

68. "Wilbur Wright Flies Nearly 92 Minutes," *New York Times*, 22 Sep. 1908, p. 1; "New Wright Record," 26 Sep. 1908, p. 1; "Wright Again Beats Record," 29 Sep. 1908, p. 1.

69. "Wright Gets More Time," *New York Times*, 30 Sep. 1908, p. 1; "Frenchmen Honor Wright," 6 Nov. 1908, p. 6; "British Medal for Wrights," 15 Nov. 1908, part 2, p. 1; "Medals for the Wrights," 11 Dec. 1908, p. 2; "Honor for Wrights," 17 Dec. 1908, p. 6; "Medals for the Wrights," 26 Jan. 1909, p. 8, and 4 Mar. 1909, p. 3; "Wrights Get Langley Medal," 14 Feb. 1909, p. 14.

70. "Wrights Fail to Fly," *New York Times*, 29 June 1909, p. 1; "Independence Carried to Excess," 30 June 1909, p. 6.

71. "Wright Aeroplane Fails, Then Flies," *New York Times*, 30 June 1909, p. 1; "Aeroplane Balks, Wright Flight Brief," 1 July 1909, p. 6; "Wright Makes Three Successful Flights," 2 July 1909, p. 1; "Wright Hits Tree, Wrecks Aeroplane," 3 July 1909, p. 1; "Trying to the Temper," 5 July 1909, p. 6.

72. "Wilbur Wright Here," *New York Times*, 7 July 1909, p. 1; "Wrights Not Moved by Officers' Pique," 8 July 1909, p. 8.

73. "Congress Frowns on Wrights' Mishaps," *New York Times*, 19 July 1909, p. 14.

74. "Wright Sets New American Record," *New York Times*, 21 July 1909, p. 1; John Goldstrom, *A Narrative History of Aviation* (New York: Macmillan, 1930), pp. 65–70.

75. "For Two Navy Aeroplanes," *New York Times*, 14 Aug. 1909, p. 6; "Navy Aeronauts Must Wait," 18 Aug. 1909, p. 4.

76. Renstrom, *Wilbur and Orville Wright*, pp. 35–42.

77. "House Votes Down Airships," *New York Times*, 3 Feb. 1909, p. 3.

CHAPTER 2

Innovation in America's Aviation Support Infrastructure

The Evolving Relationship between Airports, Cities, and Industry

JANET R. DALY BEDNAREK

T he development of municipal airports represents one of the little-appreciated chapters in aeronautical innovation in the history of twentieth-century America. The important issues and themes at work during the formative period (1918–40) of municipal airports involved experimentation and innovation at many levels, private and public organizations, people both famous and obscure, institutions rigid and innovative. The key actors included various agencies of the government in promoting and directing airport development, but more importantly, airport evolution pointed to the changing relationship between cities and the federal government.

When the first cities began to build airports in 1919, they were treading on new ground. Airports, like airplanes, were recent inventions. Cities had few examples, if any, to follow. In many ways, therefore, the earliest municipal airports grew out of very individual experimentation on the part of many cities. Over the first eight or nine years of airport development, cities had to devise ways to build and finance airports, sometimes stretching existing municipal powers to their limits. Different cities came up with different answers as to how best to accomplish the job. Although it was generally acknowledged that airports should be built locally, what exactly constituted municipal airports, how they should be built and financed, and what their relationship to their sponsoring cities should be had to be worked out gradually by cities, by the courts, and by federal agencies involved in airport promotion. Even the idea that "municipal airport" meant only an airport owned and operated by a city did not come about until the 1930s.

Several federal government agencies played important roles in encouraging municipal airport development. The Post Office and the Commerce Department both pushed cities to provide basic airport facilities and attempted to require them to provide frequently improved and updated facilities. The work relief programs of the 1930s gave cities financial aid for airport improvement. The existing literature generally acknowledges the contributions of those agencies and their roles in attempting to set uniform standards for airports. Another division of the federal government, though, was also deeply involved. The military, especially the Army Air Service (later the Army Air Corps), also strongly encouraged the construction of some of the nation's earliest municipal airports.

As airports became more complex (and more expensive), cities found that they could not hope to shoulder the total burden of airport construction, maintenance, and improvement. As part of a general trend during the 1930s toward a strong, more direct relationship between cities and the federal government, federal aid to airports (direct, rather than in the form of work relief) became an important issue pushed by cities. The end result, though less than that for which cities had hoped, was the acknowledgment of the need for a national airport plan that would include direct federal aid to cities.

PIONEER EFFORTS: WORLD WAR I TO 1926

Outside Dayton, Ohio, on a piece of land now within the confines of Wright-Patterson Air Force Base, is the location of what is arguably the world's first airport, the Huffman Prairie Flying Field.[1] After their triumph on the remote Outer Banks of North Carolina in December 1903, Wilbur and Orville Wright sought a location nearer their home to further test and refine their invention. A local landowner, Torrence Huffman, agreed to let the brothers use a pasture he owned outside of town, just off the interurban rail line, as long as they were careful not to let the horses and cows stray. The brothers agreed, and during the next two years the Huffman Prairie Flying Field witnessed the first regular takeoffs and landings of a manned, heavier-than-air flying machine. Before becoming part of Wilbur Wright Field during World War I, the flying field also served as the location of the Wright brothers' flying school and exhibition company.[2]

Calling the Huffman Prairie an airport may, indeed, be a bit of an exaggeration. The location was basically an open, level field, wide enough and long enough to accommodate the takeoff and landing requirements of the early Wright flyers, and over the years the brothers built three hangars on the site (in 1904, 1905, and 1910). Generally speaking, though, the Huffman Prairie Flying Field probably was quite similar to the other fields being used for land-based aircraft.[3] In the years before World War I, with the exception of a few military training fields and perhaps a few private fields, airfields remained rather simple, informal places. As the Wright and Curtiss exhibition companies toured the country, for example, they frequently operated out of airfields that had only become airfields in anticipation of their arrival. In the early days any flat, open pieces of land—including golf courses, racetracks, and fairgrounds—could and did serve as airfields. As long as flying remained exhibition oriented and experimental in nature, such arrangements worked fairly well. All that changed with the need for military pilots and then, more importantly, Post Office pilots to fly from one location to another on a regular basis.

During World War I the U.S. Army needed to train its fliers not just to fly, but to fly over long distances and from one location to another. In part to that end, and in part out of the need to train a large number of pilots rapidly, the War Department built a number of flying field-training bases throughout the country. While the military did create something of a network of flying fields and brought regular flying activity to a number of communities around the country, the more important program started during the conflict was that of flying the mail.

In the 1917–18 budget, Congress gave the Post Office $100,000 to conduct airmail experiments. Although it would eventually own its own planes and hire its own pilots, in order to get started as soon as possible, the Post Office borrowed both planes and pilots from the U.S. Air Service (which saw flying the mail as a training opportunity). On 15 May 1918, flying from a makeshift field between the Potomac River and the Tidal Basin in Washington, D.C., the first government airmail plane took off for New York. That first airmail flight set off in the wrong direction and then crash-landed about 25 miles away in Waldorf, Maryland. Despite the rather dismal first performance, the airmail service, sought for years by the business community, soon established itself as reliable and valuable.[4] But in order for the service to expand, it needed not only more planes and pilots but a network of airports to receive and service the planes and handle the airmail bags. Out of the dual need of the Post Office and the military (the army, especially, but also the navy) for more fields came the first municipal airports. Some of the earliest municipal fields initially served military needs; others of those established before 1927 served Post Office needs. Many eventually served both.

Several cities claim the honor of having the country's first municipal airport. One of those cities is Tucson, Arizona. While not the first,[5] it certainly was a very early municipal airport and represented an example of the military's encouragement of municipal airport construction. In early 1919 the Tucson Chamber of Commerce organized an Aviation Committee, and the local newspaper began to promote the city as "'an ideal place for aviators.'"[6] Probably coincidentally, in May 1919 the mayor of Tucson received a letter from the U.S.

Air Service requesting that the city build an airfield. A few months later a local councilman, Randolph E. Fishburn, convinced the city council to finance and build such a facility. Apparently, the Chamber of Commerce donated money to the city and the airport funding came out of that money, "with the chamber's blessings." On 20 November 1919, the municipally owned airport opened for business, both military and civilian. During its early years the Aviation Committee of the Chamber of Commerce operated the airport.[7]

Pittsburgh responded both to the needs of the U.S. Air Service and to the fact that its urban rival, Cleveland, had a place on the Post Office's developing transcontinental airmail route in working to establish its first airport. In their early arguments in favor of an airport, proponents pointed out that both the military, especially the Air Service, and the Post Office were working to expand the nation's network of airports. In part because Pittsburgh lacked a landing field, the Post Office already had passed the city by. Pittsburgh had not acted quickly enough. However, in late 1921 the city saw an opportunity to make up for its tardiness by participating in the Air Service's Reserve Flying Fields program.[8]

The Air Service's program aimed at creating a network of flying fields where both government and civilian planes could "find good landing, shelter from storms, mechanical assistance, communication by phone . . . and every other courtesy which the army can afford." Under the program cities provided fields that the Air Service leased for one dollar per year. Pittsburgh's Chamber of Commerce opened talks with the War Department. The problem was that in 1922, when negotiations began, the city lacked the power to purchase land for an airport. At that point, the Aero Club of Pittsburgh stepped in, leased the land that the city and the War Department had identified as the most suitable for an airport, and, in turn, leased it to the War Department. The new airport, Rodgers Field, was named in honor of Calbraith Rodgers, a Pittsburgh native and the first person to fly coast to coast.[9]

In 1923 Pittsburgh's solicitor drafted two bills that were sent to the state legislature. One enabled counties to purchase land for airports, and the other enabled cities of a certain class to do so as well, both within and without city limits. Why the city sent forth both bills was unclear. Perhaps proponents wanted to double their chances for success (even if the state legislature rejected one bill, it might approve the other). Or perhaps, as subsequent actions suggest, the city of Pittsburgh needed some assistance and hoped to persuade the county of Allegheny to help in the airport project by either taking it over entirely or by sharing the costs. Either way, both bills passed, and in 1923 the city and county entered into talks that produced a city-county agreement to purchase Rodgers Field and operate a city-county airport. Despite some local opposition (from the

Fox Chapel Country Club and the elite Shadyside Academy located near the site), Rodgers Field opened as a city-county airport in June 1925.[10]

Pittsburgh, though mindful of the airmail program, opened its airport primarily to help the Air Service. Atlanta, on the other hand, acted in response to both push and pull factors. The Air Service pushed Atlanta to adopt an airport program, and at the same time the pull of a possible spot on the airmail network inspired local aviation enthusiasts.

About the same time that one group of Air Service representatives opened discussions with Pittsburgh officials, another pursued a similar course of action in Atlanta. In 1921 Air Service officers arrived in the city as part of a project surveying a Washington-San Diego transcontinental air route. While a couple of local groups (reserve army officers and the Chamber of Commerce) responded favorably, Atlanta's new mayor, William Sims, declared the project too expensive, and it quietly died. Two years later, however, the Air Service again approached the city. It wanted to establish an airfield at the existing arsenal south of the city and to explore again the possibility of the city establishing an airfield. Atlanta businessmen expressed a strong desire to bring airmail service to the city. A local newspaper pointed out that the Post Office had rejected one proposed route (Atlanta to New York via Washington, D.C.) because Atlanta had no official airport.[11]

Mayor Sims remained reluctant to commit the city. He argued that the site proposed initially cost too much, even with the county picking up half the tab. In fact, as it turned out, the city did not have the money in its budget. Then in December 1924 a local aviation pioneer, Asa G. Candler, offered the city a deal on his property, an abandoned racetrack that had been the site of aviation exhibitions. The city could have the land rent-free for two years; all it had to do was pay the taxes. Still the city failed to take action. Local pressure increased, however, and in February 1925 several local civic groups, backed by the senior U.S. senator from Georgia—who promised that if Atlanta became part of a government airmail route, the government would pay for the airport—mounted a coordinated campaign to gain such a facility for the city. Asa Candler again offered his land, and on 12 April 1925 Mayor Sims, on behalf of the city, signed a lease for the property, which became Atlanta's municipal airport. The city would have to wait another year before the airmail finally arrived.[12]

Other early municipal airports sprang into existence primarily to serve the Post Office. During the first years of the airmail service, the Post Office continued to operate out of whatever landing fields were available. As noted, the first airmail flight took off from a temporary field in Washington, D.C. Like the Air Service did, in the early 1920s Post Office officials traveled across the country trying by various means, including broadly hinting at possible federal aid, to entice cities to establish municipal airports. It had few immediate takers.[13] However, as the airmail service grew during the early 1920s and the commercial potential of air travel became more easily imagined, several cities along the early airmail routes took action to build municipal airports.

Chicago, an early and important stop on the growing airmail service network, represented an early example of municipal involvement in airport finance and construction. In 1916 the Aero Club of Chicago financed and developed an airport at 83rd Street and Cicero Avenue, calling it Ashburn Field. When the Post Office announced plans for airmail service to Chicago, the club hoped that the Post Office would use Ashburn Field as its terminal. Considered too remote, it lost out to Grant Park along the Chicago waterfront, which had been used as an aviation exhibition field. In 1919 the club went to the city of Chicago hoping to persuade the city council to invest money in Ashburn Field in order to establish it as Chicago's municipal airport. That plan failed in the wake of a disastrous blimp crash that soured many on the city council to the whole idea of aviation.[14]

During the first eight years of operation, the airmail service in Chicago shifted between three airports — Grant Park, Checkerboard Field, and Maywood Field, the latter two located west of the city limits. Following the establishment of round-the-clock airmail flights in 1924, many civic leaders in Chicago pushed to build a municipal airport within the city. Charles Wacker, chairman of the City Plan Commission, went to the city council in July 1924 asking that it lease some property owned by the Board of Education for use as an airport. The city council initially took little action. But in early 1925, with the passage of the Kelly Act, the council moved quickly to sign a lease, and early the following year it approved $25,000 for improvements to the field.[15]

As noted, when the Post Office tried to recruit cities to build airports, few responded. For one thing, simple as they were (still often open fields with perhaps a single hangar; only a few airports, as yet, had lighting), the early airports still cost money, and although the Post Office (and others, according to the Atlanta example) apparently hinted at eventual government reimbursements, no money flowed into municipal coffers to help pay expenses.[16] Secondly, cities had never built airports before and, as noted in the Pittsburgh example, had no authority to begin to do so. In the United States, cities are creations of the states in which they are located. Even with home rule, the powers of cities are (and were) limited by their charters. Before a city could build an airport, it had to either find a way to stretch its existing powers (as apparently Tucson, Atlanta, and Chicago did) or be enabled by the state to specifically build an airport.

Indiana passed the first general airport enabling act in 1920. Pennsylvania also acted early (1923), along with Minnesota (1923), Ohio (1926), Washington (1925), and Wisconsin (1921). However, most states took no action before 1927. Before that date, cities employed various means to get their airports built. As a consequence, the term "municipal airport" must be viewed as being somewhat elastic during the early years. Until the 1930s, the term did not necessarily always apply to municipally owned airports. For example, answering the urgings of a local civic group, the state of Massachusetts enabled the state's department of public works to build Boston's first "municipal" airport. The state leased the facility to the army, but it remained open to civilian and commercial use as well. The city did not take over the airport until 1928. Omaha's Chamber of Commerce provided that city with its first municipal airport in 1920 by raising money to build a hangar on property it rented from another civic organization, AK-SAR-BEN, which operated a racetrack on the land. That airport, created for the use of the Post Office, helped establish Omaha as an important link on the emerging transcontinental airmail network. St. Louis civic leaders also, apparently, took action similar to that of Omaha's. Therefore, the earliest municipal airports came about by various means, including being built by a city, by a city-county combination, by the state within a city, and by a local civic group in the city's name. The general idea was, though, that airports should be built by local interests and preferably with strong ties (formal or informal) to the local government. [17]

If, indeed, cities lacked the specific power to build and operate airports, why all the early, persistent insistence upon municipal airports as the means to building a network of landing fields throughout the country? Both the military and the Post Office encouraged cities to build airports. In one way, neither had any choice, as neither had budgets large enough to build the needed facilities. In the absence of federal funds, those organizations turned to the governmental body they deemed most likely to agree (or be convinced to agree) to build airports. And the Post Office and the Air Service lobbied cities hard.

In one of the very first works published on the subject of municipal airports, the chief of the Army Air Service, Major General Charles T. Menoher, argued for municipal airport construction. He appealed to the booster element in cities by noting that any city failing to build an airport would find itself losing out in the coming age of aerial transportation. He further asserted that the nation needed a network of landing fields "established under municipal control by cities and towns" in order to promote commercial aviation and make it safer. Finally, he stated that municipal airports also contributed to national defense.[18] The article seemed to take it for granted that municipally owned airports were the way to go. It offered no real specific argument for that particular means of building and financing airports.

More specific arguments for why cities should shoulder the responsibility for airport construction appeared in two early articles by Archibald Black, a consulting engineer, who apparently ranked as one of the first, if not the first, consulting engineers specifically interested in airport construction. In the first article, written in 1923, Black argued that cities must take action to build airports as "many cities have only one or two really suitable sites for air terminals," and unless the city established its ownership over it, the site would undoubtedly come under the control of the first commercial airline to enter the city. That airline would then act to prevent others from entering the city, which Black deemed as "not a very healthy condition for the city."[19]

In a second article, written in 1925, Black appealed to the booster element. He argued that cities needed to act immediately to provide landing fields lest they lose out in the competition with their urban rivals. As in the 1923 article, Black asserted that cities could provide themselves with landing fields at minimal cost. All cities had to do was purchase the land and prepare it for use by aircraft (grading, providing drainage, etc.). Hangars and other equipment could wait, but every city that intended to remain a thriving, progressive city needed at least to have a municipal landing field on the map.[20]

Black's articles also hinted at why airports should be built by the public sector rather than the private sector. Airports, though supposedly inexpensive to build, were unlikely to make money, at least in the short run. The private sector could not be expected to provide a large number of airports if they were expected to be money-losers. As has often been the case, governments, especially local governments, were expected to step in and provide the services that could not be provided at a profit by the private sector.

The arguments in favor of municipal airports (versus commercial and/or private airports) remained somewhat vague during this early period of airport construction. In fact, commercial and/or private airports far outnumbered municipal airports until the late 1920s. But it was clear that at least two prominent forces behind aviation development in the United States, the military and the Post Office, preferred and promoted the idea of municipal airports. In the early 1920s, the Glenn L. Martin Company also produced a brochure promoting the construction of municipal airports (the brochure called them "municipal airdromes").[21] During the next phase of airport construction, the arguments favoring municipal airports would be strengthened and more clearly articulated. Cities, too, became more enthusiastic about the idea.

THE ERA OF AIRPORT ENTHUSIASM, 1926–33

The Post Office, the military, and other aviation promoters may have had a hard time convincing cities to build airports during the early years; however, between

1925 and 1927 three things happened that together contributed to an explosion of municipal airport construction activity. First, in 1925 Congress passed the Airmail Act (or Kelly Bill). Responding to pressure from the fledgling and struggling commercial airline industry in the United States, Congress voted to turn responsibility for carrying the mail to commercial carriers, who would work under contract for the Post Office. The following year Congress passed the Air Commerce Act. That piece of legislation created within the Department of Commerce and Aeronautics Bureau (later the Bureau of Air Commerce). The bureau had responsibility for constructing the nation's airway system and, in general, promoting aviation activity. Together, those two laws put the federal government in the business of aiding and promoting the growth of commercial aviation in the United States.

Those acts by themselves worked to stimulate some cities to begin to look at constructing a municipal airport. However, action remained at a rather low level until the energizing influence of Charles Lindbergh's solo flight across the Atlantic came into play. Lindbergh's feat fanned the flames of aviation enthusiasm all across the United States. In the wake of his flight, and subsequent promotional tour of the country, city after city rushed to jump on the aviation bandwagon.

First, however, states needed to respond with the necessary enabling legislation. Between 1927 and 1929 at least thirty-three states passed general or specific enabling acts. (Some state acts allowed all cities of a certain class to own airports; others enabled a specifically named city within the state to do so.)[22] Collectively, this innovation, government ownership of airports, transformed the industry. While the acts varied from state to state, all allowed cities (and some other substate jurisdictions such as counties) to own and operate airports. City ownership of airports, as a result, became familiar. "Municipal airport," however, still remained something of an elastic term. While it seems that most cities after 1926 chose to own their airports, some cities continued to lease land or to allow private interests to build and operate airports (under a certain amount of city supervision) and call the result "the municipal airport." That elasticity would remain until the New Deal era.

Wichita, Kansas, ranked among those cities inspired by the new circumstances of the late 1920s to take innovative action to build and operate a municipal airport. Aviation enthusiasts in Wichita began pushing for an airport as early as 1919. They needed a place at which to hold aerial demonstrations and service aircraft. Also, the Post Office made it clear that a city had to have an "official" airport before it could become a stop on the new airmail network. To give the city an "official" airport, the local Chamber of Commerce bought a 75-acre field just outside the city limits. Despite the fact that Wichita had a substantial amount of aviation industry activity within its boundaries (Swallow, Travel Air, Stearman, and Cessna all operated plants in Wichita), the small, suburban field remained Wichita's airport until 1929.[23]

In 1929 the Wichita Chamber of Commerce once again took action to provide its city with an airport that would live up to Wichita's claim of being "the air capital." The chamber helped convince the Kansas state legislature to pass a law enabling all cities of the first class (over 65,000 in population) to "acquire within or without the city limits a municipal airport," which would fall under the jurisdiction of the city's Board of Park Commissioners. With the enabling legislation in place, the city of Wichita purchased 640 acres of land just outside of the city limits, six and one-half miles from the downtown. The new airport had four turf landing strips, allowing for all-direction landing; two measured 4,800 feet in length and the other two measured 4,200 feet and 3,600 feet, respectively. Over the next two years the city and park commission installed an airport lighting system, completed a large brick-and-steel hangar, and began construction of a large airport administration building.[24]

San Diego, California, was another city that responded to the enthusiasm created in the wake of the Lindbergh flight. That city's Chamber of Commerce created an Aviation Committee as early as 1922. In that year, the committee urged the city to use its city plan to reserve area for an airport along the waterfront. The city took no action, though, until 1927. Especially inspired by the Lindbergh flight (Lindbergh's plane, though named "Spirit of St. Louis," had been built by Ryan Aircraft in San Diego), the citizens of San Diego approved a $650,000 bond issue to finance the initial work on an airport. The city located its new airport on basically the same site that the Chamber of Commerce had recommended in 1922. Construction involved "dredging in San Diego harbor and dumping this soil on the tideland airport area." The dredging activity reclaimed about 105 acres from San Diego Bay.[25]

Although the Air Commerce Act specifically forbade federal funding for airports, San Diego, nonetheless, received "federal aid" in the construction of its airport. In addition to the 105 acres reclaimed by city dredging efforts, the War Department also conducted dredging operations to reclaim 182 acres of land it owned adjacent to the new airport. Some of that land also became part of the new municipal airport. Adjacent to the municipal and War Department land stood a Marine Corps aviation field. In time of war, a combination of the Marine Corps field and the municipal field would allow for a two-and-one-half-mile-long runway. Named in honor of Colonel Lindbergh, San Diego's municipal airport soon became a center of both commercial and military aviation activity.[26] Thus, although the Post Office and the Department of Commerce received the most attention for promoting aviation, the military still played a role.

Not every city had to start from scratch in order to acquire a municipal (meaning municipally owned) airport. Some cities simply bought an existing airport. Atlanta, as noted earlier, created its first "official" airport when it leased land south of the city. In 1929, following the passage of a law specifically enabling Atlanta to "purchase, own and operate municipal landing fields . . . located within or without the limits of the city," the city bought Candler field, later renamed Atlanta Municipal Airport.[27]

Even with enabling laws in place, some cities continued either to have local private/commercial interests provide them with their municipal airports or to lease, rather than buy, airport property. Two such examples are Dayton, Ohio, and Los Angeles, California. Following the passage of the Air Mail Act in 1925, several private airports offered to be named Dayton's municipal airport. The city accepted a bid from the Moraine Flying Field, located south of the city, and it, while remaining in private hands, served as Dayton's "official municipal airport" for two years. Following Lindbergh's flight, the city explored the possibility of either building its own airport south of the city (enabling legislation was in place by that point) or taking over the soon-to-be-abandoned McCook Field site across from the downtown. Nothing came immediately of either initiative, and in 1928 the city signed an agreement with the Air Corps. Airmail planes destined for Dayton could land at Wright Field, located east of the city, until the city built its own airport in late 1930 or 1931.

Dayton's business leaders wanted a municipal airport much faster than the city apparently was willing to provide one. Therefore, they took matters into their own hands, incorporating the Dayton Municipal Airport Company in March 1928. They then sold shares, raising $300,000, and used the money to buy property near Vandalia, Ohio. In early 1929 the city arranged for the airmail service to transfer from Wright Field to the Vandalia airport. And in the summer of 1929 the city and the Dayton Municipal Airport Company held a dedication ceremony for the new Dayton Airport.[28]

During the 1920s the Los Angeles area witnessed the creation of a number of private and commercial airports. Those included the Venice Airport, the Chaplin Airport, and the Los Angeles Metropolitan Airport. After the passage of the Air Commerce Act, however, many civic leaders decided that the city needed a public airport, and in 1927 the California state legislature passed the needed enabling act. Inspired by Lindbergh's flight, the city council resolved to take action and began to take bids from property owners of potential airport sites. The city looked at twenty-seven different properties before narrowing the competition down to three. However, the council could come to no agreement over which site to purchase. With the idea that it might purchase up to three separate as yet unspecified airport sites (each serving a different part of the Los

Angeles area), the city council put a $6 million bond issue on the ballot in May 1928. The vague wording of the bond issue, however, contributed to its defeat.[29]

Following the bond issue defeat, the Los Angeles City Council finally settled on a site in Inglewood, which had recently been selected as the location for the upcoming 1928 National Air Races. Once the air races were over, Los Angeles took control of what became known as Mines Field (named after William W. Mines, the real estate agent who handled the property transaction). However, the city chose to lease, rather than purchase, the land. The defeat of the bond issue suggested a general lack of support for a city-owned airport. Further, many still objected to the Mines Field site. By leasing, the city could "experiment with municipal airport operations and decide whether or not the Mines site was suitable." The city council approved the lease idea on 26 September 1928, the day after it created the Los Angeles Department of Airports to administer the new municipal airport.[30]

Even more clearly than during the pioneering period, and despite the still considerable amount of variation in practices, between 1926 and 1933 municipally owned airports seemed to be the preferred method of building the nation's aviation infrastructure. Reflecting that, the arguments for municipal ownership of airports became much stronger and more elaborate.

Nearly all arguments supporting municipally owned airports began by comparing airports to other transportation terminals, such as railroad stations and harbors. The railroad example did not support municipal ownership, though. Railroad terminals were privately owned and operated by the railroad companies, which, like the airline companies, were privately owned and operated. Not deterred, proponents of municipal ownership then moved on to the example of docks and harbors. In the case of water transportation, historically dock and harbor facilities had been both privately and publicly owned. As a result, many proponents of municipal ownership of airports began to refer to airports as harbors of the air.[31] The lack of a strong, unambiguous example in favor of municipal ownership did seem to cause some to qualify their argument. In Harvard University's study of airports conducted by city planners Henry V. Hubbard, Miller McClintock, and Frank B. Williams, for example, the authors concluded that while municipal ownership appeared to be the best means of building a network of airports at present (1930), in the future airports might just as well be provided by private, commercial interests.[32]

Most of the other proponents of municipal airports, on the other hand, moved on from the transportation terminal example to provide other arguments in favor of municipal ownership. Austin MacDonald provided one of the more concise discussions of additional points brought up by several people in favor of municipal ownership. He asserted that municipally (or publicly) owned airports were most likely to treat all aviators, private and commercial, fairly and equally. At privately owned airports, on the other hand, the commercial operators owning the airport or the largest lessors of airport property were likely to be treated the best. Other lessors/users were likely to find themselves at a disadvantage.

MacDonald declared that the strongest argument in favor of municipal ownership "[was] that the airport land must be kept in public hands in order to prevent its diversion to other uses." Municipal land values changed over time. The owners of a privately owned airport situated at a prime location might find that within a few years their property might yield a greater return if used for other purposes (commercial, industrial, or residential). The owners, in that case, would be likely to sell. Only a public body could afford to withstand such a temptation.[33]

Those arguments in favor of municipal ownership coincided with the explosion of municipal action in the late 1920s. They came at a time when municipally owned airports began to exceed the number of private and commercial airports in the United States. Theory and practice thus reinforced each other. A number of court cases from the era bolstered the arguments in favor of municipal ownership of airports by declaring the establishment of a municipal airport as a public purpose.

Not surprisingly, as city after city took action to purchase and operate an airport, some people objected and challenged the actions in court. One of the earliest cases involved the city of Cleveland, Ohio. When the city proposed issuing bonds in order to finance the construction of its municipal airport, the action was challenged on the grounds "that [it] was in violation of the state constitution in that it constituted a raising of money or loaning of credit to or in the aid of a corporation or company." The court ruled in Cleveland's favor. The decision asserted that even if airports were not specifically mentioned in the part of the state constitution allowing cities to build, own and operate public utilities, the enabling act passed by the state in 1926 did confer upon cities the power to build, own, and operate airports. The court found that the enabling act violated no parts of the state constitution. In several other cases also challenging municipal authority to construct and own airports, the courts found in favor of the cities.[34]

While the cases such as the one in Cleveland dealt primarily with a city's power to build and own an airport, another set of cases touched directly upon the issue of whether or not an airport represented a public purpose. An especially important case dealing with that issue was *Dysert v. City of St. Louis*, decided in late 1928. In the St. Louis case the plaintiffs first argued that, at best, airports served the needs of a few wealthy, reckless individuals engaged in private flying activities. Perhaps a few tourists and other travelers might arrive in the city by way of the airport, but airline transportation remained so expensive as to be available only to a tiny minority. The court rejected that argument, asserting instead that in the near future airline travel had the potential to be as common as travel by railroad or motor car.

The plaintiffs also argued that airports could be "better provided through private initiative and private capital." The court rejected that as well, declaring that airports were "a necessary instrumentality in a new method or system of transportation which [required] public aid for its development and final establishment." The court compared airport construction to aid offered the railroads in the nineteenth century and concluded that, like the railroads, "the increased prosperity of a community which might be expected to result from the new means of travel and transport made the purpose a public one."[35]

Other court cases echoed the opinions expressed in the St. Louis case. The Supreme Court of Oregon, for example, provided an extensive defense of the idea of airports as public purpose. In the case of *McClintock v. City of Roseburg*, the court maintained that the definition of public purpose had and would continue to change over time given "the changing conditions of society, new appliances in the sciences and other changes brought about by increased population and modes of transportation and communication." Commercial air travel had witnessed substantial growth in the late 1920s, and the court expressed the belief that the growth was likely to continue well into the future. It then asserted: "An airport owned by the city open to the use of all aeroplanes [was] for the benefit of the city as a community, and not of any particular individuals therein. It is therefore a public enterprise." Public ownership of airports, further, would assure that no commercial airline could monopolize the air travel into and from any city.[36]

Theory, practice, and the law all came together in favor of municipally owned airports by the late 1920s. But just as cities gained such strong support for building the airports they dreamed would afford them an important place on the emerging air transportation network, several other factors came together to dampen the enthusiasm and bring the whole enterprise down to earth. First, in late 1929 the country began to experience what would become the longest and most severe economic downturn in its history. Second, cities found themselves involved in several cases that signaled the fact that owning and operating an airport was not quite as simple as some cities had hoped it would be. The late 1920s and early 1930s saw several court cases dealing with issues of liability and of whether or not an airport constituted a nuisance. The early depression years, however, also saw continued experimentation and innovation on the part of cities. They began to focus on what social functions airports could perform, which, they hoped, might also help transform airports into paying propositions.

DEPRESSION AND REALITY: THE FADING ENTHUSIASM

It was all supposed to have been so simple. Archibald Black had said so in his pioneering articles in 1923 and 1925. In 1923 the Air Service published a how-to pamphlet on airport construction that seemed to lay things out clearly.[37] By the late 1920s cities could also take advantage of a series of brochures published by the Aeronautics Branch of the Department of Commerce. Buy a property, provide for grading and drainage, build a hangar, and, basically, a city had an airport. Cities all over the country jumped at the opportunity after 1927, but by the end of the decade they were finding that their simple enterprise was not so simple after all. Almost immediately the Post Office and the commercial airline companies began to demand a series of costly improvements (lighting, all-weather landing surfaces, two-way radio communications). Coinciding with the onset of the Great Depression, cities found themselves in the position of facing growing aviation demands and shrinking municipal revenues. Airports failed to make money, and yet cities were being asked to spend more and more on their development. Cities also found themselves in court defending themselves in liability and nuisance suits, which further contributed to the deterioration of the situation.

The law states that cities cannot be held liable "for alleged injuries to the persons or property of individuals when it is engaged in the performance of public or governmental functions." Several states passed laws that either declared municipal airports a governmental function or otherwise exempted municipalities from liability. Most states, and most courts, however, viewed municipal airports as a function of cities. In other words, much as when cities operated electric, gas, and water systems, when cities owned and operated airports they "[were] engaged in a private enterprise and not a governmental function and for that reason [were] liable for any injuries sustained by a third party as a result of the municipality's fault, just as any other private airport proprietor would have to be."[38]

In examining the issue of liability, in 1932 the *National Municipal Review* opined that while cities should be held liable for injuries sustained at municipally owned airports, nonetheless such a situation increased the cost of maintenance at most municipal airports. That increased cost constituted a "discouraging element" that, along with the depression, served to put a "decided check" on municipal subsidies to aviation "in the form of the establishment of municipally owned airports."[39]

In addition to being held liable for injuries, cities also found themselves in court defending their airports against the charge that they constituted a nuisance. Many of the earliest cases dealing with that issue involved private or commercial airports. Two important cases, arising in 1932 and 1934, did involve municipal airports. The first dealt with the airport leased by the city of Santa Monica, and the second dealt with Atlanta's municipally owned airport. In the Santa Monica case the court ruled "that the ordinary use of an airport need not necessarily result in a nuisance." Therefore, airports *per se* were not nuisances. However, the case did not resolve whether or not certain airport operations might constitute a nuisance. Cities, therefore, might still find themselves faced with injunctions against their airports because certain operations might produce, among other things, dust, noise, danger, and crowds.[40]

A 1934 case in Georgia seemed to lessen the possibility of airport operations being halted by injunctions aimed at preventing nuisances. Atlanta's airport, in place since 1925, had grown during the late 1920s and early 1930s once Atlanta became a stop on the airmail network. In 1934 an adjacent property owner, a Mr. Thrasher, complained that the dust stirred up by the airport made his wife ill, that planes flying low (under 500 feet) over his property constituted a danger, and that both he and his wife suffered from the noise produced by airport operations. Thrasher wanted the airport declared a common nuisance and put out of business.

The court decision was mixed but generally supported the airport. The court ruled that the airport did have to do something about the dust and "that Mrs. Thrasher could recover for her illness caused by such dust." One the other hand, as to the issues of noise, and particularly that of overflight, the court ruled in the city's and the airport's favor. On the latter issue, the court declared "that there was no proof sufficient to show that flying at less than 500 ft. was a trespass or a nuisance, and therefore refused to grant an injunction." Cities, however, remained subject to charges that their airports constituted nuisances throughout the prewar period.[41]

Faced with economic pressures caused by the depression and an increasingly complex legal situation, cities tried to convince people that airports were more than municipal money losers, liabilities, or nuisances. In an effort to make airports pay their own way, cities began to emphasize the social aspects of airports. Airports had always attracted crowds of people. Airplanes remained enough of a novelty that people still came out to the airports, especially on weekends, to view those modern marvels.[42]

Aviation enthusiasts concerned with airport finance began to make suggestions as to how airports might provide social and recreational facilities as a means to raise revenues. An article in *The American City* in 1930 suggested that airports take advantage of the crowds they attracted by establishing concessions.

The article then listed a number of possibilities, including refreshments, hotel, swimming pool, pay toilets, merry-go-round, and barber shop. The success of those concessions depended on the size of the crowds the airport could attract on the weekend. However, if the airport provided such concessions, it might increase the number of people interested in spending part of their weekend at the airport. The article concluded: "There is no reason why airports should not have many of the features of an amusement park, as the visitors to a flying field are there principally for amusement."[43]

The issue of concessions at airports also arose at the Second National Airport Conference, held in Buffalo, New York, in May 1930. A committee at that conference looked at the issue and came to the conclusion that concessions were "one of the promising sources of airport income." However, airports needed to be careful. Concessions should not be allowed to interfere with "maintaining a dignified basis of operations." Further, "amusement concessions in any case should be separated from flying activities." In the case of restaurants, airports should be guaranteed a "monthly minimum with a percentage basis beyond that." The bottom line was, though, that airports had to find some way to make money.[44]

The idea of providing social and recreational facilities at airports as a way to make money continued well into the 1930s. In 1935, Grand Central Air Terminal (a commercial airport) in Los Angeles used radio advertisements to try to convince people that the airport was a recreation center. The managers of the airport asked: "And why shouldn't an airport profit by satisfying the same needs that have been filled by motion picture theaters, restaurants, bazaars and the higher type of cocktail dispensaries?" Grand Central advertised that it offered a bar, a sidewalk cafe, and a first-class restaurant. In addition, the Los Angeles airport had an advantage all its own that might also help attract crowds. The airport's radio announcements included a list of the Hollywood stars expected at the airport and their times of arrival or departure. Los Angelenos could go to one of their local airports to gaze not only at the airplanes, but also at the stars. As late as 1940 *Aviation* published an article that encouraged airports to build country clubs that would offer pleasant facilities for private pilots on cross-country jaunts and for other visitors to the airport.[45]

The fact of the matter was that airports had become expensive and complex facilities. Faced with the rapid advance of aviation technology, which demanded frequent updates of airport equipment (including the landing areas); the rising costs of airport operations (including those caused by the legal situation); and the financial pressures exacerbated by the deepening economic depression, by the early 1930s cities could no longer build and maintain airports on their own. They needed help.

CITIES, THE FEDERAL GOVERNMENT, AND AIRPORTS, 1933–40

Help first came in the form of federal work relief programs. When Franklin D. Roosevelt became president in March 1933, millions of Americans were unemployed. Providing immediate relief to the out-of-work ranked high on the list of priorities for his new administration. To that end Congress passed the Federal Emergency Relief Act (FERA) and Roosevelt created the Civil Works Administration (CWA). Those two agencies provided cities with the means to hire labor to work on many needed projects, including airports. While both programs were temporary in nature, the FERA and the CWA began to establish the patterns for federal aid to municipal airports.

First, both the FERA and the CWA would give money for airport projects only if the city owned or leased the airport. As noted, some cities, such as Dayton, had designated private, commercial airports as their official airport. In order to receive aid, Dayton had to agree to lease the Dayton Airport from its private owners. The city signed a lease in 1934 and received $45,000 from the FERA.[46] Thus, the advent of federal aid resulted in a narrowing of the definition of the term municipal airport.

Second, during the 1930s federal aid to airports came primarily in the form of work relief dollars. While the Public Works Administration (PWA) also engaged in airport improvement projects, its participation was relatively small in comparison with that of the FERA, the CWA, and (after 1935) the Work Projects Administration (WPA). Federal aid thus provided airports with manpower, but not materials or the latest equipment. Critics charged that mandating a link between airport aid and work relief limited the value of the program. Especially by the end of the decade, proponents of more flexible federal aid to airports argued that "the pick and shovel work [was] largely done." In other words, manpower alone could only do so much. The federal government had to realize that airports also needed help to acquire the latest equipment and facilities.[47]

The patterns established by the FERA and the CWA remained in place under the permanent work relief program established in 1935, the WPA. The WPA continued many of the projects begun under the earlier programs and initiated a new, large airport and airways improvement program.[48] The WPA also further refined federal policy toward airport aid and, in many ways, gave cities their first taste of what it would be like to run a municipal airport under federal regulation.

The definition of a municipal airport further narrowed under the WPA. The FERA and CWA had allowed aid to flow to cities as long as they leased their airports. The WPA declared that under its program "no airports may be constructed or improved unless the land on which they are built is owned by a public agency."[49] Chicago could continue to lease its airport because the Board of Education, a public agency, owned the land. Many other cities, however, had to scramble to purchase their airports in order to receive federal aid.

Los Angeles, under pressure from the airlines that served Mines Field, initiated a program of airport improvement in 1935. It applied for both FERA and WPA funds. The FERA approved the application; the WPA did not, because Los Angeles leased the land from private owners. In 1937 the city finally concluded that it had to buy the airport, and the city council took the necessary action in September.[50]

City leaders in Dayton also realized that its airport had to become municipally owned in order to receive federal aid. The Dayton Airport was in poor financial shape. The Johnson Flying Service, which had run the airport from 1929 to 1933, lost money. Frank Hill, one of the original participants in the formation of the Dayton Municipal Airport Company, took control of the airport in 1932. The company owed him $45,000 and also owed money to a local bank. Between 1932 and 1936 Hill repeatedly petitioned the city government for aid.[51]

The city could do little. It leased the airport for a nominal sum in 1934 in order to be eligible for FERA moneys, but it apparently could not afford to buy the airport in order to receive WPA funding. Dayton's business leaders decided that they would have to take action. Led by James Cox, editor of the local newspaper, a number of Dayton's most prominent businesspeople (including several who had been involved in the original Dayton Municipal Airport venture), along with businesspeople from throughout the Miami Valley, raised the money necessary to purchase the airport from Hill. The businesspeople then presented the airport to the city as a gift in April 1936. WPA funding soon followed.[52]

Although all airport projects originated at the local level, in order to receive funding all projects had to receive the blessings of both the WPA and the Bureau of Air Commerce (or after 1938 the Civil Aeronautics Authority). The Bureau of Air Commerce had attempted to set standards for airports beginning in the late 1920s. The rating system it established, however, was purely voluntary. In order to receive a rating from the bureau, an airport had to apply to be rated. Generally, only airports assured of receiving the highest rating applied.[53] As already noted, the Bureau of Air Commerce also published a series of pamphlets with recommendations on such topics as airport management and construction. With the advent of federal aid, however, the Bureau of Air Commerce and the WPA could begin to require that cities take certain actions (or not take other actions) in order to receive aid.

Tampa, Florida, one of many cities in that state receiving WPA funding, found its project suddenly canceled. The city of Tampa had signed a lease for the airport with Pan-American Airways, Inc. Civic leaders defended the action on the grounds that the lease was the only way to get Pan-American to return to Tampa. What good was an improved airport, they argued, unless it had air traffic? The exclusive lease with the airline, however, violated WPA policy. If the airport was used exclusively by Pan-America, a private corporation, then the money spent on airport improvement in Tampa would be for the benefit of a private corporation, not the general public. The city, at first, refused to cancel the contract. However, it had no money to complete the improvements, and within a week of the WPA action, Pan-American and the city canceled the lease. In the resolution announcing the cancellation the city pledged that before finalizing any future arrangement "for the general management or operation of [Peter O. Knight Airport] by other than a governmental agency," the city would submit the terms to "the bureau of aeronautics of the United States department of commerce, or other like body at that time having jurisdiction of such matters, for its study, criticism, suggestions, and recommendations." Cities still owned their airports, but now city policies had to reflect federal policies.[54]

The WPA and the Bureau of Air Commerce wanted to achieve some level of uniformity, or at the least a situation in which most public airports met certain minimum standards. Federal regulation of airports remained somewhat limited, but by wielding the power of approval, the two agencies could strongly persuade cities to make certain kinds of improvements. The WPA's division of airways and airports drew up a plan that outlined the basic airport needs of the nation. The hope was that the plan would offer guidance to local officials and inspire projects that would tend to, at the least, bring more of the nation's airports up to what the WPA and the Bureau of Air Commerce considered adequate standards. But officials in the WPA had to admit that the airport program was a relief program, and that, rather than raising standards at U.S. airports, remained the primary focus.[55]

Even though federal aid meant meeting some federal guidelines, cities generally strove to take advantage of FERA, CWA, and WPA funding. By 1937, however, despite those programs, municipal airports were still lagging behind in terms of technology, and they remained a burden on municipal budgets. All work relief project grants had to be matched by contributions at the local level. By 1937 cities had begun to complain that they could no longer afford to finance their end of airport improvement projects. National organizations representing cities, such as the American Municipal Association and the United States Conference of Mayors, started to push for new and broader aid to municipal airports.

As Mark Gelfand argued in his *A Nation of Cities*, the depression helped forge a new relationship between cities and the federal government. Before 1933 the relationship between cities and the federal government had been largely indirect. Most communication between the federal government and local governments went through the states. With the onset of the depression, however, a number of organizations representing the nation's cities began to forge direct ties to the federal government. According to Gelfand, cities especially desired direct federal aid in the areas of unemployment relief, public works, and housing. Airports represented another area in which cities wished to establish a direct relationship with the federal government—in the form of airport funding (rather than relief funding that could be spent on airport improvement projects).[56]

Organizations representing cities first took up the issue of municipal airports in early 1937. At a January meeting of the American Municipal Association (AMA) the group produced a report that called for a rethinking of federal aid to airports. The report pointed out that cities had invested large sums of money in airports. The benefits from those investments had gone not just to cities but to state and federal governments as well. The time had come, therefore, for "definite and complete Federal action . . . for a national system of civil airways and airports, in order that cities may know where they stand for the future." The report included a resolution passed by the executive committee of that organization that "[recommended] a complete projected national system of civil airways, including the establishment of financial responsibilities of the various agencies benefiting by such airports." It went on to assert that "[r]apid growth of air transportation [was] fast leaving most municipal terminal facilities in an obsolete condition," leaving most cities faced with the task of building new facilities. Because cities were not the only beneficiaries of the new facilities, the federal government should look at airports in the light of "their Federal value—as stops on the national airways or for national defense." And in that light, the federal government "should consider Federal responsibility for any projected federal airways program on a basis similar to the Federal responsibility in the national highway system and rivers and harbors."[57]

When the AMA's executive committee met again in July 1937, it reiterated the need "for a national program sharply defining the authority and responsibility of city, state and Federal governments in the future airways program." It also stated again that airports functioned at several different levels: locally, as part of interstate commerce, and as part of a system of national defense. In view of that, the committee again emphasized that each government (local, state, and federal) benefiting from airports must pay its fair share in the maintenance and improvement of airports.[58]

In late 1937 the AMA sponsored a conference of municipal representatives and the Bureau of Air Commerce. As a result of that meeting the bureau appointed a committee "to propose plans for future development of the aviation industry, and to allocate responsibility for [those] municipal projects which also benefit state and Federal governments."[59]

The United States Conference of Mayors also took up the issue of municipal airports at its 1937 meeting. Four speakers addressed the issue at a session on "The Municipal Airport Problem." Colonel J. Monroe Johnson, assistant secretary of commerce, admitted that despite federal aid to airports from the FERA, CWA, and WPA, most of the financial burden for the construction, maintenance, and improvement of airports had fallen to cities. That burden was heavy and made heavier by the fact that few municipal airports returned any profits to their sponsoring cities. Johnson echoed the sentiments of the AMA when he stated that many felt that the burden of airport development must be borne not just by cities, but shared between local, state, and federal governments. This was especially critical in light of the fact that many cities simply had no more money to devote to airport improvement; they could no longer contribute the local share required by the WPA. Johnson concluded that all those factors necessitated the creation of "some well-reasoned, comprehensive and coherent airport plan, a plan that [would] be satisfactory to all the parties involved — the airline operators, the aircraft manufacturers, the municipalities, the Post Office Department, and the Department of Commerce."[60]

Harllee Branch, Second Assistant Postmaster General, also pointed out that cities had reached their limits in terms of their ability to finance airport construction and improvement. He further described the frustration felt by many cities when, after paying for early improvements, they found themselves still lagging behind because of the extremely rapid development of aircraft and airport technologies. Branch offered few answers to those problems, however.[61]

The next two speakers, both mayors, had very strong suggestions as to what might be done. Frank Couzens, the mayor of Detroit, stated plainly "that the federal government should also share in the cost of providing a general national system of airports." He believed that direct airport aid was no different than the federal aid afforded to highway construction and river and harbor improvements. The airport problem, he declared, was a national problem, and Congress should repeal that section of the Air Commerce Act of 1926 that forbade the spending of federal moneys specifically on airports. Instead, the federal government should begin to share in the cost of the improvement and maintenance of municipal airports. R. E. Allen, the mayor of Augusta, Georgia, essentially echoed and reinforced the sentiments expressed by Couzens.[62]

At that 1937 meeting the United States Conference of Mayors adopted a resolution in favor of federal aid to airports. The resolution reiterated many of the points made by the speakers. It stated that cities had borne most of the financial burden involved in the development of the nation's airports, but that it was a burden that cities could no longer bear. Since the federal government had aided in the development of other transportation systems (railroads, waterways, highways), aid to airports would not represent a radical departure from past practices. Therefore, the mayors resolved that Congress should pass legislation "to provide for and authorize a permanent program of Federal financial cooperation in the construction, improvement, development and expansion of publicly owned airports."[63]

In 1938 Congress passed a law, the Civil Aeronautics Act, that greatly reformed the ways in which the federal government would regulate civilian aviation. Most of the act had little directly to do with municipal airports. Two sections, however, did address some of the concerns raised by cities. First, the act repealed the ban on federal aid to airports. Further, it required the newly created Civil Aeronautics Authority (CAA) to survey the nation's public airports and make recommendations to Congress "as to whether the federal government shall participate in the construction, improvement, development, operation, or maintenance of a national airport system, and if so, to what extent, and in what manner."[64] In preparing the report the CAA consulted, among other groups, the United State Conference of Mayors and the American Municipal Association.

The survey, completed in March 1939, concluded that the United States did need to develop a planned system of airports and that "[s]uch a system should be regarded, under certain circumstances, as a proper object of Federal expenditure." With that in mind, the CAA presented to Congress a complex proposal with three phases. If implemented, phase 1 required spending $128 million; phase 2 would increase total spending to $230 million; and phase 3 would result in spending a total of $435 million.[65]

City representatives and others voiced disapproval of the CAA program. It was not that the money was inadequate, but that it was not exclusively for airports. Under the CAA proposal most of the money would go to the WPA to finance work relief airport projects. As already noted, many believed that airports had already absorbed all the labor-intensive work that was possible and that the aid ought to be directed not at work relief but at airport upgrades and improvements. At a National Airport Conference held in June 1939, supporters of federal aid to airports criticized the link to work relief and again called for more direct federal aid to airports.[66]

Timing, however, was against the proponents of a large program for the improvement of civilian airports. By 1939 the United States had begun a program of war preparedness. While airport supporters usually linked airports to the issue of national defense, Congress proved reluctant to act on a program aimed at

Fig. 2.1. By the 1930s the municipal airport had evolved into a complex system. Shown here is the Las Vegas airport in 1942, essentially militarized because of World War II. Courtesy United States Air Force

civilian aviation and work relief. In late 1940, though, Congress did appropriate $40 million for airport work, separate from available work relief funds. The money would go to up to 250 airports (as determined by a board composed of representatives from the Departments of War, Navy, and Commerce) and would fund improvements "'necessary to the national defense.'"[67] The appropriation was seen as a small but important first step in the creation of a national system of airports to serve both national defense and civilian aviation needs. Though far from what supporters had hoped for, the action in 1940 established an important principle. Congress had appropriated funds for airports within a national airport system.[68]

CONCLUSION

Though cities failed to get all they desired in the late 1930s, the precedents set by the end of 1940 established the basic framework for postwar federal action toward municipal airports. After a little over two decades of experimentation and innovation at both the local and the federal levels, the familiar, sometimes welcome and sometimes uncomfortable relationships between cities and their airports and between municipal airports and the federal government had been established. The major airports in the United States would be owned and operated by cities (or by agencies created by cities), and while the financing of municipal airports would continue to be largely a municipal responsibility, the federal government would provide aid and set standards for operations.

The history of municipal airports in the United States is one of the most neglected subjects in both aviation and urban history. The subject is complex, involving a host of political, social, and economic issues. This essay only touches the surface of a few of the more obvious issues. Other works have also sketched the outline of additional dimensions of the story. Paul Barrett's 1987 article suggested many of the connections (and missed connections) between the history of airports and the history of city planning and zoning. Deborah G. Douglas explored an interesting line of inquiry in which she suggested that a system of airports emerged in the United States that closely reflected the existing urban hierarchy. She theorized that air traffic flows closely mirrored capital flows.[69] Both of these topics and all the issues touched on in this essay need further examination. For example, far more must be done on the connection between the military and the development of municipal airports. And more case studies of individual airports would certainly contribute to the fleshing out of this rich and complex subject.

NOTES

1. While technically there are differences between airports, flying fields, airfields, and landing fields, those terms were often used interchangeably, and at the risk of being a bit too general, in this paper those terms will also be considered interchangeable.

2. Lois E. Walker and Shelby E. Wickam, *From Huffman Prairie to the Moon: The History of Wright-Patterson Air Force Base* (Washington, D.C.: Government Printing Office, 1986), pp. 3–5, 10–14. 17–54.

3. While airports were built from the beginning for both land- and water-based aircraft, in the interests of simplicity this paper will concentrate almost exclusively on facilities built for land-based craft.

4. Henry Ladd Smith, *Airways: The History of Commercial Aviation in the United States* (Washington, D.C.: Smithsonian Institution Press, 1991), pp. 50–63.

5. Tucson may have claimed to be the first, but it is generally acknowledged that Atlantic City, New Jersey, opened the nation's first municipal airport on 3 May 1919.

6. Quoted in "The Story of Tucson Airport Authority 1948–1966, Tucson, Arizona" (prepared under the direction of Charles H. Broman, A.A.E., General Manager T.A.A., 31 Dec. 1966), copy in author's possession, p. 5.

7. The municipal airport-military connection remained strong in Tucson. That first municipal field was eventually replaced in 1927 by Davis-Monthan Field, then the largest municipal airport in the country, jointly used by the city and the military until after World War II. Ibid., pp. 5–6.

8. Untitled, undated, typewritten manuscript, National Air and Space Museum Technical Files, Air Transport Series, Airports, US, Pennsylvania-Pittsburgh, pp. 1–2.

9. Ibid., pp. 2–4.

10. Ibid., pp. 3–5; Charles P. Johnson, "Pittsburgh City-County Airport," *Aero Digest* 19 (Dec. 1931): 45.

11. Betsy Braden and Paul Hagan, *A Dream Takes Flight: Hartsfield Atlanta International Airport and Aviation in Atlanta* (Atlanta: Atlanta Historical Society and Athens: University of Georgia Press, 1989), pp. 16–17.

12. Ibid., pp. 23–26, 45.

13. Smith, *Airways*, p. 66; Braden and Hagan, *Dream Takes Flight*, p. 10.

14. David Young and Neal Callahan, *Fill the Heavens with Commerce: Chicago Aviation, 1855–1926* (Chicago: Chicago Review Press, 1981), pp. 83–84, 145.

15. Ibid., pp. 149–51.

16. Smith, *Airways*, p. 66.

17. Arnold Knauth et al., *U.S. Aviation Reports, 1928* (Baltimore, Md.: United States Aviation Reports, Inc., 1928), p. 484; Joseph H. Wenneman, *Municipal Airports* (Cleveland, Ohio: Flying Review Publishing Company, 1931), pp. 336, 346–47, 355, 357; William P. Long, "The Development of the Boston Airport," *American City* 48 (Apr. 1933): 51–52; John Walter Wood, *Airports: Some Design Elements and Future Developments* (New York: Coward-McCann, 1940), p. 43; "Report of the Committee on Post Office & Postal Facilities on the Airplane Landing Field Situation in Boston," 9 Jan. 1922, National Air and Space Museum Technical Files, Air Transport, Airports, US, Massachusetts; Robert E. Adwers, *Rudder, Stick, and Throttle: Research and Reminiscences on Flying in Nebraska* (Omaha, Nebr.: Making History, Inc., 1994), p. 216; *Annual Report of the Postmaster General for the Fiscal Year ended June 30, 1920* (Washington, D.C.: Government Printing Office, 1920), p. 58.

18. Major-General Charles T. Menoher, Chief of the Army Air Service, "The Need for Landing Fields," in George Seay Wheat, ed., *Municipal Landing Fields and Air Ports* (New York: G. P. Putnam's Sons, 1920), pp. 1–3.

19. Archibald Black, "Air Terminal Engineering," *Landscape Architecture* 13 (July 1923): 226–27.

20. Ibid., p. 228; Archibald Black, "Have You a Landing Field in Your Town?" *Aero Digest* 6 (Apr. 1925): 186–87.

21. Glenn L. Martin Company, "Municipal Airdromes," (Cleveland, Ohio: Glenn L. Martin Company, n.d.), in the DeWitt Clinton Ramsey Room, National Air and Space Museum, Washington, D.C.

22. See Wenneman, *Municipal Airports*, pp. 319–58.

23. Frank Joseph Rowe and Craig Miner, *Borne on the South Wind: A Century of Kansas Aviation* (Wichita, Kans.: Wichita Eagle and Beacon Publishing Company, 1994), pp. 57, 80; O. J. Swander, "Exceptional Site, Landscaping, Lighting and Buildings Characterize Wichita Airport," *American City* 44 (Apr. 1931): 109.

24. Swander, "Exceptional Site," p. 109; Wenneman, *Municipal Airports*, p. 330; Swander, "Exceptional Site," pp. 109–10; Edwin W. Pryor, "Wichita's Municipal Airport," *Aero Digest* 18 (Apr. 1931): 192–93.

25. J. W. Brennan, "Lindbergh Field," *Aero Digest* 21 (Sep. 1932): 40–41; "City and Federal Governments Cooperate in Creating Extensive Airport," *American City* 38 (Feb. 1928): 148.

26. Brennan, "Lindbergh Field."

27. Braden and Hagan, *Dream Takes Flight*, pp. 26, 53; Wenneman, *Municipal Airports*, pp. 324–25.

28. Janet R. Daly Bednarek, "Lost Opportunities and False Beacons: The Failure of Planning in Dayton, Ohio," *Proceedings of the Sixth National Conference on American Planning History* (Hilliard, Ohio: Society for American City and Regional Planning History, 1995), pp. 864–65.

29. Paul D. Friedman, "Birth of an Airport: From Mines Field to Los Angeles International, L.A. Celebrates the 50th Anniversary of Its Airport," *Journal of the American Aviation Historical Society* 23 (Winter 1978): 286–88; George N. Kramer, "From Beans to Planes in One Year: The Story of Metropolitan Airport, Los Angeles, One of the Busiest Western Air Terminals," *Airway Age* 11 (Apr. 1930): 525; Wenneman, *Municipal Airports*, pp. 320–21.

30. Friedman, "Birth of an Airport,"pp. 288–89.

31. The material in this paragraph and in the following discussion of municipal ownership of airports is drawn from a number of the most prominent examples of published arguments in favor of municipally owned airports. These include Archibald Black, *Civil Airports and Airways* (New York: Simmons-Boardman Publishing Company, 1929), pp. 3–5; Donald Duke, *Airports and Airways: Cost, Operation, and Maintenance* (New York: Ronald Press Company, 1927), pp. 5–8; Henry V. Hubbard et al., *Airports: Their Location, Administration, and Legal Basis* (Cambridge, Mass.: Harvard University Press, 1930), pp. 46–53; Austin F. MacDonald, "Airport Problems of American Cities," *Annals of the American Society of Political and Social Sciences* 151 (Sep. 1930): 225–83.

32. Hubbard et al., *Airports*, p. 53.

33. MacDonald, "Airport Problems," p. 265.

34. Harry J. Freeman, "Establishment of Municipal Airports as a 'Public Purpose,'" *National Municipal Review* 18, no. 4 (Apr. 1929): 263–64.

35. Ibid.

36. Ibid., 266.

37. "Airways and Landing Facilities," *Air Service Information Circular* 5 (1 Mar. 1923).

38. "Quarterly Review of Decisions: Aeronautics," *Air Law Review* 10 (July 1939): 310; ibid.; Solomon Rothfeld, "The Law May Get You . . . ," *Aviation* 39 (June 1940): 38; "Quarterly Review," p. 311; Rothfeld, "The Law," p. 38.

39. "Municipal Airports-Liability for Negligence in Operation," *National Municipal Review* 21 (May 1932): 330.

40. David Schlang, "Notes, Aeronautics: Airports— Operation as a Nuisance—Injunctions," *Air Law Review* 4 (Jan. 1933): 64–70.

41. Solomon Rothfeld, "To Sue or Not to Sue," *Aviation* 39 (Nov. 1940): 43.

42. The Harvard Airport Study asked the subject airports to report how many people visited the airport on an average summer day and on an average summer weekend. It also asked them to report the largest single-day crowd at the airport. The results were published in a chart in the appendix to the study. Hubbard et al., *Airports*, 146–47.

43. Stratton Coyner, "The Job of the Airport Manager," *American City* 42 (Mar. 1930): 126–28.

44. Charles H. Gale, "The Second National Airport Conference," *Aviation* 28 (24 May 1930): 1039; *Proceedings, Second National Airport Conference, Buffalo, New York, May 14–16, 1930* (New York: Aeronautical Chamber of Commerce of America), p. 74.

45. Major C. C. Moseley, "Hitch Your Airport to the Stars," *Aviation* 34 (Nov. 1935): 16–18; William D. Strohmeier, "More Fun at the Airport," *Aviation* 39 (Nov. 1940): 38–39, 106.

46. Bednarek, "Lost Opportunities and False Beacons," p. 866.

47. Speech of Major V. C. Burnett (Manager, Detroit City Airport; President, Association of Airport Executives), "Minutes of Annual Convention, National Aeronautic Association, January 1940," National Air and Space Museum Archives, National Aeronautic Association Archives, Acc. XXXX-0209, Box 3803.

48. "$45,000,000 Airport Program Launched," *National Aeronautics Association Magazine* 14 (July 1936): 20–23.

49. Works Projects Administration, *America Spreads Her Wings* (Washington, D.C.: Government Printing Office, 1937), p. 10.

50. Friedman, "Birth of an Airport," p. 291; "What About the Los Angeles Airport?" *Western Flying* 18 (Nov. 1938): 18.

51. Bednarek, "Lost Opportunities and False Beacons," pp. 865–66.

52. Ibid., 866–67; George F. Baker, "Dayton Improves Its Municipal Airport," *Aero Digest* 29 (Dec. 1936): 28–29.

53. Charles C. Rohlfing, *National Regulation of Aeronautics* (Philadelphia: University of Pennsylvania Press, 1931), pp. 133–38.

54. "City Should End Deadlock by Canceling Airport Lease," *Daily Times*, 22 July 1936, p. 4; Box 83, Florida, Work Projects Administration Division of Information Newspaper Clipping File, 1935–1942; Records of the Work Projects Administration, Record Group 69; National Archives, Washington, D.C. [hereafter WPA Newspaper File]; "A Happy Outcome for the Airport Situation," *Daily Times*, 30 July 1936, p. 6; Box 83, Florida, WPA Newspaper File; "Board Accepts Pan-Am Offer to Cancel Airport Deal," *Tribune*, 31 July 1936. Box 83, Florida, WPA Newspaper Files.

55. "$45,000,000 Airport Program Launched," pp. 20–23; W. Sumpter Smith, "The WPA Airport Program," *Journal of Air Law* 7 (Oct. 1936): 495–99.

56. See Mark I. Gelfand, *A Nation of Cities: The Federal Government and Urban America, 1933–1965* (New York: Oxford University Press, 1975), pp. 3–70. See also Robert B. Fairbanks, "A Clash of Priorities: The Federal Government and Dallas Airport Development, 1917–1964," in Joseph F. Rishel, ed., *American Cities and Towns: Historical Perspectives* (Pittsburgh, Pa.: Duquesne University Press, 1992), p. 164.

57. "Municipal Airports and Federal Responsibility," *American City* 52 (Mar. 1937): 15.

58. "Cities Seek National Airport Program," *American City* 52 (Aug. 1937): 13.

59. "A Year-End Message from the American Municipal Association," *American City* 58 (Jan. 1938): 5.

60. Col. J. Monroe Johnson, "Airports and the Bureau of Air Commerce," in *Federal-City Relations in the 1930s* (New York: Arno Press, 1978), pp. 26–29.

61. Harllee Branch, "Airmail Service and Municipal Airports," in ibid., pp. 31–38.

62. Frank Couzens, "The Municipal Airport Problem from the Viewpoint of the Larger Cities," in ibid., p. 42; R. E. Allen, "The Municipal Airport Problem from the Viewpoint of the Smaller Cities, in ibid., pp. 44–52.

63. "Federal Aid for Airports," *American City* 53 (Jan. 1938): 11.

64. A. B. McMullen, "Airports: Development and Problems," *Journal of Air Law* 9 (Oct. 1938): 651.

65. Civil Aeronautics Authority, *Airport Survey: Letter from fhe Civil Aeronautics Authority Transmitting Recommendations as to the Desirability of Federal Participation in the Construction, Improvement, Development, Operation, and Maintenance of a National System of Airports* (Washington, D.C.: Government Printing Office, 1939), pp. xiii, 129; "CAA Suggests Adoption of New Airport System," *Shreveport Times*, 23 Apr. 1939, p. 21.

66. Cy Caldwell, "Putting Our Airports on Relief," *Aero Digest* 35 (Apr. 1939): 56; "The Problem of the Airport," *National Aeronautics* 17 (July 1939): 20.

67. Quoted in "$40,000,000 Program to Improve Nation's Airports Announced," *Washington Star*, 12 Dec. 1940, p. B-4.

68. Kendall K. Hoyt, "The Airport Program Makes a Start," *National Aeronautics* 18 (Nov. 1940): 10.

69. Paul Barrett, "Cities and Their Airports: Policy Formation, 1926–1952," *Journal of Urban History* 14 (Nov. 1987): 112–37; Deborah G. Douglas, "Airports as Systems and Systems of Airports: Airports and Urban Development in America before World War II," in William M. Leary, ed., *From Air Ship to Airbus: The History of Civil and Commercial Aviation*, vol. 1, *Infrastructure and Environment* (Washington, D.C.: Smithsonian Institution Press, 1995), pp. 55–84.

CHAPTER 3

The Search for an Instrument Landing System, 1918–48

WILLIAM M. LEARY

The airline industry in the United States made remarkable progress during the years between World Wars I and II. By 1940, U.S. scheduled domestic airlines carried 2.8 million passengers and flew more than 1 billion passenger miles. Furthermore, the industry had an impressive safety record. In fact, in 1940 the Equitable Life Assurance Society of America removed all restrictions on life insurance coverage for passengers flying scheduled airlines. Thanks to advances in radio aids to navigation, airliners were able to fly from point to point in adverse weather conditions with regularity and safety. Once they arrived at their destination, however, landing often became a problem. Despite years of effort, the airline industry lacked an approved instrument landing system (ILS) that made possible landings in all types of weather. Such a system required three essential elements: a radio beam or localizer to align the aircraft with the runway; vertical radio beacons or markers to indicate the distance to touch down; and—what would prove the most challenging element—a radio beam that would be projected from the end of the runway at an angle so as to designate the proper glide path that an aircraft should follow to touch down. The search for an instrument landing system began during the First World War; it would continue for the next thirty years.[1]

Shortly after the U.S. Post Office inaugurated a scheduled airmail service in May 1918, a somewhat surprised—and chagrined—Second Assistant Postmaster General Otto Praeger began to realize that airplanes could not fly in bad weather. An aeronautical novice, Praeger had promised his boss, Postmaster General Albert S. Burleson, that the mails would be delivered without delay. The postal biplanes, however, had frequently been grounded by fog and thun-

derstorms. While most individuals would have accepted the limitations of existing aviation technology, the stubborn and determined Praeger decided to overcome them. As part of his effort to bring regularity to the airmail service, he
turned to the federal government's premier research agency, the National Bureau of Standards (NBS) for assistance.[2]

In August 1918, Praeger asked the NBS to look into the possibility of using
the known directional properties of radio waves to identify landing areas for
pilots. Praeger's request prompted an enthusiastic response from Frederick A.
Kolster, the bureau's Harvard-educated physicist and radio expert. On 3 September, Kolster suggested to NBS Director Samuel W. Stratton that a localized
radio signal could be used to mark a landing field. After initial experiments with
an induction signaling system, Kolster wound a transmitting coil—160 feet of
number 12 copper wire—around the roof of the Radio Building on the NBS
grounds in northwestern Washington, D.C.[3]

On Armistice Day, 11 November 1918, a full-scale trial of the system took
place. Kolster energized the coil at 24 amperes from a 500 watt generator. A
postal JN-4 ("Jenny"), with 40 turns of magnetic wire looped around each side
of its lower wing as an antenna and carrying a special audio-frequency amplifier,
flew toward the Radio Building. The pilot reported that he heard the audio signal when overhead at 3,000 feet.

Encouraged by the results, Kolster moved the experiment to the airmail field
at nearby College Park, Maryland. He laid a coil of single-turn wire around an
area that measured 600 by 800 feet, then impressed a radio frequency wave
on it. To receive the signal, a postal Curtiss R was equipped with an antenna
similar to the one earlier used on the Jenny, plus a French-made three-step amplifier. The test pilot had good reception for seven seconds while passing over
the field at 1,500 feet with his engine running at full speed and traveling 90 miles
per hour.[4]

By the early months of 1919 Kolster and other NBS scientists had begun
work on a directional radio system. Using a novel antenna array, they were able
to direct upward a sharply defined radio signal. "From theoretical considerations," they reported, "it appears that the field radiated from such an aerial
should be mainly in the form of an inverted cone with a hollow center, that is,
signals should be inaudible at points immediately over the center of the aerial but audible at quite a distance on either side." Although the signal pattern
showed a good deal of promise as a landing marker, work on the project soon
lapsed as bureau scientists turned their attention to developing en route radio
aids to navigation.[5]

The early 1920s saw both the NBS and the Army Air Service experimenting with directional radio beacons that led to the development of the low-

frequency, four-course radio range—allowing truly accurate air navigation for the first time—that would come into widespread use by the end of the decade. Although the low-frequency range marked a significant improvement in the ability of pilots to navigate from point to point in bad weather, the problem of landing in foggy conditions remained to be solved.[6]

In was not until the fall of 1928 that the NBS again began to focus on the development of an instrument landing system. On 4 October, J. Howard Dellinger, senior physicist and chief of the NBS Radio Section, presented a paper on "Directional Radio as an Aid to Safe Flying" at the First National Aeronautics Safety Conference in New York City. Dellinger pointed out that radio had made important contributions to safe flying. Thanks to the newly developed directional radio beacon, a pilot could now follow an invisible electronic highway in the sky from one city to another in any kind of weather. The problem of landing once the pilot arrived at his destination, however, had not been solved. The answer, Dellinger believed, lay in the development of "a field localizer and landing altimeter." Only when airplanes could land in bad weather, he concluded, would scheduled flight operations become dependable and passenger carrying be considered "a serious service."[7]

Adopting the philosophy that complex equipment should be on the ground and simple equipment in the aircraft, the NBS began experiments at College Park in November 1928 with a low-power (200 watts) directive radio beacon. Similar to the more powerful beacons used for guidance on the low-frequency radio ranges, the field localizer beacon had a useful range of ten miles.[8]

Work at College Park had hardly started, however, when representatives of the Daniel Guggenheim Foundation for the Promotion of Aeronautics approached the NBS and suggested a cooperative effort to develop an instrument landing system. In January 1929, the NBS agreed to install a localizer beacon at New York's Mitchel Field and participate with the foundation in a program of trial flights.[9]

The Guggenheim Foundation had established a Full Flight Laboratory at Mitchel Field in 1928 to study various methods of helping pilots land in fog. After considering various alternatives, it concluded that the NBS directive radio beacon offered the greatest promise. Preliminary practice flights by project pilot James H. Doolittle confirmed this judgment. Doolittle, however, found that existing aircraft instruments—the compass and turn-and-bank indicator—failed to provide adequate indications for blind landings. "An accurate, reliable, and easy-to-read instrument showing exact direction of heading and precise attitude of the aircraft was required," Doolittle concluded, "particularly for the initial and final stages of blind landing."[10]

Doolittle turned the problem over to Elmer Sperry, Jr., of the Sperry Gyroscope Company. In a remarkably short time, Sperry produced two new gyroscopic instruments: the artificial horizon and the directional gyroscope. Both performed superbly, providing Doolittle with the precise and easy-to-interpret information that he required.

Another instrument problem found an equally satisfying solution. The field localizer generated an electronic signal that guided Doolittle toward the point of touch-down at Mitchel Field, while a fan-type marker beacon indicated his distance to the landing point. But Doolittle lacked precise information on his altitude when approaching the ground for a landing. Existing barometric altimeters measured altitude to the nearest 50 to 100 feet, at best. Doolittle wanted an instrument that would measure to 10 or even 5 feet.

This time it was Paul Kollsman of the Kollsman Instrument Company who came to Doolittle's assistance. By August 1929, Kollsman had perfected a sensitive barometric altimeter that could be relied upon for measurements to 20 feet. The new Kollsman altimeter represented a significant improvement over existing instruments. While recognizing that a barometric measuring device would not be the final answer to providing a pilot with precise vertical information, Doolittle was now confident that he could land by reference to instruments alone.

On 29 September 1929, Doolittle took off from Mitchel Field to attempt a blind landing. With safety pilot Benjamin S. Kelsey in the front cockpit of the NY-2 biplane, Doolittle intercepted the localizer and then followed the radio signal toward the field. Passing over the marker beacon, he began a steady descent at 60 miles per hour until he touched down. As historian Richard P. Hallion has observed, Doolittle's flight marked "a milestone" in aeronautical research and development. For the first time in aviation history, "a plane had taken off, flown a precise flight path, and landed, controlled by a pilot observing only his cockpit instruments, without recourse to external visual reference."[11]

While the Guggenheim experiments were underway at Mitchel Field, NBS personnel continued to work at College Park, focusing on developing a directive radio beam that could be used to provide vertical guidance for pilots. Bureau scientists Harry Diamond and Francis W. Dunmore used a very high frequency (90.8 MHz) transmitter and directive antenna array to project a slightly curved beam at a small angle above the horizon. The signal—the first practical application of very high frequencies in aviation—was received by two horizontal half-wave antennas, located just forward of the leading edge of the aircraft's wings. A horizontal needle on a special instrument in the cockpit indicated to the pilot when he was on course. The pilot kept the needle centered,

Fig. 3.1. A confident
James H. Doolittle stands
in front of the N4-2
that he used during the
Guggenheim blind landing
experiments at Mitchel
Field in 1929. Courtesy
National Air and Space
Museum, 77-11836

flying a gently curved path under the landing beam. The curvature diminished
as the ground approached.[12]

In the two years following Doolittle's blind landing of September 1929, NBS
scientists worked to perfect the three-element instrument landing system. The
localizer, marker beacons, and newly developed landing beam (or glide slope) all
required modifications. Also, aircraft antennas and receiving equipment needed
further improvements. A simplified cockpit instrument evolved, with horizontal and vertical needles displaying localizer and glide slope information.[13]

After numerous flights at College Park to test the improved system, project
pilot Marshall S. Boggs, on loan from the Aeronautics Branch of the Department of Commerce, made the first completely blind landing on 5 September
1931. Like Doolittle, Boggs carried a safety pilot in the front cockpit of his
biplane. The requirements for landing at College Park, however, differed significantly from those at Mitchel Field. Doolittle had landed on a large grassy
area; Boggs had to set down on a runway that measured 2,000 x 100 feet. Also,
Doolittle had a vertical path to Mitchel Field that was free of obstructions;
Boggs had to clear a house chimney that was located 1,500 feet from the edge
of the field.

Fig. 3.2. James L. Kinney in front of a Curtiss N26 Fledgling that he flew during instrument landing trials at College Park, Maryland, and Newark, New Jersey. Courtesy National Air and Space Museum, A2199-C

The NBS instrument landing system afforded the precision that Boggs required. The sharp localizer beam gave off-course deviations of 250 feet at five miles from the transmitter and 20 feet at the approach end of the runway. At the same time, the glide slope gave deviations of plus or minus 50 feet at a distance of three miles and at an altitude of 1,600 feet, while deviations of plus or minus 5 feet could be detected when over the edge of the field at 30 feet.[14]

Boggs made over a hundred hooded landings at College Park during 1931 and 1932, demonstrating the reliability of the NBS system. The Department of Commerce was sufficiently impressed to order an operational test of the equipment at Newark Airport. The aim was to demonstrate the NBS landing system at a busy commercial airport and thereby focus attention on its practicality. Under existing legislation, however, the federal government could not fund "airport improvements." By demonstrating the NBS system to airline operators, the Department of Commerce hoped to encourage manufacturers to make the equipment commercially available.[15]

While the NBS gear was being installed at Newark, the Commerce Department suffered a tragic loss when Marshall Boggs, who had been scheduled to fly the tests, was killed in January 1933 in a landing accident in California while on vacation. Colonel Clarence D. Young, head of the Aeronautics Branch, hailed the important role that Boggs had played in the development of an instrument

Fig. 3.3. Dr. C. D. Barbulesco, Lt. Albert F. Hegenberger, and Frederick Celler pose in front of the Douglas BT-2A that was used for blind landing experiments, February 1932. Courtesy National Air and Space Museum, 156679-AC

landing system. "His work at College Park," Young told the *New York Times,* "exists as a monument to him, a great contribution toward safe flying for future generations."[16]

By the end of February, the NBS equipment had been put into place at Newark. The localizer beacon operated on a frequency of 278 KHz, with the glide slope on 100 MHz. There were two low-frequency marker beacons, one located at 2,000 feet from the end of the runway, and the other placed at the field boundary.

Demonstrations got underway on 1 March 1933. James L. Kinney, who had often flown as safety pilot for Boggs, made three hooded landings to test the newly installed equipment. The next day, with a ceiling of 200 feet in snow showers, he invited members of the press along for a flight in a Bellanca cabin monoplane. Kinney impressed the reporters when he flew a smooth instrument approach and brought the Bellanca within five feet of the ground by following radio signals.[17]

Kinney continued to demonstrate the NBS system to an appreciative audience of media representatives and aviation professionals. On 7 March he made seven consecutive hooded landings. One week later, when a ceiling of 50 feet and visibility of one-eighth of a mile grounded all flights at Newark, Kinney recorded several successful instrument landings.

Bad weather on 20 March afforded a perfect opportunity to demonstrate the advances that had been made in radio navigation. Kinney, who had gone back to College Park, departed the NBS experimental station at a time when the ceiling was 200 feet and the visibility one-quarter of a mile. He climbed in clouds to 3,000 feet and proceeded northwards on instruments. Kinney first tuned in the Washington low-frequency radio range. He followed this beam until intercepting the Hadley, New Jersey, signal. After identifying his position over the Hadley range by the cone of silence directly over the beacon, he flew a compass course toward Newark. Tuning his receiver to 278 KHz, he soon picked up the field localizer signal. He then turned on his glide slope receiver. When he was about ten miles from the airport, both radio signals registered on his cross-pointer indicator.

Kinney flew down the glide slope at a constant rate of descent, observing the needles on his dial. "As long as they formed that perfect cross," he reported, "I knew I was maintaining the proper gliding angle and that I was headed for the center of the airport." At 1,700 feet from edge of the field, he received a high-pitched beep in the earphones, indicating that he had passed over the first marker beacon. Just as he broke out of the clouds at 200 feet over the edge of the field, he received the lower pitched beep of the inner marker. Kinney proceeded to land, completing the longest-ever instrument flight in poor weather conditions.[18]

Kinney continued to showcase the NBS instrument landing system at Newark into early April, receiving extensive press coverage. At one point, Charles A. Lindbergh made two hooded landings, with Kinney acting as the safety pilot. Also, Kinney's landings were recorded by the motion picture cameras of news organizations, and the film was shown in theaters throughout the country.

The outlook for widespread adoption of the NBS system could not have been more promising. The success of the Newark tests, NBS scientist Harry Diamond reported, "has roused considerable interest on the part of air line pilots, air transport operators, radio and aircraft manufacturers, and air officials of a number of foreign countries." Several radio manufacturers had begun production of the ground and air equipment for the NBS system, while a number of foreign countries were preparing experimental installations. "It is hoped," Diamond concluded, "that service tests of the system in this country will begin in the near future."[19]

The steady progress toward the development of a practical instrument landing system, however, soon came to an abrupt halt. Under President Herbert Hoover, funding for aeronautical research had remained a priority of the federal government despite the worsening economic situation. But the new Franklin D. Roosevelt administration had different priorities. During the campaign of 1932, Roosevelt had castigated Hoover for excessive federal spending. Upon taking office in March 1933, FDR—not yet an admirer of Keynesian deficit spending—ordered a sharp cut in federal expenditures. The budget ax fell especially hard on the Aeronautics Branch of the Department of Commerce, with funding reduced from $7.7 million to $5.17 million. This unfortunate—and unwise—action by the Roosevelt administration crippled the branch's program of support for aeronautical research and development.[20]

In May 1933, Lyman J. Briggs, chief of the research division in the Aeronautics Branch, informed the NBS that the end of the fiscal year on 30 June would bring a sharp reduction in funds for aeronautical research. Dellinger, head of the Radio Section, could hardly believe the news. NBS scientists, he pointed out, had been instrumental in developing a series of vitally important radio aids to navigation. Their contributions over the past decade had included the low-frequency radio range beacon, improved antenna systems, effective aircraft ignition shielding, and, most recently, a promising instrument landing system. "I hope that it may be found possible," he wrote to Briggs, "to convey to proper officials a realization that this [budget cutback] would destroy a Government group of proved value and high efficiency, having a stock of technical knowledge and ability that will be difficult to build up again."[21]

Dellinger's pleas fell on deaf ears. Shortly after the beginning of the new fiscal year, Dellinger had to drop, transfer, or furlough nineteen members of his staff. Over the next twelve months, the NBS was forced to close its research facility at College Park and abandon most of its experimental projects.[22]

The airlines remained interested in the NBS instrument landing system but were deterred by the price. Jack Frye, president of Transcontinental & Western Airlines (TWA) informed the Department of Commerce in January 1934 that the cost of installing the NBS system at one airport to cover four runways would amount to $16,450. Also, $600 would have to be spent to equip each of TWA's aircraft with the necessary antennas and receivers. As TWA used eight airports and operated fifty airplanes, Frye concluded, "the cost of this system would be so high as to prevent its practical application."[23]

The need for an instrument landing system, however, soon came to the forefront when the actions of the Roosevelt administration raised public concern over aviation safety. In February 1934, Army Air Corps pilots began flying the mail after President Roosevelt canceled the airmail contracts held by commercial airlines. Between 19 February and 1 June, military aviators suffered twelve fatalities in sixty-six accidents. Whether deserving or not, the army—and the Roosevelt administration—received extensive criticism for the apparent inability of military pilots to cope with bad weather.[24]

Stung by the public outcry, the army appointed a special investigating board, headed by former Secretary of War Newton D. Baker, to look into the shortcomings of the Air Corps and to recommend changes. "The greatest hazard in the operation of aircraft, both military and commercial," the Baker Board concluded, "is that of landing in a fog or in the absence of visibility from other causes." The board recommended that "urgent priority" be given to the practical application of an instrument landing system that had been under development by the Materiel Division of the Air Corps.[25]

The landing system recommended by the Baker Board was primarily the work of Captain Albert F. Hegenberger, a talented army pilot and ardent proponent of instrument flying techniques. Hegenberger had conceived of a simplified instrument system that used a refinement of the radio compass, designed by army radio engineer G. G. Kreusi, that would home in on nondirectional radio beacons (NDB).

Hegenberger had begun tests of the system in September 1931. He aligned two low-frequency nondirectional beacons with the centerline of the runway at McCook Field, Ohio, one 1,500 feet from the field boundary and the other 1½ miles distant. Colocated with the NDBs were very high frequency marker beacons. Some fifty miles from McCook, Hegenberger would tune in the NDB at the inner marker ("A") and turn his aircraft until his radio compass needle pointed to zero. He then would fly toward "A" until a light illuminated in the cockpit, indicating his passage over the station. Immediately switching his receiver to the NDB at the outer marker ("B"), he would fly toward that location, noting the wind drift, until the proper light signal came on. Turning 180 degrees, Hegenberger would again tune in "A." He followed the radio compass indicator, adjusting for wind and descending at a normal glide angle, until he passed over "A." He then cut his power, placed the aircraft in a proper landing attitude, and waited for his wheels to touch the ground.

On 7 May 1932, Hegenberger made his first blind landing, carrying C.D. Carbulesco as safety pilot. The next day, he flew two more successful tests, one with Carbulesco on board and one with Kreusi. On 8 May, Hegenberger made the first solo blind landing in history. The success of the system, he reported to his superiors, "far exceeded expectations."[26]

Despite the promise of the Hegenberger system, nothing much happened for the next year. The furor created by the airmail fiasco in early 1934, however, immediately placed Hegenberger in the spotlight. In May 1934, his efforts were recognized and he received an oak leaf cluster to add to his Distinguished Flying Cross. Later in the year, the National Aeronautics Association announced that he had won the prestigious Collier Trophy for the year's outstanding contribution to the development of aeronautics.[27]

The Hegenberger system suddenly became the favored instrument landing system not only of the Army Air Corps but also of the Department of Commerce. Following a demonstration at Langley Field, Virginia, in September 1934, the Bureau of Air Commerce announced that the Hegenberger system would be adopted as the standard for civil aviation and installed along the transcontinental airway. "The advantages of the standardization of a system usable by commercial and military aviation," the bureau argued, "are too numerous and obvious to mention." Also unmentioned was the fact that the relatively inexpensive Hegenberger system did not constitute an "airport improvement" and thus could be funded by the federal government.[28]

The Department of Commerce's decision on a standard instrument landing system did not please airline operators. As Jack Frye earlier had informed Dellinger, TWA considered the NBS system "far superior to any other so far projected." TWA believed that "positive indications of lateral, longitudinal, and vertical positions of the aircraft" were necessary for safe instrument landing. The Hegenberger system failed to meet this test of precision.[29]

With the federal government apparently content with the Hegenberger system, the airlines and equipment manufacturers decided to proceed on their own. By 1934, four major developmental programs were underway, all based on the original NBS design.

At Kansas City, TWA developed and tested a combined localizer and glide slope unit that operated on a frequency of 85 MHz. Although the use of very high frequencies usually gave clearer reception, TWA encountered problems with the glide slope signal. As the signal crossed a river at the edge of the airport, it became distorted. Only later did TWA radio engineers trace the problem to vertically polarized waves.[30]

The Lorenz Company of Germany also sponsored tests of its version of the NBS system. An early proponent of the NBS system, Lorenz had installed a similar system at Berlin's Templehof Airport in 1932. During 1934 and 1935, the company had modified the original NBS design, primarily through the use of very high frequencies. The resultant Lorenz system used a single transmitting aerial system, broadcasting on 33.3 MHz, for both the localizer and glide slope. Two marker beacons, giving both aural and visual signals, operated on 38.0 MHz. After more than 1,000 training flights by pilots from Lufthansa Airlines, the Lorenz equipment went into operational service toward the end of 1935 at Berlin and Zurich.

Tested at Indianapolis in 1936 and 1937, the Lorenz system failed to impress American Airlines pilots. They considered the localizer course to be too wide. Also, the glide slope took a pronounced dip as it crossed the end of the runway. Whether the system could be modified to meet this objections remained to be seen.[31]

A third project grew out of the budgetary cuts at the NBS in 1933. Several NBS scientists who had lost their jobs organized the Washington Institute of Technology (WIT) to develop the bureau's instrument landing system into a commercially viable product. By 1935 they were testing what they called the Air-Track system. Close to the NBS original, with the localizer on 278 KHz, glide slope on 93 MHz, and aural marker beacons on 278 KHz, the Air-Track claimed a great advantage in its portability. The localizer and glide slope transmitters and antennas were contained in a trailer that could be towed from one runway to another in approximately ten minutes, while the marker beacons were carried in motorcycle sidecars.[32]

The portable Air-Track system gained the attention of the U.S. Navy. Rear Admiral Ernest J. King, chief of the Bureau of Aeronautics, wanted an instrument landing system that would enable aircraft carriers to conduct aerial operations in bad weather, and the Air-Track seemed a possible answer. King assigned Lt. Frank Akers to work with the Washington Institute of Technology to develop the system for navy use. Following tests at College Park in 1933 and 1934, WIT placed the equipment onboard the aircraft carrier USS *Langley*. On 30 July 1935, Akers (on his third pass) made a successful instrument landing on the short carrier deck. Although further trials confirmed the possibility of using the Air-Track for carrier landings in bad weather, the WIT system failed to gain acceptance for operational deployment with the fleet. The navy, however, did install similar equipment on landing fields used by its patrol planes.[33]

The most extensive and promising work on improvements to the NBS system was done by United Air Lines. In 1934 United obtained the original NBS equipment that had been stored in the corner of a hangar at Newark Airport since the conclusion of the Department of Commerce's demonstration in April 1933. Assisted by NBS technicians, the airline installed the equipment at Oakland Airport. Following initial tests, United concluded an agreement with the Bendix Radio Corporation for joint development of the project. By 1936, a modified system had emerged. In place of the NBS low-frequency localizer, the United-Bendix system featured a combined localizer and glide slope transmitter, similar to the one tested by TWA, that operated on 91 MHz.

Extensive tests of the system took place in February and March 1936, with

Fig. 3.4. Harry Huking, R. T. Freng, and J. H. Woodward of United Air Lines examine an antenna on the nose of the Boeing 247 that conducted instrument landing tests at Oakland. Courtesy National Air and Space Museum, 83-9840

R. T. Freng flying a Boeing 247. James W. Belding, the safety pilot, recalled that the main problem with the system arose when approaching the inner marker. The directional guidance of the glide slope became so tight that the signal would be lost if the aircraft deviated from its course by as little as ten feet.

Freng believed that the answer to the problem lay in coupling a Sperry hydraulic autopilot to the instrument landing system. On 11 March 1936, Freng made the first successful instrument landing by autopilot. The system worked superbly. Over the next two years, pilots from the airlines, army, navy, and Department of Commerce made more than 3,000 hooded landings by autopilot.[34]

While the airlines and equipment manufacturers were proceeding with their largely uncoordinated work on developing a practical instrument landing system, there had been growing public concern about unsafe conditions in the nation's airline industry. As *Fortune* magazine pointed out in April 1937, a series of five airline crashes between December 1936 and February 1937 had "given the travelling public a case of the jitters." Thirty-seven passengers and crew died in the accidents, most of which involved the use of radio aids to navigation.

In a lengthy analysis of the state of industry, *Fortune* concluded that the major factor contributing to the lack of safety in the air was the growing disparity between the capabilities of modern airliners—the Boeing 247 and DC-2/3—and the state of the nation's airways. The magazine castigated the Roosevelt administration for failing to meet "the demands of a highly technical industry in the process of growth and expansion." It recommended a modernization of radio aids to navigation. Also, it pointed to the need for a reliable instrument landing system. "Safe blind landing," it concluded, "obviously, would revolutionize the technique of modern flight."[35]

Responding to charges that its fiscal policy had contributed to the growing number of aircraft accidents, the Roosevelt administration announced that it would spend $5 million on airways modernization during the fiscal year that began on 1 July 1937. At the same time, officials from the Department of Commerce met with representatives of the airlines and radio manufacturers to formulate a basic set of standard specifications for an instrument landing system. As aviation writer and radio expert Henry W. Roberts later observed, the Chicago conference of 6 July 1937 "marked the real start of commercial application of instrument landing in the country."[36]

While it soon became clear that the Department of Commerce was now prepared to support some version of the NBS system over the Hegenberger system as the national standard for instrument landing, the provisions of the Air Commerce Act of 1926 still meant that the federal government could not pay for "airport improvements." Recognizing that private enterprise would have to purchase equipment located on airport property, the Commerce Department continued to hesitate about deciding exactly *which* version of the NBS system should become generally accepted. As a result of governmental indecision, 1938 saw three competing equipment manufacturers promoting their instrument landing systems as the best answer to the problem of landing in bad weather.

The Washington Institute of Technology installed the Air-Track system at Pittsburgh's Allegheny Airport. On 28 January 1938, pilot Jack Neale of Pennsylvania-Central Airlines landed in bad weather at Pittsburgh, marking—in the words of *Fortune* magazine—"the first blind landing made by a U.S. airline with a load of passengers on a regularly scheduled trip." Meanwhile, the International Telephone and Telegraph Corporation (ITT) installed Lorenz equipment at Dallas for use by American Airlines. This system had the virtue of experience: it had been used for several years in Europe by Lufthansa and Swissair to land passengers in bad weather. Finally, Bendix hastened to install the United-Bendix system, which was favored by most pilots, at Burbank, Oakland, Kansas City, Chicago, Cleveland, and Newark.[37]

On 23 June 1938, President Roosevelt signed a new Civil Aeronautics Act into law. Among other provisions, it specified that airports were not to be excluded from federal assistance as had been the case under the Act of 1926. This meant that the federal government would now fund the instrument landing system. Finally, after years of confusion and delay, it appeared that a decision would be forthcoming on a standard landing aid.

In September 1938, the newly organized Civil Aeronautics Authority (CAA) announced its design specifications for an instrument landing system. Based on the NBS model, the system would include a localizer, glide slope, and two marker beacons. All elements of the system would use very high frequencies. Unlike the curved beam of the NBS glide slope, however, the CAA specifications called for a straight line signal that could be adjusted to permit a constant rate of descent. The CAA planned to purchase and install twenty-five landing systems over a two-year period.[38]

After reviewing the bids, the CAA awarded a development contract to the International Telephone and Development Corporation (ITD), a subsidiary of ITT. Early in 1939, the CAA began to test the ITD equipment at its newly opened experimental facility at Indianapolis. Before the tests could be completed, however, President Roosevelt stepped in and added an unnecessary complication to the decision process. In August 1939, at the request of the Army Air Corps, he asked the National Academy of Sciences to study all existing landing systems and to recommend a standard system for both civil and military aviation.[39]

By the end of 1939, the CAA had completed its evaluation of the ITD equipment. After modifications to the glide slope, the system received the CAA's endorsement. At the same time, the National Academy of Sciences also selected the ITD system. It still took several months, however, to appease the Army Air Corps. Not until 2 May 1940 did President Roosevelt give final approval to deploy the ITD system.[40]

Six days later, the CAA opened bids for installation of instrument landing systems at six airports. The contract, not surprisingly, went to ITD. Thereafter, delays in the delivery of equipment slowed progress. By the time the United States entered World War II in December 1941, only one instrument landing system had been installed.

The Army Air Corps—redesignated the Army Air Forces in 1942—took over the CAA-sanctioned instrument landing system following Pearl Harbor. Manufactured during the war by the Federal Telephone and Radio Corporation, it carried the army designation of SCS-51. Eight additional civil airports and twenty-nine army fields received instrument landing system installations between 1942 and 1945.

During the war years, however, the Army Air Forces came to favor a new instrument landing system—the radar-based Ground Controlled Approach (GCA)—as a simpler and better way for pilots to be guided to a landing in bad weather. GCA employed a system of instruments that included at its heart ground radar and communications capabilities to combat the rigors of most weather conditions. At military airfields around the world, hour after hour, disciplined operators stared at green, glowing scopes in dark, cramped rooms and calmly talked pilots blinded by the weather down glide paths where only minor deviations could spell disaster. But GCA was more than equipment; it was a process that required steady nerves and mutual confidence both on the ground and in the air. The extensive use of GCA at every base was probably the most important single technical factor in the increasing flight safety by military pilots during the war.

The end of World War II witnessed a bitter struggle between military and civil authorities over the proper instrument landing system, a fight that was reminiscent of the earlier controversy over the Hegenberger system. The military, supported by private pilots, believed that GCA could be used successfully by aviators who had only limited training in instrument flying; also, the system required no special equipment on airplanes. The CAA and the Airline Pilots Association (ALPA), however, still wanted the prewar-approved instrument landing system. This would eliminate the need for operators on the ground, and commend the care of the aircraft to the pilot flying it. As historian John R. M. Wilson has observed, "The professionals were reluctant to entrust their planes, reputations, and lives to ground controllers of unknown skill."[41]

In February 1946, the Pentagon hosted a meeting of all interested parties in an attempt to reach an agreement on a landing system that could be used both by military and civilian pilots. As a result of these discussions, the Army Air Forces and CAA agreed to conduct trials of the GCA and ILS at Indianapolis. After extensive tests, a final report concluded that neither system deserved the name of "instrument landing system." Both GCA and ILS could be more properly described as "low approach systems." Of the two, GCA appeared to offer more promise than ILS.[42] The International Civil Aviation Organization (ICAO) reached a different conclusion. Following lengthy trials of GCA and various European versions of the ILS, ICAO in December 1946 selected ILS as the primary landing aid for all international trunk airports.

In an effort to settle the festering ILS-GCA controversy, the matter was turned over to the Radio Technical Commission for Aeronautics, which was composed of representatives from the military services, CAA, and civilian aviation interests. Special Committee 31 came up with a compromise solution, recommending that the precision beam radar of the GCA system be incorporated into the ILS. Pilots without ILS receivers in their aircraft could make GCA landings, while aviators using ILS would have their approaches monitored by radar.[43]

The committee's report of May 1948 finally settled the GCA-ILS controversy, although implementation of its recommendations came slowly. In the end, ILS would win out over GCA and become the principal landing aid for civil aviation throughout the world for the next half century; the last GCA unit went out of service in the 1970s.[44]

In the long search for an approved instrument landing system, technology frequently posed the least problem. Scientists Harry Diamond and Frances Dunmore of the National Bureau of Standards accomplished the basic work on what became the ILS between 1929 and 1932. By 1939, the NBS system had been modified by the use of very high frequencies for the localizer and marker beacons, and ultrahigh frequencies (in the range of 300 MHz) for the glide slope. Of all elements of the system, the glide slope proved the most troublesome. Nonetheless, by the end of the 1930s the ILS was a viable system for assisting pilots to land in bad weather.

The lengthy delay in bringing the ILS into operational use could be attributed in part to the desire for a system that could cope with zero-zero weather conditions. As Edgar A. Post, superintendent of navigational aids for United Air Lines, pointed out in 1949, "The industry was trying to run before it learned to walk well." The ILS, he emphasized, could be used with reasonable reliability when the ceiling was as low as 200 feet and visibility a half-mile. It also functioned as an important schedule aid, permitting aircraft to land at intervals of three minutes. The airlines and the government should have accepted the limitations of the ILS and proceeded with the installation of the equipment during the 1930s.[45]

Political considerations, however, were more important in causing delays than misperceptions about the precision needed for a viable landing aid. The struggle between military and civil aviation interests, both before and after World War II, prompted a seemingly endless series of tests of competing landing systems that led nowhere. Military and civil pilots had different requirements, and attempts to bridge the gap between the two were doomed to failure.

President Roosevelt's policy toward commercial aviation also merits criticism. After the unfortunate decision to cut funding for aeronautical research that crippled the NBS and the later cancellation of airmail contracts, the Roosevelt administration largely ignored the interests of commercial aviation. Only under the pressure of events, when the public became concerned over the question of air safety, did the administration respond with the Civil Aeronautics Act of 1938. For five years, however, the lack of federal coordination inhibited the orderly development of a generally acceptable instrument landing system.

Technological advances made possible the growth of a viable commercial airline industry in the United States in the years after World War I. In addition to the appearance of advanced airframes, engines, and mechanical devices that led to such modern airliners as the Boeing 247 and DC-2/3, the use of radio for a series of aids to air navigation permitted the new transports to operate with remarkable regularity and safety. But as the struggle over an instrument landing system reveals, this progress was not always smooth. All too often, political and parochial interests slowed the advance of the airline industry toward becoming a major factor in the nation's transportation system. It was a story that would be repeated in the years to come.

NOTES

1. The story of the domestic airline industry between the wars is still best told by Henry Ladd Smith, *Airways: The History of Commercial Aviation in the United States* (New York: Knopf, 1942).

2. On Praeger and the airmail service, see William M. Leary, *Aerial Pioneers: The U.S. Air Mail Service, 1918–1927* (Washington, D.C.: Smithsonian Institution Press, 1985). The best general account of the work of the NBS is Rexmond C. Cochrane, *Measures for Progress: A History of the National Bureau of Standards* (Washington, D.C.: Government Printing Office, 1966).

3. See Wilbur F. Snyder and Charles L. Bragaw, *Achievement in Radio: Seventy Years of Radio Science, Technology, Standards, and Measurements at the National Bureau of Standards* (Washington, D.C.: Government Printing Office, 1986), 148–49.

4. Radio Laboratory, National Bureau of Standards, "Localized Signalling System for Airplane Landing," 2 June 1920, in the General Records of J. Howard Dellinger, Records of the National Bureau of Standards, Record Group 167, National Archives and Records Administration, Washington, D.C. (hereafter referred to as Dellinger Records).

5. Ibid.

6. On the development of the low-frequency range, see William M. Leary, "Safety in the Air: The Impact of Instrument Flying and Radio Navigation on U.S. Commercial Air Operations between the Wars," in William M. Leary, ed., *From Airships to Airbus: The History of Civil and Commercial Aviation*, vol. 1 (Washington, D.C.: Smithsonian Institution Press, 1995), pp. 97–113.

7. A copy of the paper can be found in the Dellinger Records.

8. Dellinger notes, "Blind Landing—Historical," n.d., Dellinger Records.

9. On the Guggenheim Foundation, see Richard P. Hallion, *Legacy of Flight: The Guggenheim Contribution to American Aviation* (Seattle: University of Washington Press, 1977).

10. James H. Doolittle, "Early Experiments in Instrument Flying," *Smithsonian Report For 1961* (Washington, D.C.: Smithsonian Institution Press, 1962), pp. 337–55.

11. Hallion, *Legacy of Flight*, p. 123.

12. H. Diamond and F. W. Dunmore, "A Radio Beacon and Receiving System for Blind Landing of Aircraft," *Proceedings of the Institute of Radio Engineers* 19 (Apr. 1931): pp. 585–626; National Bureau of Standards, Radio Section, "Annual Report for Fiscal 1930," n.d., Dellinger Records; *Air Commerce Bulletin* 2 (15 Aug. 1930): 79–87.

13. H. Diamond, "Performance Tests of Radio System of Landing Aids," Research Paper RP 602, *Bureau of Standards Journal of Research* 11 (Oct. 1933): 463–90.

14. Ibid.

15. National Bureau of Standards, "Annual Report for Fiscal 1932," n.d., Dellinger Records.

16. *New York Times*, 12 Mar. 1933.

17. Ibid., 3 Mar. 1933.

18. Ibid., 20 Mar. 1933; Diamond, "Performance Tests," pp. 483–84.

19. Diamond, "Performance Tests," p. 490; see also Diamond to Dellinger, 1 Apr. 1933, Dellinger Records.

20. See Nick A. Komons, *Bonfires to Beacons: Federal Civil Aviation Policy under the Air Commerce Act, 1926–1938* (Washington, D.C.: Government Printing Office, 1978), pp. 238–39.

21. Dellinger to Briggs, 26 May 1933, Dellinger Records.

22. Dellinger, "Annual Report of the Radio Section for Fiscal 1934," n.d., Dellinger Records.

23. Frye to Eugene Vidal, 30 Jan. 1934, Dellinger Records.

24. The standard account of this episode is in Paul Tillett, *The Army Flies the Mail* (Tuscaloosa: University of Alabama Press, 1955), but see also R. E. G. Davies, *Fallacies and Fantasies of Air Transport History* (McLean, Va.: Paladwr Press, 1994), pp. 41–50.

25. U.S. Special Committee on the Army Air Corps, *Final Report of the War Department Special Committee on the Army Air Corps,* 18 July 1934 (Washington, D.C.: Government Printing Office, 1934), p. 48.

26. Hegenberger, "Engineering Section Memorandum Report on Fog or Blind Landing System," 4 Mar. 1933, Army Air Forces Central Decimal File 373, Record Group 18, National Archives.

27. William B. Courtney, "The Covered Cockpit," *Collier's,* 27 July 1935, pp. 9, 39–40. Hegenberger had received the Distinguished Flying Cross for a long-distance flight to Hawaii in 1927.

28. *Air Commerce Bulletin* 6 (15 Nov. 1934): 107–109.

29. Frye to Dellinger, 30 Jan. 1934, Dellinger Records.

30. W. E. Jackson, "Status of Instrument Landing Systems," *Proceedings of the Institute of Radio Engineers* 26 (June 1938): 681–99.

31. E. Kramer, "The Present State of the Art of Blind Landing of Airplanes Using Ultra-Short Waves in Europe," *Proceedings of the Institute of Radio Engineers* 23 (Oct. 1935): 1171–82; "Under the Weather," *Fortune* (June 1938): 62–63, 104, 106.

32. Jackson, "Instrument Landing Systems," pp. 692–95.

33. Navy Department, *U.S.S. Langley,* "Final Report on Acceptance Trials of Blind Landing Equipment Installed on U.S.S. LANGLEY by Washington Institute of Technology," 2 Dec. 1935, Bureau of Aeronautics, General Correspondence, 1939–1942, File F31-2/NA6, Record Group 72, National Archives. See also F. Akers and F. G. Kear, "Instrument Landing at Sea," *IRE Transactions on Military Electronics,* Dec. 1957, pp. 36–43.

34. "Under the Weather," *Fortune* 17 (June 1938): 62–63, 104, 106; James M. Belding to Leary, 12 July and 12 Aug. 1983. For the work done by the Army Air Corps to develop an automatic landing system, see Jacob Neufeld, "George V. Holloman: Missile Pioneer," *Aerospace Historian* 29 (1980): 101–102. Holloman made his first automatic landing on 23 Aug. 1937.

35. "The Air Is How Safe?" *Fortune* 15 (Apr. 1937): 75–80, 154, 156, 158, 163–64, 166, 168, 170, 173–76.

36. Roberts, "Instrument Landing," *Aero Digest* 35 (Oct. 1939): 74, 77.

37. "Under the Weather," *Fortune* 17 (June 1938): 62–65, 104, 106; Henry W. Roberts, "Instrument Landing—Today and Tomorrow," *Aero Digest* 32 (June 1938): 78–80, 98.

38. Henry W. Roberts, "Instrument Landing," *Aero Digest* 35 (Oct. 1939): 74, 77. The Civil Aeronautics Authority became the Civil Aeronautics Administration in 1940.

39. *Aviation* 3 (1 Oct. 1939): 1, 8.

40. John R. M. Wilson, *Turbulence Aloft: The Civil Aeronautics Administration amid Wars and Rumors of Wars, 1938–1953* (Washington, D.C.: Government Printing Office, 1979), 128–29.

41. Ibid., 219.

42. William Koger, "CAA and Airlines Versus GCA," *Air Transport*, Mar. 1947, pp. 32+.

43. Wilson, *Turbulence Aloft*, pp. 225–28.

44. See Samuel B. Fishbein, *Flight Management Systems: The Evolution of Navigation Technology* (Westport, Conn.: Praeger, 1995), pp. 84–87.

45. Edgar A. Post, "Airline Operating Experiences with the Instrument Landing System," paper presented at the Institute of Aeronautical Sciences, 22 July 1949, copy in the library of the National Air and Space Museum, Washington, D.C.

CHAPTER 4

Higher, Faster, and Farther

Fueling the Aeronautical Revolution, 1919–45

Stephen L. McFarland

When Orville Wright started his four-cylinder, 140-pound gasoline engine on 17 December 1903, it produced sixteen horsepower. As the engine heated up, power output dropped to twelve horsepower—a loss of 25 percent. The Wright Flyer still flew some one hundred feet through the air—just enough to begin a new mode of transportation and revolutionize the world. The world wanted flight that went higher, faster, and farther, however, because of the universal human compulsion for better performance and because the competitive urge demanded it. Military aviators sought increased performance because of a lesson learned at least 55,000 times in World War I: fly higher, faster, and farther than your enemy—or die.

Steps forward in flight performance came from the interaction of individual advances in drag reduction[1] and engine power, though Leonard S. Hobbs of the United Aircraft Corporation estimated that 75 percent of the 400 mph advance in fighter aircraft speed between the world wars came from the latter.[2] The Liberty aircraft engine of World War I fame and the Merlin engine of World War II fame were both V-12s with the same displacement, but the twenty-five-year older Liberty produced 420 horsepower (2.04 pounds of dry engine weight per horsepower) against the Merlin's 2,250 horsepower (0.78 pounds of dry engine weight per horsepower). Unfortunately, greater power meant greater heat, burned-out valves, cracked spark plugs, and, most importantly, engine knock or detonation.

Improved cylinder designs, new metal alloys, pressurized radiators using ethylene glycol coolants, sodium-cooled valves, stellite lining, and ceramic-platinum spark plugs were all mechanical solutions to rising temperatures, but they brought increased weight, expense, and complexity. None solved the root problem of engine knock—aviation gasoline itself. A means had to be found to control heat from inside the combustion chamber by altering the fuel's chemical composition. The pursuit of higher, faster, and farther from 1919 to 1939 became a chase to contain the ever increasing heat of the thousands of combustions taking place inside an aircraft engine every minute.

Engine knock was the villain in the pursuit of greater propulsion. In a normal combustion process, a spark plug ignites the air-fuel mixture, generating a flame front or wave that travels through the cylinder, consuming the mixture, increasing the temperature and pressure, and forcing the piston before it. If the temperature of the air-fuel mixture ahead of the flame front rises too high, the remaining unburned mixture can ignite spontaneously and violently, causing destructive vibrations in the cylinder, an excessive rise in cylinder temperature and pressure, loss of engine power, and destruction of engine parts—knock. An annoyance in an automobile engine, knock can be immediately fatal to an aircraft engine. Pound per pound, the gasoline-air mixture in an engine cylinder contains more energy than the explosive TNT. Improved performance between the world wars meant maximizing this explosive energy by one or more of three methods: increasing the cylinder's compression ratio, making the engine run at a higher number of revolutions per minute (rpms), and supercharging the cylinder with larger quantities of the air-fuel mixture.[3] The latter, supercharging or boosting the engine with more air, offered the greatest opportunities. Air was free and did not have to be carried aboard the aircraft at the cost of additional weight. Mechanics and engineers used all three to achieve higher, faster, and farther flight but in the process generated engine knock—the barrier to improved performance.

The effort to understand and conquer knock in the United States during the interwar era involved contributions from government agencies (primarily the Army Air Corps Materiel Division at Wright Field and the National Advisory Committee for Aeronautics, or NACA, established by Congress in 1915 "to supervise and direct the scientific study of the problems of flight"), private industry, universities, and foreign sources. It was largely the product of serendipitous, empirical research and development, though science played an important role.[4]

Initially knock and preignition were considered identical and treated by improved cooling or advancing the spark timing, which decreased performance because of increased engine weight or decreased power output.[5] Few blamed fuels for knock; other fuel qualities were thought to be more important, including volatility,[6] stability, freezing point, boiling point, specific gravity, caloric value, distillation range, and color.[7] Harry Ricardo and Bertram Hopkinson at Cambridge University began examining the effects of compression ratios on preignition in 1903, determining that knock and preignition were different features of the combustion cycle and that knock was a characteristic of fuel. By 1912 Ricardo had shown that knock was the spontaneous combustion of the unburnt air-gas mixture, or end gas, being compressed by the advancing flame front.[8]

During World War I the knock problem intensified because engine manufacturers increased compression ratios and rpms to achieve greater power, fuel producers used cracked gasolines with an increased tendency to knock to meet the demand for fuel, and pilots and mechanics tinkered with their engines to run them "beyond the red line" for the extra speed that might make the difference between life and death. Alcohol added to gasoline resisted knock but produced less power per gallon.[9] Benzol, a by-product of coke production, provided power and a remarkable resistance to knock. American pilots in France used French gasoline containing benzol, flying against German pilots using an 80/20 gasoline-benzol mixture. Americans developed Alcogas (38 percent methanol, 19 percent benzol, 4 percent toluol, 30 percent gasoline, and 7.5 percent ether), Hecter fuel (20 percent benzol and 80 percent hexahydrobenzol), and Taylor fuel (33 percent methanol, 40 percent gasoline, and 27 percent benzol) to defeat knock, but none received widespread use.[10]

The American pursuit of improved aviation gasoline began on 2 August 1917, when the Bureau of Mines and the Aviation Section of the Signal Corps launched a study of available fuels. Flight testing at Langley and McCook Fields showed America's best aviation gasoline, Pennsylvania "high test," was no better than regular motor gasoline in resisting knock. A 1918 NACA report on the power characteristics of aviation gasoline never considered knock—too little was yet known about the phenomenon. Benzol remained the antiknock fuel of choice, though it could only be used in small quantities because its high freezing point (34°F) clogged fuel lines in the freezing temperatures found at combat altitudes, engine starting was difficult because it did not vaporize easily, and its antiknock qualities declined at higher temperatures and rpms. Benzol also produced an abrasive carbon residue that corroded engine parts. NACA research offered little hope that benzol would solve the knock problem.[11]

Working independently for the Dayton Engineering Laboratories (DELCO), Thomas Midgley Jr. pursued a solution to knock because DELCO's battery ignition for automobiles was being incorrectly blamed for the widening knock problem in American automobiles that was actually due to the increased use of cracked gasolines. Midgley's pressure studies revealed that knock's abrupt rise in pressure occurred after ignition, confirming Ricardo's belief that knock was not preignition. He hypothesized that knock was therefore due to a natural tendency of gasoline to resist ignition, leading to the buildup of excessive pressure in the unburned air-gas mixture that would explode as knock. Adding iodine to the gasoline, Midgley believed the dyed gasoline would absorb more radiant heat and burn more readily without the spontaneous ignition of knock. Serendipity intervened as iodine eliminated knock, but for the wrong reason. Follow-up tests showed that other dyes had no effect on knock, but colorless ethyl iodide did. Midgley had discovered "doping"—adding a nonfuel compound to gasoline to increase its antiknock qualities. Continued research produced a number of such compounds, including nitrogen, phosphorus, arsenic, antimony, selenium, and tellurium, but all had shortcomings.[12]

In late 1921 Midgley's research team tried tetraethyl lead (TEL), which proved to have especially effective antiknock qualities. Extensive testing of what was officially called GM Anti-Knock No. 501 began at McCook Field in Dayton, Ohio, the location of the Army Air Service's Engineering Division, revealing dramatic reductions in knock, but also serious problems with spark plug fouling and valve erosion. A year later Midgley determined that adding ethyl bromide to TEL prevented such effects and together with Graham Edgar developed a method of extracting this compound from seawater. Charles Kettering of General Motors labeled the new TEL-ethyl bromide compound "ethyl" fluid. Used in quantities as small as one molecule of TEL in 80,000 molecules of gasoline, it eliminated knock in the gasolines being burned in the engines of the day.[13]

Doping with TEL could improve the qualities of 1920s fuels, but only to a degree. Further improvements would be dependent on raising the quality of the gasoline itself. In the early 1920s the Army Air Service standardized four grades of gasoline on the basis of color, boiling point, and specific gravity. These grades, from lowest to highest "test," were Motor Gasoline, Domestic Aviation Gasoline, Export Aviation Gasoline, and Fighting Aviation Gasoline. Any effect these had on preventing knock was purely coincidental. Harold Harris, chief test pilot at McCook Field in the early 1920s knew, as did other air racers, that California aviation gasoline suppressed knock better than Pennsylvania gas. In July 1923 the Power Plant Laboratory at McCook and Midgley, first at DELCO and then at the Ethyl Gasoline Corporation, compared California gasoline to standard aviation fuels and revealed the difference to be a high concentration of aromatics in California gas.[14] West Coast aviation gasoline was no answer to the knock problem by itself, however, because pilots had to use whatever fuel was available where they landed and because California alone could not produce sufficient gasoline to power the nation's aircraft. Tests also indicated that aromatic fuels were prone to preignition, had less energy per unit of weight than other hydrocarbons, produced nauseating fumes, and were powerful solvents that dissolved rubber fuel system and engine components. Continued research revealed the antiknock qualities of benzene, toluene, xylene, and other aromatics, but the efficiency and economy of TEL made such compounds unnecessary, especially in light of the aromatics' deficiencies.[15]

A daunting challenge facing researchers in the 1920s was how to identify and specify the antiknock qualities of fuels, especially because they did not know what knock was, just the effect it had on engines. Harry Ricardo started the process after World War I, designing a variable compression ratio single-cylinder test engine (the E-35). Test engines were necessary because full-size engines required too much fuel and because to be accurate the engines had to be made to knock, which destroyed these expensive motors. Ricardo suggested burning a test fuel in the engine while adjusting the compression ratio upward until knock began, establishing the fuel's highest useful compression ratio, or HUCR. HUCR was dependent on atmospheric conditions and the condition of the test engine, however. Next, while working for the Shell Oil Company, Ricardo identified heptane as the hydrocarbon most likely to cause knock and toluene as the least. He suggested using a mixture of toluene and heptane as a reference standard against which to measure the tendency of other fuels to knock. The resulting Toluene Number, used mainly in England, was the first attempt to measure the knocking qualities of different fuels. Unfortunately, these qualities varied greatly from one batch of reference fuels to another, and toluene demonstrated a tendency to preignite, ruining test results.[16]

In the United States the Army Air Service's Engineering Division and the Ethyl Gasoline Corporation's Midgley and Thomas A. Boyd collaborated to build a standard test engine, the Series 30, converted from a single-cylinder DELCO lighting engine. Testing at the General Motors Research Laboratories, the Engineering Division, the Bureau of Standards, the Standard Oil Development Company, the Ethyl Gasoline Corporation, and several universities revealed some of the difficulties associated with developing standards. Research showed that, among others, carburetor adjustment, spark plug timing, lubricating oil temperature, the condition of the piston rings, coolant temperature, and atmospheric temperature and humidity affected a fuel's tendency to knock. Such variables made standardization problematic.[17]

A breakthrough came in 1926, when Graham Edgar of the Ethyl Gasoline Corporation synthesized the isooctane hydrocarbon using tertiary butyl alcohol heated with sulfuric acid to produce di-isobutylene and hydrogenated to form isooctane. Testing showed that the new compound had high antiknock qualities, but there was no question of using isooctane as a commercial fuel, not at $30 ($216 in 1996 dollars) per gallon. Edgar suggested his synthesized isooctane and Ricardo's heptane as fuel knock and antiknock standards. On the Edgar octane scale, heptane would have a value of zero because it caused knock at even low compression ratios. Isooctane would have a value of 100 because it resisted knock at even the highest compression ratios. Octane ratings would be expressed as the percentage of isooctane that had to be mixed in a heptane fuel to prevent knock in a standard test engine. All fuels would be evaluated for their antiknock qualities in test engines by equating their performance to a combination of isooctane and heptane.[18]

The United States Navy began using the octane scale in late 1927 and the Army Air Corps in 1929, guaranteeing the widespread adoption of Edgar's system. By this scale, the gasoline used in the Wright Flyer rated about 38 octane. World War I aviation gasoline was about 40 to 60 octane. Samuel Heron of the Ethyl Gasoline Corporation tested aviation fuels advertised as "high test" in the Series 30 engine, discovering that most rated about 50 octane—inferior in terms of antiknock value to most "low-test" automotive fuels.[19]

The Army Air Corps led the way in issuing the first specification for aviation gasoline using Edgar's octane system. Specification Y-3559 of 30 June 1930 required gasolines to have an octane rating of no less than 65, raised to 87 octane with no more than 6 ml of TEL per gallon, as tested in a Series 30 engine.[20] Specification Y-3557 that same year required a minimum octane rating of 72 raised to 87 octane with TEL. Wright Field's Materiel Division carried out knock tests on available fuels and published the results to assist all producers and consumers in understanding the importance of antiknock qualities.[21]

Agreement to define a fuel's antiknock qualities by the octane scale was only a first step. Test engines and procedures for determining octane ratings varied. Fuel manufacturers wanted simple testing procedures to reduce their costs, while engine manufacturers and users wanted tests run under complex service conditions of high temperatures and full-sized engines. Standard Oil of New Jersey produced 76 octane gasoline that when combined with 1.1 ml TEL achieved an 87 octane rating when tested in a Series 30 engine running at 600 rpm and 300°F. The Army Air Corps' Materiel Division at Wright Field, replacing the old Engineering Division at McCook Field in 1927, tested the fuel at closer-to-service conditions (a Series 30 engine running at 900 rpm and 375°F) and discovered that the same Standard Oil 76 octane gasoline required 4 ml TEL to achieve the 87 octane rating because most fuels lost antiknock values at high cylinder temperatures and pressures. The Series 30 test engine, a fixed compression engine, was too sensitive to slight changes in operating conditions to allow standardization.[22]

In pursuit of standardization, Wright Field agreed at a meeting on 28 August 1930 to cooperate with the Ethyl Gasoline corporation and the Stanavo Specification Board (representing all Standard Oil companies) in rating aviation fuels with a modified test engine, the Series 30-B. Materiel Division personnel soon realized that such standardization was impossible because of the number of variables in the process. Rich and lean mixtures and different temperature and rpm settings all produced different results. Worst of all, the results differed markedly when compared to the same fuels run in full-size engines. Fortunately, the Materiel Division took failure as an incentive to try harder.[23]

Representatives of the Bureau of Standards, the Ethyl Gasoline Corporation, the Army Air Corps, and the navy met in Detroit on 23 January 1931 to unify specifications for aviation gasoline. All agreed that Wright Field should issue standardized testing specifications because it was the center for aviation fuels research and development and the largest single purchaser of aviation gasolines. Meeting again on 16 April, the Wright Field group could report little progress after three months' work. The Air Corps had to run its test engine at "very high cylinder and piston temperatures and high compression pressures" to duplicate the tendency of aromatic and cracked gasolines to cause overheating, preignition, and knocking. Such conditions made the test engine "exceedingly sensitive to the influence of carbon and other deposits, to oil pumping, and to the presence of other liquids within the combustion chamber which may result in changing cylinder wall, piston and charge temperature." Any attempt to standardize at this time, the Materiel Division was forced to conclude, was liable to produce misleading results. Wright Field could not adapt the Series 30 engine to duplicate operational conditions. For the time being, the United States would retain the old specifications that required testing in a Series 30 or Series 30-B engine at 600 rpm rather than the 900 rpm that more closely duplicated operational conditions.[24]

Two new test engines competed to fill the gap. NACA offered an expensive Universal Variable Compression Engine that attracted few users. The second engine then under development by the Cooperative Fuel Research Committee, formed by the Society of Automotive Engineers, the American Petroleum Institute, and the National Bureau of Standards, offered hope of more accurate testing and standardization in the future. Manufactured by the Waukesha Motor Company, a member of the Cooperative Fuel Research Committee, this new CFR engine automatically varied spark advance with the compression ratio, which was adjustable while the engine was operating. The cylinder was one piece to prevent coolant leakage into the combustion space, and the entire engine was overbuilt for ruggedness, including a one-inch-thick crankcase. The Materiel Division struggled through 1932 to develop testing procedures for this new CFR engine, which it had begun using in 1931. Representatives from the Society of Automotive Engineers, the Bureau of Standards, the navy, ten oil companies, and six engine manufacturers met at Wright Field to standardize these procedures, but the November 1932 meeting produced agreement only on the CFR engine, not the testing procedures. At the Cooperative Fuel Research Committee meeting in Detroit from 24 to 27 January 1933, a near-consensus agreed to continue using the Series 30 engine running at 600 rpm and 300°F until testing procedures for the new CFR engine were available. Only the Air Corps disagreed, complaining that such conditions did not reflect service conditions and gave "too favorable ratings" to alcohols and aromatic fuels. It had plans for higher-octane aviation fuels and knew that above 80 octane the old testing methods were not accurate. The Air Corps preferred to wait for the completion of new procedures it was developing for the CFR engine.[25]

Stakes in the dispute were high as fuels with more aromatic hydrocarbons were cheaper and showed higher octane values at lower engine speeds and cooler operating conditions, but showed lower octane values under service conditions. In 1933 the American Society for Testing Materials (ASTM) declared a set of standards for determining octane ratings. Producers and consumers would use the CFR engine at 900 rpm and 209–215°F as the ASTM-CFR "Motor Method" that best represented automotive needs. When tests were run at 600 rpm and 209–215°F, octane values would be given as the "Research Method" that best served research laboratory purposes. Octane ratings would specify which method was used. With the Series 30 engine, tests had been run with a fixed compression ratio while knock conditions were varied by adjusting the mixture and spark advance. With the CFR engine, tests were run by varying the compression ratio and the air-fuel mixture ratio. Technicians determined when knock occurred by using Midgley's bouncing pin. These procedures were initially called the 1-C method and later the ASTM F3 method.[26]

Here the Army Air Corps, later joined by the navy, parted company with other government agencies and industry. Wright Field wanted the new CFR engine, but with a smaller 2⅝″ bore and other modifications, at 1,200 rpm and 330°F temperature and using a thermal plug to measure the onset of knock as a way of better representing the conditions of a full-sized service engine. It compared data gained from these test conditions to octane rating tests run in full-size multicylinder engines. The results were sufficiently close for the Air Corps to declare that the CFR engine run under the army's new Y-3566 specification, issued on 1 July 1933, was "very satisfactory and the method is easy and rapid to work with." No tests could exactly duplicate what happened to fuels in a full-size aircraft engine under service conditions, but specification Y-3566 and the Air Corps method was a "fair average." Despite intense pressure from oil, engine, and automobile industries, Chief of the Air Corps Major General Benjamin Foulois declared that the 1-C/ASTM F3 method did "not meet requirements in all cases for military engines." Furthermore, he claimed there was not "sufficient data on the testing of multi-cylinder engines by organizations other than the Air Corps to arrive at a common method of testing."[27]

The Cooperative Fuel Research Committee's Aviation Gasoline Detonation Subcommittee supported the Air Corps and the navy against the ASTM's Motor and Research Methods. Using multicylinder aviation engines under 1-C/ASTM F3 requirements, the subcommittee, dominated by the Air Corps but including oil and engine companies, the National Bureau of Standards, the National Research Council of Canada, and the U.S. Navy, concluded that the "Motor-Method rating incorrectly predicts the full-scale engine performance of the test fuel." The CFR engine and standardized procedures ignored the fact that major gains in engine power in the 1930s were the product of increased supercharging absent in test engines. Raising the intake pressure via supercharging boosted rpms and engine temperatures, creating special stresses on a fuel's antiknock qualities that could not be duplicated in the test engines of the time. Testing in unsupercharged engines was subject to changing air density, temperature, and humidity. Shell, for example, delivered 87 octane fuel tested in a CFR engine at 212°F to Wright Field, which tested it at 85 octane in the same engine run at 300°F. Wright Field shipped some to the navy, which tested it in a Series 30 engine at 89 octane. Standardized octane ratings and testing specifications would remain at best only an indication of a fuel's antiknock qualities.[28]

Other laboratories attempted to use chemical analysis to predict the antiknock qualities of a fuel, without success. Determining the percentage of paraffins, naphthenes, aromatics, and olefins in a fuel to identify an octane value did not match the results of engine testing. Engine testing was a complicated and imprecise method, but as researchers at the University of Pittsburgh concluded, "We do not know of any dependable method for determining the detonating tendency of motor fuels except that of direct engine tests."[29] Knowledge of knock would remain not in the world of science, but in the empirical realm.

Wright Field also determined that the best consistency in testing occurred when a test fuel was compared to the performance of a standard reference fuel rather than when compared to the octane scale. Fuel tested in the winter at 87 octane with cold air flowing into the cylinder could not meet the 87 octane standard when tested again in the summer with hot air flowing into the cylinder. Materiel Division personnel discovered that when fuels were compared to a standardized fuel under the same conditions, the results were generally equal: "anti-knock cannot be properly expressed as absolute standard of octane numbers, but instead only in comparison to standard fuel performance." In conjunction with the Standard Oil Development Company, the Air Corps produced Standard Reference Fuel C-6, which when combined with 1.1 ml TEL performed equal to 87 parts laboratory-grade isooctane and 13 parts laboratory-grade heptane or 87 octane. The Air Corps cared less about the actual octane rating of the fuels it was buying than about how much TEL had to be added to achieve 87 octane. It therefore wrote its specifications to require suppliers to express their fuels' antiknock qualities as the amount of TEL that had to be added to perform equal to or better than Standard Reference Fuel C-6 with 1.1 ml TEL, instead of dictating that the fuel be 87 octane. The world used the CFR Motor Method to identify a fuel as 87 octane, but for the Army Air Corps it was Standard Reference Fuel C-6 plus 1.1 ml TEL.[30]

Between the wars the Army Air Corps had performed the key role of catalyst in the pursuit of higher, faster, and farther flight. Under the direction of Samuel D. Heron, Wright Field had shown that knock was related to cylinder temperature, not just spark advance or fuel quality. It had refined the octane rating system based on standardized Reference Fuels. It performed tens of thousands of free tests on fuel samples from all over the United States to try to standardize quality. It was the single largest purchaser of aviation gasoline and of aviation engines. Navy development policy was to procure engines and try to match them to the best fuel then available. Air Corps policy was to encourage the development of the best fuels possible and then convince manufacturers to develop engines to take advantage of the improved fuels. Naval policies further inhibited the development of better fuels because the navy insisted on buying aviation gasoline without TEL, preferring to add the ethyl fluid as it was being pumped into aircraft fuel tanks. Other users objected because navy policies drove up the price of aviation gasoline and discouraged the oil industry from expanding production. The Air Corps and commercial users demanded 87 octane but allowed producers to mix and match lower- and higher-quality gasolines, making up the difference with TEL. The navy demanded 73 octane without TEL, forcing suppliers to deliver the highest-quality straight gasolines to the navy, thereby reducing the overall availability of such gasolines.[31]

Since 1928 the Air Corps had led the world in fuel research and in methods for rating fuels. While other consumers were satisfied with the 52 octane fuel then available, the Air Corps demanded 87 octane and, for a few more cents per gallon, got a 33 percent increase in power. Once Wright Field proved its value, the world adopted 87 octane gasoline. Only NACA supported the Air Corps in this effort. Assistant Chief of the Air Corps Oscar Westover declared, "This leadership displayed by the Air Corps contributed more to aeronautical development in the world than any other single accomplishment in the past eight years."[32]

The Air Corps never paused after its successes with 87 octane but began encouraging the research and development of a super fuel produced synthetically through chemical hydrogenation, or the adding of hydrogen to hydrocarbon compounds. The Materiel Division provided laboratories, test engines, some funding through purchases, and coordination. Standard Oil of New Jersey and the Shell Oil Company provided the rest. Ironically, Shell had financed Friedreich Bergius's hydrogenation experiments in Germany after World War I, only to lose access to them when Standard Oil purchased rights to the patents from Germany's I. G. Farbenindustrie for $35 million ($273 million in 1996 dollars) on 9 November 1929. Samuel Heron, the Ethyl Gasoline Corporation, and Wright Field personnel produced the first batch of this new isooctane-based aviation gasoline for a series of tests in specially modified full-scale aircraft engines in 1930. The results revealed the promise of hydrogenated high-octane gasoline, though no manufacturers would build an engine to take advantage of it because the fuel was too expensive and available only in laboratory-scale quantities. It tested at 74.6 octane without TEL and 92 with TEL, encouraging the Air Corps to issue specification Y-3557-G for the new high-octane fuel early in 1931. By creating a requirement for 92 octane fuel, the Air Corps encouraged the Wright Aeronautical Corporation to design the Cyclone R-1820-33 engine with a 6.4:1 compression ratio and an 8.31:1 supercharger gear ratio. These engines, made possible only because of the availability of 92 octane gasoline, propelled the revolutionary Martin B-10 Air Corps bomber through the air at 210 miles per hour, with no knock, launching a revolution in airplane performance.[33]

Standard Oil improved the Bergius cold acid process when it discovered that heating isobutylene and normal butylenes with sulfuric acid increased the amount of resulting di-isobutylenes available for hydrogenation into isooctane. Isooctane combined with aviation gasoline tested at 87 octane, raised to 100 octane with TEL. Heron convinced Standard Oil to produce a model hydrogenation plant at Bayway, New Jersey, that could produce "iso paraffins of extremely condensed structure such as iso-octane," identified by the Materiel Division as the "best possibility" for improving the octane ratings of aviation gasoline. In January 1934 the Power Plant Branch at the Materiel Division asked Shell, Standard Oil of New Jersey, and other oil companies to each produce two thousand gallons of 100 octane fuel for tests in supercharged service engines. Testing continued through 1934, with such promising results that contracting personnel negotiated with James H. Doolittle of Shell and Edwin E. Aldrin of Standard Oil of New Jersey for future service purchases. Wright Field issued a temporary specification, X-3575, to govern the purchases on 1 February 1934, and sought industry interest in supplying the fuel in large quantities in December 1934. Standard Oil of New Jersey, Shell, and Phillips expressed interest, estimating the cost at 75 percent more than then current 87 octane.[34]

In 1929 and 1930 Shell had readied itself to move into the high-octane market by hiring three former Air Corps officers to run its U.S. operations, coordinated from St. Louis by Doolittle. In 1931 Shell purchased the hydrogenation technology from Standard Oil in order to convert waste gases from its oil refineries into usable compounds. While trying to produce butyl alcohol, the Shell Development Company accidentally discovered polymerization, by which waste gases were converted into di-isobutylene, which was converted into isooctane via hydrogenation. The process offered the potential to mass produce the 100 octane fuel at a price much lower than Edgar's laboratory-produced isooctane. Doolittle convinced Shell to build pilot production plants and the Air Corps to order one thousand gallons at $2 ($17.20 in 1996 dollars) per gallon as a test run in 1934. In April 1934 Shell delivered the order to Wright Field at a price of only $0.71 ($6.11 in 1996 dollars) per gallon. Initial tests at Wright Field indicated a 20 to 30 percent increase in power, with no increase in cylinder temperature, encouraging Doolittle to send 70,000 gallons of the new isooctane to fuel laboratories and users across the nation. The navy and commercial airlines initially indicated that they did not want 100 octane gasoline because of the additional expense. Doolittle and Wright Field were confident, however, that adoption of the new fuel would become universal because it was "by far the cheapest way of making possible a marked improvement in airplane performance."[35]

Standard Oil delivered its first batch of the new 100 octane aviation fuel to Wright Field for testing in March 1935, one year later than Shell, and its first shipment for service use in September 1935. Wright Field had also sought contracts with Socony-Vacuum, Texaco, Humble, Phillips, Richfield, and Standard Oil of Indiana, but all refused because there was no market for it.[36] If the Air Corps could help it, the market would be there. In March 1935 Chief of the Air Corps Major General Benjamin D. Foulois and Chief of the Engineering Section at Wright Field Major Clinton W. Howard met with representatives of Shell and Standard Oil to discuss the possibilities of standardizing hydrogenated isooctane and 100 octane gasoline. Both companies notified the Air Corps representatives that the feeder stock for isooctane (isobutylene) was in short supply and would not support full-scale production. Foulois's decision to proceed anyway, based on his faith in the oil industry, guaranteed that American aviation would be at the forefront of the aeronautical revolution of the 1930s that carried through World War II. On 20 June 1935, Wright Field issued final specifications for 100 octane aviation gasoline and invited bids for one million gallons. The first delivery was to Selfridge Field in Michigan on 20 September 1935, at a price of $0.30 ($2.55 in 1996 dollars) per gallon.[37]

Despite a budget that left his service with only $4.3 million ($37 million in 1996 dollars) for fuel purchases in FY 1936, Foulois ordered the Materiel Division to buy exclusively 100 octane gasoline at $0.30 ($2.55 in 1996 dollars) per gallon rather than 92 octane at $0.16 ($1.38 in 1996 dollars) per gallon as a way of encouraging oil companies to produce the new gasoline and engine manufacturers to redesign their engines to exploit its additional antiknock capabilities. Secretary of War George H. Dern learned of the Air Corps plan and ordered the acquisition of 100 octane limited to no more than 10 percent of total aviation gasoline purchased that year. His logic was sound, though hardly farsighted: "to use a more expensive gasoline than needed for present day engines appears wasteful." The secretary, expressing the opinion of the General Staff, opposed 100 octane because the United States did not want to start a "gas race" with other countries and complicate the supply situation in the rest of the army, for which 87 octane gasoline was more than enough. And in an age when government subsidies to the private sector were the exception, he argued that "to ask the War Department alone to subsidize the oil industry . . . seems needless."[38]

Stymied by War Department myopia, the Air Corps called together its experts and representatives from the navy's Bureau of Aeronautics, NACA, oil companies, and aircraft and engine manufacturers for four days in November 1936 at Wright Field to establish a policy on the standardization of 100 octane fuel and the development of aircraft engines to exploit its potential. It reported that Air Corps units had by then used 3.5 million gallons of 100 octane fuel consisting of about 50 percent isooctane and 50 percent regular aviation gasoline plus 3 ml TEL. The super fuel allowed Air Corps units to run their engines at higher power settings without knock, producing average increases over 92 octane fuel of 20 percent in horsepower, 6 percent in speed, and 50 percent in climb rates for existing engines not designed for the higher octane. Without the funding to back up their requests, Air Corps representatives at the meeting could do little more than plead with the assembled oil companies to build more plants and engine manufacturers to design new engines to exploit this new fuel.[39]

On 26 February 1937, the army finally agreed to standardize 100 octane aviation gasoline for Air Corps use, effective 1 January 1938. The new chief of the Air Corps, Major General Oscar Westover, was less than gratified by this tardy action: "It is unfortunate that whereas the initiative in this matter was taken by the U.S. Army Air Corps, foreign development has been allowed to pass ours in its exploitation." He also complained that the navy had already converted to 100 octane exclusively, completing the process by the start of 1938. Even commercial airliners were using it for takeoffs. And as a final irritation, the army's adjutant general notified the Air Corps that the additional costs of any 100 octane purchases made in FY 1937 and 1938 would have to be absorbed by the Air Corps using existing funds. Nevertheless, Wright Field notified all U.S. engine manufacturers on 1 May 1937 that "[e]ngines, other than Primary Training engines to be procured on invitations opening after 30 April 1937, shall be designed, rated, tested, and accepted for use with 100 octane fuel."[40]

The Air Corps' commitment to 100 octane was apparent in its procurement policy for FY 1938 (1 July 1937 to 30 June 1938). For training and testing, 29 percent of Air Corps fuel purchases would be 65 and 92 octane gasoline. The remaining 71 percent for operational aircraft would be 100 octane. As a further sign of this commitment, the Air Corps refused to modify its specifications when the engine manufacturer Wright Aeronautical Corporation reported that reducing the amount of isooctane in 100 octane gasoline and boosting the amount of TEL from 3 ml to 4 ml to maintain a 100 octane rating would be cheaper and require less of the then scarce synthetic isooctane. The Air Corps was afraid that the resulting reduced demand would encourage oil companies to cut back on plant expansion.[41]

Expanded production was the result of not only demand but also new production techniques. In addition to hydrogenation, oil companies developed alkylation, polymerization, isomerization, and aromatization techniques to produce isooctane or isooctane substitutes and catalytic cracking to produce high-quality aviation gasolines. By the fall of 1938, with war on the horizon, U.S. production of 100 octane aviation gasoline was 4.2 million gallons per month, coming from seven plants (owned by Phillips, Standard Oil of California, Gulf, Standard Oil of New Jersey, and Shell, itself responsible for 62 percent of total production). With critical implications for the eventual outcome of the impending war, some of this production went to England and the Battle of Britain, where Royal Air Force Spitfire pilots could as a result run their Merlin engines beyond the throttle stop to get 1,700 horsepower instead of the rated 1,000 horsepower, allowing them to outfly German Messerschmitt pilots.[42] By the start of the war in Europe, the United States had fifteen plants producing 24 million gallons per month.

Mass production also affected the price of high-octane fuels. In 1940, 100 octane cost the Air Corps 16.5 cents ($1.89 in 1996 dollars) per gallon and 92 octane 7.5 cents ($0.86 in 1996 dollars). This compared favorably to the 6.36 to

8.5 cents ($0.73–$0.97 in 1996 dollars) per gallon it paid for regular automobile gasolines (70 octane) and the 7.21 to 10.5 cents ($0.83–$1.20 in 1996 dollars) it paid for premium automobile gasolines (77 octane).[43]

Mindful of the possibility of war and of the advantages 100 octane fuel gave the United States, the Air Corps tried to keep its specifications and the manufacturing processes secret. On 25 June 1935, the Air Corps asked the army's adjutant general to declare the release of information concerning the new super fuel to any foreign nation a violation of the Espionage Act (40 Stat. 217). Despite Air Corps arguments that the process was a "matter of importance to National Defense" and that it be held a "trade secret" on the "basis of patriotism and Americanism," the adjutant general rejected the Air Corps's request on 30 July 1935, declaring that the disadvantages of withholding this information outweighed the advantages. Assistant Chief of the Air Corps Brigadier General Oscar Westover then asked for at least one year of protection to give the United States a head start in exploiting this breakthrough, but again the adjutant general rejected the request, officially declaring 100 octane fuel a "non-secret." After Shell and Standard Oil requested permission to export the process, Wright Field notified all manufacturers of the adjutant general's decision on 23 December 1935. By February 1936, Germany, Japan, Italy, England, France, and the Soviet Union had inquired about specifications, prices, manufacturing methods, and quantities available for purchase. In April 1936 Universal Oil Products Company of Chicago contracted to build three isooctane plants in the Soviet Union. As evidence of its continuing view of 100 octane as a weapon, the Air Corps initiated a research project in 1940 to identify compounds that could be sprayed on enemy airfields to reduce the antiknock qualities of their fuels, thus destroying their aircraft engines on takeoff.[44]

The advantages 100 octane fuel offered became quickly apparent when the three aircraft manufacturers bidding in a competition for a new Air Corps bomber all wanted to use the Wright Cyclone R-1820-39 engine, specifically designed to burn it. The winner, the YB-17, could fly 3,000 miles on 1,700 gallons of 92 octane fuel, but required 400 gallons less when burning 100 octane. The fuel's high knock resistance allowed engines to run with lean mixtures for increased fuel economy without knock.

This fuel also had an impact on commercial aviation. It allowed airliners to cut their takeoff distance by up to 45 percent or to take off with greater loads. For cruising, 100 octane fuel gave a 15 to 20 percent boost in range over 87 octane. Shell's Jimmy Doolittle told the Air Transport Association of America in 1938 that over the life of an aircraft 100 octane could save an airline $800,000 ($7.2 million in 1996 dollars) despite the increased cost of the fuel. Other observers not associated with the petroleum industry suggested a more conservative, though still impressive, savings of $153,000 ($1.4 million in 1996 dollars). The evolution of the Wright Cyclone engine demonstrated the impact of higher-octane fuels (see Table 4.1).[45]

Table 4.1
Impact of Octane on Wright Cyclone Engine Performance

Year	Horsepower	Rpm	Fuel Consumption*	Octane
1929	535	1,900	0.5	73
1930	580	1,900	0.5	80
1931	600	1,960	0.5	80
1932	650	1,950	0.5	87
1933	700	1,950	0.48	87
1934	780	2,100	0.46	87
1935	820	2,100	0.46	87
1936	1,000	2,200	0.44	87
1937	1,100	2,300	0.43	92
1938	1,150	2,400	0.41	92
1939	1,200	2,500	0.4	100

*Pounds of fuel per horsepower per hour

As the world prepared for war and the United States expanded its 100 octane production facilities, a new problem with standardization appeared. Testing and octane determination of fuels in the United States was still being done in standard unsupercharged CFR test engines running on lean (cruise power) mixtures using the 1-C/ASTM F3 method because engines tended to knock at lean settings before they knocked at rich settings. American researchers worried little about rich mixture properties because American fuels contained only small amounts of aromatics, whose octane values depreciated rapidly at high temperatures, and were so uniform in composition that rich mixture results varied little from lean. Other nations were not so fortunate, however, and even the United States had to begin using more aromatics to increase production. Harvey Mansell of the Bristol Airplane Company tested 100 octane fuel in a supercharged cylinder removed from a Bristol radial engine and discovered that the octane level of the fuel fluctuated depending on whether a rich or lean mixture was used. Work began at Wright Field to develop a means of judging rich mixture performance in a new supercharged test CFR engine designed by Ethyl Gasoline Corporation capable of 1,800 rpm and 400°F, which more closely simulated the operating conditions of a full-sized service engine. Technicians expressed its results in the amount of supercharging used. Testing at NACA showed that rich mixtures had higher end-gas temperatures before the initiation of knock than lean mixtures, demonstrating that the same fuel had a different sensitivity to knock based on the gas/air mixture.[46]

Mansell's work had shown the need for a rich and lean scale, so the Army Air Forces began issuing two antiknock ratings, one for lean and one for rich mixtures. In 1942, for example, the army issued specifications for 100(lean)/130(rich) aviation fuel. Testing with the 1-C/ASTM F3 method, however, penalized fuels high in aromatics. Under that system 100/130 fuel might test as 100/100. Wright Field and the American Society for Testing Materials issued a new method, 3-C/ASTM F4, which tested rich mixtures under the old 1-C/ASTM F3 system, but required lean mixtures to be tested in a CFR engine set at a fixed 7:1 compression ratio, with operating conditions varied by increasing or decreasing the manifold pressure with a supercharger.[47]

Mansell's work indicated that rich mixture fuels suppressed knock better than isooctane. At the same time, continuing work at Wright Field, General Motors, and the Ethyl Corporation offered the prospect of fuels such as triptane that would also resist knock better than pure isooctane. Because Edgar's octane scale was based on a percentage of isooctane in a fuel, the scale could not go beyond 100. Initially the Materiel Division labeled fuels rated above 100 octane "Pursuit Grade." As more became known, the Air Corps adopted a scale based on the "S" secondary reference fuel. "S" was pure isooctane used for engine testing. A fuel having an antiknock quality above that of isooctane was therefore expressed as the amount of TEL that had to be added to the "S" reference fuel to be of equal antiknock ability. An S + 1 fuel was therefore equal to isooctane plus 1 ml TEL.[48]

Not everyone used "S" reference fuel, however. The octane scale had shown the advisability of a universal standard. Samuel D. Heron and Harold A. Beatty of the Ethyl Corporation and Lieutenant F. D. Klein of Wright Field offered such a standard beginning in 1935. Their "Performance Number" (PN) system expressed a fuel's antiknock performance as a percentage of the maximum power produced in a test engine using the test fuel relative to the same engine using isooctane. Adopted by the Army Air Forces in late 1942, a PN of 100 was equal to an octane rating of 100 while a PN of 130 had 130 percent of the knock-suppressing value of 100 octane. A fuel at lean mixture equal to the first and at rich mixture equal to the second was identified as 100/130 PN fuel. Using Wright Field's "S" scale, S + 1 was equivalent to 125 PN, S + 1.25 to 130 PN.[49]

Concerned with possible confusion, Wright Field decided that the rich mixture rating was sufficient in specifying an aviation gasoline because most combat operations were carried out at rich settings. In late 1942 it therefore revised

fuel specifications to drop the lean mixture rating. All American aviation gasolines thereafter would be identified by a grade number corresponding to the Performance Number rounded to the closest five. What would have been "high test"
or Fighting Grade fuel in the 1920s became S + 2 fuel (a fuel equal in antiknock
quality to the "S" standard reference fuel plus 2 ml TEL) in the 1930s. In 1942
it became 100/138.2 PN fuel (equal to 100 percent of the knock-suppressing
value of isooctane at a lean mixture and equal to 138.2 percent of the knock-
suppressing value of isooctane at a rich mixture) and then Grade 140 (PN
rounded to the closest five in rich mixture only) aviation gasoline.[50]

One last obstacle to exploiting the potential of high-octane aviation fuel in
World War II remained. Fuels with high knock resistance allowed engines with
high compression ratios to run with lean mixtures for increased fuel economy
and caused increased power for takeoff and War Emergency ratings that pushed
an engine beyond its normal rated power. To permit such power increases that
would otherwise exceed the cooling ability of the engine, the Air Corps turned
to water injection. Injecting water, and usually alcohol to keep the water from
freezing, into the cylinders along with the air-fuel mixture directly cooled the
cylinders and pistons as the water absorbed heat, evaporated, and was discharged
as steam in the exhaust. Water injection allowed a 15 to 25 percent increase in
rich mixture power, in effect turning 100/130 PN fuel into 100/150 PN. With
water injection, the engine received the benefit of increased resistance to knock
with increased power without the need for additional cooling. The technique
improved power, but not range — there was an increase in fuel consumption because of the additional weight of the water supply and because more fuel had to
be sprayed into the cylinder to increase power. The technique had not been used
earlier because American development agencies were trying to increase range,
relying on higher octane alone for greater power.[51]

Water injection had been used to fight knock as early as 1880 and had been
tested in the United States for use in aircraft in 1918.[52] The success of American
attempts to develop high-octane fuels and antiknock compounds had driven
water injection into disuse. High-octane fuels and improved cooling systems reduced the outer temperature of the cylinder, but the temperature of parts inside
the cylinder were reaching the danger point as engine manufacturers extracted
as much power as possible with increased compression ratios, rpms, and supercharging. Wright Field's J. F. Campbell injected straight grain alcohol into cylinders to boost power in the early 1930s, but the result was preignition due to the
increased cylinder temperatures. Campbell therefore added water to the alcohol in the ratio of 1 : 5 to stop the preignition. In 1935 Ford L. Prescott of Wright
Field also injected water while testing supercharged engines that overheated
with 93 PN fuel. In 1942 Pratt & Whitney personnel were testing to see how

much rain an engine could take in before it quit when they discovered that water injection allowed a 20 to 30 percent increase in power. NACA research determined that the optimum amount of water for injection was one pound for every two pounds of fuel. Full-scale tests showed a 2,100 horsepower engine could be boosted to 2,800 horsepower for short periods of five to six minutes. NACA research also showed that water injection prevented knock by speeding the movement of the flame front through the cylinder.[53]

By the end of the interwar period, aviation in the United States had reached higher, faster, and farther, powered by fuels that were products of empirical work by engineers and mechanics, as science lagged behind. Mechanical fixes, fuel dopes, and higher-quality fuels helped solve the knock problem but did little to advance any understanding of the basic underlying phenomenon of knock. Science would need seventy-some years to catch up to empiricism.

First to propose an explanation for the knock phenomenon was the Englishman Harry R. Ricardo. Beginning in 1919 he hypothesized that knock was the result of the spontaneous explosion of the last part of the air-gas mixture, or end gas, heated and compressed by the initial, spark-initiated explosion. Streak photographs of bomb combustion by an E. I. DuPont team provided the first evidence of Ricardo's spontaneous ignition, or autoignition, theory. While not refuting this explanation, G. L. Clark and W. C. Thee of MIT revealed its limitations in 1926 by identifying fuels that did not autoignite yet still caused knock.[54]

Thomas Midgley Jr. and Thomas A. Boyd of DELCO theorized that knock was a product of a pressure wave traveling through the air-gas mixture, based on French discoveries dating from 1881 that the propagation of a flame through an air-fuel mixture generated an instantaneous detonation wave. The wave moved so fast that the energy liberated by the burning fuel could not dissipate, causing pressure to build up and adding more energy to the burning flame front, which then hit the cylinder sides with a heavy blow, causing the vibrations of knock. Relying on spectroscopic observation of combustion through a quartz window, Midgley concluded that the flame front contacted weak molecules in the mixture and robbed them of their hydrogen to get stronger. During combustion fuels broke down into secondary or intermediate compounds of an extremely explosive nature, especially acetylene, through dissociation. Fuels such as benzol, according to this argument, were strong enough to resist the robbing process and therefore did not knock. TEL and other dopes delayed the breakdown until the flame front arrived, preventing knock in fuels that would otherwise knock. Supporters of Ricardo's autoignition theory doubted that a detonation wave existed but argued that if it did, it was the product of autoignition. Others insisted that Midgley's dissociation theory involved intermediate products too small to cause knock.[55]

A process as complex as knock attracted many explanations through the 1920s and 1930s. The electron theory viewed the flame front as a wave of electrons, creating knock when sufficient collisions with other electrons took place. The absolute density theory argued that an excess of oxygen in the cylinder accelerated the combustion's velocity. The molecular collision theory argued that molecules of carbon, hydrogen, and oxygen raced ahead of the flame front, bombarding the unburned gas and causing an explosion. None of these explanations matched the actual, observed conditions of knock.[56]

In 1929 Lloyd Withrow, Thomas A. Boyd, and W. G. Lovell of the General Motors Research Laboratories used multiple sampling valves to check the chemical content of gases withdrawn from different areas of the cylinder during combustion, revealing that the flame front proceeded from the spark plug through the cylinder at a constant rate, speeding up only if the engine speed increased. Knock, this analysis showed, was confined to the end gas and was associated with an accelerated rate of oxygen consumption.[57]

Success in this endeavor encouraged Withrow and another General Motors employee, Gerald M. Rassweiler, using Air Corps Materiel Division equipment and personnel, to photograph the combustion process through a quartz window at 2,250 to 5,000 frames per second. The project revealed that rising pressure and temperature in the end gas caused autoignition and knock well ahead of the flame front. Withrow also did simultaneous flame and pressure studies, showing the relation between the rate of flame travel and resulting rise in pressure. Previously the onset of knock had been identified by sound and pressure, but Withrow and Boyd showed that knock was due to a "many-fold increase in the rate of inflammation within the latter portion of the end gas," which appeared in their relatively slow photographs as a simultaneous explosion. This explosion was accompanied by a pressure increase, which produced the visible and auditory effects of knock. Withrow and Rassweiler's photographs seemed to disprove the detonation wave theory, though their camera was in fact too slow to reveal such a wave if it existed.[58]

These General Motors researchers also showed that Ricardo's autoignition could occur without knock.[59] This did not preclude an autoignition-knock connection, but it did suggest that autoignition and knock were not the same reaction. Others had observed vibrations in engine cylinders but had thought they were not connected to knock or were simply caused by knock. Withrow, Rassweiler, and Boyd proved that autoignition alone was insufficient to explain knock.[60]

Two decades of research by the National Advisory Committee for Aeronautics (NACA) forced a revision of the Ricardo theory of autoignition that by the early 1930s seemed to be becoming the consensus explanation for knock despite its weaknesses. In 1933 Langley personnel unveiled a special camera shutter arrangement able to photograph combustion in a cylinder at 2,400 frames per second through a glass window. The camera produced interesting results, as had Withrow and Rassweiler's camera, but was too slow to identify what went on in the engine cylinder. These photographs from the mid-1930s showed incorrectly that no sonic or supersonic compression shock waves occurred with knock, but correctly that the knock reaction could occur not only in the unburnt end gases but also in the partially burned area behind the wave front.[61]

Beginning in February 1936 at NACA's Langley Laboratory, Cearcy D. Miller endeavored to design a camera capable of 40,000 images per second. First tested at Langley in December 1938, Miller's high-speed camera showed that the flame front compressed the end gas to the point of spontaneous ignition. Knock was the "sudden completion of burning in a region in which partial combustion has taken place . . . a marked increase in the rate of pressure rise followed by the reverse motion of the combustion front, which actually drove the explosion back upon itself, which is primary cause of vibration." Adding a cathode ray oscillograph operating on a piezoelectric pickup inside the combustion chamber showed that knock, despite all previous evidence, did not necessarily originate in the end gas, but might also occur in areas of the cylinder already ignited by the flame front or by autoignition, as theorized in previous NACA studies. Autoignition might cause knock, but autoignition might also occur "a considerable length of time before knock occurs." The knock reaction itself lasted only 0.00005 seconds, was sufficiently intense to emit visible light, and was too fast for Withrow and Rassweiler to have observed knock with their slow camera; they had observed autoignition, not knock.[62]

The autoignition theory of knock needed revising because autoignition required about 1,000 microseconds to occur while NACA photographs showed that the knock reaction took place in only 50 microseconds. Autoignition was too slow to cause the gas vibrations that were characteristic of knock; something else had to be occurring to cause knock. NACA returned to Midgley's out-of-favor theory of the detonation wave, which would be sufficiently powerful to produce gas vibrations, but too fast for detection by previous methods. The first real evidence for a detonation wave came from two Soviet scientists, A. Sokolik and A. Voinov, who used streak photographs to show that the normal flame front moved through the cylinder at about 20 meters per second before accelerating suddenly to 2,000 meters per second to complete the combustion cycle and cause knock. Their measurements might have been inaccurate, however, because of a simple trick of angle: the flame front was moving away from their camera.[63]

As the world went to war, a synthesis of the autoignition and detonation wave theories began to evolve at NACA, from research done at Langley, the National Bureau of Standards, and the NACA Aircraft Engine Research Laboratory in Cleveland (now the Lewis Laboratory). This research suggested that autoignition produced "natural vibrations of engine parts," which produced knock whether a detonation wave were present or not. With some fuels, however, the fuel continued to burn after the flame front had passed, retaining enough energy behind the flame front to generate a detonation wave. This wave caused gas vibrations of sufficient intensity to vibrate the cylinder wall at the same frequency. Knock of a low pitch was the product of autoignition at a rate too slow to generate audible gas vibrations. Knock of a high pitch was caused by a detonation wave traveling at 3,000 to 5,500 feet per second (one to two times the speed of sound) in gases burning after the passage of the flame front, generating gas vibrations. Knock of a low and high pitch was caused by autoignition followed by a detonation wave. This synthesis was in harmony with the conditions revealed in Miller's 40,000-frame-per-second camera.[64]

Miller began improving his camera in 1939, assisted by Alois Krsek and Newell D. Sanders. By 1941 NACA researchers could photograph the detonation process at 200,000 photographs per second, though it took the rest of the war years to perfect the device. These photographs revealed violent gas vibrations originating as a self-propagating disturbance starting in the burning or in the autoignition gases. This disturbance spread through the unburned end gas at up to 6,800 feet per second, or over twice the speed of sound, confirming the earlier synthesis.[65]

Late in the war, Miller boosted his camera's performance to 400,000 frames per second. His ultraspeed photographs, taken at Cleveland's NACA laboratory, allowed viewers to observe the combustion phenomenon that had retarded the pursuit of higher, faster, and farther travel since the origins of flight. "Knock," Miller concluded, "is produced by the sudden inflammation of the end gas, the gas that has not yet been ignited at the time knock occurs by the normal travel of the flame from the spark plug" and by "the subsequent expansion of the end gas [that] sets up a violent vibration or system of standing waves throughout the entire contents of the combustion chamber."[66]

Knowledge of what happened in a cylinder during knock was the penultimate step in solving the problem. An understanding of what went on at the molecular level during knock remained beyond reach, not to be revealed until the 1980s and 1990s through chemical kinetics. The process required powerful computers to examine the thousands of elementary reactions occurring between up to four hundred distinct chemical species of even a single isomer of a single hydrocarbon such as heptane. These computations have shown that straight carbon chains are more knock prone than branched carbon structures, allowing predictions of the temperature and pressure conditions that will cause a particular fuel to knock. They have also revealed why TEL (it deactivates the chain branching sequence) and more modern compounds such as MTBE (methyl tert-butyl ether) and MMT (methylcyclopentadienyl manganese tricarbonyl) suppress knock.[67]

These answers would not help the Allies win World War II—that work had already been done. World War II was as much an economic as a military war, and aviation gasoline was a critical component behind the Allied victory. According to a postwar Army Air Forces study, Germany had to invest $12.8 billion ($135 billion in 1996 dollars) to produce one million barrels of aviation gasoline per day using the Bergius coal hydrogenation technique. The United States needed only $700 million ($7.4 billion in 1996 dollars) to produce similar fuel from petroleum. The Army Air Forces flew to victory on $1.2 billion ($12.7 billion in 1996 dollars) worth of high-octane aviation gasoline. For the Luftwaffe to have matched U.S. production would have required an investment of over $22.6 billion ($238.6 billion in 1996 dollars).[68]

There were other costs. The Bergius process produced aviation gasoline of only 72 octane that was not particularly responsive to TEL. Germany could only reach 87 octane by adding 15 to 18 percent aromatic hydrocarbons and 95-97 octane by adding nearly 40 percent aromatics.[69] Such fuels forced the Luftwaffe into a vicious spiral. Higher-quality fuels meant a decrease in quantity. Aromatics provided greater resistance to knock but increased the tendency of engine gases to preignite. They tended to overheat engines because of increased heat transfer to the cylinder walls by radiation and the high luminosity of their flames, as NACA and Wright Field had discovered twenty years earlier, destroying some of their antiknock qualities.[70] Luftwaffe pilots therefore had to run their engines on rich mixtures, dumping expensive and precious fuel into engine cylinders, knowing that the additional fuel would not combust but rather would vaporize and cool overheated engines, producing no additional power. Because aromatic hydrocarbons were high in carbon and low in hydrogen, they had reduced specific energies, requiring richer mixtures to provide the power for high performance.[71] Paraffinic hydrocarbons used by the United States provided that power at lean mixtures because of their greater ratio of hydrogen to carbon. Rich mixtures provided power and cooling for German engines, but at the cost of range and efficiency. The aromatics were less volatile than paraffinic hydrocarbons, resulting in incomplete ignition that deposited gum on valves and rings and further reduced the efficiency of the combustion process. Reduced volatility forced Germany to use expensive and complex fuel injection systems. Aromatics also caused neoprene hoses, fuel tank linings, seals, gaskets, and diaphragms to deteriorate and leak.[72]

World War II was also a scientific war, and the United States continued fuels research to push the internal combustion piston engine to even greater performance. Late in the war the Army Air Forces added 3 percent xylidine to boost Grade 130 (100/130 PN) fuel to Grade 150 (100/150 PN) so its fighters could better chase the German Me 262 jet and V-1 cruise missile. With such fuels and water-alcohol injection, the rated War Emergency Power of the P-47 Thunderbolt increased from 2,200 to 2,600 horsepower. The Ethyl Corporation identified triptane as potentially one of the most powerful antiknock fuels. So powerful were its antiknock qualities when combined with TEL that Wright Field's test engines exploded before technicians could get the engines to knock. A 1944 NACA study estimated triptane to have an antiknock rating of 200/300 PN. Triptane and four other fuels with even higher antiknock values identified by NACA were exceedingly expensive but might have been used to fly even higher, faster, and farther had the turbojet not made the whole problem of knock largely irrelevant to the future of high-performance aviation.[73]

NOTES

1. The technologies of drag reduction included flush riveting, cantilevered single wings, retractable landing gear, engine cowlings, flaps, new airfoil designs, enclosed cockpits, and metal stressed-skin monocoque construction.

2. Israel Katz, *Principles of Aircraft Propulsion Machinery* (New York: Pitman, 1949), p. v.

3. The compression ratio is the ratio of the volume inside a cylinder at the beginning of the compression stroke to the volume at the end of the stroke.

4. There was similar work underway in other nations, notably the United Kingdom. This has been described in Andrew Nahum, "Two-stroke or Turbine? The Aeronautical Research Committee and British Aero Engine Development in World War II," *Technology and Culture* 39 (Apr. 1997): 312–54.

5. Preignition is the premature ignition of the fuel-air mixture before the firing of the spark plug, resulting from the mixture coming into contact with spots in the cylinder sufficiently hot (about 1,500°F) to start combustion.

6. Volatility is the ease of fuel vaporization, or becoming gaseous, which is directly related to the fuel's boiling point. Early engines used carburetors that required fuels of extremely high volatility. With straight-run gasolines, volatility was related to specific gravity. The lower the specific gravity, the better the volatility and the better the engine ran. Early specifications for aviation gasoline therefore emphasized a low specific gravity as the most important characteristic. See E. L. Bass, "Piston Engine Fuels," *Journal of the Royal Aeronautical Society* 70 (Jan. 1966): 184.

7. When the United States entered World War I, the army used French specifications for gasoline calling for "smooth, of mild odor, colorless, clear and without deposit" products "of the distillation of natural, unrefined petroleum." It had to be "high grade, refined and free from water and all impurities," with "a vapor tension not greater than 10 pounds per square inch at 100°F" and a boiling point not over 120°F. The specific gravity had to be 0.735 at 15°C. "Specifications for Gasoline for Airplanes," 26 Jan. 1917 (French specification dated from 16 Aug. 1916), and "Specifications Governing the Purchase of Gasoline and Areoplane Naphtha by the United States Government," n.d., File 463.7, Folder—Gasoline 1917–1919, Box 39, RD-3093, Record Group 342, Records of the Engineering Di-

vision, Central Decimal Correspondence File, Material Command, Wright Field, 1917–51, Suitland National Records Center (hereafter RG342).

8. Harry R. Ricardo, *The Ricardo Story: The Autobiography of Sir Harry Ricardo, Pioneer of Engine Research* (Warrendale, Pa.: Society of Automobile Engineers, 1990), pp. 92–206.

9. Methanol contains 9,500 Btu of heat per pound, gasoline about 20,000.

10. United States Army, *Bulletin of the Airplane Engineering Department*, Sep. 1918, File 216.2103, United States Air Force Historical Research Agency, Maxwell AFB, AL (hereafter HRA); Engineering Division of Air Service to Assistant Post Master General, 30 Dec. 1919, File 463.8, Folder—Fuel Airplane 1919, Box 39, RD-3093, RG342; Division of Military Aeronautics memo, 29 Aug. 1918, File 463.7, Folder—Hector Fuel 1918, Box 39, RD-3093, RG342; David R. Winans, "World War One Aircraft Fuels and Lubricating Oils," *Cross & Cockade Journal* 2 (Autumn 1961): 230; Division of Military Aeronautics memo, 7 Sep. 1918, File 463.8, Folder—Fuel 1920, Box 39, RD-3093, RG342.

11. Matthew Van Winkle, *Aviation Gasoline Manufacture* (New York: McGraw-Hill, 1944), p. 3; H. C. Dickinson et. al., "Power Characteristics of Fuels for Aircraft Engines," Report No. 47, pts. 1, 2, and 3, in NACA, *4th Annual Report, 1918* (Washington, D.C.: Government Printing Office, 1920), pp. 560–89; Power Plant Section Memo, 20 Feb. 1924, File 463.7, Folder—Gasoline 1924, Box 204, RD-3139, RG342; BuAer Technical Note No. 219, 25 Apr. 1922, File 463.7, Folder—Gasoline 1923, Box 166, RD-3127, RG342; and NACA, *Technical Note No. 93* (Washington, D.C.: Government Printing Office, 1922).

12. Thomas Midgley Jr., "The Combustion of Fuels in the Internal-Combustion Engine," *SAE Transactions* 15 (1920): 659–96. Selenium, for example, proved too corrosive to engine parts. Tellurium produced a terribly foul smell.

13. Chief of Air Service to Engineering Division, 16 Dec. 1921, File 463.8, Folder—Fuel 1921–1922, Box 132, RD-3118, RG342, Suitland; Power Plant Laboratory memo, 25 May 1922, File 463.8, Folder—Anti-Knock Fuel Compound 1922, Box 132, RD-3118, RG342; and Charles F. Kettering, "Biographical Memoir of Thomas Midgley, Jr., 1889–1944," *National Academy of Sciences Biographical Memoirs* 24 (1947): 361–80. During the combustion process ethyl bromide converted the lead in tetraethyl lead into lead oxide, which was ejected from the combustion chamber in the exhaust, thus preventing lead deposits on cylinder parts. Ethyl fluid was, by weight, 61.42 percent TEL, 35.68 percent ethylene-dibromide, 0.17 percent dye, and 2.73 percent kerosene and impurities. C. A. Kraus of Clark University developed a technique for the cheap production of TEL and sold the rights to Standard Oil Development Company. General Motors owned the patent on using TEL in fuel, so the two companies together launched the Ethyl Gasoline Corporation to produce ethyl fluid and to continue research into the causes and cures for knock. Midgley became vice president and general manager.

14. Hydrocarbons consist of five separate groups, based on their molecular shape and carbon bonding: olefins, paraffins, napthenes, acetylenes, and aromatics. On the Ethyl Corporation, see Joseph Robert, *Ethyl: A History of the Corporation and the People Who Made It* (Charlottesville: University of Virginia Press, 1985).

15. Engineering Division Memo, 15 Aug. 1921, File 463.7, Folder—Gasoline 1921, Box 95, RD-3106, RG342; Interview of James Doolittle, 1965, File K239.0512-623, HRA; Insley to Macready, 19 July 1923, File 463.7, Folder—Gasoline 1923, Box 166, RD-3127, RG342; Power Plant Section to Office of the Chief of Air Service, 18 Aug. 1924, File 463.8, Folder—Fuel 1924, Box 204, RD-3139, RG342; "The Development of Aviation Gasoline and Lubricants," n.d., File 106-7, HRA; Engineering Division to Midgley, GM Research Corporation, Moraine City, Ohio, 18 Oct. 1920, File 463.8, Folder—Anti-Knock Fuel Compound 1922, Box 132, RD-3118, RG342; and Bureau of Mines to Engineering Division, 16 Aug. 1921, File 463.8, Folder—Fuel, Box 95, RD-3106, RG342.

16. Ricardo, *Ricardo Story*, pp. 202–206; and S. D. Heron, *Development of Aviation Fuels* (Boston: Graduate School of Business Administration, Harvard University, 1950), p. 579. Harold Moore of

Great Britain had built the first variable compression ratio engine during World War I, but Harry
Ricardo was the first to use such an engine for testing fuels.

   17. John M. Campbell, Wheeler G. Lovell, and T. A. Boyd, "Influence of Carburetor Setting
and Spark Timing on Knock Ratings," *SAE Transactions* 25-26 (1930–31): 459–63; H.R. Stacey, "Effect of Oil Consumption and Temperature on Octane-Number Ratings," *SAE Transactions* 25-26
(1930–31): 457–58; Graham Edgar, "Jacket and Cylinder-Head Temperature Effects upon Relative
Knock-Ratings," *SAE Transactions* 25-26 (1930–31): 452–56; and D. B. Brooks, N. R. White, and
G. C. Rodgers, "Effect of Humidity and Air Temperature on Octane Numbers of Secondary Detona-
tion-Standards," *SAE Transactions* 25-26 (1930–31): 445–51. The Series 30 engine ran at 600 rpm
with a fixed compression ratio of 6.5:1 for fuel testing. The test apparatus relied on a bouncing pin between two electrical contacts developed by Midgley to detect knock rather than relying on the human ear as in the Ricardo method. See Engineering Section Memo, 8 Jan. 1934, File 463.7, Folder—
Ethyl Gasoline 1928–1934, Box 637, RD-3252, RG342.

   18. Graham Edgar, "Comparison of Methods of Measuring Knock Characteristics of Fuels," *SAE
Transactions* 23 (1928): 74–89; and Graham Edgar, "Detonation Specifications for Automotive Fuels," *SAE Transactions* 22 (1927): 55–57.

   19. S. D. Heron, "Fuel Requirements of the Gasoline Aircraft Engine," *SAE Transactions* 25-26
(1930–31): 164–69.

   20. Military and commercial specifications and documentation from the 1920s and 1930s used cubic centimeters (cc) to measure TEL. In the late 1930s and during World War II, these same sources
switched to milliliters (ml).

   21. Heron, "Fuel Requirements."

   22. Engineering Section to Standard Oil of New Jersey, 10 Apr. 1931, and Engineering Section to
Bureau of Standards, 6 June 1931, File 463.7, Folder—Gasoline 1931, Box 481, RD-3209, RG342.

   23. Experimental Engineering Section to Graham Edgar, 5 Dec. 1930, File 463.7, Folder—Ethyl
Gasoline 1928–1934, Box 637, RD-3252, RG342. The Series 30 engine tended to leak coolant into
the combustion chamber, affecting octane ratings. The Materiel Division modified the cylinder head
so that the coolant leaked into the open air rather than the combustion chamber, producing the Series 30-B engine.

   24. Experimental Engineering Section to Bureau of Standards, 11 and 29 Feb. 1931, and Engineering Section to Society of Automotive Engineers, 25 Apr. 1931, File 463.7, Folder—Ethyl Gasoline
1928–1934, Box 637, RD-3252, RG342.

   25. H. L. Horning, "The Cooperative Fuel-Research Committee Engine," *SAE Transactions* 25-26
(1930–31): 436–40; Engineering Section to SAE, 11 Oct. 1932, and Engineering Section memo,
7 Feb. 1933, File 463.7, Folder—Ethyl Gasoline 1928–1934, Box 637, RD-3252, RG342.

   26. Waukesha Motor Company to Wright Field, 1 Apr. 1933, File 463.7, Folder—Ethyl Gasoline
1928–1934, Box 637, RD-3252, RG342; and Ethyl Corporation, *Aviation Fuels and Their Effects on Engine Performance* (n.p.: Ethyl Corporation, 1951), p. 86. According to the CFR Motor Method, the
CFR test engine was run on 65 octane fuel while the compression ratio was increased until knock first
became detectable with a bouncing pin gauge. The engine was then run on the test fuel, which was
then compared to the knocking of reference fuels one octane above and one below the test fuel. Octane ratings for automotive fuel today are the average of the two methods. Gas pumps usually have
a sticker stating "Octane rating determined by (R + M)/2 method." "R" stands for the Research
Method: a test engine running at 600 rpm and 209–215°F. "M" stands for the Motor Method: a test
engine running at 900 rpm and 209–215°F.

   27. Engineering Section Memo, 4 Apr. 1933, and Foulois to Aeronautical Chamber of Commerce
of America, 12 June 1933, File 463.7, Folder—Ethyl Gasoline 1928–1934, Box 637, RD-3252,
RG342. The results of the Air Corps' aircraft engine testing are contained in Engineering Section

Memo, 3 Apr. 1933, File 463.7, Folder—Ethyl Gasoline 1928–1934, Box 637, RD-3252, RG342. These tests used both air-cooled radial and liquid-cooled V-engines under varying conditions of full and partial throttle and varying amounts of supercharging. Most were destroyed by the testing. The results showed the frustration of attempting to establish standard specifications for aviation fuels as mid-continent natural gasolines, for example, gave 81 octane at 600 rpm, but 67 octane at 900 rpm. Partially cracked California gasoline gave 87 at 600 rpm, but 81 octane at 900 rpm.

28. C. B. Veal, "Rating Aviation Fuels—in Full-Scale Aircraft Engines," SAE Transactions 31 (1936): 161–75; Navy Engineering Experiment Station to BuAer, 3 Oct. 1930, File 463.7, Folder— Gasoline Aug–Dec 1930, Box 438, RD-3197, RG342; and F. D. Klein and Robert V. Kerley, "A Comparison of Octane Ratings by Air Corps Method and C.F.R. Motor Method for Various Types of Fuel," n.d. (1936) File JJ 7G 1, Vol. 10, Box 2587, BuAer General Correspondence 1925–1942, Record Group 72, Records of the Bureau of Aeronautics, Suitland National Records Center (hereafter RG72).

29. Samuel P. Marley, Donald R. Stevens, and W. A. Gruse, "Detonation Characteristics of Petroleum Motor-Fuels," SAE Transactions 22 (1927): 44–54; and Robert E. Wilson, "Significance of Tests for Motor Fuels," SAE Transactions 25-26 (1930–31): 151–60.

30. Engineering Section, "Study of Knock Test Methods for Aircraft Fuel," 8 Sep. 1932, and Materiel Division to Oil Companies, 26 June 1933, File 463.7, Folder—Ethyl Gasoline 1928–1934, Box 637, RD-3252, RG342.

In Jan. 1940 the Aviation Fuels Division of the Cooperative Fuel Research Committee met in New York to try to convince the Army Air Corps to adopt the proposed AFD 1-C Method developed by Shell and the Ethyl Corporation for testing aviation fuels. It used the same techniques as the 1-C/ASTM F3 method, including the CFR engine's 3.25″ bore cylinder rather than the Air Corps' 2⅝″ bore, but ran at 1,800 rpm instead of the Air Corps' speed of 1,200 rpm. The Air Corps voted against the method, joined by the Phillips Oil Company, the Standard Oil Development Company, and the Navy's Bureau of Aeronautics. Eleven other members voted in favor. The Air Corps was still the largest consumer of aviation gasoline, however, and its negative vote effectively vetoed the standardization attempt. In January 1941, however, compromise was achieved and the Aviation Fuels Division, with Air Corps support, approved the newly designated 3-C method of antiknock testing in a supercharged CFR engine. See Materiel Division, "Conference Relative to Adoption of Proposed Knock Test Method for Aircraft Engine Fuels," 5 Feb. 1940, File 463.8, Folder—Fuel Knock Ratings, Box 1276, RD-3414, RG342; and Materiel Division, "Knock Tests on Fuel," 20 Oct. 1941, File 463.8, Folder—Fuels Anti-Knock 1938–1941, Box 1416, RD-3467, RG342.

31. Edwin E. Aldrin to BuAer, 24 Nov. 1931, and BuAer memo, 19 Jan. 1932, File JJ 7G 1, Vol. 2, Box 2584, BuAer General Correspondence 1925–1942, RG72.

32. Westover to Commander GHQAF, 28 Feb. 1935, File 463.8, Folder—100 Octane Gasoline 1936, Box 772, RD-3287, RG342.

33. Interview of James Doolittle, File K239.0512-623, 1965, HRA; Materiel Division to BuAer, 14 Mar. 1931, File JJ 7G 1, Vol. 2, Box 2584, BuAer General Correspondence 1925–1942, RG72; and Bernard C. Nalty, "Milestone from the Middle River: Martin's B-10—America's First Modern Bomber," Air Power History 41 (Spring 1994): 30–35.

34. Engineering Section, "Mr. S. D. Heron's Visit to New York on Sep. 20 to 24, 1932," 15 Oct. 1932, File 463.8, Folder—Fuels Anti-Knock Knock Tests 1929–1937, Box 869, RD-3311, RG342.

Furthering the Air Corps connection, Aldrin was a major in the Air Corps Reserve. Doolittle had resigned his Air Corps commission in 1930.

From 1930 to 1935 the Materiel Division issued aviation gasoline specifications designated by Y-numbers. From 1935 to 1940, however, the War Department insisted on issuing specifications under a War Department number such as 2-92. One hundred octane fuel was Specification Y-3575 in March 1935, but then became 2-92 fuel. Beginning in July 1940, the joint Army-Navy Aeronautical Board issued specifications designated by an AN (Army-Navy) number to standardize specifications. During

World War II this designation was changed to an AN-F number, meaning it met Army, Navy, and British specifications. So Army Spec 2-95 fuel became AN-VV-F-776 fuel in July 1940 and AN-F-26 fuel on Apr. 15, 1943. These designations referred to specifications, not antiknock capabilities.

35. Kendall Beaton, *Enterprise in Oil: A History of Shell in the United States* (New York: Appleton-Century-Crofts, 1957), pp. 404–405, 531–50; Engineering Section, "100 Octane Fuel," 25 Mar. 1935, File 463.8, Folder—100 Octane Gasoline 1936, Box 772, RD-3287, RG342; and Engineering Section, "Multi-Cylinder Engine Tests of High Anti-Knock Fuels in R-1830-9 Engine," 7 Aug. 1937, File 463.8, Folder—Fuel 100 Octane Iso-Propyl Blends 1937–1939, Box 973, RD-3337, RG342. The Shell process involved heating butane and isobutane to form isobutylene (C_4H_8). Polymerization combined the molecules of isobutylene to form di-isobutylene (C_8H_{16}). Hydrogenation added two atoms of hydrogen by running the di-isobutylene over a nickel catalyst to produce isooctane (C_8H_{18}). Synthetic isooctane produced by hydrogenation and combined with straight-run gasoline and 3 ml TEL and rated at 100 octane was superior to 100 octane "Technical" isooctane produced by traditional methods in suppressing knock at low power (700 horsepower in the R-1830-9 engine with 8.06:1 compression ratio and 10.12:1 supercharger ratio), equal at medium power (1,000 horsepower), and "considerably inferior" at maximum power (above 1,000 horsepower).

36. Power Plant Branch to Engineering Section, 18 Jan. 1934, Procurement Section to Oil Companies, 18 Dec. 1934, Standard Oil to Procurement Section, 7 Jan. 1935, and Shell to Procurement Section, 9 Feb. 1935, File 463.8, Folder—100 Octane Gasoline 1936, Box 772, RD-3287, RG342. Phillips shipped its version of 100 octane fuel to the Materiel Division in May 1934, but the supply consisted of 89 percent isopentane, 9 percent n-pentane, and 2 percent n-butane of 91 octane, raised to 100 octane with TEL. Wright Field rejected the mixture because it contained too many aromatics. It also rejected Phillips's offer to use 80 percent toluene and 20 percent isopentane because toluene was needed for explosives production. See Engineering Section, "Conference on Iso-Pentane Held at Materiel Division on May 25, 1934," 6 June 1934, File 463.8, Folder—Fuels Anti-Knock Knock Tests 1929–1937, Box 869, RD-3311, RG342.

37. Charles Sterling Popple, *Standard Oil Company (New Jersey) in World War II* (New York: Standard Oil Company, 1952), p. 21.

38. Chief of Materiel Division to Chief of Air Corps, 28 May 1935, and "Report of Sub-Committee of Air Corps Technical Committee on 100 Octane Fuel," Nov. 1936, File 463.8, Folder—100 Octane Gasoline 1936, Box 772, RD-3287, RG342. The $4.3 million budgeted would have allowed the Air Corps to buy 14.3 million gallons of 100 octane in FY 1936. The navy's first interest in the new fuel came in Dec. 1935 when it ordered 50,000 gallons through the Materiel Division for testing purposes. See Klein to Engineering Section, 17 Dec. 1935, File 463.8, Folder—Fuel Anti-Knock 100 Octane 1935–1940, Box 1276, RD-3414, RG342; and Chief BuAer to Standard Oil of California, 27 Nov. 1937, File 463.7, Folder—Gasoline 1936–1937, Box 868, RD-3311, RG342.

39. "Report of Sub-Committee of Air Corps Technical Committee on 100 Octane Fuel," Nov. 1936, File 463.8, Folder—100 Octane Gasoline 1936, Box 772, RD-3287, RG342.

40. Chief of Air Corps to Adjutant General, 18 Jan. 1937, Adjutant General to Chief of Air Corps, 26 Feb. 1937, and various letters, 1 May 1937, File 463.8, Folder—Fuel 100 Octane Iso-Propyl Blends 1937–1938, Box 973, RD-3337, RG342. Commercial airliners carried two sets of tanks, one for 100 octane and takeoffs, the other for 87 octane and cruising. When Wiley Post flew solo around the world in 1933, he burned 87 octane gasoline in his supercharged Pratt & Whitney Wasp engine to produce 500 horsepower and 2,200 rpm for takeoffs. He used 80 octane for 420 horsepower and 2,000 rpm while cruising.

41. Materiel Division to Chief of Air Corps, 10 May 1937, File 463.7, Folder—Gas and Oil Requirements FY1938, Box 973, RD-3337, RG342; Engineering Section, "Conference with Representative of Wright Aeronautical Corporation on 100 Octane Fuel Specification," 25 Aug. 1937, and Engineering Section to Wright Aeronautical Corporation, 14 Sep. 1937, File 463.8, Folder—Fuel

100 Octane Iso-Propyl Blends 1937–1939, Box 973, RD-3337, RG342. After having just completed two years of intense and difficult negotiations with the navy over specifications for 100 octane aviation gasoline, the Air Corps was also reluctant to make modifications.

42. Engineering Section, "Conference with Mr. J. H. Doolittle of Shell Petroleum Corp., Regarding European Aircraft and Power Plants, and Fuel and Lubricants," 12 Jan. 1938, File 463.8, Folder—Fuels 1938, Box 973, RD-3337, RG342.

43. Engineering Section, "Grades of Aircraft Engine Fuel," File 463.8, Folder—Fuels 1939–1940, Box 1276, RD-3414, RG342.

44. Engineering Section to Asiatic Petroleum Corporation, 5 June 1935, File 463.8, Folder—100 Octane Gasoline 1936, Box 772, RD-3287, RG342; Chief of Air Corps to Adjutant General, 25 June 1935, Adjutant General to Chief of Air Corps, 30 July 1935, Shell Oil Company to Adjutant General, Oct. 4, 1935, Assistant Chief of Air Corps to Adjutant General, Oct. 24, 1935, Adjutant General to Air Corps, Dec. 10, 1935, Standard Oil Development Company to Assistant Chief of Air Corps, Dec. 11, 1935, Air Corps to Shell and Standard Oil, Dec. 23, 1935, Air Corps to BuAer, Jan. 3, 1936, SAE to Air Corps, Feb. 18, 1936, File 463.8, Folder—Fuel Anti-Knock 100 Octane 1935–1940, Box 1276, RD-3414, RG342; and Universal Oil Products Company to Secretary of War Harry H. Woodring, 4 May 1937, File 463.7, Folder—Isopentane toluene 1934–1951, Box 4101, RD-3905, RG342.

Research identified several possible antiknock-destroying compounds, called "proknocks"— iodoform, acetylene tetrachloride, chloroform, and others—though testing indicated that a reasonable concentration of these compounds would cause only a maximum 10 octane reduction in the antiknock qualities of fuels. See Engineering Section, "Notes on Effect of Proknock Compound on AntiKnock Value of 100 Octane Number Fuel," 29 Sep. 1938, File 463.8, Folder—Compounds Aniline and Related Compounds 1942, Box 1878, RD-2448, RG342; Materiel Division to Chief of Air Corps, 24 Jan. 1939, and Chemical Warfare Service memo, 5 Aug. 1938, File 463.8, Folder—Compounds Aniline and Related Compounds 1942, Box 1878, RD-2448, RG342; and AAF Historical Division Draft Study, "Aviation Gasoline," n.d., File 106-7, HRA.

45. Jane's All the World's Aircraft, 1930 (London: Sampson Low Marston, 1930); Jane's All the World's Aircraft, 1935 (London: Sampson Low Marston, 1935); Jane's All the World's Aircraft, 1940 (London: Sampson Low Marston, 1940); Van Winkle, Aviation Gasoline Manufacture, pp. 234, 253; and Pilot's Manual for Boeing B-17 Flying Fortress (Appleton, Wisc.: Aviation Publications, 1984).

46. S. D. Heron and Harold A. Beatty, "Aircraft Fuels," Journal of Aeronautical Sciences 5 (Oct. 1938): 463–79; and E. S. Taylor, W. A. Leary, and J. R. Diver, "Effect of Fuel-Air Ratio, Inlet Temperature and Exhaust Pressure on Detonation," NACA Report No. 699, 1940, File 159.853-699, HRA.

47. Bass, "Piston Engine Fuels," 185; Heron, Development of Aviation Fuels, p. 604; and Ethyl Corporation, Aviation Fuels, p. 89.

48. Engineering Section Memo of Conference with S. D. Heron of Ethyl Gasoline Corp., 13 June 1935 (meeting 20 May 1935), File 463.8, Folder—Fuels 1930–1937, Box 868, RD-3311, RG342; and Wheeler G. Lovell, John M. Campbell, and T. A. Boyd, "Knocking Characteristics of Hydrocarbons," Industrial and Engineering Chemistry 26 (Oct. 1934): 1105.

49. Heron and Beatty, "Aircraft Fuels," pp. 463–79; and Power Plant Design Section to Plans, 19 Oct. 1942, File JJ 7G 1, Vol. 4, Box 962, BuAer Confidential Correspondence 1922–1944, RG72. Technically, the PN was given as the ratio of the knock-limited indicated mean effective pressure of a given fuel to the knock-limited indicated mean effective pressure of isooctane in a test engine.

50. Materiel Division, "Analysis of Aircraft Engine Test Data Relative to Pursuit Grade Fuel," 15 Oct. 1942, File 463.8, Folder—Fuel Dimethyl Butane Superior Engine, Box 2877, RD-2881, RG342.

51. Ethyl Corporation, Aviation Fuels, p. 26; and interview of C. W. Schnare, 1975, File K239.0512-863, 1975, HRA.

52. W. A. Reichle of the McCook Field Airplane Engineering Department examined water injection in 1918 but concluded that "there is no apparent advantage to be gained by injecting water into the intake header" because horsepower output dropped. See Airplane Engineering Department, "Report on Water Injection into Intake Headers of 12-Cylinder Liberty Engine," 7 Nov. 1918, File 216.21051-151, HRA.

53. Ford L. Prescott, "Military Aircraft Engines of the Future," *Mechanical Engineering* 58 (Mar. 1936): 157–61; Heron, *Development of Aviation Fuels*, p. 647; Addison M. Rothrock, Alois Krsek, and Anthony W. Jones, "The Induction of Water to the Inlet Air as a Means of Internal Cooling in Aircraft-Engine Cylinders," Report No. 756, in NACA, *29th Annual Report, 1943* (Washington, D.C.: Government Printing Office, 1948), pp. 59–70; and Earnest F. Fiock and H. Kendall King, "The Effect of Water Vapor on Flame Velocity in Equivalent CO-O_2 Mixtures," *Report No. 531, in NACA, 21st Annual Report 1935 (Washington, D.C.: Government Printing Office, 1936), pp. 445–50.*

54. Ricardo, *Ricardo Story*, pp. 126–27; H. R. Ricardo, "Paraffin as Fuel," *Automotive Engineering* 9 (Jan. 1919): 2–5; C. A. Woodbury, H. A. Lewis, and A. T. Canby, "The Nature of Flame Movement in a Closed Cylinder," *SAE Journal* 8 (Mar. 1921): 209–18; and G. L. Clark and W. C. Thee, "Present Status of the Facts and Theories of Detonation," *Industrial and Engineering Chemistry* 17 (Dec. 1925): 1219–26.

55. Thomas Midgley Jr. and T. A. Boyd, "The Chemical Control of Gaseous Detonation with Particular Reference to the Internal-Combustion Engine" *Industrial and Engineering Chemistry* 14 (Oct. 1922): 894–98; Midgley, "Combustion of Fuels," pp. 659–96; Charles F. Kettering, "More Efficient Utilization of Fuel," *SAE Transactions* 14 (1919): 201–19; Woodbury, Lewis, and Canby, "Nature of Flame Movement," pp. 209–18; and Clark and Thee, "Present Status," pp. 1219–26.

56. Clark and Thee, "Present Status."

57. Lloyd Withrow, W. G. Lovell, and T. A. Boyd, "Following Combustion in the Gasoline Engine by Chemical Means," *Industrial and Engineering Chemistry* 22 (1930): 945–51.

58. Lloyd Withrow and Gerald M. Rassweiler, "Slow Motion Shows Knocking and Non-Knocking Explosions," *SAE Transactions* 31 (1936): 297–303, 312; and Lloyd Withrow and T. A. Boyd, "Photographic Flame Studies in the Gasoline Engine," *Industrial and Engineering Chemistry* 23 (1931): 539–47.

59. This was a phenomenon already observed by G. B. Maxwell and R. V. Wheeler in "Flame Characteristics of 'Pinking' and 'Non-Pinking' Fuels," *Industrial and Engineering Chemistry* 20 (Oct. 1928): 1041–44.

60. Lloyd Withrow and Gerald M. Rassweiler, "Engine Knock," *Automotive Engineering* 24 (Aug. 1934): 281–84.

61. F. E. Tuttle, "Non-Intermittent High-Speed 16mm Camera," *Journal of Society of Motion Picture Engineers* 21 (Dec. 1933): 474–77; A. M. Rothrock and C. D. Waldron, "Some Effects of Injection Advance Angle, Engine-Jacket Temperature, and Speed on Combustion in a Compression-Ignition Engine," Report No. 525, in NACA, *21st Annual Report 1935* (Washington, D.C.: Government Printing Office, 1936), pp. 343–57; and A. M. Rothrock and R. C. Spencer, "A Photographic Study of Combustion and Knock in a Spark-Ignition Engine," Report No. 622, in NACA, *24th Annual Report, 1938* (Washington, D.C.: Government Printing Office, 1939), 213–33.

62. Cearcy D. Miller, "The NACA High-Speed Motion-Picture Camera Optical Compensation at 40,000 Photographs per Second," Report No. 856, in NACA, *32nd Annual Report, 1946* (Washington, D.C.: Government Printing Office, 1949), pp. 345–61; A. M. Rothrock, R. C. Spencer, and Cearcy D. Miller, "A High-Speed Motion-Picture Study of Normal Combustion, Knock, and Preignition in a Spark-Ignition Engine," Report No. 704, in NACA, *27th Annual Report, 1941* (Washington, D.C.: Government Printing Office, 1942), pp. 15–30; Cearcy D. Miller, "A Study of High-Speed Photography of Combustion and Knock in a Spark-Ignition Engine," Report No. 727, in NACA, *28th Annual Report, 1942* (Washington, D.C.: Government Printing Office, 1946), pp. 15–37; Cearcy D.

Miller and H. Lowell Olsen, "Identification of Knock in NACA High-Speed Photographs of Combustion in a Spark-Ignition Engine," Report No. 761, in NACA, *29th Annual Report, 1943* (Washington, D.C.: Government Printing Office, 1948), pp. 125–43; and Cearcy D. Miller and Walter O. Logan, "Preknock Vibrations in a Spark-Ignition Engine Cylinder as Revealed by High-Speed Photography," Report No. 785, in NACA, *30th Annual Report, 1944* (Washington, D.C.: Government Printing Office, 1949), pp. 223–42.

63. A. Sokolik and A. Voinov, "Knocking in an Internal Combustion Engine," NACA *Technical Memorandum* No. 928 (Washington, D.C.: NACA, 1940).

Previously the German researchers Kurt Schnauffer and H. Weinhart had used ionized gaps and an oscillograph to conclude that the flame front progressed at 265 to 300 meters per second, sufficient to cause gas vibration, and that therefore knock was the autoignition of the end gas. See Kurt Schnauffer, "Engine-Cylinder Flame Propagation Studied by New Methods," *SAE Transactions* 29 (1934): 17–24; and H. Weinhart, "Knocking in the Otto-Cycle Engine," *Technical Memorandum* No. 911 (Washington, D.C.: NACA, 1939). Other researchers were unable to verify their results, however, suggesting that the Germans were observing simple autoignition and not vibratory knock. See Cearcy D. Miller, "Relation between Spark-Ignition Engine Knock, Detonation Waves, and Autoignition as shown by High-Speed Photography," Report No. 855, in NACA, *32nd Annual Report, 1946* (Washington, D.C.: Government Printing Office, 1949), pp. 317–43.

64. Ernest F. Fiock, Charles F. Marvin Jr., Frank R. Caldwell, and Carl H. Roeder, "Flame Speeds and Energy Considerations for Explosions in a Spherical Bomb," Report No. 682, in NACA, *26th Annual Report, 1940* (Washington, D.C.: Government Printing Office, 1941), pp. 39–58; A. M. Rothrock and R. C. Spencer, "A Photographic Study of Combustion and Knock in a Spark-Ignition Engine," Report No. 622, in NACA, *24th Annual Report, 1938* (Washington, D.C.: Government Printing Office, 1939), pp. 213–33; and G. D. Boerlage, "Detonation and Autoignition," *Technical Memorandum* No. 843 (Washington, D.C.: NACA, 1937).

65. Cearcy D. Miller, H. Lowell Olsen, Walter O. Logan, and Gordon E. Osterstrom, "Analysis of Spark-Ignition Engine Knock as Seen in Photographs Taken at 200,000 frames per second," Report No. 857, in NACA, *32nd Annual Report, 1946* (Washington, D.C.: Government Printing Office, 1949), pp. 363–73.

66. Miller, "Relation between Spark-Ignition Knock."

67. Charles K. Westbrook, "The Chemistry behind Engine Knock," *Chemistry and Industry*, 3 Aug. 1992, pp. 562–66; "Knock Observed Via New Device," *Automotive Engineering* 93 (Apr. 1985): 56–63; Lyle D. Burns, "Organic Antiknock Chemicals," *Chemtech* 14 (Dec. 1984): 744–48; William R. Leppard, "A Detailed Chemical Kinetics Simulation of Engine Knock," *Combustion Science and Technology* 43 (1985): 1–20; V. E. Pierce and B. B. Bansal, "Lead Phase-Out and Octane Enhancement," *Chemical Engineering Progress* 82 (Mar. 1986): 27–33; and Sidney W. Benson, "The Mechanism of Inhibition of Knock by Lead Additives: A Chain Debranching Reaction," *Journal of Physical Chemistry* 92 (Mar. 25, 1988): 1531–33.

68. AAF Scientific Advisory Group, "Aircraft Fuels and Propellants," May 1946, 17, Document M-30479-R, United States Air Force Air University Library, Maxwell AFB, Ala.; and *Army Air Forces Statistical Digest, World War II* (Washington, D.C.: Office of Statistical Control, 1945), p. 298. From Pearl Harbor until V-J Day the Allies produced 19 billion gallons of 100/130 PN aviation fuel at a cost of about $3 billion ($31.7 billion in 1996 dollars). Refinery expansion cost nearly $1 billion ($10.6 billion in 1996 dollars), with 75 percent borne by private companies and 25 percent by the Defense Plant Corporation. See Heron, *Development of Aviation Fuels*, p. 659.

69. German engine manufacturers also resorted to water-methanol and nitrous oxide injection to produce additional power.

70. NACA, *Technical Note No. 93* (Washington, D.C.: Government Printing Office, 1922); and

Engineering Section, "Study of Knock Test Methods for Aircraft Fuel," 8 Sep. 1932, File 463.8, Folder—Fuels Anti-Knock Knock Tests 1929–1937, Box 869, RD-3311, RG342.

71. Isooctane is C_8H_{18}, or one carbon atom for every 2.25 atoms of hydrogen. Benzene, one of the major aromatics in German aviation gasoline, is C_6H_6, or one carbon atom for every one atom of hydrogen.

72. Stephen L. McFarland and Wesley Phillips Newton, *To Command the Sky: The Battle for Air Superiority over Germany, 1942–1944* (Washington, D.C.: Smithsonian Institution Press, 1991), pp. 57–58; Engineering Division to Air Transport Command, 27 July 1944, File 463.8, Folder—Fuel Dimethyl Butane Superior Engine 1944, Box 2875, RD-2880, RG342; Wright Aeronautical Corporation, "Evolution of Aviation Gasoline," 23 Dec. 1943, File 463.8, Folder—Fuels 1944–1945, Box 3363, RD-3042, RG342; and BuAer memo, "Meeting of Joint Aircraft Committee, Technical Sub-Committee on Self-Sealing Tanks and Hoses, 26 May 1942," 2 June 1942, File JJ 7G 1, Vol. 4, Box 962, BuAer Confidential Correspondence 1922–1944, RG72. The United States slowly increased the aromatic content of its aviation fuel to 20 percent during the war as a means of increasing available supplies, using primarily cumene (isopropyl benzene).

73. Heron, *Development of Aviation Fuels,* pp. 644–46, 657; and George W. Gray, *Frontiers of Flight: The Story of NACA Research* (New York: Knopf, 1948), pp. 245–46.

CHAPTER 5

Engineering Successful Innovation

Pratt & Whitney Aircraft Engines, 1925–40

Bayla Singer

Put all your eggs in one basket—and then watch that basket!

—Andrew Carnegie

The Pratt & Whitney Aircraft Company was incorporated in 1925, dedicating itself for the next generation to the production of radial piston engines for aircraft. As a case study, the spectacular success of the first fifteen years of the company illustrates the interdependence of technical innovation, market conditions, and managerial decision making. Guided by the vision of Frederick B. Rentschler and the engineering skill of George J. Mead, the company focused on design and production of air-cooled radial engines, the type that dominated the aviation industry in the period between the world wars.

In the years between the two world wars, aviation became firmly established as an integral part of America's economic and military environments. It followed the trajectory of many other technological systems, beginning as a novelty and developing to young maturity under the formative influences of the social roles it seemed fitted to play. As happened with other technological systems, aviation in the process of its own development also helped modify the structure of American society.

The character of the aeronautical engine is crucial to this story. It is at least equal in importance to the more obvious influences of airframe design and pilot skill in determining the capabilities of aircraft and thus their potential for social utility. Range, altitude, speed, reliability, and maneuverability all begin with the engine.

BACKGROUND AND GENEALOGY: 1910–25

Prior to World War I, civilian aviation in the United States had been primarily a matter of barnstorming and stunt flying. There was little motivation to improve engines, nor an extensive market to spur competitive engineering. Although powered flight had been pioneered in the United States (with the Wright brothers manufacturing their own engine), by 1916 the complaint could legitimately be made that "there is not a good American motor made."

With war brewing in Europe and American involvement increasingly likely, the armed forces became a potential large market for improved aeronautical engines. Two separate lines of development ensued, each having strong influences on the eventual formation of Pratt & Whitney Aircraft.

One line began with a meeting between the engine manufacturers and representatives of the military air arms on 8 June 1916. Arranging the meeting and providing an atmosphere in which cooperation could be achieved were early triumphs for the National Advisory Committee for Aeronautics (NACA). In this spirit of cooperation, "J. G. Vincent, of the Packard Motor Car Company, and E. J. Hall, of the Hall-Scott Motor Car Company, took over a hotel room in Washington for nearly a week and designed the 8- and 12- cylinder Liberty power plants with prevalent engineering and mass-production procedures in mind." The intimate association between the aeronautical manufacturers and their military clients continued through and after the war, becoming one important ingredient in the strength of the industry. The U.S. Navy's continuing direct communication with industry executives was a strong factor in the subsequent establishment of Pratt & Whitney Aircraft.[1]

The second line of development began with a license to produce Hispano-Suiza ("Hisso") engines. The Wright Company (later Wright-Martin, Wright Aeronautical, and Curtiss-Wright) acquired the license in 1916; the company also acquired the Crane-Simplex Company, whose automotive-engine facilities were thought to be well suited to aircraft engine production.[2]

Adapting the Hisso took far more time than designing the Liberty from scratch; the engineering problems that arose illuminate the state of the industry and its infrastructure in America. As summarized by an article in *Aviation*, the industry's trade periodical:

> The French drawings . . . were all in metric measure, and very few, if
> any, limits or tolerances were stated. This meant at first, that the draw-
> ings must be entirely redrawn to American standards, and that limits
> had to be established for the fit of the various parts. Tools and fixtures
> had to be designed for the production of these parts. The castings, par-

ticularly the cylinder block and upper crankcase, involved intricate foundry problems. The best foundries in this country were unable to solve them. At that time very little experience was available in the aluminum industry with anything but very simple castings, and therefore a foundry had to be developed for their production. The French standards of steel had to be translated into commercially procurable material in this country, and the heat treatment of these materials developed, . . . in order to reduce the weight as much as possible. Suitable accessories, such as magnetos, carburetors and spark plugs, were not at first available in this country. . . . By the time all these matters had been straightened out, the problem of the proper testing equipment came up.[3]

Henry Crane had followed his company into the Wright-Martin organization and served as head of the engineering section. Under his leadership, his team developed a series of improved engines from the basic Hisso: by 1918, performance had risen from an initial 150 hp at 1,450 rpm to 325 hp at 1,800 rpm, and the weight/power ratio (specific weight) had been reduced to 1.92 lbs/hp from 2.9. During the War, the Wright Company worked closely with the military Aircraft Production Board. One navy officer detailed from the board to Wright-Martin was Frederick B. Rentschler, a Princeton graduate with a strong background in automotive engines.[4]

Born 8 November 1887, thirty years old in 1918, Rentschler had qualified as a machinist, an artisan, and a moulder, working in the family business in Hamilton, Ohio. He enlisted in the navy when the United States entered the First World War, fully expecting to return to the Hooven-Owen-Rentschler Company and eventually take his place at its head. At Wright-Martin, Rentschler decided that his future lay with the new aeronautical engines, though his father "grumbled that aviation was 'a damn-fool business, mostly for sportsmen.'"[5] His main activities at Wright-Martin were administrative, though he became intimately familiar with the quality of work done by such hands-on engineers as George J. Mead, an MIT graduate who later joined Rentschler in founding the Pratt & Whitney Aircraft Company.

Although large-scale production of the Liberty and the Wright-Hisso engines did not occur in time to "darken the skies over Europe" (in Howard Coffin's colorful phrase), aviation's contribution to the war effort was significant enough to convince the U.S. military that strong air forces would be crucial to the successful prosecution of future wars. Strong air forces, in turn, would depend on a thriving domestic aviation industry.[6]

After the armistice, however, the military weakened the aviation industry by abruptly canceling contracts and by dumping surplus aircraft on the civilian market. The aircraft construction industry shrank to a bare tenth of its wartime size. Rentschler later commented, "when the Armistice came all the companies who carried on our chief aviation activities blithely went back to automobile manufacture, so the aviation industry did not even get any real or lasting results." In the face of the subsequent reduced economic environment for aircraft production, the armed forces nevertheless insisted that their future purchases would look toward improvements in fighter, trainer, and bomber aircraft. The Wright-Martin assets had been sold to the Mack Truck Company, with approximately three million dollars set aside "for the possible formation of a small postwar aviation company." Rentschler was asked to assemble personnel for the new Wright Aeronautical Company.[7]

To head the engineering section, he approached George Mead, who had worked so successfully under Henry Crane in adapting the Hispano-Suiza. Mead at first demurred, preferring to take a position at the army's McCook Field as chief of the Power Plant Laboratory. Rentschler then turned to Crane, who accepted the position; Andrew Wilgoos, Charles Marks, and John Borrup also came to Wright Aeronautical from Wright-Martin. After about a year, Crane resigned to join General Motors, and Mead accepted the chief engineer's position as Crane's replacement. The principal client continued to be the military, and Rentschler's contacts with the navy were an additional asset over and beyond his demonstrated managerial skills.[8]

Lack of a large and stable market had been one important factor hobbling American aviation before the war. Since the military were accustomed to purchasing in quantity, they were attractive clients, and their demands proved a strong motivation for aviation manufacturers' research and development. The engineering search began: which of the many possible engine types was capable of the sort of improvements that would be attractive to the military? Some engine types proved to have intractable negative characteristics when attempts were made to scale them up.

For example, the rotary engine had been almost satisfactory at the low speeds typical of World War I aircraft, although the castor-oil fumes billowing from the engines into the open cockpits were reputed to have caused more than one pilot to make an emergency landing in order to answer the call of nature. (If the delicate moment occurred over enemy territory, the hapless pilot might find himself a POW.) When the rotary was scaled up, the gyroscopic effect of the rotating engine became unmanageable and the aircraft could not be easily steered.[9]

In other cases, superiority of one engine type over another could not be so easily established. This was the situation with the competition between air-cooled and liquid-cooled engines, and between radial and in-line (straight or V) configurations. While liquid-cooled engines were heavier and more subject to mechanical failures, for example, the lighter air-cooled engines (usually radials or rotaries) presented severe problems with power loss due to drag. Radial engines in single-engine planes generally allowed a shorter-nosed fuselage, with better visibility and maneuverability, than did in-line engines. Incremental technical advances could swing the balance between one type and another.

The newly reorganized Wright Aeronautical Company began operations by providing improved Hisso-type engines to the army. George Mead had made a comprehensive study of engines during his stint at McCook and felt that this was the most promising avenue; the results were the Wright H-3 and H-3 "super-fighter" liquid-cooled V-8s. The standard "pursuit airplane" (fighter) in 1921 carried the Wright H-3.[10]

Meanwhile, Charles Lawrance had developed a workable air-cooled radial engine. His company was very small, and it ran into financial trouble. The directors approached Wright Aeronautical about a merger, which Rentschler at first opposed. As Rentschler later recalled, "Admiral [William F.] Moffett, then the head of the Bureau of Aeronautics, asked me to come down and talk with him about the Lawrance situation. He said definitely the Navy was interested in the type and was proposing to concentrate on air-cooled radials for that size." Rentschler reversed his recommendation, and Wright Aeronautical acquired the Lawrance Aero-Engine Corporation. However, he "revised the design under Mead's direction. . . . After a few months the only Lawrance personnel retained were Mr. Lawrance himself and one excellent serviceman. Charles Lawrance . . . proved to be an asset in general and sales relations." Rentschler continued to keep a tight rein on the company, and a weather eye on the requirements of the U.S. Navy. When it became apparent that the navy would insist on continued development of the air-cooled radial, and the directors at Wright Aeronautical balked at the level of attendant expense and effort that Rentschler thought appropriate, Rentschler resigned as president.[11]

FORMATION OF PRATT & WHITNEY AIRCRAFT

About a year later, in the spring of 1925, Rentschler was ready to reenter the aeronautical engine business. The year was one of transition for the industry as a whole, as one analyst commented:

> The commercial flyer of today faces a most critical situation. It is the period of transition from the use of war surplus material to the pur-

chase of new planes of a more modern and efficient character. . . .
Within a period of three to five years at the longest it is believed that
the whole stock of cheap war surplus material will be exhausted and
the commercial flyer who does not realize this and does not now lay
plans to meet the new conditions will be forced out of business. . . .
Stunt flying is no longer a star attraction. . . . The novelty of riding in
an airplane and the day when the passenger was a hero among his
friends for months to come has passed. The day when the gypsy flier
could drop into a town and get passengers at $15 a trip is now ancient
history. The question is what will replace this business?

The only possible answer is a careful study of the possibilities of
new equipment. What will it do and what will it cost?[12]

The Curtiss Exhibition Company advertised in 1925 that they had now
"disposed of their surplus JN airplanes under their offer of a free plane with each
flying course" and went on to suggest that patrons consider the "Complete
Course, including Flying and Mechanical Training . . . $300" (this was accom-
plished in ten hours) or "Flying instruction by the hour . . . $35 (no deposit re-
quired to cover breakage)." Curtiss still had some planes for sale, and would-be
aviators could "arrange for *instruction on their own machines at $10.00 per hour*"
(emphasis in the original)[13] Robertson Aircraft Corporation advertised that
eight to ten hours of instruction "should complete the most stubborn case,
and from then on, the refinements . . . can be gained only from experience."
Robertson's ad went on to say, "Commercial aviation is a rapidly growing industry. Don't delay! Enroll now!"[14]

It is worthwhile to pause a moment and consider some implications of these
offers and others like it. "Commercial aviation" is clearly envisioned as an enterprise for independent businessmen flying short hauls. Crop-dusting operations are one such opportunity mentioned in an advertisement for the Wright
Whirlwind 200 hp J-4 engine. The advertisement explicitly cites military adoption of the Whirlwind as a positive selling point, evidence of the engine's "unusual dependability, high performance, ease of inspection, adjustment and minor repairs and the low cost per flying hour."[15]

Foresight is always risky: there are always predictions, plausible enough at
the time they are made, that turn out to be spectacularly off the mark; a 1925
editorial saw a poor market outlook for planes to be flown by highly paid professionals (commercial aviation), and opined that "the largest potential field for
planes is the amateur user . . . until a plane is built which is safe for the amateur
there will only be a limited market for specialized planes."[16]

The largest sector of the limited market was still the military, and Rentschler was positioned to make the most of it. He had retained his connection with the navy and had been reassured by Admiral Moffett that the navy remained eager to purchase air-cooled radial engines in the 400 hp class. Moffett desired to bring healthy competition to the aeronautical engine industry; the alternative would be to develop the navy's own design and production capacities far beyond that required for peacetime. Rentschler's plans offered an opportunity to strengthen the civilian industry, to promote equitable pricing policies, and to stimulate further innovation.[17]

Rentschler was also well connected to the business establishment: his elder brother Gordon was executive vice-president of the National City Bank of New York, and Frederick Rentschler himself was acquainted with many influential people both through his family's business and through friendships and acquaintances made at Princeton and in the navy. There was risk, as always, in starting a new company, but Frederick Rentschler was the type of man who would please the heart of any capitalist. As one of the longtime Pratt & Whitney engineers, Leonard S. Hobbs, later recalled, "He worked very hard, and he fixed it so he knew everybody. This was back in the early days more, but he knew everybody in the Air Force and the government, the Navy particularly. . . Forrestal was his brother's roommate in Princeton; he was an old friend of Lovett's, the second Secretary of Defense . . ."[18]

Gordon Rentschler suggested that Frederick see their family friend James K. Cullen, who in turn gave him a letter of introduction to Clayton Burt, general manager of the Pratt & Whitney division of the Niles-Bemont-Pond Company. Pratt & Whitney was an established name in the tool business and had both idle capital and an idle plant in Hartford. Within days, the deal was done: Rentschler should assemble his team, and the Pratt & Whitney Tool Company would provide capital and work space.

Rentschler recruited a half-dozen men in the next few weeks. His first hire was George Mead, to be vice-president and to head the engineering department. Knowing that Wright Aeronautical would enter its new Simoon air-cooled radial for the U.S. Navy's consideration by early 1926, the engineers felt the pressure of time. If Pratt & Whitney Aircraft couldn't submit its own contender before the navy standardized on the Wright entry, all would be lost.

George Mead and Andrew Wilgoos worked through June and July in Wilgoos's garage to design the company's new engine, well before Pratt & Whitney Aircraft's official incorporation on 1 August. Earle Ryder, another of the "first official employees," assisted Wilgoos in July. Ryder recalled, "We set up a couple of drawing boards on packing cases" and laid out the "essentials for the engine":

Oh, the crankshaft, the connecting rod and so forth. This engine had a novel crankshaft construction which was a little different from anything else being made then. . . . I guess Andy laid down the sizes of the main parts and probably made some layouts showing the general arrangement of the thing.

[Design of a new engine] begins on the inside and works out. One would determine the stroke and the bore and lay out one cylinder with the connecting rod and the piston; and then the valves and valve operating gear would come next. . . . [Y]ou make up your mind to build an engine of a certain horsepower and you know from experience with other engines about how many horsepower per cubic inch [displacement] you can count on for a certain type of cylinder construction. So, you make up your mind that this would be a 1600 cubic inch engine, or whatever else you may choose for it. . . . You have to design your inner parts so that they'll miss each other.[19]

In the 1920s, design was more art than science:

You apportioned your parts so they looked right and a good mechanic could pretty well tell what they needed. That was one of Andy Willgoos's strong points. He was a natural mechanic and had a feel for machinery of all kinds. He didn't need any pencil work to tell him how a thing ought to be made.

Interviewer: Did you give much thought to the mechanic and the nuts he had to take off and if he had adequate working room and space in the engine? I guess it was always a consideration, but not a controlling one.[20]

Pratt & Whitney's new engine, the Wasp, was ready for testing within six months. It performed extremely well, and the navy chose it for its standard in the 400 hp class. The less powerful Wright Whirlwinds (150–200 hp class) continued to be used for army and navy trainers.

Ryder's casual recollection makes it seem easy, almost routine, but several important technical problems had to be solved. One of the most vexing was that of crankshaft speed. Since the "big end" of the master connecting rod circles a narrow portion of the irregularly shaped crankshaft, either rod or crankshaft must be made in two pieces to allow assembly. Customary practice in 1925 was to make a solid crankshaft and split master rod; at high speeds, the master rod tended to pull itself apart. Mead and Wilgoos designed a solid master rod and split crankshaft, which allowed the engine to run at much higher rpm, thereby increasing its power. (All other things being equal, at higher speeds the num-

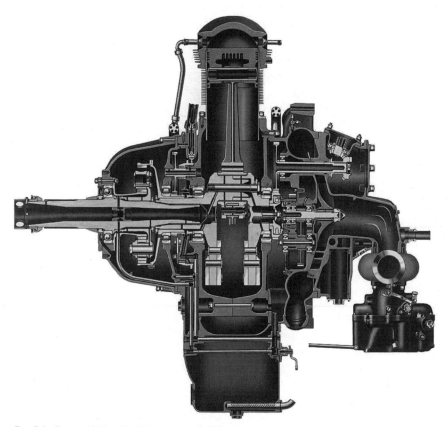

Fig. 5.1. Original Wasp R-1340 engine, sectional view. Courtesy United Technologies Archives, #D-201

ber of power strokes each piston can make per unit time is increased, and therefore the total power developed by the engine is increased.)

Mead and Wilgoos also changed the crankcase fabrication from a casting to a forging and designed it to be symmetrical across the plane of the cylinders, allowing identical forgings to be used for either the front or rear half. This provided a reduction in weight without loss of strength, distributed the load more evenly, and improved the ease of assembly and maintenance.[21]

Another technical problem was encountered when the Wasp was put into flight:

> We didn't know much about vibration. But I guess one of the first airplanes [a Curtiss F6C-4] to have a Wasp engine threw a counterweight over some flying field in Long Island. We went out and rescued the

things from the dirt and decided we had crankshaft vibrations and didn't know it. So the cure for that was to make the cheeks of the crankshaft a little thicker. Anything you would do would cure it because it would cure the vibration period but, of course, we put a lot of thought on it and thought we were doing the right thing. . . . Any change whatever probably would have fixed it. In fact, if we had made the cheeks thinner instead of thicker, that probably would have fixed it too.[22]

The Wright Simoon engine was announced in the 1 February 1926 issue of *Aviation;* the Pratt & Whitney Wasp made its debut in the issue of 15 February. Each was tested by the U.S. Navy in the standard bench procedure and flight-tested in actual aircraft, in this case the Wright Apache. The Wasp far outperformed the Simoon and went on to become the parent of an extremely successful family of engines.

Although the Wasp was designed to suit the navy's requirements, Pratt & Whitney marketed it to general aviation as well. The 15 February issue of *Aviation* carried an elegantly spare advertisement: a frontal view of the engine, resembling a sunburst, with the simple caption "Introducing the 'Wasp.'" The descriptive article in the same issue stressed such qualities as reliability, durability, high safety factor, and ease of maintenance. The article also notes, "The efficient cooling enables the engine to develop full power on domestic aviation gasoline, which is an important consideration."[23]

By August, the advertising for the Wasp showed a detailed side view of the engine, ticking off "Exclusive Reasons for Leadership: Valve Mechanism—completely enclosed; Nose—clean and free from accessories providing for excellent cowl lines; Solid Master Rod and Split Crankshaft—provides for high speed; Main Crankcase—Divided—maximum strength with minimum weight; Accessories—all located behind mounting—accessible and weather proof; Mounting Flange—approximately on center of gravity; Supercharger—built in G.E. type; Cylinders—Unusual provision for cooling; Lifting Hooks—on center of gravity."[24]

Another descriptive article appeared in May 1926, with additional details of the bench and flight test results. "For the first time, a radial type engine in the 400 hp class compares more than favorably with the efficient water-cooled types of engines on a dry weight per horsepower basis." The Office of the Secretary of the Navy is quoted: "A number of new airplanes for shipboard use are being built around this engine. . . . There is every assurance that, as a result of this development, the fleet will soon have aircraft whose performance is far in excess of anything available elsewhere." Tucked inconspicuously near the end of the article is Frederick Rentschler's announcement that Pratt & Whitney Aircraft has added two men to its Board of Directors: Charles F. Kettering of General Motors and William B. Mayo of Ford. The choice is well calculated; both men are trained engineers and not likely to be short-sighted about the need for continued research and product development. Further, Mayo had "directed the . . . aviation operations of that company"; the Wasp engine was soon installed in a Ford airplane.[25]

Again, it is useful to digress briefly. The mutual influence of engine and airframe are explicitly addressed in the navy statement quoted above. Some aircraft were designed with a particular engine in mind, but capable of utilizing others; the Wright Apache was one of these, intended to carry the Whirlwind engine but equally hospitable to Simoon or Wasp radials as well. Another member of this group is the Vought Corsair, "designed around the P & W 'Wasp' Engine."[26] In these cases, the airframe once established then constrained the choice of engine; improved performance would depend on incremental changes in engine design within a given type.

Other planes were literally "built around" their engines; to this group belongs the Granville Gee Bee R-1. As Colonel Fletcher Prouty recounted in his reminiscence about his boyhood infatuation with planes, the Granville brothers purchased Wasp engines from the factory and constructed their planes one at a time, designing as they went along. "To almost all who came in contact with it, in that heyday of daredevil flying, the Gee Bee was to bring meteoric fame, fortune, and—for some—tragedy." Prouty added that "the big new Wasp would require an airframe of totally new design and concept. The resulting airplane would be unique, incorporating the revolutionary 'teardrop' streamline design."[27] Here the engine called forth modifications in the airframe in order to fully realize its potential. In either case, neither the engine nor the airframe evolved in complete independence from the other.

Rentschler had been unhappy with what he saw as Wright Aeronautical's lack of commitment to continued improvements in their engines; he did not let his Pratt and Whitney team make that mistake. Almost immediately after inauguration of the Wasp engine, Pratt & Whitney introduced a larger and more powerful sibling, the Hornet. At 1900 rpm, the Hornet developed 525 horsepower compared to the Wasp's 425. Although the Hornet's displacement was approximately 1,700 cubic inches, compared with the Wasp's 1,300, the Hornet was only a few inches larger in diameter. As *Aviation* noted, "From a service . . . standpoint, it is of unusual interest to know that approximately 80 per cent of the total parts of the Hornet and Wasp are identical. . . . The entire accessory ends of the engines are exactly alike, including even the mounting flange, so that Wasp and Hornet engines can even be interchanged readily in the same type of airplane."[28]

DEVELOPING MARKETS

In the period 1925–30, aviation was still the glamorous province of individuals, but the early phases of the more mundane workaday industry were beginning to appear. Aircraft manufacturing increased dramatically; the number of establishments producing aircraft grew from 44 in 1925 to 132 in 1929, and the value added grew from $9,654,752 to $43,784,821 in the same period. The number of persons employed in aircraft manufacture increased as well, from 2,701 in 1925 to 14,710 in 1929. Pratt & Whitney Aircraft shipped 260 Wasps in 1927; by 1929, the number shipped rose to 1,656.[29]

The exploits of aeronautical record setters drew attention to aviation; such commercial enterprises as cargo transport, airmail, and passenger service rode their public-relations coattails while military clients provided the economic foundation for continued development of the industry. *Aviation* was moved to editorialize on the "real beginning" of commercial air transport in 1926, and the regularity and reliability of airmail. "New uses for aircraft and new commercial types have put America in the lead in this branch of aviation."[30] Airmail contracts directly subsidized and encouraged passenger traffic, and flying began to acquire a new image in the public consciousness. Speed-minded businessmen braved the perils of open-cockpit planes, or later enjoyed the relative comfort of small, unpressurized closed cabins. The Hisso, Liberty, and OX-5 engines were still the workhorses of commercial aviation at this stage, with the Wright Whirlwind representing the state of the art.

The nascent commercial market and the established military role are evident in a 15 April 1927 advertisement for the Wasp: "In a Ford Air Line Transport the 'Wasp' has demonstrated its ability to carry 33-1/3% greater pay load than the previously used water cooled powerplant of approximately the same power. It is becoming apparent that the 'Wasp' will find the same useful application in the commercial field as it has in Naval aeronautics."[31]

However, the major market for Pratt & Whitney's 400 hp engine remained the U.S. Navy; Congress in 1926 funded five-year aircraft procurement programs for the military, which provided the security and stability needed by the manufacturers.[32] Pratt & Whitney gave the navy the highest priority; shipping records for 1926 show that all but one of the first 213 Wasps were sold to the navy (the odd one was sold to Ford, and was probably the engine referred to in the advertisement mentioned above). Not until 1927 were 25 Wasps sold to Boeing, to replace the Liberty engines in Boeing's Model 40A. Pratt & Whitney's first and second "commercial series" of 55 Wasps were shipped between January and June of 1928. Of the first thousand Wasps, just under 74 percent went to the navy. Substantial sales to commercial aviation had to wait until the field matured enough to need and demand the higher-powered engine.[33]

Charles Lindbergh's dramatic transatlantic flight of 20–21 May 1927 was just one entry in that year's commercial exploitation of aviation record setting. Pratt & Whitney took a two-page spread in *Aviation* to illustrate various Wasp-powered aircraft "in which the recent load carrying speed and altitude records were set up" and "in which the recent World records were made." Wright Aeronautical, which had previously trumpeted "It was a COMMERCIAL WRIGHT WHIRLWIND MODEL J-5C ENGINE that established the new World's Endurance Record of 51 Hours, 11 Minutes, 20 Seconds on April 14th, 1927," wasted no time in putting Lindbergh's cable "WRIGHT WHIRLWIND FUNCTIONED PERFECTLY DURING ENTIRE FLIGHT INCLUDING OVER ONE THOUSAND MILES OF RAIN SLEET AND FOG STOP COMPLETE REPORT WILL FOLLOW" into an advertisement. Chance Vought, a friend of Rentschler's, countered with "FOUR WORLD'S RECORDS for the VOUGHT 'CORSAIR' . . . The 'Corsair' is designed around the P.& W. 'Wasp' Engine."[34]

Personal associations were as economically important among the various segments of the aeronautical industry as they were between the industry and their clients. Frederick Rentschler had asked advice of Chance Vought before organizing Pratt & Whitney Aircraft; he had been acquainted with William Boeing since 1918. It is not surprising that in 1928 William Boeing began to institutionalize some of the informal arrangements by purchasing companies and consolidating them under the umbrella of a holding company, eventually named United Aircraft & Transport. He first expanded his own operations, adding subsidiaries to carry airmail. Early in 1929, he acquired Pratt & Whitney Aircraft and Chance Vought Aircraft Corporation. Later that year five other manufacturers and designers of aviation equipment were added: Sikorsky Aircraft Corporation, Northrop Aircraft Corporation, Stearman Aircraft Corporation, Hamilton Aircraft Corporation, and Standard Steel Propeller. Three other airlines were also acquired: Stout Air Services, National Air Transport, and Varney Airlines. Rentschler became president of the holding company, Mead and Vought vice presidents, and Boeing held the chair.[35] United Aircraft & Transport was well positioned to respond to all aspects of both military and civilian aviation. This vertical integration provided sufficient strength to weather the financial storms of the 1929 stock market crash and the ensuing Great Depression.

MATCHING MACHINES TO MARKETS

The military, unlike the commercial market, required a constant stream of improvements in engine and airframe. As these were incorporated into production models, the smaller commercial market reaped the benefits—lower cost and higher quality—of the quantity production runs supported by the military.

Some of Pratt & Whitney's innovations were easily visible, such as the two-row radial design of the Twin Wasp, whose first model was rated at 1,350 horsepower. Other developments to the entire Pratt & Whitney line, while improving performance sufficiently to warrant new model numbers, were less obvious: thinner cooling fins, improved superchargers and carburetors, new compositions for bearings. Most of the hardware was fabricated to order, since materials had to be of high grade and the specifications were more exact than those of ordinary stock (for example, bolt lengths to the nearest eighth of an inch). Sometimes special treatment of the supplier was in order: "The way to get finer fins was to design the stuff, take the drawings down to the Pattern Shop [at Aluminum Company of America, in Bridgeport, Connecticut], and then go away on vacation so they couldn't complain about it. If you would keep well away for the next couple of months, you'd probably get what you wanted."[36]

There are two main types of aeronautical engineering research, one which might be called "cut-and-try" (systematic parameter variation) and the other "pencil-and-paper" (focusing on basic theory and its application). Although the two types are not completely independent, the professional atmosphere of a shop will usually emphasize and even idealize one over the other. Each has its advantages and shortcomings: parameter variation can lead to impressive improvements in the absence of a deeper understanding of complex problems, while analysis and application of theory can illuminate counterintuitive realities.

An excellent example of the two systems applied to the same problem may be found in the National Advisory Committee for Aeronautics (NACA) work on engine cowling. Parameter variation had led to the development in 1928 of the NACA cowling for radial engines. On the test plane, "the maximum speed was increased from 118 to 137 mph. This is equivalent to providing approximately 83 additional horsepower without additional weight or cost of engine, fuel consumption, or weight of structure."[37] (The dramatic improvement in performance also illustrates the interdependence of engine and airframe.) However, further improvement was dependent on theoretical analysis, and in 1937 research "demonstrated as fact something that everyone had unconsciously assumed to be physically impossible . . . a proper engine cowling could . . . lower operating temperatures more than could full exposure of cylinders in the airstream" by "making the enclosed baffled engine act in essence as a ducted radiator for cooling."[38]

In the period between the two world wars, aviation was a complex art whose parameters were not yet well understood. The interactions among engine components within a single engine, the mutual influences of engine and airframe, and the differing requirements of military and civilian operations all conspired to favor the "informed guesswork" of the experienced engineer over the calculations of the theorist. Within the Pratt & Whitney shop, the "cut-and-try" school was the dominant feature of the professional culture. We have already seen one example in Ryder's description of the initial work of Mead and Wilgoos on the Wasp; Guy Beardsley's description of his own work provides additional evidence. One problem was the float carburetor: "We were having more trouble because you couldn't fly inverted with a float type carburetor for very long. You had to be at the right horsepower so it could absorb the fuel which went through a fixed jet when you inverted. If you went faster it was too lean. If the engine went slower it was too rich. It was a very poor setup. We were trying to get something which would work in all positions . . . but it never panned out."[39]

Another challenge was the supercharger, an essential ingredient in compensating for the thin air of high altitudes (engines as well as pilots require sufficient oxygen for proper function):

> [W]e depended entirely on the General Electric Company to build our superchargers. . . . We put it together and it didn't work well . . . Parkins said, 'Well, why don't we just put in a higher gear ratio? That ought to cure it.' We put in a higher gear ratio and it was worse. It turns out that the airflow was not properly matched to the areas at the exit of the supercharger at the inlet and exit . . .
>
> The compression through the supercharger—these were all radial superchargers at that time. The compression going through it didn't match up with the reduction in the area and you'd get all kinds of problems. You'd tip the backflow and everything else. So we finally decided this was for the birds, that GE didn't know as much as they thought they did about it. So we got into it in a very serious way and started doing some very basic work on superchargers . . .
>
> We had some valves on the exit side which we were going to use later on with trying to make some altitude tests on it. We just closed those valves down and all of a sudden the pressure just jumped up. In other words, the diffuser was completely out of match with the supercharger because the flow was too great through it. When we restricted the flow coming out of it, the pressure just built up like mad. That's

when early in the game we found out that you had to absolutely match everything right through from one end to the other.

The big problem was that nobody wanted to spend much money on that stupid research work in blowing air through things but when they'd come around and wanted to know what they were supposed to do for the new engine that was coming out. . . . Finally we got to the point where you really started and designed the engine on the basis of what your supercharger had to do beforehand and that's when we got superchargers which would go up to twenty and twenty-five thousand feet. Prior to that, you know, ten to twelve thousand feet was the highest that they ever got supercharged.[40]

Flight testing, and then actual operation, brought out additional considerations. In a 1929 joint paper, Leonard S. Hobbs of Pratt & Whitney and Edward Hubbard of Boeing addressed some issues of engine-airframe interaction: "The control of cylinder temperature must be effected by a cowling arrangement, which has generally been left to the airplane designer and the operator to work out. This attitude was the result of a genuine lack of knowledge on the part of the engine builder as to just what the requirements were. . . . Sufficient experience has now been gained to enable the engine manufacturer to advise the user . . . when conditions of operation are known." Hobbs and Hubbard also described the routine and special conditions of operation in particular circumstances which could significantly affect performance:

> The fuel situation is aggravated by a serious lack of knowledge on the part of both the engine manufacturer and the refiner. The former does not know what actually occurs in the cylinder, and the latter has no real yardstick for measuring the quality of his fuel . . .
>
> Our experience [with cooling the engine] has conclusively proved that all controls must be operated from the cockpit, as the conditions encountered during one flight will sometimes require wide variation in adjustment . . .
>
> Special equipment to meet some special condition must in almost every case be worked out by the operator in conjunction with the engine manufacturer.[41]

THE BALANCING ACT, 1930–35

The transition noted in 1926 persisted into the 1930s. The growth and improvement of infrastructure elements such as airports, radio, and navigational instruments helped support concurrent evolution of civilian aviation. As civilian aviation began to answer a wider variety of social functions, the legacy of World War I surplus engines and airframes was only slowly displaced by the newer models.[42] Aeronautical manufacturing industries trod a precarious path, dependent on government subsidy and struggling to establish a stable civilian business environment. Military procurement remained the economic backbone of the industry.

Encouraged by the U.S. Navy, Pratt & Whitney began development of the Twin Wasp and a smaller version, the Twin Wasp Jr., in 1929. The primary advantages of the two-row configuration were smoother operation, higher operating speeds (and hence higher power), and smaller frontal diameter. Flight tests "in a long series of Navy airplanes" were conducted in 1931 through 1933. Production "was commenced in 1934 and from that time on . . . further improvements to these engines, including automatic mixture and power control carburetors, fully automatic valve gear lubrication, [and] improved cylinder cooling [resulted in] increased power and even greater dependability." The Twin Wasp and Twin Wasp Jr. were eventually purchased in significant quantities by both the army and the navy.[43]

Celebrity endorsement and record-setting achievements continued to be important throughout the 1930s. After the Granville Gee Bee taxed Jimmy Doolittle's piloting skill to the utmost in August and September 1932, he nevertheless sent Pratt & Whitney a letter on Shell Petroleum letterhead, saying: "I wanted to tell you that the Wasp Senior functioned perfectly during the Shell Speed Dashes and the Thomson Trophy Race. I have never flown a sweeter running engine and want to congratulate you and the Pratt & Whitney Company on the development of the big 6:1 12:1 Wasp."[44]

Amelia Earhart owned and flew a Wasp-powered Lockheed Vega; the plane in which she made her last flight in 1937 was a Lockheed 10 E Electra, with two Wasp engines. In spite of impressive individual achievements, the strong future often forecast for individually owned and operated planes ("flying flivvers," as it were) never materialized. The public never quite lost its collective fear of flying, though it became increasingly willing to trust its life to professional pilots.[45]

Passenger traffic continued to grow with the increasing comfort and convenience of the airlines' planes and schedules. Advertising in *Aviation* acknowledged the new markets; for example, one illustration shows over a dozen men and fashionably attired women waiting to board a trimotor, another advertisement touts new materials that "bring valuable refinements in passenger planes," and yet another, showing a chic young woman at ease in her airline seat, simply offers "Latest Upholstery Fabrics for Modern Transportation."[46]

Passenger traffic still did not generate enough revenue to support the service,

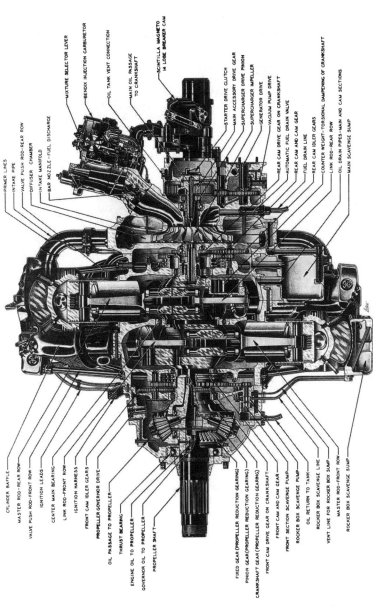

Labels (top, left to right along rotated text):
PRIMER LINES
INTAKE PIPE
VALVE PUSH ROD—REAR ROW
DIFFUSER CHAMBER
INTAKE MANIFOLD
BAR NOZZLE—FUEL DISCHARGE

MIXTURE SELECTOR LEVER
BENDIX INJECTION CARBURETOR
OIL TANK VENT CONNECTION
MAIN OIL PASSAGE TO CRANKSHAFT
SCINTILLA MAGNETO 14 LOBE BREAKER CAM

STARTER DRIVE CLUTCH
MAIN ACCESSORY DRIVE GEAR
SUPERCHARGER DRIVE PINION
SUPERCHARGER IMPELLER
GENERATOR DRIVE
VACUUM PUMP DRIVE
REAR CAM DRIVE GEAR ON CRANKSHAFT
AUTOMATIC FUEL DRAIN VALVE
REAR CAM AND CAM GEAR
FUEL DRAIN LINE
REAR CAM IDLER GEARS
LINK ROD—REAR ROW
COUNTER WEIGHT—TORSIONAL DAMPENING OF CRANKSHAFT
OIL DRAIN PIPES—MAIN AND CAM SECTIONS
MAIN SCAVENGE SUMP

Labels (bottom, left to right):
CYLINDER BAFFLE
MASTER ROD—REAR ROW
VALVE PUSH ROD—FRONT ROW
IGNITION LEADS
CENTER MAIN BEARING
LINK ROD—FRONT ROW
IGNITION HARNESS
FRONT CAM IDLER GEARS
PROPELLER GOVERNOR DRIVE
OIL PASSAGE TO PROPELLER
THRUST BEARING
ENGINE OIL TO PROPELLER
GOVERNOR OIL TO PROPELLER
PROPELLER SHAFT

FIXED GEAR (PROPELLER REDUCTION GEARING)
PINION GEAR (PROPELLER REDUCTION GEARING)
CRANKSHAFT GEAR (PROPELLER REDUCTION GEARING)
FRONT CAM DRIVE GEAR ON CRANKSHAFT
FRONT CAM AND CAM GEAR
FRONT SECTION SCAVENGE PUMP
ROCKER BOX SCAVENGE PUMP
OIL RETURN TO TANK
ROCKER BOX SCAVENGE LINE
VENT LINE FOR ROCKER BOX SUMP
MASTER ROD—FRONT ROW
ROCKER BOX SCAVENGE SUMP

PRATT & WHITNEY SIC3-G TWIN WASP ENGINE

Fig. 5.2. SIG 3-G Twin Wasp Engine (R-1830), sectional view. Courtesy United Technologies Archives, #D-6385

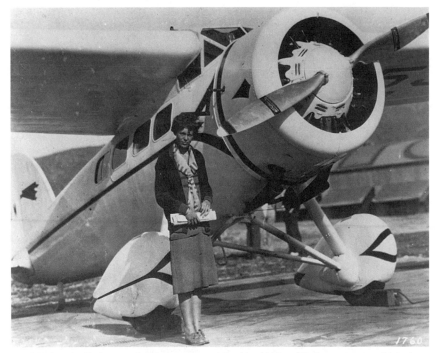

Fig. 5.3. Amelia Earhart with Wasp-powered Lockheed Vega 5A Executive in which she set the women's speed record of 184.7 mph in November 1929. Note cowling on engine and fairing on landing gear. Courtesy United Technologies Archives, #Gooch 2423

however. Government support, in the form of subsidized airmail contracts, was sought and obtained by United and other airline operators. This proved a source of notoriety in 1934, when Senator Hugo L. Black directed an investigation into what seemed inordinate, not to say obscene, profits made by the aviation industry at a time when other sectors of the U.S. economy were suffering.[47]

INTERDEPENDENCE, 1920–40

Both the aviation industry and the federal government were caught in mutual dependence throughout this period. Companies such as Pratt & Whitney Aircraft prospered by employing demonstrated technical excellence together with personal connections in a timely fashion.

Civilian designers and manufacturers needed large markets to provide economic support for innovation, while the military saw the importance of a well-developed civilian manufacturing capability long before civil aviation emerged from the barnstorming stage. The industry chafed at the restrictions attendant upon receipt of public money yet relied on government contracts and subsidies during this period of pioneering growth.

Vertical integration, an effective tool in adapting to the uncertain civilian market, rendered United and others vulnerable to deeply held public antitrust sentiments. The government could not afford to ignore this and indeed used these sentiments as a political brake on the degree to which it accommodated the aeronautical industry.

The emergence of a self-sufficient civilian airline industry awaited the development of aircraft that were safe and comfortable enough to attract a large number of passengers, but such development required a sizable investment in research and innovation. Since the civilian market could not yet support this investment, federal recognition of the national interest prompted long-term economic support. With this stable support, Pratt & Whitney could concentrate on solving the technical problems encountered with increasing demands for higher engine performance.

NOTES

1. Alex Roland, *Model Research: The National Advisory Committee for Aeronautics 1915–1958* (Washington, D.C.: NASA SP-4103, 1985), vol. 1:, p. 35; Roger E. Bilstein, *Flight in America, 1900–1983: From the Wrights to the Astronauts* (Baltimore, Md.: Johns Hopkins University Press, 1984). For a more detailed account of the Liberty engine's development, see Robert Schlaifer, *Development of Aircraft Engines* (Andover, Mass.: Andover Press, 1950), and Herschel Smith, *Aircraft Piston Engines: From the Manly Balzer to the Continental Tiara* (Manhattan: Kans.: Sunflower University Press, 1981).

2. Smith, *Aircraft Piston Engines*, p. 68.

3. "Development of an American Pursuit Engine," *Aviation*, 26 Dec. 1921, pp. 735–38.

4. Frederick B. Rentschler, *An Account of Pratt & Whitney Aircraft Company, 1925–1950* (privately printed), p. 8; *The Pratt & Whitney Aircraft Story* (privately printed, Aug. 1950), pp. 16–18.

5. Ibid., p. 17.

6. Rentschler, *An Account of Pratt & Whitney*, pp. 5–8. See also William F. Trimble, *Admiral William A. Moffett, Architect of Naval Aviation* (Washington, D.C.: Smithsonian Institution Press, 1994), p. 116; Schlaifer, *Development of Aircraft Engines*, pp. 7–14; William F. Trimble, *Wings for the Navy: A History of the Naval Aircraft Factory, 1917–1956* (Annapolis, Md.: Naval Institute Press, 1990), chapter 4.

7. Roland, *Model Research*, pp. 51; Rentschler, *Account of Pratt & Whitney*, pp. 6, 7.

8. Rentschler, *Account of Pratt & Whitney*, pp. 7–8; "Pratt and Whitney Aircraft Co. Formed," *Aviation*, 3 Aug. 1925.

9. Smith, *Aircraft Piston Engines*, p. 63. It should be noted that the rotary engine of the 1910–20 period differed significantly from the modern automotive engine bearing the same designation, especially in the fact that the early engine rotated in its entirety around the crankshaft. Ibid., p. 58.

10. "Development of an American Pursuit Engine," *Aviation*, 26 Dec. 1921.

11. Rentschler, *Account of Pratt & Whitney*, pp. 9–10; Hugo T. Byttebier, *The Curtiss D-12 Aero Engine*, Smithsonian Annals of Flight no. 7 (Washington, D.C.: Smithsonian Institution Press, 1972), p. 75. See also Rentschler, *Account of Pratt & Whitney*, p. 10. Lawrance was in fact a vice president of Wright Aeronautical and became president after Rentschler's departure. It would not be surprising if

there were some coolness between Lawrance and Rentschler, reflected in the subsequent rivalry between their firms. In an address before the Royal Aeronautical Society in England, Lawrance mentioned the Simoon, "which has just completed a full 50-hour test" and two other American radial engines under development in the 400 hp class, but omitted any notice at all of the Wasp. Charles L. Lawrance, "Modern American Aircraft Engine Development" *Aviation*, 22 Mar. 1926, pp. 411–15.

12. Earl D. Osborn, "Modern Planes vs War Surplus Equipment," *Aviation*, 12 Jan. 1925, p. 47.

13. *Aviation*, 5 Jan. 1925, p. 4. See also Schlaifer, *Development of Aircraft Engines*, p. 160.

14. *Aviation*, 15 June 1925, p. 659.

15. Ibid., p. 660.

16. *Aviation*, 30 Mar. 1925, editorial, p. 341.

17. William F. Trimble, Moffett's biographer, describes Moffett's dilemma in the early 1920s: "[I]t was the government's responsibility, in the absence of a viable commercial outlet for the products of the aviation business, to do all it could to encourage the industry, knowing that 'if war should break out there would be a tremendous urge to get what we need in the shortest possible space of time.'" William F. Trimble, *Admiral William A. Moffett*, p. 116. See also William F. Trimble, *Wings for the Navy*, p. 66.

18. Leonard S. Hobbs, interview with John H. Martin, 19 Mar. 1970, United Technologies Archives, East Hartford, Conn.

19. Earle A. Ryder, interview with Harvey Lippincott, United Technology Archives, East Hartford, Conn., pp. 12–13.

20. Ibid., p. 41.

21. *Pratt & Whitney Aircraft*, pp. 36–37; Schlaifer, *Development of Aircraft Engines*, pp. 186–87.

22. Ryder interview, p. 20. Editorial note inserted by Lippincott.

23. *Aviation*, 15 Feb. 1926, pp. 228–30. For further discussion of aviation fuels, see S. D. Heron, *Development of Aviation Fuels* (Andover, Mass.: Andover Press, 1950).

24. *Aviation*, 2 Aug. 1926, p. 199.

25. Ibid., 31 May 1926, pp. 827–28; ibid., 25 Apr. 1927. Pratt & Whitney shipping records show, however, only one Wasp engine sold to Ford in 1926 (United Technologies Archives).

26. *Aviation*, 20 June 1927, advertisement featuring "Four World's Records for the Vought 'Corsair.'" It should be noted that the four record-setting pilots were U.S. Navy officers.

27. Fletcher Prouty, "Jimmy Doolittle and the Gee Bee," *Air Force Magazine*, Feb. 1977, pp. 77–81, United Technologies Archives, cabinet 922A, folder "Prouty, 'Jimmy Doolittle and the Gee Bee'." Recalls an airshow in Springfield, Mass., 1930.

28. *Aviation*, 28 May 1927, p. 897.

29. *Fifteenth Census of the United States: 1930: Manufactures 1929*, vol. 2, *Reports by Industries: Group 14*, pp. 1189–92; *Sixteenth Census of the United States: 1940: Manufactures: 1939*, volume 2, part 2, *Reports by Industries Groups 11 to 20*, pp. 540–42; Records of the Special Committee of the Senate to Investigate Air-Mail and Ocean-Mail Contracts, 1933–35. National Archives and Records Administration (NARA) Record Group # 46, Box 153, folder "United Aircraft Pratt & Whitney."

30. *Aviation*, 3 Jan. 1927, p. 13.

31. Ibid., 15 Apr. 1927.

32. See Trimble, *Wings for the Navy*.

33. United Technologies Archives. Serial numbers 216 through 240 sold to Boeing, shipping dates 17 Feb. 1927 through 18 May 1927. The record bears the comment "first commercial airline engine." Serial numbers 683–727, "first commercial series," shipped 1/9/28–5/14/28; "second commercial series," numbers 729–40, shipped 4/15/28–5/21/28, to various manufacturers. Of the first thousand serial numbers, 738 are recorded as sold to the navy.

34. Ibid.

35. Paula Kepos, ed., *International Directory of Company Histories* (Detroit, Mich.: St. James Press, 1994), vol. 9, p. 416; *Pratt & Whitney Aircraft Story*, pp. 31, 73; United Aircraft & Transport Corporation, *First Annual Report to Stockholders*, Dec. 1929.

36. Ryder interview, p. 18.

37. Smithsonian report, 1955, p. 257.

38. James R. Hansen, *Engineer-in-Charge: A History of the Langley Aeronautical Laboratory, 1917–1958* (Washington, D.C.: NASA SP-4305, 1987), p. 137.

39. Guy E. Beardsley, interviewed with Harvey Lippincott, 28 Mar. 1983, United Technologies Archives, p. 13.

40. Ibid., pp. 15–20.

41. Edward Hubbard and L. S. Hobbs, "Maintenance of Air-Cooled Engines in Commercial Operation," *Society of Automotive Engineers Journal* 26 (Jan. 1930): 91–94.

42. See *Aviation*, Mar. 1934, pp. 72–76; May 1935, pp. 178–80; May 1935, p. 201.

43. J. Olligainen, "Pratt & Whitney 2-Row 14-Cylinder Engines," typescript, datelined The Hague, 1 Oct. 1938, United Technologies Archives, drawer 910 B, folder "Twin Wasp (R-1830)-7, Engine Model History General." According to Pratt & Whitney figures, the R-1830 Twin Wasp "production totalled 173,618 engines, more than any other aircraft engine."

44. Prouty, "Doolittle and the Gee Bee," pp. 77–81; James H. Doolittle to Donald L. Brown, 16 Sep. 1932, United Technologies Archives, cabinet 922A, folder "Doolittle, James H."

45. Roy Blay, "Amelia Earhart's Last Flight," *Lockheed Horizons*, May 1988, p. 22; Joseph J. Corn, "Making Flying 'Thinkable': Women Pilots and the Selling of Aviation, 1927–1940," *American Quarterly* 31 (1979): 556–71.

46. *Aviation*, 9 Feb. 1929, p. 394; 6 Apr. 1929, p. 1136; 15 June 1929, p. 2186.

47. *Hearings Before a Special Committee on Investigation of Air Mail and Ocean Mail Contracts: United States Senate: 73rd Congress, 2nd Session*, transcripts of the investigation; see especially parts 4, 5, SUDOC: Y4.Ai7/2:H35.

CHAPTER 6

Three-Miles-a-Minute

The National Advisory Committee for Aeronautics
and the Development of the Modern Airliner

Deborah G. Douglas

Everyone in the American aviation community believed 1933 would be
a pivotal year in the development of commercial aviation. Under the
leadership of Postmaster General Walter Folger Brown, the outgoing
Hoover administration had forged a national system of air transportation. One could now fly an airplane "somewhere to somewhere."[1] Airways, airports, weather stations, strings of electric light beacons, and a new system of
radio navigation were being constructed at a steady clip, enabling increasing
numbers of Americans to criss-cross the nation.[2] The Depression had hardly
dimmed the nation's desire to travel, either. In 1920, the average American traveled five hundred miles per year. In 1930 that figure climbed to two thousand
and, in spite of three years of desperate economic circumstances, had dropped
only to seventeen hundred miles in 1933.[3] Air travel made up only a tiny fraction of those miles but had been steadily increasing. Still, the entire air transportation system was sustained by politically fragile federal subsidies, and many
feared it might collapse if steep budget cuts were enacted.[4]

Most scholars interested in the relationship between the federal government and the commercial aviation industry have focused on the role played by
the Post Office. The Air Mail Service represented the largest number of federal
dollars directed toward the development of commercial aviation. In addition,
historians have delighted in recounting what could be considered some of aviation's most colorful stories (e.g. the Black Hearings).[5] This is not the full story,
however of how the federal government in the United States "aided" the development of commercial aviation. The work of engineers at the National Advisory Committee for Aeronautics (NACA) during the interwar period, for in-

stance, contributed significantly to the development of the "modern" airliner. This short historiographical essay explores the role of NACA in fostering this important innovation in the 1930s.[6]

These aircraft—collectively and notably the Boeing 247, the Douglas DC-3, and the Lockheed Electra—received a blizzard of publicity, flying at a then "blistering" speed of three-miles-a-minute. Even today, the DC-3 remains one of the most celebrated aircraft in history. It has been fabled in story and legend, and several are still flying. But the persistence of the DC-3 and other "modern airliners" are less important for fond memories and longterm use than they are as outward manifestations of enormous changes taking place within the discipline of aeronautical engineering. The late 1920s saw the maturation of the U.S. aeronautical engineering community, a process which was largely mediated by the National Advisory Committee for Aeronautics.

Most descriptions of the technical development of these aircraft, however, have focused almost entirely on the work of industry engineers. While no one would dispute the hard work and creative effort of engineers such as Jack Northrop, Arthur Raymond (Douglas), or C. N. Montieth (Boeing), the near exclusive focus of aviation historians on them has resulted in a misleading narrative of what is a more rounded history of aeronautical engineering design in the production of these aircraft.

The most influential account of this subject is still Peter Brooks's late-1950s series of articles that culminated with the publication of *The Modern Airliner: Its Origins And Development*.[7] There is hardly a book in aviation history written since that does not bear the mark of Brooks's interpretative influence.[8] Brooks and subsequent authors have amassed an impressive collection of technical accounts and woven them into a coherent narrative to explain the origins of the innovative all-metal, monocoque transport aircraft that emerged to revolutionize air transportation in the 1930s. It is useful to note, however, that Brooks had a much more contemporary agenda when he wrote his articles and book. As an executive of British European Airways (BEA), he felt a special compulsion to "consider why America had such a monopoly in pioneering the successful transport aeroplane." His is a heroic tale with the hardly surprising conclusion that the locus of American technical genius was to be found in private industry and that American leadership resulted from vigorous free market competition among manufacturers.[9]

Over the years, Brooks's version has come to represent the dominant interpretation among aviation historians. Yet for all the power of the detail that Brooks and other writers have presented, this version of history is deeply deterministic. The sense of predestination hovers all over these narratives, as if the invisible hand of the marketplace were the only ingredient shaping the industry and prodding American aeronautical engineers along the path to the development of the Boeing 247, the Douglas 1, 2, 3 series, or the Lockheed Electra. The problem with this interpretation is that it denies the fact that the participants had control over their actions. Further, it has pushed to the periphery the contributions made by anyone or any institution outside private industry. Fairly modest queries reveal a much more complex historical reality.[10]

The NACA was established by Congress in 1915 "to supervise and direct the scientific study of the problems of flight, with a view to their practical solution, and to determine the problems which should be experimentally attacked, and to discuss their solution and their application to practical questions."[11] Two years later, the NACA broke ground for a laboratory on the same site as the Army Air Service's first permanent airfield being built in Hampton, Virginia. By the late 1920s, the NACA's Langley Aeronautical Laboratory had begun to earn an international reputation, largely due to the construction of a trio of pioneering wind tunnels (the Variable Density Tunnel that became operational in 1922, the Propeller Research Tunnel in 1927, and the Full Scale Tunnel in 1931). In 1929, the NACA won U.S. aviation's most prestigious award, the Robert J. Collier Trophy, for the development of the "NACA" cowling—the metal covering of radial engines that managed simultaneously to decrease drag and increase cooling, thereby providing significant improvement in aircraft performance.

But many in industry felt alienated from NACA. When the Langley lab was first being planned, the members of the Main Committee thought that the way to do this was to emulate the great research laboratories of Europe—in particular the National Physical Laboratory and Royal Aircraft Factory in Great Britain; the Institut Aérotechnique de l'Université de Paris and Gustav Eiffel's Laboratoire Aérodynamique in France; and the Deutsche Versuchsanstalt für Luftfahrt zu Adlershof and Ludwig Prandtl's Aerodynamischen Versuchsanstalt zu Göttingen in Germany.[12]

The NACA made a conscious decision to keep an arm's length from industry. The fear of co-optation apparently motivated those leading the NACA. Still, they recognized the importance of the industry, and the NACA's relationship to it, almost from the beginning of the organization. Accordingly, aircraft manufacturers were encouraged to submit proposals for research projects, and NACA was as eager to work on projects for civil aviation as military, but attempts by industry to gain membership on NACA's Main Committee and principal technical committees were repeatedly rebuffed. There were a few engineers employed by industry on technical subcommittees, but it was a source of discontent that industry was not welcome on the Main Committee. It was the

Main Committee that made the final decisions as to which research problems would be pursued and which would not.[13]

This was antithetical to Herbert Hoover's associative philosophy of the state. The activist secretary of commerce believed industry ought to govern itself. The federal government had an important role in bringing corporations together and in issuing the necessary regulations. This was the approach taken by the Aeronautics Branch of the Department of Commerce as well as the National Bureau of Standards (NBS).[14] George Lewis, NACA's director of research, staunchly resisted integrating industry representatives. He believed that it would be impossible to achieve equitable levels of representation, which would serve the best interest of science and engineering research, without making the NACA committees too large and therefore unresponsive to any organization's needs.[15]

As the aircraft industry recovered from its post-World War I slump, the pressure from industry to open up increased. Complaints about the NACA had begun as early as 1921, and though this sentiment persisted it did not receive much attention until Edward Pearson Warner, the onetime chief physicist at the Langley Aeronautical Laboratory, then MIT professor and assistant secretary of the navy for aeronautics, urged NACA to appoint industry engineers.[16] Warner was an "insider"—not just a former employee but also a member of NACA subcommittees (in 1929, he was invited to join the Main Committee). He was a highly respected engineer and author of the new standard textbook for aeronautical engineers (*Airplane Design: Aerodynamics*, 1927). Thus, when Warner made his recommendations to NACA Chairman Joseph Ames, he got a substantial hearing.

The answer from Lewis was still "no," but important changes were instituted. In general, Lewis and the other members of the Main Committee recognized the need to improve communication with industry. All saw the benefit of greater publicity and improved distribution of NACA technical reports. They conceded more slots on the technical subcommittees. NACA engineers were encouraged to make regular field visits to industry plants and allied research organizations (such as the Forest Products Laboratory of the Department of Agriculture or the NBS). These changes were viewed as positive, especially in light of the success that NACA had had with the start of annual conferences or "inspections" at Langley in 1926. The 1929 Collier Trophy seemed to confirm industry approval of the NACA's new openness.[17]

During the 1930s engineers in industry, at various universities, and employed by the NACA formed a cohesive technical community. The process of creating this community was not a straight-forward development. A good example of this which suggests the complex interconnections between social, cultural, and economic factors is the firing of the NACA's preeminent employee, Max Munk. Munk was the German "genius" recruited from Ludwig Prandtl's Göttingen lab. Inventor of the Variable Density wind tunnel and creative genius behind the propeller research tunnel, Munk transformed the NACA's Langley laboratory into a major research facility. However Munk's autocratic cult of personality had not found fertile soil at Langley. Further, many in industry had found him difficult to work with.[18]

For example, C. N. Montieth commented in a meeting of the United Aircraft Technical Advisory Group in 1929: "I might state that in that particular model we made for the NACA, I was instrumental in building this set of wings for the test. We had one set arranged with internal bracing so we could put the struts in or take them out, but they let Doctor Monk [sic] get hold of it finally and he held it so long we never did get the complete test. We were trying to find out what that interplane bracing interference amounted to on the ship but we never got the data."[19]

After all the engineers at Langley submitted letters of resignation to George Lewis, the NACA's director of research — threatening "him or us"—Munk was gone. The new modus operandi replaced the "research genius" paradigm with a research style based on teamwork with an emphasis on the problems of aeronautical engineering knowledge (rather than theoretical problems of aerodynamics). This change altered significantly the relationship between the engineers in industry and those working for NACA. Thus, the termination of Max Munk can be viewed as a critical turning point in the maturation of the aviation community.

At this point, it is useful to interject a clearer definition of the term "technological community." Technology, like science generally, is practiced in groups. Edward Constant has written that "technological knowledge comprises traditions of practice which are properties of communities of technological practitioners." These communities have specific ways of communicating, educational and career paths, and special interest groups such as engineering societies. Again, as Constant writes, these communities are more than simple aggregates of individuals and institutions. The most important attributes of a technological community are the knowledge and "traditions of practice" that "define an accepted mode of technical operation, the conventional system for accomplishing a specified technical task."[20]

Constant's insights are vital to this story and to a fuller understanding of the NACA. Contrary to popular assertion, the NACA was not subservient to industry but rather a full-fledged member of this technological community. Langley engineers soon found themselves central players helping establish traditions of practice that come to define what it meant to be an aeronautical engineer. This is a very different interpretation from Brooks's version, which pits corporate engineers against each other in a kind of Darwinian survival-of-the-fittest drama.

In other words, invention and design are not processes of discovering pre-existing solutions. The Douglas DC-3 was not a "better" airplane than the Boeing 247 because the engineers at Douglas were "smarter" than engineers at Boeing. Yet this is precisely what is often asserted. Airplanes do not develop in isolation; they are immensely complex technological systems built by engineers working within a broad-based community of engineers from industry, government agencies, university departments, and civil and military users.

As noted earlier the aeronautical community began a process of substantial reconfiguration in the late 1920s. Many of the elements that constituted the "traditions" and "practice" of this group were undergoing change. Eric Schatzberg has introduced the idea that technological communities also have ideological commitments. His research on the shift from wood to metal airplanes examines the aeronautical community's association of metal with "progress." In particular, Schatzberg writes: "Leading figures in the aviation community made their beliefs quite explicit, articulating these symbolic associations into a specific ideology of technical progress that I term the progress ideology of metal. According to this ideology, the shift to metal was an inevitable consequence of technical progress, part of the shift of engineering from art to science."[21]

In the history of the aeronautical community in the 1930s, ideology is indeed important, However, unlike Schatzberg, I do not see a single ideology; rather, I believe that there are many smaller, and sometimes competitive, ideologies. In addition to the ideology of progress, aeronautical engineers also had ideological commitments (in varying degrees) to a broad range of ideals, including safety, economy, control, materials (including manipulability or availability), professional status, and corporate or institutional success. The reconfiguration of the aeronautical community mentioned earlier, then, represents the emergence of a new ideological coalition (in which the "progress ideology of metal" was, perhaps, one of the most important). In other words, as the aeronautical community matured in the late 1920s, the social relations within that community changed, as did the ideas of what constituted technological practice and tradition.

The Langley laboratory in Hampton, Virginia, is important to this account because it is there that the NACA defined itself as the member of the aeronautical community that should be expected to be the leader in the creation "technological knowledge." There were three main ways in which NACA and industry related with each other during the late 1920s and 1930s. What follows is a working typology, classifying specific interactions according whether the NACA was acting as (a) Technology Benefactor, (b) Technology Servant, or (c) Technology Gatekeeper. These are not as rigid groupings. Indeed, certain interactions might fit under more than one heading.

The NACA did not found the Langley laboratory with the Edisonian expectations of an invention factory. The premise for establishing its own laboratory was essentially the cultivation of experts in the search for "practical" or rather, "engineering," solutions for the problems that the fledgling American aircraft industry could not figure out. The NACA was to be the supplier of conceptual tools and information that would enable other engineers to do their work better. In practice, the NACA did not limit itself to a responsive mode of action. Langley engineers were quick to apprehend technical problems and undertake a research program without any input from industry. Inquisitive and eager to make use of the incredible equipment, these researchers demonstrated little passivity. Still, the idea that Langley might become a "benefactor" of hardware to the industry initially did not find much fertile soil.

Gradually, this changed. One reason was a growing public acceptance of a federal role in scientific research. A decade of Republican enthusiasm for business and technology had altered the political and economic environment. Then too was the fact that the NACA's director of research George Lewis liked engineers who demonstrated intellectual initiative (within certain limits). While the NACA had never intended to provide "off-the-shelf" technologies, Lewis and John Victory (the NACA's secretary) were nonetheless extremely happy to have NACA research results praised by industry. By the late 1920s the NACA began to seek actively to have the "NACA" moniker attached to a specific aeronautical technology. The airfoil and cowling research are two especially good examples of the way the NACA began to embrace a new role as technological "benefactor."[22]

It is important to recognize that while most industry engineers cherished their NACA technical reports detailing the latest family of airfoils, not all the work of the NACA was held in such high esteem. In 1929, C. N. Montieth attended NACA's annual inspection at Langley and managed to instigate a fight during the usual "lovefest" session held at the end of the tour (ostensibly for the visitors to offer comments to NACA engineers and officials). Montieth posed a problem related to the design of the rudder and fin of an airplane and asked if NACA might provide a generalized solution. Professor Alexander Klemin of New York University said snidely that such theoretical work had been done in 1913 and why didn't the Boeing engineers just run some wind tunnel tests. Montieth snapped back that "he was very well aware that the fact that dihedral and fin area were interrelated was one of the fundamentals of airplane design, but the designer did not have time to make these classical investigations nor to wait for wind-tunnel results to answer these questions, as he was constantly being pushed to get the airplane out."[23]

Tempers were eventually calmed, but Montieth's comments revealed an emerging controversy in the aeronautical engineering community between engineers who identified themselves as "theorists" and those who called themselves "practical men." Many observers of the situation were beginning to call for a compromise. Lockwood Marsh, editor of the British journal *Aircraft Engineering*, wrote, using the example of the NACA cowling research program, that "it would be a bold man who would set himself up as the infallible arbiter of what is likely to prove of practical utility and what is not."[24]

As suggested earlier, over the decade, George Lewis began to permit more and more research projects that seemed more like industrial development than "basic" research. In fact in 1931, NACA announced that it had "decided to permit the use of the facilities of its Langley Field laboratory by individuals in the aircraft industry, providing they are willing to bear the expense of the research. Test projects not of general interest to the industry, yet capable of being carried out only at the Langley laboratory may now be conducted for the benefit of individual manufacturers, who will receive the results, though the Committee reserves the privileges of releasing them for general distribution at its discretion."[25] This is the new version of the NACA's original mission to serve industry. As a technological "servant," Langley engineers devised research programs that directly responded to the needs of industry. Increasingly however, these programs were cooperative endeavors that brought industry engineers to Virginia to participate in tests. Two particularly good examples of work fitting the "Technological Servant" category are its confidential studies of the stall characteristics of the DC-3 and de-icing studies, which began in the late 1930s (and which received the Collier trophy after World War II).[26]

Current scholarship on the history of NACA largely emphasizes aerodynamics research work. However, inspired by the new all-metal, stressed-skin monoplanes, two innovative and entrepreneurial engineers at Langley — Eugene Lundquist and Paul Kuhn — spent a decade creating a research program that they intended to be the central source of disciplinary knowledge about aircraft structures. Before the 1930s, NACA played a much more modest gatekeeping function — it advised, it suggested, and it distributed technological knowledge. But the development of a structures research program represented a shift from passive to active and even aggressive.

Prior to this period, if another government laboratory had facilities or expertise in a particular field, NACA would defer to it (and transfer the cash so the lab could undertake the desired research). George Lewis initially was furious with Eugene Lundquist when he learned that Lundquist had set in motion the events that would lead to Langley's acquiring its own structures laboratory in the late 1930s. "I've talked to you about NACA policy more times than with anyone else," Lewis angrily told Lundquist."[27] But Langley had made changes over the decade, including changes in how its engineers perceived the lab's relationship with industry. George Lewis could not control everything—much to his dismay—and initially he was unhappy about this development unleashed by Lundquist and Kuhn.

How Langley got its structures lab is a fascinating story. Briefly, the introduction of new designs for commercial transports placed tremendous technical demands on the engineers at the Bureau of Air Commerce (later the Civil Aeronautics Authority). The Langley engineers who had become deeply interested in structures seized the immediate opportunity to become the bureau's source for expert knowledge on aircraft structural engineering (and also as a means to get a structures lab). Almost immediately Langley's vision of its role in structures research became much more ambitious. In the following decade, the intellectual locus of structures engineering research (especially in the difficult area, compression studies) would shift from the U.S. Army's research facilities at Wright Field to Langley.

This short explication of the three types of research would be incomplete without some mention of the larger context of federal-corporate relations. While general studies by business historians such as Alfred Chandler and Louis Galambos are enormously helpful, historians have had a difficult time characterizing the nature of institutional relationships between business and government in the aviation sector. So too did contemporaries, however. The multiyear research project "Public Aids to Transportation," conducted by the Office of the Federal Coordinator for Transportation during the 1930s, summarized the work of NACA in a single footnote buried in the middle of its volume on "Public Aids to Scheduled Air Transportation":

> There would be some justification for including the cost of research work of the National Advisory Committee for Aeronautics. . . . Aviation research has been emphasized by the Government over research that would benefit other forms of transportation. Owing to the importance of defense considerations in these research activities and to the fact that no aid has been set up against other forms of transportation for such limited Government research as is conducted directly for their benefit, it is considered unnecessary to include a portion of the Committee's expenditures among the costs charged against scheduled air transportation.[28]

This report represented the single most comprehensive analysis to date on the nature and extent of federal contributions to commercial aviation, yet its authors (most of the report was prepared by Douglas L. Cullison and economist Paul T. David) made a categorical decision to exclude NACA from their study, asserting that it was too difficult to assess its contributions in conventional terms. Historians today should try harder. I hope this brief chapter has suggested a general methodical approach and a framework that will be useful to understanding the problem of the linkage between aviation, the business community, and the federal government in the interwar period.

NOTES

1. This expression has been attributed to Brown by R. E. G. Davies in *Airlines of the Unites States* (Washington, D.C.: Smithsonian Institution Press, 1984), p. 130. This work is based on research performed under contract with the National Aeronautics and Space Administration. A slightly different version was presented at the American Historical Association's annual meeting in New York City, January, 1997. The assistance of A. Gary Price, Roger D. Launius, Marion Kidwell, and Richard D. Layman is acknowledged. In addition to materials housed in the Langley Archives, some sources came from the library and archives of the National Air and Space Museum, Smithsonian Institution, Washington, D.C.; the Herbert Hoover Presidential Library, West Branch, Iowa; and the corporate archives of the Boeing Company, Seattle, Wash.

2. For a general survey of this period, see Roger E. Bilstein, *Flight in America: From the Wrights to the Astronauts*, rev. ed. (Baltimore, Md.: Johns Hopkins University Press, 1994), and Bilstein's detailed study of the 1920s, *Flight Patterns: Trends of Aeronautical Development in the United States, 1918–1929* (Athens: University of Georgia Press, 1983).

3. United States, Federal Coordinator of Transportation, Section of Transportation Service, "Passenger Traffic Report," 17 Jan. 1935, p. 21.

4. Evidence of this can be found in the annual reviews of the aviation industry published in *Aviation* or the Aeronautical Chamber of Commerce of America's *Aircraft Year Book*. See, for example, Edward P. Warner, "What Way, Air Transport?" *Aviation* 31 (Aug. 1932): 340–43; "Air Transport Gains Favor," *Aviation* 32 (Mar. 1933): 68–76; "The Old Year: The Turning Point Was Passed in 1933 and All Forces Are Moving Upward," *Aviation* 33 (Jan. 1934): 1–4; Edward P. Warner, "Aviation and the Government's Spending," *Aviation* 33 (Feb. 1934): 37–39; and *The Aircraft Year Book, 1934* (New York: Aeronautical Chamber of Commerce of America, 1934), pp. 1–6.

5. See William M. Leary, *Aerial Pioneers: The U.S. Air Mail Service, 1918–1927* (Washington, D.C.: Smithsonian Institution Press, 1985), and F. Robert van der Linden, "Progressives and the Post Office: Walter Folger Brown and the Creation of United States Air Transportation," in William F. Trimble, ed, *From Airships to Airbus: The History of Civil and Commercial Aviation*, vol. 2, *Pioneers and Operations* (Washington, D.C.: Smithsonian Institution Press, 1995). Also, it should be noted that this is the core narrative of two standard reference works for commercial aviation history, Henry Ladd Smith, *Airways: The History Commercial Aviation in the United States* (Washington, D.C.: Smithsonian Institution Press, 1991), and R. E. G. Davies, *Airlines of the Unites States*. For an excellent account of the impact of the Department of Commerce, see Nick Komons, *Bonfires to Beacons: Federal Civil Aviation Policy under the Air Commerce Act, 1926–38* (Washington, D.C.: Federal Aviation Administration, 1977). Thomas Worth Walterman, "Airpower and Private Enterprise: Federal-Industrial Re-

lations in the Aeronautics Field, 1918–1926," Ph.D. diss., Washington University, 1970, is a fascinating and detailed account of the origins of federal aviation legislation. Rexmond Cochrane, *Measures for Progress: A History of the National Bureau of Standards* (Washington, D.C.: Government Printing Office, 1966), includes information about the aeronautical research conducted by the National
Bureau of Standards.

6. The standard work on the NACA is Alex Roland, *Model Research: The National Advisory Committee for Aeronautics, 1915–1958* (Washington, D.C.: NASA SP-4405, 1985); see also James Hansen,
Engineer in Charge: A History of the Langley Aeronautical Laboratory, 1917–1958 (Washington, DC:
NASA SP-4307, 1987). A. Hunter Dupree's classic *Science in the Federal Government: A History of Policies and Activities to 1940* (Cambridge, Mass.: Belknap Press of Harvard University Press, 1957), makes
brief mention of the NACA.

7. Peter Brooks, *The Modern Airliner: Its Origins and Development* (London: Putnam, 1961).

8. In fact, the lone exceptions among serious scholarship are the works of Walter Vincenti, *What
Engineers Know and How They Know It: Analytical Studies From Aeronautical History* (Baltimore, Md.:
Johns Hopkins University Press, 1990), and Eric Schatzberg, whose doctoral dissertation and subsequent writings present an immensely valuable alternative interpretation. Schatzberg's study of the
shift from wood to metal is a fascinating account of the indeterminancy of technical choice. See Eric
M. Schatzberg, "Ideology and Technical Change: The Choice of Materials in American Aircraft Design between the World Wars," Ph.D. diss., University of Pennsylvania, 1990, and "Ideology and Technical Choice: The Decline of the Wooden Airplane in the United States, 1920–1945," *Technology and
Culture* 35 (Jan. 1994): 34–69.

9. Brooks, *Modern Airliner*, pp. 89–90.

10. Again, Vincenti and Schatzberg have included a strong call for a historical reassessment of the
1930s.

11. From Public Law 271, 63rd Congress, approved 3 Mar. 1915.

12. Roland, *Model Research*, chapter 1; A. Klemin and T. H. Huff, "Course in Aerodynamics and
Aeroplane Design, Part I., Section 1., 'Modern Aeronautical Laboratories,'" *Aviation* 1 (1 Aug. 1916):
9–16.

13. Roland, *Model Research*, p. 109.

14. Ellis Hawley, "Three Facets of Hooverian Associationalism: Lumber, Aviation, and Movies,
1921–1930," in Thomas K. McCraw, ed., *Regulation in Perspective: Historical Essays* (Cambridge, Mass.:
Harvard University Press, 1981); Ellis W. Hawley, "Herbert Hoover, the Commerce Secretariat and
the Vision of an 'Associative State,' 1921–1928," *Journal of American History* 61 (June 1974): 116–
40; and Gary Dean Best, *The Politics of American Individualism: Herbert Hoover in Transition, 1918–
1921* (Westport, Conn.: Greenwood Press, 1975).

15. J. C. Hunsaker, "Forty Years of Aeronautical Research," from the Smithsonian Report for 1955,
reprinted in National Advisory Committee for Aeronautics, *Forty-Fourth Annual Report, 1958* (Washington, D.C.: Government Printing Office, 1959), p. 10.

16. "Notes for Meeting of the Air Craft Men Monday, July 16, 1921," Herbert Hoover Papers, Herbert Hoover—Commerce Papers, Herbert Hoover Presidential Library, West Branch, Iowa, Box 39.

17. Roland, *Model Research*, pp. 108–10, 111–13.

18. For a full accounting of the firing of Max Munk at NACA, see Hansen, *Engineer in Charge*, esp.
pp. 84–95, 119–22.

19. Minutes of the Second Meeting of the Technical Advisory Committee of the United Aircraft
and Transport Corporation, 5 Dec. 1929, Boeing Historical Archives, Seattle, Wash., p. 214,

20. Edward W. Constant II, *The Origins of the Turbojet Revolution* (Baltimore, Md.: Johns Hopkins
University Press, 1980), pp. 8–10. Constant writes: "Such traditions encompass aspects of relevant
scientific theory, engineering design formulae, accepted procedures and methods, specialized instru-

mentation, and often, elements of ideological rationale. A tradition of technological practice is proximately tautological with the community which embodies it; each serves to define the other" (p. 10).

21. Schatzberg, "Ideology and Technical Choice," p. 52.

22. See for example, Norriss S. Hetherington's "Public Perception, Politics, and War: The National Advisory Committee for Aeronautics and Government Patronage for Scientific Research," unpublished manuscript, NASA History Office, Washington, D.C.

23. C. N. Montieth to G. W. Carr, memorandum, "Continued Report on Trip East," June 6, 1930, Boeing Historical Archives, Seattle, Wash.; NACA, Report of Proceedings of Fifth Annual Aircraft Engineering Research Conference, 13 May 1930, p. 21.

24. "Theory and Practice: Some New Thoughts on an Old Battle," *Aircraft Engineering* 1 (May 1929): 79.

25. "N.A.C.A. Opens Doors," *Aviation* 30 (Dec. 1931): 670.

26. For more information see NACA Research Authorization File 476, Langley Historical Archives as well as accounts in Hansen.

27. Eugene Lundquist, telephone interview with author, 6 May 1996. The policy was that Langley should not duplicate research performed elsewhere in the federal government. Lewis interpreted that restriction broadly and discouraged the construction of facilities that duplicated those found in other government labs. This had a profound effect on the type and conduct of research at Langley. Most aerodynamic and flight research proceeded unfettered, but propulsion and structures research had a stunted development path. This was later whitewashed by Jerome Hunsaker, who rationalized that NACA could not do everything and that structures and propulsion facilities were too expensive. Hunsaker, "Forty Years of Aeronautical Research," p. 23.

28. U.S. Federal Coordinator of Transportation, Section of Research, *Public Aids to Transportation*, vol. 1, *General Comparative Analysis, and Public Aids to Scheduled Air Transportation* (Washington, D.C.: Government Printing Office, 1940), p. 148.

CHAPTER 7

An Airplane for Everyman

*The Department of Commerce and
the Light Airplane Industry, 1933–37*

Tom D. Crouch

I
n spite of the warning signals, it was hard to believe that the crisis was actually at hand. By the end of 1992, American manufacturers had virtually ceased
production of single-engine light aircraft. The industry had emerged from the
tribulations of the immediate postwar years with a basic lock on the international market for personal aircraft and bright hopes for a "golden age" of private
flying. Half a century later, Piper, Cessna, Beech, and the other legendary giants
of the American light aircraft industry seemed to have abandoned the shrinking market for private airplanes.[1]

M. Stuart Millar, hailed as the "savior" of Piper Aircraft when he took over
the company in 1987, filed for Chapter 11 bankruptcy protection in 1991.
Cessna, purchased by General Dynamics in January 1992 and sold to Textron
three months later, had ceased production of single-engine light aircraft. Like
Cessna, Beech Aircraft was concentrating on the stable and lucrative corporate
market for twin-engine aircraft, turboprops, and turbojets. The Mooney Aircraft
Corporation, which continued to produce traditional light aircraft, was controlled by French interests.[2]

The immediate cause of the collapse was clear enough. Since the mid-
1980s, the threat of product liability suits against the manufacturers of light airplanes had led to a steady increase in purchase price. In 1993, the cost of well-
equipped, reasonably high-performance, single-engine aircraft could run as high
as $250,000. The passage of statute-of-repose legislation in the fall of 1994, lim-
iting the number of years for which a manufacturer could be held responsible
for a product, led Cessna and others to announce plans for the resumption of

single-engine aircraft production. It was clear, however, that a host of fundamental problems remained unresolved.

With the exception of avionics, the manufacturers of personal aircraft had proven remarkably resistant to technological advance. The past thirty years had produced only marginal improvements in the safety, comfort, and performance of light aircraft. The cost of flight instruction, fuel, hangar space, and maintenance remained very high. The need to develop competence in the use of the latest communications gear and avionics packages had become an absolute requirement, particularly for pilots who operate in the neighborhood of busy commercial airports.

Worse, the aura of romance that had once attracted young and old alike to aviation seemed to be slipping away. As one industry observer noted: "Unlike 40 or even 20 years ago, young people today are rarely seen climbing the airport fence for a closer look at aviation, and the kid who begs to wash aircraft in return for a flight is as extinct as a dinosaur."[3]

Puzzled aviation enthusiasts regarded it as a sad state of affairs for a nation where a significant number of people had once looked forward to the prospect of an airplane in every garage. But the reality of the situation had always been more complex than the aviation boosters supposed. For over half a century, the history of the light aircraft industry has been shaped by a fundamental tension between the rosy vision and high expectations of the aviation enthusiasts and the cautious restraint of manufacturers who must test their judgment-and risk their investment-in an unforgiving marketplace.

As Joseph Corn and others have noted, the notion that Americans would take to the skies in extraordinary numbers if only they were given access to appropriate (and appropriately priced) technology was an article of faith for air-minded dreamers of the 1930s.[4] More than any other American of the era, Eugene Luther Vidal was determined to transform that dream into a reality. During his tenure as director of the Bureau of Air Commerce, Vidal employed the full resources of his agency to encourage the development of a safe and inexpensive "airplane for everyman." A study of his effort illuminates the basic nature of the dream, the illusions on which it was based, and some of the practical realities faced by the aircraft manufacturers whom Vidal sought to enlist. In the end, the episode tells us a great deal about the nature of technological enthusiasms and innovations and attempts to artificially encourage their realization.

The Air Commerce Act of 1926 established a Bureau of Air Commerce within the Department of Commerce. Signed by President Coolidge on 20 May 1926, the legislation specifically empowered the bureau to establish airways; develop, operate, and maintain aids to navigation; license pilots; certify the airworthiness of aircraft and components; investigate accidents; and take other steps to foster the growth of air commerce. Under William P. McCracken, Jr. and Clarence M. Young, the first assistant secretaries for aeronautics, the organization functioned as a typical regulatory agency in the Progressive mold.

With the appointment of Eugene L. Vidal as director on 1 October 1933, however, of the Bureau of Air Commerce, expanded its area of responsibility to include the stimulation of light aircraft sales as a contribution to national recovery. An essential element of Vidal's "New Deal for Aeronautics," the bureau's attempts to guide aircraft manufacturers onto unfamiliar paths would have important implications for the aviation industry and help shape the public vision of the future of the airplane.[5]

As the son-in-law of Senator Thomas Gore, and a close friend of Elliot Roosevelt and Amelia Earhart, aviatrix heroine of Eleanor Roosevelt, Vidal had been a natural choice as an aeronautical adviser for the new administration. A graduate of the University of South Dakota with a degree in civil engineering, he had entered West Point in 1916, receiving a commission in the Corps of Engineers two years later. He transferred to the Air Service in 1920 and remained an army pilot until 1926. Following a season as football coach with the University of Oregon and a brief stint as a real estate salesman during the Florida land boom, he accepted a post as assistant general manager of Transcontinental Air Transport in 1928. The following year he became an organizer and general manager of the Ludington Lines, formed to operate hourly freight and passenger flights between New York and Washington.[6]

In February 1933 Vidal traveled to Warm Springs, Georgia, with Elliot and Eleanor Roosevelt and Louis M. Howe to confer with the president-elect on aviation policy. The visit prompted newspaper speculation that he was likely to be placed in charge of aeronautics in the "little cabinet" being planned by the president. He was named assistant director of the Aeronautics Branch early in 1933 and replaced Clarence M. Young as director the following September. J. Carroll Cone and Rex Martin, senior officials of the branch, had also gained congressional support for the appointment but had been unable to overcome Vidal's close ties to the administration.[7]

With Vidal's appointment, "the aviation industry found itself staring into the vivid face of the New Deal." The new director planned to transform his agency from a body whose primary concern had been the safety of the airways to one that could lead the industry back to prosperity through increased employment and sales. He provided a clear expression of his aims in a speech to the Society of Automotive Engineers in April 1934: "If there is such a thing as a New Deal for aviation, it is the recognition of the Government's additional duty to aid in the development of a sound aviation industry, which means above all other things, the development of greater markets for the products of that industry."[8] Vidal was certain that he had found just such a market in that symbol of depression-era America, the "forgotten man."

> The forgotten man of aviation is the private flyer, and his brothers are legion. They work at manual training branches in high schools and at engineering tables in colleges, and each dreams of the day when his inspired design will revolutionize aeronautics. They build model planes by the millions and trudge out to local airports each week-end to worship their idols from the ground and long for the day when they will have saved enough wherewith to buy a hop. They are the young business women and men who travel by air and would like to fly for recreation or sport or pleasure but cannot afford to. They are the older folks, who would like to include air travel in their daily social and business lives but have not yet met it within the ken of their experiences. They are the multitudes who admire Lindbergh and his wife and all others to whom the air is as commonplace as Sunday roads, and stand on the edge longingly-physically and mentally worthy of the kingdom of flight, but financially unprepared.[9]

Vidal was prepared to "unlock the gates of this paradise" by convincing the aviation industry of the existence of this enormous untapped market for very cheap aircraft and by assisting manufacturers to design, produce, and sell a "Poor Man's Airplane."

Little attention had been paid to the needs of the amateur pilot or to the possibility of a mass market for relatively inexpensive light planes in the United States prior to 1932. In America flying had remained a business for professionals. American aircraft manufacturers, who emerged from World War I much weaker and less experienced than their European counterparts, turned to the military services, commercial flying operations, and a growing number of business aviators as the most obvious markets for their products. The production of light aircraft for a potential market of sportsmen pilots seemed far too speculative a venture for firms that were devoting all of their energies to increasing the speed and carrying capacity of the airplane in an effort to meet the needs of an existing body of professional airmen.

Sport flying did become a popular activity in Europe during these years, however. Established aeronautical companies employed their increased productive capacity by supplying light airplanes for sale to large numbers of amateur pilots. In England alone De Havilland, Short, Parnall, Hawker, and Avro marketed one- and two-place machines powered by converted motorcycle engines or specially developed lightweight power plants like the 32 horsepower (hp)

Bristol Cherub. Flying clubs were organized, enabling novice aviators to obtain inexpensive flying instruction while sharing the cost of airplane ownership and maintenance. The British government, sensing the value of the movement to airplane manufacturers and recognizing the importance of a reserve of potential military pilots, encouraged the growth of private flying.

Sport aviation in Germany, where the manufacture of large aircraft was forbidden, followed a similar course. In this case state-sponsored glider clubs and competitions provided basic flight training for a generation of young German airmen.[10]

The enormous enthusiasm for aviation that swept over the United States in the wake of Charles Lindbergh's transatlantic solo flight of 1927 convinced a number of manufacturers that the time was at last ripe to offer light private airplanes to the public. Many of this first generation of American private aircraft were standard biplane models priced from $1,800 to $2,500. Specially designed closed cabin airplanes like the Velie Monocoupe ran as high as $2,675 in 1928. The expense of airplane ownership was not the only problem facing the sport aviator of the period, however. Very little thought had been given to the unique requirements of amateur flying. The airplanes available to the private pilot of the 1920s were designed to provide the increased power, speed, carrying capacity, and range demanded by professional business and commercial flyers. The resulting aircraft were not only priced beyond the range that the average pilot could afford but also were difficult for less experienced aviators to operate safely.

With the appearance of the Heath Parasol, the Aeronca C-2, the Curtiss-Wright Junior, and the American Eaglet by 1930, airplanes designed for private pilots were at last available in the $1,000 to $2,000 range. After 1933 other firms, including Porterfield, Rearwin, Welch, Taylor, and Piper were also offering closed-cabin airplanes for less than $2,000.[11]

In the minds of most Americans, however, sport flying remained an activity for the very rich. The absence of flying clubs such as those developed in Europe meant that a pilot had to bear the expenses of flying instruction and the purchase price of the airplane, as well as storage and maintenance costs, by himself (or, more rarely, herself). Manufacturers gauged their advertising accordingly, presenting airplane ownership as a symbol of social status. A Keystone-Loening ad in the *Sportsman Pilot* urged readers to "Join the 400" in "flying into the arms of Spring" in one of the firm's amphibians, while the Whittelsey Avion was touted as the perfect vehicle in which to travel to "the polo games at Rumson, a quiet week-end at Bar Harbor, or Newport in a Vampish mood." In an effort to interest aircraft companies in advertising in their magazine, the editors of *Country Life* argued that their readers were a perfect market for private planes. They pointed out that 98.7 percent of their readers were home owners, 80 percent traveled frequently, and 52 percent owned automobiles. When such a man buys a plane, the editors continued, "Price will not be an object."[12]

Eugene Vidal, however, was convinced that price should become a very important object. Soon after taking office as director of the Aeronautics Branch, he expressed his hope that "the New Deal may do for the airplane what the pioneers of mass production did for the automobile; convert it from a rich man's hobby to a daily utility or inexpensive pleasure for the average American citizen."[13]

Vidal believed that the most obvious route to recovery from depression for the aviation industry lay in the development of an airplane so inexpensive that private flying would no longer be the preserve of the wealthy. He envisioned a light, cheap machine that could be flown safely after minimum instruction. Such a craft, priced at current automobile levels of from $500 to $1,000, would make possible "an airplane in every garage." He outlined his thoughts on the prerequisites for meeting this goal in February 1934:

> The family airplane will arrive on the transportation scene in this
> country just as the family automobile made its entrance, by way of vol-
> ume production. There can be no substantial growth and development
> in private flying until there are low priced airplanes which can be eas-
> ily operated and maintained. Such an airplane can be made available,
> but if the price is to be within the reach of the average person, it must
> be produced and sold in large numbers. Ease of maintenance and cost
> of replacing parts are important, and these also are problems which
> depend upon large scale manufacturing.[14]

Vidal believed that his agency should assume the task of assisting industry to begin volume production of such a "poor man's airplane." He justified federal intervention in private industry by pointing to Post Office Department subsidies for commercial flying services carrying the mail. Moreover, he was able to cite the example of European governmental support for private flying. Nevertheless, the entry of the Aeronautics Branch into the field of light aircraft development was a radical departure from its traditional emphasis on the regulation of commercial aeronautics and the provision of aids for navigation. While Vidal believed that he was legally empowered to encourage the design of particular aircraft types by the original injunction to "foster the growth of air commerce," he sought specific congressional approval for the development program. John H. Geisse, a Vidal assistant, led the successful drive for an amendment to the Air Commerce Act of 1926 that enabled the Department of Commerce to "encourage and participate in such research and development work as tends to create improved aircraft, aircraft power plant, and accessories."[15]

Vidal had launched his plan to bring producer and consumer together even before legislative approval had been received, however. The first problem was to demonstrate that the market for inexpensive private airplanes was as large as Vidal suggested. In November 1934 he mailed a questionnaire to each of the 34,000 licensed pilots, student pilots, and aircraft mechanics in the nation. Those surveyed were asked if they would be interested in purchasing an all-metal, low-wing, two-place monoplane with a maximum speed of 100 miles per hour, equipped with flaps to drop the landing speed to 25 miles per hour. The cost of this craft would be only $700. At the same time, questionnaires were sent to industry leaders asking if they would be willing to produce this machine given financial support to retool for automotive-style mass production and a guaranteed market for 10,000 airplanes.[16]

During discussions with President Roosevelt, Vidal had not only been given approval to proceed with his program to encourage the manufacture of this "airplane for everyman," but he had also received a promise of a $998,000 Public Works Administration (PWA) grant to assist the aircraft industry during the first year's production. The president later reduced this sum to $500,000 during discussions with PWA authorities. A special committee was created to assist the branch in developing the most effective method of distributing the grant to industry. J. Carroll Cone, of the Aeronautics Branch; Amelia Earhart; George W. Lewis, of the National Advisory Committee for Aeronautics (NACA); Robert B. Renfro and Leighton Rogers of the Aeronautical Chamber of Commerce; Fred L. Smith of the National Association of State Aviation Officials; Edward P. Warner, editor of *Aviation* magazine; and Major Al Williams of the American Petroleum Institute were all named to the group. At an initial meeting of the committee on 4 January 1934, three subcommittees were appointed. The first of these, chaired by Vidal, was to cooperate with industry representatives in developing a plan for producing the airplanes. Another group was to concentrate on the selection of a suitable power plant, while a third would develop promotional literature. In addition, a technical board composed of three Aeronautics Branch officials was named to advise the full committee on engineering problems.[17]

By February 1934, 18,000 replies to the original questionnaires had been received. Of these, 14,000 expressed a desire to purchase the "$700 Airplane." A total of 9,000 respondents promised immediate purchase, while an additional 5,000 made their decision contingent on financial status, satisfaction with the final design, or other conditions. More important, 64,000 friends or acquaintances of the survey group also expressed interest in buying the airplane. It was clear that, as the journal *Western Flying* reported, amateur pilots and operators of small airports and flying schools were "almost rabid in their endorsement" of

Vidal's plan to revitalize the industry. In addition, many state aviation authorities and aeronautical parts manufacturers seemed to favor the scheme.[18]

While the popular press offered some support for the Vidal plan, aeronautical trade and professional journals generally viewed the possibility of a $700 airplane with guarded skepticism, underlining the economic and technical difficulties involved in building and selling so inexpensive an airplane on so large a scale. *Aero Digest*, for example, commented that the cost of distribution and marketing, subtracted from the $700 purchase price, would force production costs to less than $400. The *Sportsman Pilot* complained that the Vidal questionnaire raised "false hopes." The editor wondered, "where 10,000 pilots are to get hold of $700."[19]

The initial response from the aircraft industry was sharply negative. A reporter for *Aviation*, the most widely read periodical in the industry, remarked that manufacturers met the plan "with a shower of dead cats and brickbats."[20] A *Time* correspondent called attention to "the shrill yelp of suspicion, terror, and ridicule" emanating from the aircraft industry.[21] A *Western Flying* study of industrial reaction revealed that most aircraft manufacturers were either noncommittal or openly hostile toward the idea of a $700 airplane. Much skepticism was also reported among professional pilots. An *Aviation* survey of opinion in the aircraft industry showed that 64 percent of the airframe manufacturers and over 54 percent of the engine manufacturers were opposed to the Vidal program.[22]

It is not difficult to explain this negative response on the part of the aircraft industry. Many manufacturers and journalists believed that Vidal's $700 airplane was not a realistic goal. William B. Stout, a leading spokesman for the industry and president of the Society of Automotive Engineers, argued that the belief "one can 'build' a cheap airplane and sell it for $700 or anything near that price indicates a pathetic ignorance of the problem at hand."[23] An *Aero Digest* critic attacked the "just imagine" attitude of bureau officials. He recalled the story of two men discussing local restaurants. The first one exclaimed "Oh boy, just imagine-a thick sirloin steak, fried sweet potatoes, bread, coffee, and a piece of pie-all for fifteen cents!" "Yeah! Where can you get it?" asked his companion. The reply was-"I don't know, but just *imagine* it."[24] Another editor commented that the technical problems of producing an aircraft such as that described by Vidal for only $700 could be solved by reducing its size. "The dwarf who sat on J. P. Morgan's knee will be the pilot. This $700 airplane is for dwarfs. Under the New Deal a dwarf is going to amount to something in aviation."[25]

While journalists and industry leaders might joke about the Vidal plan, there was genuine fear that talk of a $700 dream ship by federal officials would

encourage prospective buyers of standard light airplanes to postpone their purchase until prices dropped. They pointed to the drop in auto sales in 1928 when
Ford announced plans for the Model A. Almost 70 percent of those surveyed by
Aviation expressed concern that the publicity surrounding the project had already retarded sales in a similar fashion. Grover Loening, E. E. Porterfield, and
other aircraft manufacturers decried the long-range effect of the "ballyhoo" and
"propaganda" on the industry. In addition, *Business Week* reported a general fear
among "experts of long aeronautical experience" that the private airplane was
not a sufficiently useful vehicle to command a mass market. Some authorities
believed that the production of a $700 airplane would lead to an increased num-
ber of crashes that would frighten potential airline passengers. Katherine Brown
Collings, for example, argued in a *Reader's Digest* article that Vidal's talk of a
"safe" airplane was premature and dangerous. A number of industry commen-
tators pointed out that the price of the airplane was being held at a high level
because of material, engine, and instrument costs. These men suggested the expenditure of the $500,000 in an attempt to reduce costs in these key areas. Un-
derlying all of this criticism was a general feeling in the industry that the federal aviation officials housed on the "Pennsylvaniaski Prospekt" would be well
advised to return to the development of improved navigational aids and aircraft
inspections and allow the aviation industry to proceed on its own course.[26]

In spite of their vocal opposition to the $700 airplane program, most air-
craft manufacturers chose to cooperate with the Aeronautics Branch in taking
the first steps toward implementing the scheme. Industry leaders found that
they could not afford to ignore the prospect of a $500,000 government contract.
Moreover, many manufacturers were unwilling to oppose the Department of
Commerce, "which, they hoped, might soon offer them a tastier dish." Thus,
members of the Aeronautical Chamber of Commerce, the aircraft industry trade
association, attempted to guide Vidal and his $500,000 grant down the path
that would prove most advantageous to the manufacturers.[27]

Meeting in New York on 9 January 1934, 22 members of the group adopted
a resolution of "wholehearted" endorsement for Vidal's proposal, on the condition that the PWA grant be made available. The manufacturers immediately appointed two industry committees. One, including representatives from the Curtiss-Wright Airplane Company, the Waco Aircraft Company, the Consolidated
Aircraft Corporation, and the Taylor Aircraft Company, was to develop performance specifications and the technical details of the new airplane. The second
committee was to establish a program for producing the airplanes. The Fairchild
Aviation Corporation, North American Aviation, United Aircraft and Transport, Curtiss-Wright, and the Aeronautical Corporation of America were represented on this committee. Industry leaders, speaking through the Aeronauti-

cal Chamber of Commerce Committees, recommended the creation of a new company to manufacture the "poor man's airplane." The entire $500,000 grant would be made available to the new firm, which would then offer stock to existing airframe and engine manufacturers. The established aircraft firms would provide business and technical guidance and personnel for the jointly held firm. In this way, any profit or loss that might accrue from the scheme would be spread evenly through the industry.[28]

News of the plan to use PWA funds to establish a new firm controlled by the aircraft industry reached administration officials already deeply concerned with the possibility of collusion between the large holding companies that dominated American aviation and the government officials who controlled the airmail contracts that were so vital to the economic success of the airlines. Since 1929 large firms like the United Aircraft and Transportation Corporation, North American Aviation, and the Aviation Corporation (AVCO) had built vertical combinations of major airframe manufacturers, parts and accessory suppliers, and commercial air carriers. By 1934, using their power to distribute the all-important airmail contracts, federal officials had forced the breakup of the large combinations. In such an environment, the Bureau of Air Commerce proposal to use federal dollars to create a new company that would be jointly held by the already tainted aircraft industry was bound to look suspicious.[29]

As early as 24 January 1934, Harold Ickes told President Roosevelt that he had heard rumors "indicating collusion between men in the government and outside interests as a result of which this money [the $500,000 PWA grant] will really be expended for the benefit of outside interests." Roosevelt expressed concern and suggested that Ickes continue to withhold money voted by the PWA.[30]

At a meeting of the Special Board for Public Works on 1 February 1934, Ickes advised Secretary of Commerce Daniel Roper that President Roosevelt had rescinded his approval of the $500,000 grant. Rather than broach the possibility of collusion without evidence, Ickes remarked that Roosevelt questioned the wisdom of the expenditure, pointing out that the government had provided similar subsidies for the automobile industry. Vidal's $700 airplane program had fallen victim to the Administration's mistrust of the aircraft industry and the desire to bring equity to the process of awarding government grants and contracts.[31]

With the collapse of the "poor man's airplane," the Bureau of Air Commerce shifted the emphasis of its development program from the subsidized production of very cheap aircraft to a well-publicized plan for purchasing light airplanes that met rigid performance and safety standards for use by bureau inspectors. This competitive purchase program had been devised some months earlier and was originally intended to operate as an adjunct to the $700 airplane plan.

While the new program was designed to produce a relatively inexpensive airplane, the question of price was now to be subordinated in order to encourage innovative designs that could be flown safely by novice pilots. Once such a craft was in existence, Vidal believed that consumer pressure would force manufacturers to produce the airplane for the general market, thus meeting the original goal of increased sales and employment while satisfying the administration's requirement for competitive bidding. With increased sales he hoped prices would drop back to the $700 level. Of the new procurement effort, a total of $180,000, drawn from bureau funds already earmarked for the purchase of aircraft to be used by inspectors and from War Department allocations to the development program, was spent by 1936.[32]

The Bureau of Air Commerce released the specifications to be met by the competitors in July 1934. The lowest bidder meeting the requirements was to be awarded a contract for twenty-five airplanes and publicity that might lead to the sale of thousands more. The aircraft to be purchased had to be all-metal machines with dual controls and side-by-side seating for a pilot and passenger. The requirements called for a useful load of 380 pounds, with a minimum range of 300 miles. A maximum speed of at least 110 miles per hour was specified. The airplane was required to take off and clear a 35 foot obstacle in 800 feet and land in 400 feet. Special emphasis was placed on ease of control on the ground and on full visibility for the pilot. Stalling and spinning were to be minimized. A full complement of instruments, including a turn-and-bank indicator, fuel gauge, altimeter, oil pressure and temperature gauges, compass, and tachometer were to be furnished.[33]

While preparing the specifications for the competition, bureau officials became aware of the work of a group of NACA engineers at the Langley Aeronautical Laboratory. In 1931, Fred E. Weick, a senior NACA engineer, had persuaded nine Langley engineers and mechanics to join an informal seminar, the object of which was to design an inexpensive light airplane to meet the needs of amateur pilots. In spite of industry indifference to the market potential of light aircraft, Weick's interest in the field was shared by a number of other American aeronautical engineers who had long been intrigued by the problems of designing a safe airplane for private pilots. Jean Roché and Harold Morehouse had designed and built the airframe and engine for the influential Aeronca C-2 in 1928, while employed at the Air Service Engineering Division at McCook Field in Dayton, Ohio. The Aeronca was later to become one of the first popular, closed-cabin light planes on the market. Robert T. Jones, now senior scientist with NASA's Ames Research Laboratory, recalls staying "up late nights in the small cafes . . . designing 'flivver' airplanes to be stamped out of metal."[34]

The Langley group first considered the uses to which such an airplane would be put and then developed the performance and flying characteristics best suited to amateur pilots. They believed that short field landings and takeoffs, spins and stall, and the incorrect coordination of the rudder and ailerons were the most important sources of difficulty for the novice aviator. They also determined that conventional light aircraft were frequently deficient in the areas of cockpit comfort and pilot visibility. A period of discussion and computation followed, during which the engineers devised alternative solutions to these problems. Three large flying models were constructed of the most promising designs.[35]

The most successful of these was Weick's contribution, which was to become known as the W-1. At the conclusion of the seminar, Weick invited the participants to carry the work to a conclusion by constructing a prototype W-1 in his garage. This aircraft was nearing completion in January 1934 when Bureau of Air Commerce officials visited Langley seeking advice on the specifications to be met by competing airplanes. In order to encourage the efforts of the Weick team, Department of Commerce officials requested that NACA conduct wind tunnel and flying tests of the W-1 to determine its performance and handling characteristics.[36]

As it entered the test program, the W-1 was not a revolutionary airplane. It did include a number of features that reduced the level of skill and judgment required of the pilot, however. A high wing pusher monoplane, it featured an auxiliary airfoil, or slat, fixed to the leading edge of the wing to facilitate low-speed flight and short field landing performance. The introduction of sufficient longitudinal stability, the presence of the slat, the limitation of the upward travel of the elevator, and the arrangement of the engine and propeller made it difficult to maintain the W-1 in stall, the condition in which the loss of air speed leads to decreased lift and usually forces the airplane to fall off in a spin. This was recognized as one of the most frequent causes of fatal crashes for amateur pilots.[37]

Perhaps the most notable innovation in the W-1 was the introduction of the tricycle landing gear. In normal aircraft, inexperienced pilots exhibited a tendency to force the nose down on landing and often had difficulty in controlling their machines on the ground, especially when winds were blowing across the runway. The steerable nose wheel and differential wheel brakes featured on the W-1 made it very difficult to nose the airplane over on landing and made steering during takeoff and landing a much simpler task. While many very early aircraft had featured three landing wheels, only the 1908 Curtiss June Bug had featured a steerable castering nose wheel that could be used to guide the craft on the ground. Weick's reintroduction of the tricycle concept was a key innovation.[38]

When first flown, the W-1 featured a standard three-axis control system, with a stick to control the airplane in the pitch-and-roll axis, and a swiveling foot bar that operated the rudder. Weick hoped to convert this to a two-control system in which movement of a wheel controlled the airplane in all axes of motion, freeing the pilot from the necessity of properly coordinating a stick and rudder pedals. The two-control system would certainly simplify the operation of the airplane, but it also severely limited the aerobatic potential of the craft.[39]

An engine failure during a W-1 flight test in September 1934 led to a forced landing and some damage to the airplane. The Bureau of Air Commerce funded the reconstruction of the airplane by the Kreider-Reisner Division of the Fairchild Aircraft Company under Weick's direction. The resulting W-1A differed from its predecessor in several significant respects. The fixed slat was replaced by flaps positioned on the trailing edge of the wings. Controlled by a lever in the cockpit, the flaps had the advantage of being used only when needed and made control of the airplane during landing easier than had the slat. Because of the size of the flaps, the normal ailerons employed on the W-1 were replaced by newly developed mid-wing slot-lip ailerons in the rebuilt machine. The most important alteration, however, was the installation of the two-control system in which the use of the rudder was eliminated.[40]

While *Aviation* touted the W-1 as Vidal's long-sought "safe" airplane, the Weick machine was not entered in the competition. This was primarily because of its experimental nature, fabric construction, and the fact that no plans had been made to produce the craft for sale. It was, however, purchased by the bureau and returned to NACA for continued testing. Many of the features demonstrated on the W-1A, including the simplified control system, the tricycle landing gear, and flaps were to appear on other entries in the competition.[41]

The official announcement of the competitive purchase program and the release of the specifications drew less initial criticism from industry than had the $700 airplane. The attempt to influence the direction in which manufacturers would move seemed much subtler and less dictatorial. The subsidized creation of a new market was to be replaced by an effort to publicize an airplane type so superior that a market would naturally coalesce around it. Convinced that the specifications for the competition were unrealistic, most experienced manufacturers chose not to take the radical step away from their standard designs required for entry. In the absence of the specter of a $500,000 grant being awarded to a competitor, large firms simply chose to ignore the program. As the publicity generated by the competition grew during the summer and fall of 1935, however, the industry would once again join aviation journalists in heaping ridicule on Vidal and his "all-mental" airplane.[42]

The sixteen bids submitted to the competition were opened on 27 August 1934. The low bid, of $750 offered by Arthur Williams, a tavern owner from Indianapolis, was rejected when it became apparent that Williams's "Safety Air Transportation Company" had no manufacturing experience. The remaining bids ranged form $1,650 to $16,425.[43]

The Hammond Model Y, manufactured by the Hammond Aircraft Corporation of Ypsilanti, Michigan, was declared the winner of the competition. The firm promptly received the promised contract for twenty-five machines at $3,190 each, the first of which was delivered to the bureau the following summer. The Model Y was a low wing pusher monoplane powered by a 124 hp engine. It featured a two-place completely enclosed cockpit and sported tricycle landing gear and flaps to shorten landing distances. It had a cruising speed of less than 110 miles per hour and a range of 500 miles. Perhaps the most interesting similarity to the Weick airplane, however, was the application of a simplified control system. This arrangement made the use of the rudder pedals unnecessary and led Dean Hammond, designer of the Model Y, to explain that the aircraft could be flown by any automobile driver after twenty minutes of practice. To climb or dive, the wheel was moved to the front or rear. Banking was accomplished by turning the wheel to the right or left as in an automobile.[44]

The first Model Y delivered did prove to be a safe airplane to fly, but its low speed and rate of climb disappointed bureau inspectors. Commerce officials also considered the original finish and workmanship unacceptable. Lloyd Stearman was assigned by the bureau's development section to supervise the construction of an improved version of the Model Y, which was delivered to Vidal on 16 April 1936. The reengineered craft featured a duralumin fuselage and had been sufficiently improved aerodynamically to meet the bureau requirements. As a commentator in *Aviation* noted, however, the Model Y was neither "(a) a $700 airplane or (b) the final answer to the problem of an airplane in every garage." Now known as the Stearman-Hammond Y1S, the airplane was produced in small numbers between 1936 and 1938. While the craft did excite much public comment and was the subject of several favorable articles in popular magazines, the promised mass market failed to develop.[45]

In addition to the Stearman-Hammond purchased under the rules of the competition and the W-1A acquired for experimental purposes, the Bureau of Air Commerce bought three other airplanes entered in the competitive bidding. Vidal took this step in an effort to publicize the potential of these machines as "family cars of tomorrow." The first of these aircraft to be purchased by the bureau was the Waterman Arrowplane, a tailless pusher prototype for a roadable airplane. Such a craft could be flown as a plane, then landed, and, with the wings folded, driven as an automobile. Designed and built by California aeronautical pioneer Waldo Waterman, the Arrowplane was purchased for $12,500 in January 1935. Bureau inspectors reported that the workmanship on the craft was poor and that the Arrowplane showed a dangerous tendency to stall and spin. They believed, however, that the roadable concept deserved further study. The Studebaker Company became interested in the Arrowplane and financed the construction of an improved version that it hoped to market, but it allowed the project to lapse prior to World War II. William Stout, director of research for Consolidated Vultee, attempted to revive the Waterman roadable several years later but enjoyed little success.[46]

The third experimental aircraft acquired as a result of the competition was a roadable autogiro manufactured by the Autogiro Company of America. Purchased in March 1935 for $12,500, this machine attracted a great deal of public attention. James G. Ray, vice-president of the firm and pilot for the delivery flight in the fall of 1936, landed the craft in a downtown park near the Commerce Building. He then folded the rotors, disengaged the propeller, and drove to the front door of the Commerce Department. Designed to combat the problem of inaccessible airports, the machine featured a single large wheel at the rear of the fuselage to power it on the highway. It had an airspeed of ninety miles per hour and a cruising range of three and one half hours. Although underpowered, it flew well as a one-man craft and made a number of publicity flights for the bureau. On one trip the roadability of the machine demonstrated its worth by allowing the pilot to land and drive to a filling station when oil pressure dropped dangerously low. In the eyes of Commerce officials, the autogiro "clearly demonstrated the utility of such a means of transport."[47]

A final competition entry, the Curtiss-Wright Coupe, was also purchased for use by inspectors. This airplane was acquired to study the application of its stressed metal skin to light plane construction.[48]

By 1936 the Bureau of Air Commerce light aircraft experiments were coming to a close. The development program had failed to achieve the basic goal of assisting the recovery of the aircraft industry by encouraging the growth of a mass market for light aircraft. Commerce officials had been extraordinarily successful in drawing attention to the special requirements of the private pilot, however. The most important technical innovation popularized by the program, the tricycle landing gear with steerable nose wheel, was adapted to military and commercial aircraft. Moreover, continued bureau efforts in this area led to the development of the cross-wind landing gear that was to add to aviation safety and save millions of dollars in airport design and construction costs. The gear obviated the need to reorient runways to overcome problems with prevailing winds. The emphasis on safe handling characteristics, all-metal construction, cockpit comfort, and improved field of vision for the pilot, as well as the reduction of stall-spin accidents, was an important factor leading to the introduction of these features in production-model light aircraft. Bureau efforts to encourage the construction of local airports and to create improved navigation aids and inspection procedures for pilots and airplanes also helped to create a firm foundation on which private flying could develop.

In addition to influencing the development of light aircraft technology, the Bureau of Air Commerce experiments played an important role in shaping the public attitude toward the future of private flying. As industry leaders feared, the enormous publicity engendered by the $700 airplane plan and the competitive purchase program was enthusiastically received by the general public. The idea of an airplane that was safe and simple to fly-and available at a price that would be competitive with that of an automobile-made the Bureau of Air Commerce airplanes a natural subject for newspaper and magazine feature stories. Articles with titles like "Flying as Simply as Driving-Almost" lauded the goals of the Vidal effort and forecast the day when the airplane would rival the automobile as a means of mass transportation. News reports of the potential of "revolutionary" safe aircraft, autogiros, and roadable airplanes led many readers to suppose that the postwar world would witness the age of an airplane for everyone. The flood of popular articles did not cease with the conclusion of the programs. Mass circulation magazines continued to talk of "Planes for All," "Wings for the Average Man," and "Your Family Plane of Tomorrow" in the wake of the experiments. A 1944 *Collier's* survey of the postwar market for private aircraft revealed that 65 percent of the civilians who hoped to purchase airplanes preferred roadable or helicopter types. It is clear that Vidal's vision of a future that included safe, easily flown, inexpensive airplanes had been accepted by the reading public.[49]

In spite of these long-range benefits resulting from the Vidal effort, aviation journalists, politicians, and aircraft industry officials continued their bitter attacks on the Bureau of Air Commerce programs. The manufacturer's response to an Aeronautical Chamber of Commerce request for comment on the status of the light aircraft competition in April 1936 left little doubt as to the complete opposition of the industry. C. N. Montieth, vice-president of Boeing, spoke for many when he remarked: "Making 'light' and 'cheap' the range lights of the development will give us nothing but an aerodrome toy. . . ." William Crosswell, sales manager for Curtiss, believed that "the Government's development of an entire airplane is . . . in direct competition with and not favorable to a healthy aircraft industry." Carl de Ganahl, president of Fleetwing, was totally opposed to the bureau effort, suggesting that Vidal's time would be better spent in promoting improved airports, weather reporting facilities, and radio aids to navigation. Great Lakes Aircraft officials argued that the market envisioned by Vidal did not exist, while Walter H. Beech, a pioneer producer of business airplanes, doubted that "government expenditures of this kind are ever beneficial." Even accessories manufacturers like Hamilton Standard Propellers saw little benefit in the Department of Commerce project. W. C. Jamoneau, vice president of the Taylor Aircraft Company, summed up the feeling of the industry in his comment, "Enough blundering has been done to suffice for a considerable time."[50]

E. E. Porterfield, president of Porterfield Aircraft Corporation, publicly assailed Vidal and the light airplane programs at the All-American Aircraft Show in Detroit in August 1935. In an article published the following month, Porterfield remarked, "Publicity on this subject has been looked upon with suspicion by practically everyone who has read it this year, as the Development Section of the Bureau of Air Commerce has definitely proved that there is not a possibility of getting a 'safe $700 airplane' at this time."[51]

Cy Caldwell, an aviation writer who had long been a bitter critic of Department of Commerce aviation policy, commented on the damage that he believed the program had done to Vidal and his agency:

> Vidal got the small airplane by the tail, and the man with the bear's tail in his grasp is afraid to let go. The future of the Bureau of Air Commerce under his direction is bound up with the fate of his $700 airplane experiment. Publicity has almost ruined him . . . and he must accept the blame for it. But the $700 airplane must be a nightmare to him as it is to the industry. It has turned and bitten us all, and we will not be safe until it is laid low.[52]

During the course of the 1936 Senate hearings that preceded Vidal's resignation the following March, Senator Royal S. Copeland (D-N.Y.), an opponent of Roosevelt Administration aeronautical policy, offered another particularly harsh criticism of the director as "[t]he appointee who has (and still is) clamoring for a 'safe' $700 airplane, and damning all our present airplanes as unsafe. Mr. Vidal has demonstrated the very essence of bureaucratic ineptitude and pusillanimous poltroonery. The President once stated that if any of his experiments did not work, that he would admit it. The Vidal experiment has not worked."[53]

Frank Tichenor, editor of *Aero Digest*, a journal that had consistently opposed almost every phase of Vidal's program, joined Senator Copeland in his judgment of the "silly $700 airplane fiasco." He cited the experiments as a major element in the failure of New Deal aviation policy. He placed the blame for this failure on the shoulders of

> [l]ittle officials trying to make big names for themselves, even though they nearly wrecked the market for private aircraft. Men who have

never been successful in any commercial aviation venture discrediting, by means of their public position, the business sense of manufacturers turning out sound products on the only financially feasible basis possible at the present time.

... Do you think it was easy for the private manufacturers to go on improving their ships with these bureaucrats barking at the heels of their prospects about "foolproof" airplanes at $700?[54]

It would be difficult to find a series of condemnations of any government program harsher than those directed against the Bureau of Air Commerce. Clearly, Vidal had touched a raw nerve in the industry.

The violent reaction of the airframe and engine manufacturers to the Department of Commerce effort focuses attention on a central contradiction in New Deal industrial policy. While administration officials sought to aid business recovery and promote increased employment, they were also determined to protect the interests of the small businessperson and the citizen. In dealing with the oligopolistic firms that dominated aviation, these two goals proved irreconcilable. In directing the growth of the private airplane programs, the interests of the consumer, as interpreted by the Bureau of Air Commerce, were clearly more important to the Roosevelt Administration than were those of the aircraft industry. Vidal's initial $700 airplane scheme attempted to blend the needs of both groups. For the citizen it promised a superior product at low cost. The industry would benefit by a direct subsidy to be applied in a manner chosen by manufacturers. While industry leaders were not enthusiastic, they were willing to go through the motions of cooperation, for they perceived the plan as an honest, if impractical, attempt to deal with the needs of both business and the public. Ickes and Roosevelt rejected the proposal, however, because of a fear that the leaders of the giant aeronautical firms would accept the subsidy while continuing to ignore the requirements of the private pilot.[55]

The alternative competitive purchase plan was much closer to the ideological center of New Deal business philosophy, emphasizing product safety, consumer needs, and the right of the small businessperson to compete for government contracts. Spokespersons for established aeronautical firms viewed the new effort as a direct attack on their industry and its product, however. The implication that airframe and engine manufacturers were not making an honest effort to produce the best possible airplanes at reasonable prices was unmistakable. Industry leaders feared that the publicity surrounding the airplanes involved in the competition would persuade the public that the intransigence and conservatism of the manufacturers was all that stood in the way of vast technical improvements in light aircraft technology. The attack on Vidal was, therefore, a defense of current efforts to produce moderately priced airplanes that were safe and met the reasonable requirements of private flying. Manufacturers were convinced that the private airplane "enthusiasts," led by Vidal, were attempting to wrest control of economic decision making from the business community by creating public pressure calling for the realization of impractical goals.

This tension between the vision of the innovative enthusiast and the economic and technical realities faced by the businessperson remains in force today. At a fundamental level, Eugene Vidal was wrong. While a great many Americans may well dream of taking to the skies, formidable difficulties bar their way. Flying is not like driving an automobile. It is an unforgiving pursuit that demands a high degree of concentration and specialized skill. The difficulties and the costs of acquiring appropriate training and maintaining the required skills are high enough to dissuade most would-be aviators.

Moreover, the market for light aircraft is not particularly elastic. The basic costs of an airplane, flight training, fuel, and maintenance are major factors limiting the number of active pilots. Recognizing this fact, postwar manufacturers of light aircraft were rarely willing to raise the basic purchase price of their machines by undertaking major programs of research and development or by adding expensive improvements to their existing products. In such a cost-sensitive market, the advent of a new and unforeseen problem, such as a sudden rise in product liability suits, was bound to have a catastrophic impact.

The manufacturers of single-engine light aircraft, fully aware of the limitations of their market, would not soon forget the lessons of the Bureau of Air Commerce programs. When discussions of renewed work on light plane control systems were held at the bureau in 1939, one veteran of the earlier episode counseled that "no steps be taken to participate in the proposed type of experimental development until an account of what occurred a few years ago be made available for study. . . . Any appreciable publicity, we believe, would be fatal, due to the anti-climax of actual results obtained."[56]

NOTES

1. "Obsolete Designs, Shrinking Customer Base Spell Doom for U.S. Light-Aircraft Industry," *Aviation Week and Space Technology*, 24 Dec. 1990, pp. 68–69.

2. Ibid.; "Piper Seeks Bankruptcy Protection, Ceases Operations Pending Reorganization," *Aviation Week and Space Technology*, 8 July 1991, p. 24; "Who Will Build New Light Airplanes," *Flying*, Apr. 1991, p. 44; "Textron Buys Cessna from General Dynamics," *Flying*, Apr. 1992, p. 24.

3. "Obsolete Designs," p. 68.

4. Joseph J. Corn, *The Winged Gospel: America's Romance with Aviation, 1900–1950* (New York: Oxford University Press, 1983).

5. Donald R. Whitnah, *Safer Skyways: Federal Control of Aviation, 1926–1966* (Ames: Iowa State University Press, 1966); Nick Komons, *The Cutting Air Crash: A Case Study in Early Federal Aviation Policy* (Washington, D.C.: Government Printing Office, 1973).

6. W. B. Courtney, "Wings of the New Deal," *Collier's* 93 (17 Feb. 1934): 12; "Eugene Vidal Named Head of Aeronautics," *New York Times*, 20 Sep. 1933; "Vidal Made Chief of Air," *New York Times*, 1 Oct. 1933; Eugene Vidal Biographical File, National Air and Space Museum Library, Smithsonian Institution, Washington, D.C.; "Chief of Airways," *Time*, 18 Dec. 1933, p. 46.

7. "Roosevelt Due to Coordinate Air Activities," *Washington Herald*, 1 Feb. 1933; "Vidal, Former Army Flier, Urged for Aviation Post," *Washington Herald*, 20 Feb. 1933; Whitnah, *Skyways*; Komons, *Cutting Crash*.

8. Eugene Vidal, Address to Michigan Aeronautical Activities Association and the Detroit Section, Society of Automotive Engineers, 16 Apr. 1934.

9. Courtney, "Wings," p. 48.

10. Terence Boughton, *The Story of the British Light Aeroplane* (London: Aerofax, 1963).

11. Paul Matt, "Aeronca C-2," *Historical Aviation Album* 10 (Temple City, CO, 1971); Walter J. Boyne, "Those Anonymous Cubs," *Aviation Quarterly* 1 (Winter 1975): 252–81; "The Light Plane Situation," *Aviation* 30 (Feb. 1931): 80.

12. "Profile of a Prospect for a Private Plane," *Sportsman Pilot* 11 (Sep. 1929): 11.

13. Vidal, "Address."

14. Eugene Vidal, "The Poor Man's Airplane," *Western Flying* 14 (Feb. 1934): 9.

15. *Congressional Record* 80 (16 June 1934): 12203.

16. Edward P. Warner, "$700—And How?" *Aviation* 32 (Dec. 1933): 379–80; "$700 Private Plane," ibid.; Eugene L. Vidal, "Low Priced Airplane, "*Aviation* 33 (Feb. 1934): 40; Vidal, "Poor Man's Airplane"; Eugene Vidal, interview with Charles E. Planck, Apr. 19, 1962, transcript in National Air and Space Museum Library; "A Memo to Commercial Aviation, Dec. 1933," in box 344 Record Group 237, CAA Central Files, National Archives. Hereafter cited as CAA Files.

17. "A Memo"; "Dept. of Commerce New Release, Jan. 4, 1934," CAA files; Vidal, "Poor Man's Airplane"; Vidal interview; "Release No. 362—Federal Emergency Administration of Public Works," CAA Files; *Aircraft Yearbook*.

18. Vidal, "Poor Man's Airplane"; Vidal, "Low Priced Airplane"; "News of the Month," *Aviation* 33 (Jan. 1934): 25; "What the Industry Thinks," *Western Flying* 14 (Feb. 1934): 11.

19. Courtney, "Wings." For trade journal reaction, see "Chief of Airways."

20. "This Light Plane Business," *Aviation* 34 (Dec. 1935): 25.

21. "Chief of Airways."

22. "What the Industry Thinks"; "This Light Plane Business."

23. William Stout, "A Few Fallacies Concerning the Cheap Airplane Idea," *Aero Digest* 27 (Sep. 1935): 15.

24. Frank A. Tichenor, "A Questionable Questionnaire," *Aero Digest* 23 (Dec. 1933): 13.

25. Cy Caldwell, "Little Rollo Goes to Washington," *Aero Digest* 24 (May 1934): 20.

26. "What Industry Thinks"; "What Price Family Planes?" *The National Aeronautic Magazine* 13 (Sep. 1935): 5; E. E. Porterfield, "No Possibility of Safe $700 Plane at This Time," ibid., 6; Grover Loening, "Industry Will Produce Cheap and Safe Plane Not Government," ibid., p. 7; Caldwell, "Little Rollo"; Stout, "A Few Fallacies"; "$700 Airplanes," *Business Week*, 3 Feb. 1934, p. 12; "Flivver Plane," *Business Week*, 1 Sep. 1934, p. 10; Katherine Brown Collings, "Flying Is Still Dangerous," *Readers' Digest* 25 (July 1934),: 40–43.

27. "700 Plane," *Time* 22 (6 Jan. 1934): 46; "Chief of Airway"; "Flivver Plane," *Business Week*, 1 Sep. 1934, p. 10.

28. "700 Plane"; Digest of Minutes, Aeronautical Chamber of Commerce of America, Inc., 4 Dec.

1933; 9 Jan. 1934, Library Aerospace Industries Association of America, Inc.; *Aircraft Year Book For 1933* (New York: National Aeronautic Association, 1934), pp. 81–85.

29. For a detailed account of the merger period, see John B. Rae, *Climb to Greatness: The American Aircraft Industry, 1920–1960* (Cambridge, Mass.: MIT Press, 1968), pp. 39–49.

30. Harold L. Ickes, *The Secret Diary of Harold L. Ickes* (New York, 1953), vol. 1,pp. 142–43.

31. Minutes of the Special Board for Public Works, 1 Feb. 1934, Record Group 135, National Archive and Record Administration, Washington, D.C.

32. *Department of Commerce Appropriations Bill for 1937, House Hearings* (Washington, D.C.: Government Printing Office, 1937), pp. 192–95; Vidal, "Address."

33. "The Department of Commerce Light Plane Specifications," *Aviation* 33 (July 1934): 208; "Wanted—25 Planes," *Western Flying,* 14 (June 1934): 8; Edward P. Warner, "The Bureau of Aeronautics Writes a Specification," *Aviation* 33 (July 1934): 218.

34. Matt, "Aeronca"; Robert T. Jones, "Recollections from an Earlier Period in American Aeronautics," *American Review of Fluid Mechanics* (1977, Paper 8094), p. 7; Updated Memorandum, John Geisse to W. S. Campbell, CAA Files; "The Status of the Vidal Plane," *Western Flying* 14 (Mar. 1934): 19; Planck interview; Vidal, "Address."

35. Fred E. Weick to Tom D. Crouch, Aug. 12, 1976; Fred E. Weick to John H. Geisse, Jan. 19, 1934; Fred E. Weick, "The W-1 Airplane," *Aviation* 33 (July 1934): 209–12.

36. Weick to Crouch; Weick to Geisse; Weick, "W-1"; Fred E. Weick, interview, transcript in NASA History Office, Washington, D.C.

37. Weick to Geisse; Weick, "W-1"; see Oliver Stewart, *Aviation: The Creative Ideas* (New York, 1966), for a discussion of slots, slats, flaps, and other devices to control air flow at low speeds.

38. Weick interview; Weick to Geisse; Weick, "W-1."

39. Ibid.

40. Fred E. Weick, "The W-1A Airplane," *Aviation* 35 (Jan. 1936): 17–20; Weick to Crouch.

41. Weick resigned his NACA post in 1936 to join a firm interested in producing an airplane based on the advantages demonstrated by the W-1A. The resulting Ercoupe was introduced in 1940 and proved to be a very popular airplane prior to and following World War II.

42. Cy Caldwell, "Boners of a Bureau Bungler," *Aero Digest* 27 (3 Feb. 1934): 9.

43. "Flivver Plane"; "Arup Flivver Plane for Private Flying," *Newsweek,* 3 Feb. 1934, p. 9.

44. *Now You Can Fly: The Stearman-Hammond Model Y,* sales brochure, n.d.; "Building the Model Y Airplane," *Western Machinery,* May 1937, 19–26; "The Hammond Model Y Airplane," undated press release, National Air and Space Museum aircraft files; "A New Tool for Business in the Air," Stearman-Hammond news release, 29 Dec. 1936, National Air and Space Museum aircraft files; "Foolproof Plane for Novice Is Easy to Fly," *Popular Mechanics,* July 1936, p. 17; "Flying Equipment," *Aviation* 35 (May 1936): 31. The Stearman-Hammond Model Y is now in the collection of the National Air and Space Museum.

45. "Flying Equipment"; Avery McBee, "Flying as Simple as Driving—Almost," *Readers' Digest* 30 (Jan. 1937).

46. "Waterman Arrowbile," *Historical Aviation Album* 13 (Temple City, Colo., 1965), pp. 132–38; John H. Geisse, "Airplanes for Private Owners," *National Aeronautic Magazine* 13 (Sep. 1935): 5–7; Fred D. Fagg Jr. to Assist. Sect. Johnson, 6 July 1937, CAA Files. The Waterman Aerobile, a development of the Arrowplane, is in the collection of the National Air and Space Museum.

47. Fagg to Johnson; John H. Geisse, Memo to Chief, Safety and Planning Division, 14 Aug. 1937, CAA Files; "Flying Equipment," *Aviation* 35 (Nov. 1936): 33. The roadable autogiro is now on exhibit in the National Air and Space Museum.

48. Eugene Vidal to Sen. Royal S. Copeland, 3 Mar. 1936, in *Safety in the Air,* part 2 (Washington, D.C.: Government Printing Office, 1936), p. 842.

49. "Planes for All," *Business Week,* 12 June 1943, pp. 105–106; "Wings for the Average Man,"

American Explorer 132 (May 1943): 32; "Your Family Plane of Tomorrow," *Better Homes and Gardens* 22 (Sep. 1942): 30.

50. Leighton Rogers to all manufacturing members, Aeronautical Chamber of Commerce of America, 30 Apr. 1936; C. W. Monteith to L. Rogers, 6 May 1936; W. J. Crosswell to L. Rogers, 13 May 1936; G. W. Vaughan to L. Rogers, 12 May 1936; C. de Ganahl to L. Rogers, 1 May 1936; C. Barandt to L. Rogers, 5 May 1936; W. H. Beech to L. Rogers, 2 May 1936; R. Welsh to L. Rogers, 12 May 1936; W. C. Jamouneau to L. Rogers, 5 May 1936. All memos and letters in the collection of the Aerospace Research Center, Aerospace Industries Association of America, Inc. The author wishes to express his thanks to Ms. B. A. Perry of the AIAA Library for her assistance in uncovering these and other materials.

51. Porterfield, "No Possibility"; "Seeking Flying Flivver: Bureau of Air Commerce Meets Opposition from Aircraft Manufacturers," *Literary Digest* 120 (3 Aug. 1935): 16.

52. Caldwell, "Boners," p. 16.

53. Royal S. Copeland, quoted in "Vidal Statistics," *Aero Digest* 28 (June 1936): 25.

54. Frank Tichenor, "Air—Hot and Otherwise," *Aero Digest* 27 (Nov. 1935): 13.

55. Frank Friedel, *Franklin D. Roosevelt: Launching the New Deal* (Boston: Little, Brown, 1973), provides the best introduction to New Deal business policy.

56. E. P. Warner to members of the CAA, 14 Nov. 1939, CAA Files; see also Clinton M. Hesto to E. P. Warner, 9 Jan. 1940, CAA Files.

CHAPTER 8

Paths for Flight

Innovation and the Origin of Radar

Louis Brown

ANTECEDENTS

F ew things have altered the way modern civilization functions more than air transport, and certainly nothing has transformed the nature of warfare so much as air power. For these phenomena to have happened to the extent we know them required two inventions: powered aircraft and radar. This is sufficiently well understood, both by the technically trained and the generally educated public, to be considered common knowledge. The origins of powered flight have been studied and reported to the smallest details and are appreciated and understood by a respectably large portion of the population, while the origins of radar have had substantially less study and are known to very few, and to them in forms that seldom have historical balance. This is a direct consequence of the secrecy that enveloped radar's development before and during World War II, which prevented any of the engineers and scientists who wrote of their experiences afterward from knowing what happened in other laboratories, friendly or enemy.

When war came to Europe in 1939, eight nations had radio location projects under way: the United States, Britain, Germany, France, Holland, Italy, Japan, and Russia. Of these, the first three developed technically advanced equipment and deployed them in large quantities, but the mere existence of the other five demonstrates clearly the operation of a technical imperative. Radar had been "in the air" during the decades before the outbreak of war, and its invention and early evolution cannot be properly understood from a national point of view.

Heinrich Hertz reported phenomena in his 1887 demonstrations of the existence of electromagnetic waves suggestive of radar. Indeed, the continuous bands he employed were just those of early radar, wavelengths too short for the communication techniques that evolved from his work and soon neglected by experimenters. Only a few years later, Christian Hülsmeyer used similar apparatus to construct a transmitter-receiver set that allowed navigators to observe the direction to obstacles that a ship might encounter. He demonstrated it to ship owners in the harbor at Amsterdam in 1904, but a short range, which he was also unable to measure, produced no buyers.[1]

In 1922 Dr. Hoyt Taylor and Leo Young were experimenting with five-meter wavelength in the District of Columbia, moving a portable receiver on the opposite side of the river from the transmitter and noting variations in intensity caused by buildings and trees for small changes of position. A wooden steamer chanced to pass between the two units and produced large variations in the received signal. Taylor and Young were engineers in what was soon to become the U.S. Naval Research Laboratory (NRL) and were alert to any new method of locating a ship. Memoranda were filed and discussions held, but nothing more.[2] The reason for this was neither lack of imagination nor bureaucratic ineptness but the absence of the electronic components needed to make a radar set.

The introduction of the triode into wireless communication had removed the need for spark, arc, and mechanical alternator methods of generating high frequencies. It was also found capable of producing continuous waves of only a few meters. This was a basic need for a radio location technique, but the pulse method of determining range required a receiver capable of following the rapid changes in amplitude of the signal, and this was beyond the limits of triode circuits. In addition to a receiver, the apparatus would have had to have some way of measuring the time between the transmission and return of the reflected high-frequency pulse, and this required a cathode-ray tube that did not yet exist. This last statement requires some elaboration because Professor Karl Ferdinand Braun, the early radio eminence, had invented such a device in 1897, and it had seen continuous research use. Braun's tube as well as subsequent modifications operated at tens of kilovolts, as use of lower voltages resulted in the electron beam blowing itself apart through mutual repulsion of like charges, thereby producing a diffuse spot; it also needed the high voltage to make the spot on the glass glow. The high-voltage beam needed correspondingly high voltages to deflect it, voltages that the receivers of the time could not generate. Furthermore, using it was a laboratory experiment in itself.

The Western Electric company marketed in 1921 an oscilloscope that seemed to be just the trick: it accelerated the electrons with only a few hundred volts, incorporated a phosphor at the face that was easily illuminated by the beam, and could be deflected by voltages from the output of the electronic amplifiers of the day.[3] It had one disadvantage: it contained argon at low pressure from which a core of positive ions was formed by the electrons that neutralized their mutual repulsion and preserved a nice, thin beam. Unfortunately, the beam had to carry the positive ions with it to remain focused, and that, in effect, made the beam 80,000 times slower than an electron beam unencumbered by gas focusing. This tube became a favorite of experimenters working at wavelengths greater than three hundred meters and inspired designers to work on high-vacuum versions that focused the beam with the new science of electron optics.

Those working in government communications laboratories, where radio location was being considered, had very limited funds and depended on the fast-growing radio-broadcast business for the components with which to improve military equipment. There was, however, a part of what is now called the electronics industry that was obtaining generous amounts of money for research during the 1920s: television. The extreme popularity of the movies and radio broadcasting pointed strongly toward the combination of the two as a financial winner, and the requirements of television for components and circuitry were basically the same as for radar. In 1929 three engineers were independently working out the details of all-electronic, high-definition television: David Zworykin in the United States, Manfred von Ardenne in Germany, and Kenjiro Takayanagi in Japan.[4] High-definition television became possible with the invention of two critical components needed to follow rapidly changing video signals: (1) a receiver with a band width of about 6 MHz, which required multigrid electron tubes, and (2) a fast picture presentation, which required electrostatically focused cathode-ray tubes. These critical components were ready in 1929. In 1935 the BBC began operating broadcast television in London, and the 1936 Olympic Games in Berlin could be seen through the new medium. Radar grew from the availability of these new high-frequency components—a military technique that grew out of the development of civilian usage and the rare circumstance of a military use being of greater benefit to civilization than the civilian.

Electrical engineers working with meter-wave equipment during those years often found their signals affected by the presence of aircraft, and some published reports of this.[5] No one watching the amplitude-modulated television sets of the 1930s could have missed seeing the effects of the passage of an airplane. Modern television is frequency modulated and has automatic gain control that suppresses these effects, but a set operating at the limit of sensitivity can have its reception disturbed by the passage of aircraft, and the basic phenomenon is easily observed by persons walking around the room. That radar was indeed "in the air" is demonstrated by the papers published and patents issued before the war describing methods of determining distance by radio.[6]

UNITED STATES

In June 1930 Leo Young and Lawrence Hyland carried out experiments at NRL using 9.1 m communication equipment and noticed pronounced reflections from aircraft and obtained authorization to investigate radio location at low priority. They envisioned some kind of radio searchlight, which required centimetric wavelengths for a reasonable-sized mirror, wavelengths they did not have, so they continued with the longer wavelengths they did have. They were rewarded with more reflections, big ones from the airship *Akron,* and devised a system of transmitters and receivers spaced tens of kilometers apart that could detect the passage of aircraft, something of a "radio screen." Such a method of detection had no use for the U.S. Navy but was thought to be of use for the defense of cities, so Hoyt Taylor invited Major William Blair, director of the Signal Corps Laboratories, for a demonstration.

The Coast Artillery Corps had been given the responsibility of antiaircraft defense and had pressed the Signal Corps for methods of detection and gun laying that did not depend on vision. It was a subject that interested Blair, who had readily instituted research in microwaves and infrared, so he eagerly accepted Taylor's invitation. Blair found in the NRL "radio sensor" nothing new, which illustrates the general understanding of the fundamentals of radio location in 1930, and nothing of value in a method that did no more than indicate the presence of one or more airplanes somewhere within 50 kilometers. Blair's comments were evidently unfortunately worded; the meeting ended acrimoniously.[7]

Similar radio detection methods sprang up about this time in France and Russia and later in Japan; all three deployed them for air defense, but nothing from their experience can be found that invalidates Blair's snap judgment. The source of his statement that reflections from aircraft were not new is not recorded but very likely came from discussions with engineers of both RCA and Bell Telephone Labs, who had been working on meter-wave propagation during the late 1920s.[8] The Signal Corps Laboratory at Fort Monmouth was in the metropolitan New York area, where these tests were being carried out; this might also explain why the people at NRL, who probably missed these informal exchanges, considered their observations new.

In July 1934 Blair secured the approval of the chief of the Signal Corps to investigate a radio echo technique for the U.S. Army. He invited Dr. Irving Wolff of RCA to demonstrate his 10 cm equipment on Sandy Hook, the isolated spit in New York harbor. Wolff used parabolic reflectors for transmitter and receiver. He and Blair were able to determine the direction to ships moving in the harbor, but the power was insufficient for any practical use. They had reached the same position as Hülsmeyer had thirty years earlier, although they far surpassed him in being able to determine the speeds of automobiles through the formation of a beat-frequency signal resulting from the interference of the direct wave of the transmitter and the wave reflected from a moving target, which was shifted in frequency as a consequence of the Doppler effect, the basis also for Young and Hyland's experiment and the "radio sensor."

Wolff was certainly not the only experimenter working with microwaves. Dr. C. W. Rice was doing similar work at General Electric. In France, Camille Gutton experimented with 16 cm waves beginning in 1927 and mounted a collision avoidance set in 1935 aboard the new liner *Normandie* for a single trans-Atlantic crossing that left no desire among the deck officers to keep the equipment. In Germany Rudolph Kühnhold at the Nachrichtenmittel-versuchs-anstalt (NVA), the research laboratory of the navy, attempted in 1933 to use 13.5 cm equipment purchased from the firm of Julius Pintsch for radio location but with no more success than others.[9] All of these failures resulted from inadequate transmitter power. The oscillator used was the Barkhausen positive-grid tube in which output power was restricted in a fundamental way to less than a watt. Some began using the split-anode magnetron as a transmitter for very short waves, but its poor frequency stability prevented it from forming the basis of a useful system.

The people at NRL lost patience with microwaves first, as they saw no way to design anything without having substantially more power. Hyland left NRL and Taylor assigned a new man, Robert Page, to the task of radio location, but only part-time. In December 1934 he had succeeded in observing the reflection of pulsed waves from an airplane, but his use of a communication receiver had yielded a very blurred reflected signal. He ascertained the cause of the problem and designed the necessary broad-band receiver to remove it. His antenna was an array of dipoles with a mesh reflector that formed a moderately narrow beam. The work was not authorized and used funds intended for other projects. It is said that Page kept a pair of earphones connected to the receiver as a disguise.[10]

By December 1935 the Signal Corps had nothing to show for the microwave work and decided to try longer wavelengths, so William Hershberger visited NRL to see what Page had accomplished. The Signal Corps people were sufficiently impressed to push meter-waves immediately. At about this time Blair had had to retire because of ill health, and Lieutenant Colonel Roger Colton replaced him as laboratory director. Blair's strengths had lain in scientific insight, Colton's in getting things done, so the change worked out well, especially because Colton was enthusiastic about radar from his first encounter with it.

Both laboratories were working with scavenged funds for radio location during those years. Taylor found it necessary to go to an influential member of the House Naval Appropriations Committee for help and secured $100,000 in 1935.

Major General James Allison, chief signal officer, requested $40,000 for radio location from the War Department and was refused. He told Blair to use funds from $75,000 appropriated for another project, but, please, have something to show by the end of the fiscal year, June 1937! What was shown was the result of much unpaid overtime and weekends and proved capable of obtaining $250,000 with no serious questions about misuse of funds.[11]

In mid-1937 NRL showed its equipment to two electronics companies, RCA and Bell Telephone, in order to interest them in the new technique, either for production or for development. RCA had continued the 10 cm work by Wolff, which in 1939 would prove capable of ranging ships and buildings at distances of one or two kilometers with a pulsed system. They were interested in producing the set NRL was preparing for the navy exercises in early 1939 but preferred to enter a meter-wave design of their own. Radio location was new to the representatives of Bell Labs, who left to discuss the matter with their administrators. Their decision was to work on radar on their own, as the government did not enter into development contracts; Bell set up a laboratory at Whippany, New Jersey, to study the technique at their own expense. They were impressed with the NRL 1.5 m equipment and decided it would be better to attempt shorter wavelengths, using their skills in the design of appropriate new vacuum tubes.

The NRL demonstrated its 1.5 m air- and surface-warning radar, XAF, in the Caribbean fleet exercises of early 1939. It was mounted on the USS *New York*, and the rival RCA set, CXZ, on USS *Texas*. The line officers who were permitted to see XAF in operation were enthusiastic in the extreme, especially aircraft carrier men. No one was favorably impressed with CXZ, which liked neither the sea nor gunfire.[12]

The Signal Corps demonstrated their antiaircraft radar, SCR-268, at Fort Monroe in November 1938 to representatives of the Coast Artillery and the Air Corps. It pointed a searchlight at a B-10 bomber at 6,000 m altitude, which was perfectly illuminated when the light cleared a low cloud cover. The demonstration was unintentionally dramatic. The first attempts seemed to fail completely because the aircraft had been carried by a strong unknown wind out over the Atlantic, where the prototype radar finally found it, very likely preventing its loss. Not surprisingly, the Army Air Corps wanted an air-warning set, which became SCR-270.[13] Engineers from Westinghouse and Western Electric had been in residence at the Signal Corps Lab well before these tests.

By early 1940 the service radars were in production, XAF under the designation CXAM. In July 1939 Bell Labs demonstrated to the army and navy a set, CXAS, intended for main battery fire control using either 40 or 60 cm waves. A wavelength shorter than 1.5 m was required because reflection off the ocean causes the radiation pattern to extend upward, an effect that increases with wavelength and that allows long-wave sets to see aircraft at 100 km while missing a ship at a tenth that distance. The navy requested that the CXAS be further developed using the lobe-switching technique that it had seen in the Signal Corps SCR-268, which allowed a rather wide beam to locate targets accurately enough for aiming. The army ordered a few sets for coast defense but was not interested in it for antiaircraft work because its range was much shorter than the 268. In lobe switching a radiated beam of a few degrees' angular extent is directed slightly to the left and right (or up and down, or both) cyclically. By equalizing the received signal, the operator is able to determine direction to a small fraction of a degree.

One of many myths about early American radar is that the two service labs were so locked in military secrecy that they were unaware of their common interests and never consulted with the electronics industry.[14] This has been repeated so often that it seems to be regarded as revealed truth, but it has no basis in fact. The two labs had different goals: the Signal Corps sought a gun-laying or searchlight-directing radar for antiaircraft artillery, NRL an air- and surface-warning radar for ships. The engineers of the two labs discussed matters whenever they found it useful. If no other evidence were at hand, the use by the Signal Corps of Page's unique and clever 1.5 m oscillator in the SCR-268 stands as very strong material proof.

GERMANY

German radar has its origin with Dr. Rudolf Kühnhold, the technical head of the Nachrichtenmittel-versuchs-anstalt (NVA), a research laboratory operated by the Kriegsmarine at Kiel with responsibilities similar to those of NRL. In working with underwater sound Kühnhold had considered the possibility of locating a ship by reflecting radio waves from it, instead of acoustic waves, with which he had not had much success. He had done some experiments with 13.5 cm waves, which had not shown much promise, so he approached Dr. Wilhelm Runge, acting laboratory director at the electronics firm of Telefunken, with his ideas and was told that such things could not be done because the vacuum tubes required lay years in the future.[15] Runge voiced the opinion to others that the ideas were "utopian" or worse. Kühnhold voiced the opinion that Runge was rude and did not forget.

At the time Kühnhold had had satisfactory dealings with a Berlin company owned and operated by two very young engineers, Paul-Günther Erbslöh and Hans-Karl Freiherr von Willisen. The two had entered the new art of electronic sound recording, and their company, Tonographie, was very profitable. They had made underwater sound apparatus for NVA, were looking for new markets for their skills, and needed no persuasion to try their hands at radio location. This appealed to Kühnhold, not only because of the dynamic nature of the two engineers but because their company had ready funds for a development project and it was free of the bureaucratic hindrances of NVA. During the coming years the three men worked closely together, but Kühnhold never left government service and continued experimental work at NVA.

In November 1933 von Willisen noticed an advertisement by Philips for a commercially produced split-anode magnetron that produced 70 watts at 50 cm wavelength and ordered one immediately. News of this restored Kühnhold's spirits markedly from the gloom that had set in after his first 13.5 cm experiment. While waiting for construction of the circuitry for the magnetron, the two engineers built apparatus to find reflections with a 75 cm apparatus and secured as consultants two high-frequency experts from the Heinrich Hertz Institute, Dr. Hans E. Hollmann and Dr. Theodor Schultes.[16] Both the 75 cm equipment, which operated with triodes, and the 50 cm were connected to Yagi antennas to exploit their directionality. Both experiments failed because of their use of continuous waves on stationary targets. The transmitter signal overwhelmed the receiver, and it was impossible to see the small differences generated.

Kühnhold discovered in June 1934 the key to Doppler-induced beats from moving targets when he tracked a steamer with his 13.5 cm equipment. The Tonographie equipment quickly duplicated this, and the way to the future seemed clear. These continuous-wave experiments observed the fortuitous passage of an airplane through the beam, and the Kriegsmarine was sufficiently impressed to grant the work Rm70,000 ($16,500).

The Tonographie plant was ill suited for secret work, so the two engineers incorporated a new company located in another part of the city, named it Gesellschaft für elektro-akustische und mechanische Apparate, and immediately began referring to it by the acronym Gema. Schultes joined the company, but Hollmann withdrew. He had been forced to delete portions of a book he had just completed because of his association with radar, and it soured him on military work.[17] He was also distressed by the political directions of the Nazi regime.[18]

By October 1934 it was obvious to all that nothing useful could be done with continuous waves, so on Schultes's and Hollmann's advice they tried pulsed signals. By May 1935 they had a notable success with a set working on 52 cm with 2μsec pulses repeated 2,000 times per second. The antenna was now a dipole array, one of the many mattresses seen in German and American radar sets of the 1930s. By September they could follow a trawler for 8 km. It was time to demonstrate the set for Admiral Raeder.[19]

This demonstration went quite well but disclosed aspects of the German naval command that were to have consequences for the future. The Gema engineers demonstrated lobe switching with an angular accuracy sufficient to allow blind fire, but they were told to leave that out as it would be much too complicated for use at sea.[20] This was accompanied by a ban on the use of cathode-ray tubes in equipment intended for use aboard ship, as they were seen as too fragile. The cathode-ray tube was accepted after one was salvaged in operating condition from the wreck of a small research vessel on which radar was being tested, thereby saving the Gema engineers from having to design near impossible circuits, but lobe switching remained on the forbidden list. German cruisers and battleships would begin the war equipped with surface search radar superior by far to any other, yet only for ranging, searching, and navigation. Lobe switching, available in 1935, would come too late for any of the engagements the Kriegsmarine fought with radar.

The demonstration secured better funding for continuation, which proceeded along three lines. At Gema the 50 cm work was directed toward a sea-search set, and new work that quickly settled on the 2.4 m band was directed toward air warning. The 50 cm project dropped the magnetron as too unstable in frequency and substituted the very-high-frequency triode TS1 that Gema made of a kind that were being developed elsewhere at the time. Triodes forced them to longer wavelengths, finally ending at 80 cm, a set given the code designation DeTe-I (Dezimetertelegraphie), and the basis for a long line of naval equipment referred to as Seetakt. The 2.4 meter project took the code name DeTe-II. When the Luftwaffe learned of it at a demonstration for Hitler, Göring, and other notables in July 1938, they placed an order for it — over strong objections from the Kriegsmarine! From the Luftwaffe it acquired the name Freya and underwent countless variations.[21] The third line was Kühnhold's continued research on microwaves at his own NVA laboratory, the band where he thought the future of radar lay.

Wilhelm Runge, who had dismissed Kühnhold's early suggestions about radar, was designing a 50 cm directed beam communication system that used arrays of dipole antennas. Out of curiosity in 1935 he set a transmitting antenna on the ground pointing straight up with a receiving antenna to the side. When a Telefunken airplane flew straight overhead he was rewarded with a most satisfactory Doppler-beat signal. His immediate superior showed no interest, which was just the kind of inspiration to which Runge responded. The company did make a press release that was picked up by the American journal *Electronics* as "Microwaves to Detect Aircraft," which startles modern readers who encounter it.[22]

Runge's apparatus quickly grew into a small pulsed radar that he and Wilhelm

Stepp developed on the Baltic coast in the summer of 1936. The need for a beam similar to a searchlight caused them to replace the dipole array with a parabolic mirror. Stepp, who took over much of the design detail, named it Darmstadt after his hometown and started the Telefunken tradition of naming their equipment after geographical locations. Darmstadt had a range of only 5 km for an airplane but could determine its three dimensional coordinates and needed only more transmitter power to reach tactically significant distances. The additional power came through the offices of Rudolf Kühnhold, who turned the tables on Runge and criticized the work as futile because the set had only 15 W peak power. The Telefunken administration answered this rebuke by ordering the tube department to design Runge the triode that he wanted, the LS180. The new transmitter gave 8 kW of power and boosted the range to 40 km. Someone stuck a pin in the map and came up with the name of Würzburg.[23] Stepp pushed the design to make it the best antiaircraft radar in the world until 1944. It had all the elements of good World War II radars: a well-defined beam capable of high directional accuracy, excellent range accuracy, and use of a common antenna.

Gema and Telefunken were not the only companies interested in radar. Lorenz had marketed a popular form of beam navigation using overlapping lobes that allowed the pilot to determine from dot-dash signals in his earphones whether he was to the left or right of the path leading to the airport. Because of this experience Erbslöh and von Willisen had approached them rather early as collaborators on radar, and useful exchanges began. The Kreigsmarine quickly put a stop to this because of Lorenz's wide international dealings — their system was licensed in Britain and used by the Royal Air Force — to the regret of both companies. This did not end Lorenz's interest, and they initiated radar research on their own, which yielded a 60 cm set somewhat similar to the Würzburg for pointing searchlights or antiaircraft guns. The walls of military and industrial secrecy kept Lorenz from using Gema's TS1 or Telefunken's LS180, so they designed their own decimeter-wave triode, the DS320.[24] Colonel Wolfgang Martini, the chief of Luftwaffe signals, had taken an immediate and deep interest in the Gema DeTe-II, which he had adopted for the Luftwaffe as Freya, and ordered some of the Lorenz equipment, which he called Kurfürst, to compete with the Würzburg. Martini swept aside the Kriegsmarine concerns about foreign entanglements, not seeing that as a reason to ignore Lorenz's own design. Würzburg proved a better set than Kurfürst, and Lorenz left the radar business for a time except as a production contractor.

German radar in 1940 had settled on two companies for design and construction and on three wavelength bands: Gema used 80 cm for Seetakt (sea search) and 2.4 m for Freya (air warning); Telefunken used 50 cm for the Würzburg (antiaircraft). Many more pieces would be designed using the basic electronics of these bands.

GREAT BRITAIN

The similarities of U.S. and German radar invention and development are readily seen. In both countries radar started in service laboratories with varying connection to the electronic industries, which entered their own designs. Both had initially very limited financial support from the military, which began after successful demonstration. Both tried microwaves first and gave up (although Kühnhold persevered) only when forced to longer waves by the constraints of the vacuum tubes available. Both built air-warning sets with large dipole arrays and gun-laying sets for decimeter waves that had parabolic reflectors, cylindrical for the Bell Labs and paraboloid for the Telefunken. Neither had more than a handful of sets when war broke out. One is tempted to say that both were driven to similar solutions by a technical imperative that operated through the common disciplines of communications engineering.

Great Britain presents us with almost the inverse. By late 1934 many persons in the British government had realized the danger that Hitler presented, the weakness of British arms and the vulnerability of the island to air attack. Airships and bombers had attacked Britain in the 1914–18 war, causing death and damage that was not small, although in no way decisive. It had forced the government to place an air defense system in operation that deployed 376 airplanes, 469 antiaircraft guns, 622 searchlights, 258 height finders, 10 sound locators, and a balloon apron and required a force of 13,400 men and women.[25] Nothing remained of it after the war. The British Army did not even have regular antiaircraft units.

The Air Ministry approached the problem through Harry Wimperis, director of scientific research, who formed a committee to study the scientific defense of Great Britain, which informally took on the name of its chairman, Henry Tizard. Wimperis had initiated work by asking Robert Watson Watt, superintendent of the government's Radio Research Station at Slough, if there were any value for air defense in the numerous "death ray" schemes that filled the popular press. Watt's answer was, as expected, an unequivocal no, but he held out the possibility of a method of radio detection. Watt and his assistant Arnold Wilkins had turned the question around while doing the "death ray" calculations. They approximated an airplane—idealized as physicists are wont—as a wire of length equal to the wing span of a bomber. When irradiated at a wavelength double the length of the wire, the calculations showed that it reradiated enough to be detected by a conventional receiver, and this held the possibility of determining the position of the origin of the re-radiation. The idea found a good reception in the committee, and Watt set out to do a simple experiment.

This approach was quite different from the Americans and Germans, who either knew from experience or had confidence that an aircraft would re-radiate. There was also a difference in the wavelength band that the two groups considered. The American and German work was carried out by communications engineers accustomed to meter waves; Watt and Wilkins had done research that probed the ionosphere and triangulated thunderstorms—both fields of study that involved wavelengths in tens or hundreds of meters. Nether Watt nor Wilkins gave any thought to microwaves, the subject that had dominated the earlier American and German plans.

Reflections from aircraft were sufficiently unusual for Watt—he had obviously not talked to television people—that he insisted that a failure of his first, lashed up experiment not be taken as the end of the project. The experiment set up a receiver a few kilometers distant from the Daventry station that transmitted to the far-flung parts of the Empire on the 50 meter band. The experimental antenna was so arranged as to reduce through phase reversal the amplitude of the direct signal but receive signals from the bomber that flew over. The experiment of 26 February 1935 was a success. It was the same "radio sensor" experiment that had been done earlier by others; but where the Americans, French, and Russians had not known how to develop the idea further, Watt and Wilkins quickly knew how to make it a system of radio location. The result was the famous Battle-of-Britain radar, CH for Chain Home.[26]

The research carried out at Slough had involved measuring the height of the ionosphere by measuring the time between a pulse of high-frequency waves leaving the transmitter and returning to the receiver, a technique devised by Gregory Breit and Merle Tuve a decade earlier.[27] This same technique could be used to determine the range of the target. Obtaining its direction, thereby securing its position in two coordinates, made use of Watt's early lightning studies. He had determined the positions of thunderstorms by triangulation that had obtained direction by mounting two loop antennas at right angles, connecting each loop to a receiver, and applying the output of the receivers to the horizontal and vertical deflection plates of one of Western Electric's gas-focused cathode-ray tubes. A line resulted whose orientation gave the direction—with 180° ambiguity, of course. Determining the direction to the radar target would use a similar method but with loop antennas replaced by dipoles, owing to the shorter wavelength.

Within days Watt and Wilkins had devised a method from well-founded design principles based on their own knowledge and experience. It was a design of heroic proportion. Early experiments and technical matters soon forced them from 50 m to 10 through 15 m. Arrays of eight dipoles were mounted on or suspended between two 100 m steel towers from which they broadcast a useful signal through 120° horizontally with a much narrower vertical distribution. Crossed dipole receiver antennas were mounted at various levels in 75 m wooden towers that were located a few hundred meters distant from the transmitter and that allowed estimates of the target's height from relative antenna-pair amplitudes. The transmitter required an enormous amount of power, because the target would be illuminated by a very small fraction of the emitted radiation and the receiver dipoles were nondirectional; radio engineers would refer to both as low-gain antennas, in contrast to the American and German systems, which used high-gain antennas; that is, they formed beams of perhaps 10° width, concentrating power in an attempt to imitate a searchlight.

Construction of Chain Home on a grand scale began toward the end of 1936, and here is where Britain differs again from the other two. The stations were built as one part of a complete air defense system, behind which was Air Vice-Marshal Hugh Dowding, the most scientifically minded military officer of the time. He and Tizard realized that to be effective the information about the attackers gained by radar must be transformed into orders to fighter squadrons within minutes, if the information was to be of any value, for it took about twenty minutes to position the defenders at the ambush point. Thus the first observations must be communicated to filter centers for evaluation and, if determined to be an enemy formation, transmitted as combat orders in mere minutes.[28]

The first station was turned over to Royal Air Force personnel for operation in May 1937, and as practice the stations around the Thames estuary began having fighters "discretely," but initially not always successfully, intercepting KLM and Lufthansa airliners. These operations required a tremendous effort in installing secure communications, building the filter and command centers, training radar operators and mechanics and center personnel, and exercising Fighter Command in their new way of waging aerial warfare. Almost as important as radar was the introduction of very-high-frequency radios for fighter communication. In this the RAF led every other force by years. Such radios operate in a much quieter part of the frequency spectrum than the high-frequency equipment previously used and were able to have a much larger number of channels, allowing many independent messages. (The U.S. Navy's air arm suffered well into 1943 with the older system, which seriously affected its carrier fighter direction.)[29] Watching over every detail was Dowding, chief of the newly created Fighter Command, who had begun planning the Battle of Britain in 1935. When battle came in August 1940, radar was technically and tactically ready and Fighter Command knew how to use it.

Tizard had determined early that radar would put a stop to daylight attacks and that defense at night would require airborne radar. Given the gargantuan size of CH, this would seem to have been a tall order indeed. E. G. Bowen, a physicist and one of the first to join Watt's staff, obtained the task and pursued it with all the resources the director, by then A. P. Rowe, who had replaced Watt, provided. It was not the top priority, but nevertheless Bowen observed a large ship at sea in May 1938 with the makings of a 1.5 m airborne radar. By fall 1940 this grew to prototypes of sets useful for locating bombers at night or ships at any time.

The British Army was responsible for antiaircraft and coast defense and formed a small "Army Cell" at the Bawdsey Research Station where radar work was carried out. The enlightened attitudes toward science that prevailed in the Air Ministry did not carry over into the War Office. Their scientists were not to initiate projects but to develop the equipment ordered; they were not to work closely with serving officers to gain understanding of the strengths and weaknesses of their inventions and not to voice their opinions of how best to employ the new weapons. Cell efforts in designing an antiaircraft radar resulted in a "gun-assisting," not a gun-laying set, GL Marks I and II, poor things compared with SCR-268 or the Würzburg, but it was what had been ordered, a device for accurate measurement of range. The same engineers showed the high quality of their skills in the coast defense set CD, a 1.5 m radar with lobe switching capable of blind fire, techniques that easily could have been transferred to an antiaircraft radar. CD took on much greater importance as the means of detecting aircraft that could fly below the radiation patterns of the long-wave CH equipment. Stations to this end, designated CHL for Chain Home Low, began to supplement CH in late 1939. Its design was strikingly similar to SCR-268 or CXAM.[30]

The Royal Navy had become alert to the possibilities of radio location relatively early, as evidenced by a provisional patent having been granted in 1928 to a member of His Majesty's Signal School, the organization entrusted with navy electronics. The lack of electronic components suitable to allow this idea to mature led to its being neglected until the activities triggered by Watt renewed interest. The navy rejected the proposals to have them create a navy cell at Bawdsey similar to that of the army because of their awareness of the constraints placed on electronics by the harsh conditions of a warship.

Signal School engineers soon had two projects underway: a 7.5 m air-

warning radar and a 50 cm fire-direction radar.[31] The latter resulted in equipment remarkably similar to Bell Telephone's FC and FD sets and Telefunken's
Würzburg, a striking example of the technical imperative.

COMPARISONS

The development of three independent programs for constructing the means of
radio location at the same time is an unusual, possibly unique occurrence in engineering history, and it demonstrates the idea of progress through a technical
imperative in a superb manner. The similarity of the German and American
programs is apparent and has been noted, and they make a striking contrast with
the British. German and American designs followed very similar lines, and experimental models had trials separated in time by about a year, with the Germans ahead. British engineers followed American and German use of dipole
arrays a bit later and independently. Although secret from one another, the engineers of the three countries had open communication with the electronics
techniques of the day, which guided their thinking.

In Britain a call for scientific help came from the Air Ministry and was directed toward the government laboratory from which help could be expected,
and in this they were not disappointed. It was a radio laboratory with experience at much longer wavelengths than those used by much of the communication industry, and naturally from it came a different solution to the problem. The
enthusiasm of Watson Watt and the group of physicists who assembled about
him at Bawdsey was phenomenal and belongs to a class of heroic engineering.
Initially, Watt did not want electrical engineers for fear their ideas would be too
conventional, but the most advanced British design to emerge from the prewar
work was CD/CHL, the product of experienced electrical engineers.

DEPLOYMENT

In 1940 the invention of the cavity magnetron appeared to the great surprise of
radar engineers in Britain and a few months later in the United States. It was
known before in Russia, where it was ignored; in Japan, where its exploitation
was held back by the rigid minds of military authorities, and in Switzerland,
where it was used for directed-beam communication.[32] Given the dominance of
microwaves in subsequent radar, it is worthwhile to examine the use to which
the meter-wave sets described here were put, specifically their effect on the outcome of World War II. Examination of the military histories of that conflict with
radar in mind discloses three major engagements for which radar tipped the balance, all in favor of the Allies and all in the early, critical years.

Radar's part in the Battle of Britain has been studied and reported by numerous scholars and popular authors, leading to a near universal conclusion that Britain would have lost without the narrow margin that Chain Home supplied.[33]

Two other engagements were critical in preventing Allied defeat. Britain was extraordinarily hard pressed in the Mediterranean in 1941 and 1942. Loss of the Middle East to Rommel would have given Germany Britain's petroleum and cut a supply line through Iran to the Soviet Union. It could have opened the possibility of a link of Axis forces, which the Japanese rejected after the defeat of the German-Italian army at El Alamein. Rommel's defeat came about through the inability of the Axis to control the sea and supply the Africa Corps, a direct result of the neutralization of the Italian fleet and the destruction of North Africa-bound convoys that can be attributed to the British radar superiority. The 1.5 m airborne radar carried by the Swordfish torpedo bombers removed the possibility of the convoys passing unnoticed at night; the air warning radar on Malta prevented their base from being destroyed; shipborne radar located an Italian fleet off Cape Matapan that was destroyed, after which Italian surface units were of no consequence.[34]

The destruction of the U.S. battleships at Pearl Harbor left carriers as the only striking power that remained for the United States in the Pacific. These vessels had been relegated by naval authorities to a secondary role. In initial phases of a major fleet action, they were to be extremely important for the intelligence they would supply and the long-range damage they might inflict, but they were extraordinarily fragile craft with thin decks covering aircraft being fueled and armed—gasoline and explosives lying about in a deadly mix. To be surprised was to be destroyed. Their function in a battle was expected to be brief but glorious, and heavily armored ships would then continue the fight. Radar changed this suddenly. The CXAM radar of the U.S. fleet gave the carriers consistently at least twenty minutes' warning of an impending air attack, enough time to fly planes off the deck and clear fuel lines and bombs from the highly vulnerable hangar deck. Radar provided U.S. carriers with the equivalent of armor plate, and during the first two years none of them suffered the fiery fate of the Japanese carriers at Midway, which had no radar and no warning.[35]

The U.S. Army's SCR-268 and 270 were equally important during those crucial years. In his careful study of the extended and desperate struggle for Guadalcanal, Richard Frank states without qualification: "Without these warnings, Henderson Field, and ultimately Guadalcanal, could not have been defended."[36]

Germany's technical superiority in radar at the start of the war was extended to a tactical superiority only for the Kriegsmarine, whose capital ships carried the 80 cm Seetakt sets that gave excellent ranging, search, and navigation but not blind-fire capability.[37] They used these sets effectively in the cruiser warfare of 1940–41, but this manner of destroying Britain's merchant navy had too many flaws in its concept for radar to save.

When the Royal Air Force began taking the war to German cities, the equipment designed at Gema and Telefunken was quickly adapted to the unexpected task of defense. Freya was used in its original form but also altered into superb long-range air-warning equipment by the simple expedient of adding many dipoles to the arrays, creating Wassermann and Mummut, equipment capable of locating aircraft accurately in direction and height and limited in range only by the horizon.[38] A great electronic war began between the engineers of the two countries, who committed all the ingenuity that technical minds could provide.

NOTES

1. Hülsmeyer's work is described in several books. The most accessible is Alfred Price, *Instruments of Darkness: The History of Electronic Warfare*, 2d rev. ed. (London: Macdonald and Jane's Publishers, 1978), pp. 55–57.

2. David Kite Allison, *New Eye for the Navy: The Origin of Radar at the Naval Research Laboratory*, *NRL Report 8466* (Washington, D.C.: Government Printing Office, 1981), pp. 39–41.

3. J. B. Johnson, "A Low Voltage Cathode Ray Oscillograph," *Journal of the Optical Society of America and the Review of Scientific Instruments* 6 (1922): 701–12. For a beautiful history of cathode-ray tubes, see Peter A. Keller, *The Cathode-Ray Tube: Technology, History, and Applications* (New York: Palisades Institute for Research Studies, 1991).

4. L. F. Jones, "A Study of the Propagation of Wavelengths between Three and Eight Meters," *Proceedings of the Institute of Radio Engineers* 21 (1933): 349–86; V. K. Zworykin, "Description of an Experimental Television System and the Kinescope," *Proceedings of the IRE* 21 (1933): 1655–73; Manfred von Ardenne, "Die Braunsche Röhre als Fernsehemfänger," *Fernsehen* 1 (1930): 193–202; Kenjiro Takayanagi, *Pioneering Television: The Autobiography of Kenjiro Takayanagi*, trans. Mayumi Yoshida (San Francisco, Calif.: San Francisco Press, 1993).

5. Carl R. Englund, Arthur B. Crawford, and William W. Mumford, "Some Results of a Study of Ultra-short-wave Transmission Phenomena," *Proceedings of the IRE* 21 (1933): 464–92.

6. C. D. Tuska, "Historical Notes on the Determination of Distance by Timing Radio Waves," *Journal of the Franklin Institute* 237 (1944): 1–20, 83–102; C. D. Tuska, "Pictorial Radio," *Journal of the Franklin Institute* 253 (1952): 1–20, 95–124; Ulrich Kern, "Die Entstehung des Radarverfahrens: Zur Geschichte der Radartechnik bis 1945," Ph.D. diss., Universität Stuttgart, Historisches Institut der Universität Stuttgart, 1984.

7. Col. John B. McKinney, "Radar: A Reluctant Miracle," pp. 84–87, paper written for the Research Seminar in Technological Innovation at the Harvard Business School, 1960.

8. The pronounced reflection and interference effects of meter waves during these studies is described in George C. Southworth, *Forty Years of Radio Research: A Reportorial* (New York: Gordon and Breach Science Publishers, 1962), pp. 79–81.

9. J. Bion, "Le Radar," *La Revue Maritime*, July–Aug. 1946, pp. 330–46, 456–71; R. B. Molyneux-Berry, "Dr. Henri Gutton, French Radar Pioneer," *Radar Development to 1945*, ed. Russell Burns (London: Peter Peregrinus [for IEE], 1988), pp. 45–52; Fritz Trenkle, *Die deutschen Funkmessverfahren bis 1945* (Heidelberg, Germany: Alfred Hüthig Verlag, 1986), pp. 23–24.

10. Allison, *New Eye*, pp. 78–90.

11. Ibid., pp. 90–93; Dulany Terrett, *United States Army in World War II: The Signal Corps: The*

Emergency (To December 1941) (Washington, D.C.: Office of the Chief of Military History, 1956), pp. 42–48; McKinney, "Radar," pp. 136–37, 155–57.

12. Albert Hoyt Taylor, *Radio Reminiscences: A Half Century* (Washington, D.C.: U.S. Naval Research Laboratory, 1960), p. 192.

13. Roger B. Colton, "Radar in the United States Army," *Proceedings of the IRE* 33 (1945): 740–53; Terrett, *Emergency*, pp. 125–27.

14. Henry E. Guerlac, *Radar in World War II* (New York: Tomash-American Institute of Physics Publishers, 1987), p. 249. For this accusation in a more recent and virulent form, see Luis W. Alvarez, "Alfred Lee Loomis—Last Great Adventurer of Science," *Physics Today* 36 (Jan. 1983): 25–34.

15. Frank Reuter, *Funkmess: Die Entwicklung und Einsatz des RADAR-Verfahrens in Deutschland bis zum Ende des Zweiten Weltkrieges* (Opladen, Germany: Westdeutscher Verlag, 1971), pp. 18–19.

16. Harry von Kroge, *GEMA—Berlin: Geburtsstätte der deutschen aktiven Wasseschall-und Funkortungstechnik* (Hamburg: Lühmanndruck, 1998), pp. 17–26.

17. The book came to be the standard reference on microwaves throughout the decade. Hans E. Hollmann, *Physik und Technik der ultrakurzen Wellen* (Berlin, Germany: Springer Verlag, 1936).

18. H. Frühauf, "H. E. Hollmann zum 60. Geburtstag," *Hochfrequenztechnik und Elektroakustik* 68 (Dec. 1959): 141–43. Noted through the courtesy of Dr. Frederick Seitz.

19. Von Kroge, *GEMA*, pp. 37–45; Trenkle, *Funkmess*, pp. 26–30; Reuter, *Funkmess*, p. 23.

20. Von Kroge, *GEMA*, p. 55–56; P.-G. Erbslöh and H.-K. Freiherr von Willisen, patent declaration dated 27 Apr. 1935.

21. Von Kroge, *GEMA*, pp. 77, 87–89, 119.

22. *Electronics* 8 (Sep. 1935): 18–19.

23. Wilhelm Runge, "Ich und Telefunken," unpublished manuscript, 1971, pp. 42–44.

24. See William E. Jackson, *The Federal Airways System* (New York: Institute of Electrical and Electronic Engineers, 1970), pp. 219–27; Robert I. Colin, "Otto Scheller: The Radio Range Principle," *IEEE Transactions on Aerospace and Electronic Systems* AES-1 (1966): 481–87; Von Kroge, *GEMA*, p. 45; Gotthard Müller, "Funkmessgeräte-Entwicklung bei der C. Lorenz AG, 1935–1945," (Stuttgart, Germany: Standard Elektrik Lorenz AG [Technisch-wissenschaftliches Schriftum], 1979), p. 5.

25. H. A. Jones, *The War in the Air* (Oxford, Eng.: Clarendon Press, 1935), vol. 5, pp. 153–54.

26. Sir Robert Watson-Watt, *The Pulse of Radar: The Autobiography of Robert Watson-Watt* (U.S. edition of *Three Steps to Victory*) (New York: Dial Press, 1959).

27. Gregory Breit and Merle A. Tuve, "A Radio Method of Estimating the Height of the Conducting Layer," *Nature* 116 (1935): 357. Tuve later described these experiments and remembered the interference caused by aircraft taking off and landing near the NRL transmitter that they used. M. A. Tuve, "Early Days of Pulse Radio at the Carnegie Institution," *Journal of Atmospheric and Terrestrial Physics* 36 (1974): 2079–83.

28. John Terraine, *A Time for Courage: The Royal Air Force in the European War, 1939–1945* (U.S. edition of *The Right of the Line*) (New York: Macmillan, 1985), pp. 70–77, 137–222.

29. Albert Percival Rowe, *One Story of Radar* (Cambridge, Eng.: University Press, 1948), p. 23; Derek Wood and Derek Dempster, *The Narrow Margin: The Battle of Britain and the Rise of Air Power, 1930–1940* (Washington, D.C.: Smithsonian Institution Press, 1990), p. 208; Watson-Watt, *Pulse of Radar*, pp. 141–43; James H. Belote and William M. Belote, *Titans of the Sea: The Development and Operations of Japanese and American Carrier Task Forces during World War II* (New York: Harper and Rowe, 1975), pp. 125–26.

30. K. E. B. Jay, "History of the Development of Radio and Radar," part 1, para. 186–88. Unpublished manuscript prepared for contribution to the *Official History of the Second World War*, 1946, located at Library of the DRA, Malvern, Eng.; Brigadier A. P. Sayer, *The Second World War, 1939–1945: Army Radar* (London: War Office, 1950), pp. 120–25.

31. J. F. Coales, "The Origins and Development of Radar in the Royal Navy," *The Development of*

Radar Equipment for the Royal Navy, 1935–45, ed. F. A. Kingsley (London: Macmillan [for the Naval Radar Trust], 1995), pp. 11–29.

32. N. F. Alekseev and D. D. Malairov, "Generation of High-power Oscillations with a Magnetron in the Centimeter Band," *Zhurnal Tekhnicheskoi Fiziki* 10 (1940): 1297–1300; S. Nakajima, "The History of Japanese Radar Development to 1945," *Radar Development to 1945*, ed. Russell Burns (London: Peter Peregrinus [for the IEE], 1988), pp. 243–58. For a study of the entire Japanese effort, see Yasuzo Nakagawa, *Japanese Radar and Related Weapons of World War II* (Laguna Hills, Calif.: Aegean Park Press, 1997); F. Fischer and F. Lüdi, "Die Posthumus-Schwingungen im Magnetron," *Schweizerischer Elektrotechnischer Verein Bulletin* 28 (1937): 277–83.

33. See Wood and Dempster, *The Narrow Margin*.

34. Donald Macintyre, *The Battle for the Mediterranean* (New York: W. W. Norton, 1964).

35. John B. Lundstrom, *The First Team: Pacific Naval Air Combat from Pearl Harbor to Midway* (Annapolis, Md.: Naval Institute Press, 1984), pp. 307–419.

36. Richard B. Frank, *Guadalcanal: The Definitive Account of the Landmark Battle* (New York: Random House, 1990), p. 207.

37. Von Kroge, *GEMA*, pp. 55, 69, 92–93.

38. Trenkle, *Funkmess*, pp. 93–98; Reuter, *Funkmess*, pp. 91, 98.

CHAPTER 9

Rocket Aircraft and the "Turbojet Revolution"

The Luftwaffe's Quest for High-Speed Flight, 1935–39

MICHAEL J. NEUFELD

On 15 June 1939, Erich Warsitz made a brief and shaky flight around the Peenemünde-West airfield in the Heinkel He 176, the world's first pure rocket aircraft.[1] Ten weeks later, on 27 August, Warsitz took off from the Heinkel works at Rostock-Marienehe in the world's first turbojet airplane, the He 178. These two highly secret flights symbolized the dramatic advances that the Third Reich and its aviation industry had achieved in only a half-dozen years, and they made Germany the leader in advanced aeropropulsion. The second flight was also a milestone in what Edward Constant has called the "turbojet revolution"—a fundamental transformation of aircraft propulsion, design, and performance that began in the 1930s.[2]

That these two aviation "firsts" were achieved in Nazi Germany is well known. Yet for fifty years their military-organizational context has been misunderstood. To a great extent, the ghost-written memoirs of Ernst Heinkel, whose company built the He 176 and 178, have determined that context. Heinkel depicted both aircraft as his private initiatives, carried through against official indifference and even hostility on the part of the Luftwaffe (air force) and its bureaucratic arm, the *Reichsluftfahrtministerium* (Reich Air Ministry, or RLM). Heinkel was willing to share the credit only with Erich Warsitz and with the brilliant engineering physicists who pioneered rocket and turbojet propulsion in Germany: Dr. Wernher von Braun and Dr. Hans von Ohain, respectively.[3]

Heinkel's memoirs were shaped, not surprisingly, by the egotism of an energetic industrialist, and they contain errors typical of a book based on later interviews. But Heinkel's specific views of the Air Ministry were molded first and foremost by anger and injured pride. Despite his historic role in ushering in a

Fig. 9.1. Ernst Heinkel (center) speaks, probably at a celebration of the first turbojet flight in history in August 1939. At left is the test pilot Erich Warsitz, and at right the physicist-inventor Dr. Hans von Ohain. Courtesy National Air and Space Museum, 80-1894

new era of flight, the RLM gave a rival, the designer Willi Messerschmitt, the contracts for the Me 163 rocket interceptor and Me 262 jet fighter that entered combat in mid-1944. According to his biographer, Heinkel never got over his disappointment.[4]

Heinkel's account of the origins of German rocket and jet aircraft has been often repeated. Popular histories have mostly followed him without question, depicting the Luftwaffe as bumbling and slow in taking up the new technologies.[5] The more recent scholarly works of Edward Constant and Ralf Schabel have corrected Heinkel insofar as they have discussed the Air Ministry's active intervention in turbojet development after the spring of 1938—in the wake of its discovery that Heinkel had been funding von Ohain's revolutionary engine work since April 1936. But these valuable monographs only repeat Heinkel's claim that he had first begun supporting reaction-propulsion research in November 1935, after making an essentially private arrangement with von Braun, the key engineer in Army Ordnance's liquid-fuel rocket project.[6]

The organizational improbability of this arrangement should have raised questions, but no easily available sources clearly contradicted Heinkel's story.[7] Long overlooked, however, were Army Ordnance rocket files now in Freiburg and Munich, many of which are accessible on microfilm.[8] Although dominated by army concerns, these records reveal that the Air Ministry, not Heinkel, originated research into aircraft reaction propulsion in 1935. The air force began an energetic rocket program in collaboration with Ordnance, financed ramjet and pulsejet engine research as well, and then added an independent rocket development capability. When RLM officials discovered the turbojet work at Heinkel, I will argue, their longstanding interest in reaction propulsion facilitated a quick decision to promote the new technology. In Britain, by contrast, the inventor Frank Whittle had already envisioned the gas turbine as a jet engine in 1929–30, but he struggled for years against official indifference. To understand the context of the "turbojet revolution" in Nazi Germany, it is therefore important to examine the origins of the Luftwaffe's quest for high-speed flight.

THE RISE OF AN INTERSERVICE ROCKET-AIRCRAFT PROGRAM

Before 1935, the Air Ministry Technical Office and its chief precursor, Section 8 (aviation) of Army Ordnance Testing Division, had shown little interest in the rocket. According to an October 1934 document, the RLM had made "agreements" with Ordnance, leaving the army in exclusive control of it. These agreements reflected not only Air Ministry indifference but also Ordnance's campaign to eliminate amateur rocket groups and monopolize the technology. Army artillery specialists, led by Testing Division Chief Gen. Karl Becker, felt that absolute secrecy was necessary to conceal from the world Germany's interest in a potentially revolutionary new weapon: the long-range ballistic missile. In late 1932 Becker set up a small liquid-fuel rocket project at the Kummersdorf artillery range outside Berlin, as liquid fuels promised much higher performance than existing solid propellants.[9]

Because the Air Ministry had only existed since the Nazi seizure of power in 1933, when Hitler had created it for Hermann Göring, RLM officials had to focus on their main task: forging a clandestine air force as a minimal deterrent against attack during the early phases of rearmament. (The Versailles Treaty had forbidden Germany any military aviation, although the army had carried out some covert training and purchase of aircraft.) Under the circumstances, exotic new propulsion systems that might allow flight at speeds of over 800 km/h (500 mph), the practical upper limit for propeller-driven, piston-engine aircraft, must have seemed distant, utopian, even absurd. Germany scarcely possessed adequate combat aircraft that could fly at half that speed.[10]

Yet there were reasons why the new service would quickly become receptive to radical new technologies like the rocket. Lacking an entrenched establishment, the Luftwaffe was more open to revolutionary technological ideas than western air forces. It was also imbued, as were the army and navy, with a desire to quickly make Germany competitive with, or superior to, other powers; technological zeal combined easily with a nationalist or National Socialist zeal for rearmament. Moreover, the improving economy, Hitler's aggressive rearmament policy, and the weak Western response to his violations of Versailles, meant ever-expanding resources for the Luftwaffe, especially after its official unveiling in March 1935. Finally, German theoreticians closely connected to the Air Ministry were the international leaders in high-speed aerodynamics. They, as much as anyone, recognized that the propeller-driven aircraft would in a decade or less reach the limits of its performance.[11]

But the proximate cause for the Luftwaffe's sudden interest in the rocket appears to have been a single individual: Maj. Wolfram Freiherr von Richthofen. A cousin and squadronmate of the Red Baron of World War I fame, he was an ace himself, having shot down eight enemy airplanes in 1917–18. Later a Field Marshal and one of the Luftwaffe's most successful operational commanders, von Richthofen had acquired an engineering doctorate in the 1920s and become head of the Technical Office's Development Division in 1933. According to von Braun, von Richthofen came to Kummersdorf in January 1935 and showed a lively interest in Army Ordnance's liquid-fuel rocket work. Not coincidentally perhaps, in mid-January Ordnance had presented films and lectures about the successful launches of two A-2 rockets to a group that included at least one unnamed RLM official.[12]

On 5 February, von Richthofen discussed rocket development in a meeting at his office. The next day, he wrote to Testing Division's ballistics and munitions section, which ran the army rocket project, about an accident in Dessau. An explosion there had injured an official of Germany's largest aircraft firm, Junkers, revealing its financing of liquid-fuel rocket development by Johannes Winkler, a pioneer of the spaceflight movement of the late Weimar Republic. A week later von Braun and one of his superiors, Capt. Leo Zanssen, went to Dessau to investigate and to impress upon Junkers Ordnance's obsession with secrecy. The results of the investigation, plus a company report probably written by Winkler, were passed along to the Air Ministry, which awaited them with interest.[13]

The relationship between the two services deepened in March, when Zanssen and von Braun, Dr. Lorenz of the Technical Office's Research Division, the aerodynamicist Dr. Adolf Busemann, the designer Willi Messerschmitt, and others observed Paul Schmidt's pulsejet experiments in Munich. Schmidt was an independent inventor who had been working since 1930 on the pulsejet, a form of air-breathing reaction propulsion with intermittent combustion. In heavily modified form, his invention would propel the Luftwaffe's V-1 cruise missile or "buzz bomb" launched by the thousands against Britain and Belgium in 1944–45. But in 1935 the Luftwaffe was mainly interested in the pulsejet's possibilities for aircraft propulsion. Zanssen and von Braun attended because it was thought that the army might wish to pursue an automatic "aerial torpedo"— what we would now call a cruise missile—a concept seen as closer to an artillery projectile than an unmanned airplane. The upshot was that Ordnance contributed half of the research funds in a joint agreement with the Air Ministry, which would supervise the work. But both sides saw that Schmidt was years away from a practical propulsion system.[14]

It was not the first time the cruise missile idea had been broached. In October 1934 the engineer-inventor Hellmuth Walter had contacted Gen. Becker about the possibility of an "aerial torpedo" based on a ramjet. (A ramjet is essentially a tube that compresses air solely by the ram effect of the inlet at high speeds. The air is then burned with a fuel—Walter suggested oil—to produce thrust.) Since a ramjet, like a pulsejet, has to be boosted to a high velocity to work, Walter had proposed burning the fuel in a rocket engine with highly concentrated hydrogen peroxide until supersonic cruise velocity was reached. He had already been working with the navy since 1933 on hydrogen peroxide as a propellant for U-boat turbines and torpedoes.[15]

Before contacting Becker, Walter also had discussions with the Air Ministry on using the rocket/ramjet combination in "high-speed aircraft," and later claimed to have proposed some sort of turbojet engine as well. But his ideas had no apparent impact on the RLM. No one had yet demonstrated that a gas turbine would be adequately efficient for aircraft propulsion, and the ramjet concept, which had been known since at least 1913, was still beyond the existing technology. With Luftwaffe support, Walter did carry out exploratory experiments several years later. Meanwhile, Ordnance began to act as a consultant to his hydrogen-peroxide rocket development in late 1934, without investing any money.[16]

While the ideas of Walter and Schmidt must have seemed technically immature, the Technical Office's growing contacts with Kummersdorf had converted von Richthofen into a believer in the rocket—the one reaction-propulsion technology that appeared within reach. On 10 May 1935, he met Zanssen to discuss the possibility of a Luftwaffe-Army-Junkers experimental rocket-plane program. Zanssen explicitly mentioned the aviation section's earlier lack of interest. Von Richthofen was of quite another opinion. In the future, he argued, bombers could attack at high speeds and at altitudes of over 10,000 meters (33,000 feet). They would be above the ceiling of antiaircraft fire, and it would be difficult for slow-climbing, propeller-driven fighters to intercept them. A rapid-reaction, high-speed interceptor would therefore become essential. It was basically the concept that would later appear as the Me 163 "Komet."[17]

On 22 May, Ordnance replied, endorsing the feasibility of a joint rocket-aircraft program but expressing reluctance about revealing anything to Junkers. Ordnance ruled out working with the Winkler group altogether because the primary application of the rocket was the "liquid-fuel long-range missile," and its secrecy had to be protected at all costs.[18]

A little over a month later, on 27 June 1935, the Technical Office, Ballistics and Munitions, and Junkers met at Kummersdorf to view a rocket firing and discuss terms. Prof. Otto Mader, the head of development at the Junkers Engine Company, attended, as did von Richthofen and von Braun. For this meeting the twenty-three-year-old von Braun wrote a seminal position paper. Because a missile rocket engine was little different than one for an aircraft, he stated, it is "therefore advantageous that in the future as well, the development of the free-flying liquid-fuel rocket and the aircraft rocket engine could be carried out by the same center. Wa.Prw.1 [Ballistics and Munitions] believes that this goal can be achieved through the future creation of an 'experimental rocket establishment.'" This center should have some air force personnel, but they would be transferred to the employment of the army or the center.[19]

At the 27 June meeting, von Richthofen let it be known that the Luftwaffe was not going to be a junior partner in any joint "experimental rocket establishment." He also objected to the restrictive conditions that von Braun and Zanssen had laid down for cooperation with an aircraft firm like Junkers. But he made these remarks in a friendly way only after explaining his rocket interceptor concept: the goal should be an aircraft that could, after a forty-five-second boost, coast up to 15,000 m (50,000 ft) and then glide or cruise at high altitude for some minutes. As a preliminary step, a small experimental rocket plane could be tested, perhaps by towing it into the air and igniting the engine. Junkers would begin the preliminary design; von Richthofen had earlier cleared this arrangement with Mader.[20]

During the summer, the RLM brought Ernst Heinkel Aircraft into the program as well. Heinkel's fascination with high-speed flight was well known; it is also possible that the airframe side of Junkers—technically a separate company until 1936—may not have supported Mader. At the beginning of September, Army Ordnance, the Air Ministry, Heinkel, and Junkers signed a joint agreement protecting the secrecy of Ordnance's rocket development. Only five or six people at each firm were to be informed, and rocket-aircraft development was to be carried out in closed workshops. In late October or November, the Kummersdorf group received a Junkers "Junior" single-engine light plane to experiment by installing a 300 kg thrust liquid-oxygen/alcohol engine in the tail—the motor that had been used to power the A-2s. The funding and arrangements for these tests were made through Dr. Adolf Baeumker's Research Division of the Technical Office in collaboration with the quasi-governmental German Research Establishment for Aviation (*Deutsche Versuchsanstalt für Luftfahrt*, or DVL) in Berlin-Adlershof. These experiments aimed at developing takeoff-assist rockets for overloaded bombers as well as gaining experience in rocket-plane work. Junkers itself dropped out in fall 1935. The reasons are unknown, but Prof. Mader, who was a conservative piston-engine specialist, may have been unenthusiastic, or perhaps he did not see the point of Junkers Engine participating if Winkler's in-house group was excluded and propulsion development was run by Kummersdorf.[21]

Thus Heinkel's firm became the sole airframe contractor. On 16 October, von Braun and his chief designer, along with two RLM engineers, met Heinkel and his top designers at the Marienehe plant. They discussed the character of Ordnance's rocket technology and how it might be adapted to an airplane. The ultimate decision was to pursue an interim project before the construction of a pure rocket aircraft. A rocket engine would be installed in the tail of an He 112, the loser to the soon-to-be-famous Messerschmitt Bf 109 in the single-engine fighter competition of 1935. In December the firm specified an engine thrust of 1,000 kg (2,200 lb). That same month von Braun requested 200,000 marks (about $50,000) from the RLM for "Project 112 R," noting that speed was crucial since the work had already begun.[22]

MASSIVE INVESTMENTS—
AND MOVES TOWARD INDEPENDENCE

By the end of 1935, both the Junkers Junior and the He 112 projects had been launched. But the most important product of the army-Luftwaffe alliance was yet to come. Shortly after New Year's, Wernher von Braun's concept of a secret "experimental rocket establishment" would bear fruit. Following his discovery after Christmas of a suitable site for an airfield and missile test range—near the fishing village of Peenemünde on the Baltic island of Usedom—the two services agreed to jointly fund it. The projected construction cost was 11 million marks for the first year alone—roughly ten times the Third Reich's expenditure on liquid-fuel rocket research for 1935. By April 1936, both services' leaderships had approved the deal, the land was purchased, and construction began. Only a year later, in spring 1937, von Braun and members of his Kummersdorf group would begin moving into the army section, Peenemünde-East. The Luftwaffe group began forming at Peenemünde-West later in 1937, and Uvo Pauls, who had been responsible for rocket engines in the Technical Office since mid-1936, became head in early 1938.[23]

The Air Ministry's commitment to Peenemünde—which began with a promise of 5 million marks from Research Division Chief Baeumker at a time when he had a virtual carte blanche from Göring to expand his facilities—was not the RLM's only new investment in rocketry in 1936.[24] Baeumker's division also lured an Austrian, Dr. Eugen Sänger, to set up an institute at a huge aeronautical research complex to be built near Braunschweig, and both the Research and Development Divisions began to fund Hellmuth Walter's hydrogen peroxide work in Kiel. While the destruction of the Luftwaffe archive in 1945 makes it difficult to discern the policy decisions that lay behind these initiatives, let alone the role of high-ranking leaders like Göring, the air force was clearly ensuring that it had a liquid-fuel-rocket capability independent of the army.

Sänger's hiring came first. A rocket experimenter and professional engineer, he submitted a rocket-aircraft proposal to the Germans in 1934 after its rejection by the Austrian military. Ordnance was not highly interested but eventually suggested that the Air Ministry might want to look into his theoretical investigations of rocket aircraft—indeed, Sänger's 1933 book had discussed his lifelong obsession, an orbital space plane, and a December 1934 article outlined a rocket-fighter concept that might have influenced von Richthofen. But in October 1935, after the founding of the alliance, von Braun recommended against the ministry hiring him on the grounds that his efforts would be duplicative.[25]

Research Division ignored this advice and offered Sänger a contract. Assigned to the DVL in Berlin, starting in February 1936, Sänger's first task was to search for a location for a rocket institute and test center to be affiliated with Braunschweig. Construction of this institute, near Trauen, began in 1937 under a cover name, with the apparent intent of obscuring its existence as much from the army as from foreign intelligence services! The Trauen facilities, built at a reported cost of 8 million marks, included a massive liquid-oxygen plant and a test stand for rocket motors of up to a 100 metric tons (220,000 lb) of thrust— both duplicating facilities at Peenemünde-East. Sänger's group began work there in 1938, tested a 1,000 kg thrust liquid-oxygen/diesel-oil rocket motor in 1939, and drew up a design for the 100 metric ton thrust engine for his space plane, now in the guise of an intercontinental rocket bomber. But the RLM never gave

Sänger adequate resources for the high-stakes rocket business and terminated his program in 1942.[26]

Lack of documentation makes it impossible to know when the Technical Office decided to make Sänger's institute into a secret competitor with the army. It could have been at the outset, but it may be relevant that the architect of the interservice alliance, Development Division Chief von Richthofen, left in November 1936 to become chief-of-staff of the Luftwaffe's Condor Legion, which was fighting for Franco in the Spanish Civil War. He asked for reassignment in part because of disagreements with Ernst Udet, the famous World War I fighter ace, whom Göring had cavalierly appointed to head the office in June 1936, even though he knew Udet to be a poor administrator. The major expenditure on Sänger's facility at Trauen could not have been made without Udet's approval, and it would have been consistent with Göring's desire to assert independence from the army.[27]

Shortly after the Air Ministry brought Sänger to Germany as a long-term investment, it also began to finance Walter's hydrogen peroxide rocket development, in the hope of more immediate results. In March 1936 Walter notified Ordnance that he no longer needed consultation because he had received from the RLM "a number of larger contracts for the development of hydrogen peroxide rocket devices, aerial torpedoes, jet reaction motors [ramjets?] and take-off-assist devices based on the catalytic decomposition of hydrogen peroxide." These contracts would finance the construction of a rocket test stand at Kiel as well, making the use of Kummersdorf facilities unnecessary.[28]

For military use in the field, hydrogen peroxide (H_2O_2) had a number of advantages over liquid oxygen. The latter cryogenic liquid, with a boiling point of $-183°C$ ($-297°F$), is difficult to handle and hard to store for long periods; any aircraft or weapon could only be fueled immediately before use. Peroxide in high concentrations (80 percent or more) was not easy to handle either, because of its tendency to explode when in contact with organic contaminants. But it could be stored at normal temperatures, and Walter, together with a Munich chemical firm, had developed a system for producing and handling it. He could also offer two different engine types: "hot" and "cold." In the "cold" version, the inherently unstable peroxide was run over or mixed with a catalyst, often calcium or sodium permanganate, and decomposed into super-heated steam and oxygen. He demonstrated just such a system to representatives from the army, Heinkel, and the Luftwaffe, including von Richthofen, on 30 June–1 July 1936 (not without problems, one might add; erratic decomposition of the peroxide produced small explosions). The "hot" engine would be longer in coming; it burned the free oxygen in the catalyzed peroxide with a hydrocarbon fuel, producing more thrust. Fuel efficiency would be improved too, although hydrogen peroxide would always be a markedly inferior oxidizer to liquid oxygen.[29]

Attracted by peroxide's flexibility and potential, the Air Ministry began taking an intense interest in Walter no later than December 1935; the first contract came from the DVL, which wanted a small rocket motor for mounting on an aircraft wingtip for roll tests.[30] During 1936 the RLM rapidly turned Walter's development into a parallel program with von Braun's liquid-oxygen/alcohol project at Kummersdorf. The Development Division decided sometime in 1936 or early 1937 to install a Walter motor in another He 112, while both it and the Research Division were interested in assisted-takeoff systems for heavily loaded airplanes. Eventually hydrogen peroxide would become the dominant rocket propellant in the Luftwaffe, freeing that service almost completely from dependence on army technology.

THE FIRST ROCKET-ASSISTED FLIGHTS

While Walter's engines began to interest the RLM more and more, the Ordnance liquid-oxygen/alcohol project was still the primary rocket-aircraft propulsion program in 1936. Engine tests on the Junkers Junior began early in the year. In April von Braun wrote to the Research Division noting that a number of test firings had already been made, but the 300 kg thrust engine needed to be redesigned, and it shifted the airplane's center of gravity too far back. Plans to fly the Junior were then canceled following numerous explosions and burnthroughs of the new lightweight engine design. Many additional changes were needed, and the experiments lasted until at least August 1936.[31]

The Junior ground tests primarily became a pathfinder program for the He 112 project, which was funded by Development Division. During 1936 Kummersdorf designed, constructed, and test-fired the new 1000 kg thrust engines. Toward the end of the year, the von Braun group installed one in an He 112 rear fuselage, but there were still explosions and "hard starts" caused by delayed ignition. At least one fuselage was wrecked and replaced. As a result, the ignition system was changed to a small flame in the middle of the injector. In February 1937, von Braun reported that "tests with the He 112 partial fuselage are now [proceeding] without setbacks. So far 20 tests have been made."[32]

The time had come to install an engine in the first flight aircraft. The Luftwaffe or Heinkel provided the He 112 V4, the fourth prototype. Von Braun reported in February that the "first burn tests with the He 112 V4 should begin in the coming week." At the next monthly meeting, on 1 March, he noted that Erich Warsitz from the main Luftwaffe test facility at Rechlin had been named as test pilot.[33]

Fig. 9.2. An He 112 rear fuselage with a liquid-oxygen/alcohol rocket engine is tested at Kummersdorf, 1936–37. Courtesy Ernst-Karl Heinkel

Fig. 9.3. The He 112 V4 aircraft immediately after completion at the Heinkel factory, probably in early 1936. Courtesy National Air and Space Museum, 72-8494

Fig. 9.4. The Focke-Wulf Fw 56 with a small Walter motor being tested at Neuhardenberg in the spring of 1937. Courtesy Public Record Office, London

The successful static tests notwithstanding, the Ordnance group did not have much confidence in the engine. To fit a rocket to a manned airplane meant that the thrust had to be throttleable and the controls simple. But the system was still tricky and hard starts were always a possibility. When Warsitz first came to Kummersdorf, he stood beside the aircraft and watched as von Braun ignited the engine from the cockpit. The noise was ear-splitting. Later that night he found out from von Braun in a Berlin bar that this was the first time that it had ever been done from the aircraft. Usually the engine was controlled from a bunker many meters away, but von Braun and Walter Künzel, the Heinkel engineer responsible for the rocket-aircraft program, were afraid that Warsitz would never get in the cockpit if he observed the engine test that way![34]

While the He 112 V4 was being prepared for flight, the Walter "cold" hydrogen peroxide program was rapidly catching up. In fact, the Luftwaffe's first rocket-assisted flight was made with such an engine in January or February 1937. Watched by Technical Office Chief Ernst Udet, a Heinkel He 72 Kadett biplane trainer owned by the DVL was boosted by a Walter motor of about 130 kg thrust. According to Hellmuth Walter, Udet himself piloted the third flight. Beginning in April, the RLM planned a concentrated, highly secret test program at the isolated Neuhardenberg airfield, east of Berlin (Peenemünde-West was not yet ready). In addition to the He 112 V4, there was a Focke-Wulf Fw 56 with a Heinkel-installed Walter engine; an He 111 two-engine bomber with the first Walter takeoff-assist rockets designed to be dropped off and reused; and an He

72, probably with a smaller Kummersdorf liquid-oxygen/alcohol engine. Thirty flights were made with this aircraft. The latter project was likely dropped, and virtually nothing is known about the Walter experiments, but there were static tests of the Fw 56.[35]

After numerous delays and twenty-eight static tests and flights under normal engine power, the He 112 was finally ready on 3 June 1937. With Pauls, von Braun, and Künzel as witnesses, Warsitz for the first time tested the ignition system in the air. He started the ignition flame and then attempted to turn it off. Since it would not go out, he ignited the engine at half-power to prevent overheating. The acceleration was mild, and after ten seconds he stopped it again. But Warsitz soon, in the words of the official report, "noticed a strong acrid odor of burning rubber and paint and clearly perceptible hot gases flowed under the pilot's seat." He looked back to see the tail on fire! Since he was very low, he decided on an immediate belly landing. Damage was significant. An unanticipated region of low aerodynamic pressure around the tail had sucked alcohol fumes back into the fuselage, where they were ignited by heating or the ignition flame.[36]

The aircraft had to be sent back to the Heinkel works for repairs and modifications, with a target date for completion of 15 July. The rocket engine also needed a number of technical improvements to prevent a reoccurrence of the accident. For secrecy reasons, Ordnance at first insisted that the engine be reinstalled at Peenemünde-East but eventually relented and allowed it to be done in a closed building at Marienehe. Warsitz flew the He 112 V4 at Neuhardenberg later in the year, but no records of these flights have yet come to light.[37]

In spite of this success, the safety of the V4's nitrogen-pressurized tankage system was doubtful, so the RLM, Ordnance, and Heinkel decided to rebuild the aircraft. The propellants would instead be pumped, using a turbopump powered by catalyzed hydrogen peroxide from a "steam generator." The Ordnance rocket group had begun developing turbopumps in 1935, because of the need for them in large rocket engines, and had contracted with Hellmuth Walter for a steam generator in spring 1936. The He 112 V4 system was to be derived from the preliminary design for a Heinkel pure rocket aircraft, as well as from the turbopump/steam generator in the Walter-engined version of the He 112. Again, no concrete data is available, but Warsitz piloted the He 112 V3 before the end of 1937. Flights continued into 1938, culminating in takeoffs solely under "cold" hydrogen peroxide rocket power, with the piston engine turned off. The V3's successes and technical problems with Ordnance's system, in conjunction with the RLM's policy of fostering an independent rocket capability, no doubt strengthened its growing preference for hydrogen peroxide.[38]

Fig. 9.5. The He 112 V3 at Neuhardenberg or Peenemünde-West, 1937–38. Courtesy Public Record Office, London

THE HE 176

With the completion in the fall of 1937 of successful rocket-assisted flights, the RLM was finally ready to approve the pure rocket aircraft. In October 1937 it assigned the designation He 176 to the Heinkel company's Project "P 1033," a concept on the drawing boards since about December 1936.[39] Ignoring the RLM's interest in a rocket interceptor—a decision that would later be fateful— Ernst Heinkel and his designers, Walter and Siegfried Günter, together with Erich Warsitz, laid out the He 176 with one purpose in mind: speed. They were enthralled with the idea of creating the world's fastest aircraft and saw that the rocket plane might even put the magic number of 1,000 km/h (621 mph) in their grasp. At the time, the world's record barely exceeded 700 km/h. To save weight, the He 176 was tiny: it had a wingspan of about 5 m (16.4 ft), a length of about 6 m (19.7 ft), and a total loaded weight of under two tons. In accordance with the aerodynamic knowledge of the time, the wings were thin, but not swept back. Their total area of only 5.5 square meters meant very high wing loading, and thus a high landing and stall speed. As a result, the He 176 was tricky to fly and difficult to glide if the propellants ran out, which was not un-likely given that there was only enough to last two minutes. Finally, the cockpit

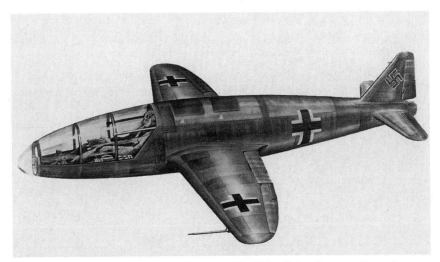

Fig. 9.6. A post-1945 artist's conception of the He 176 in flight. Courtesy Deutsches Museum

was so tight, it was literally designed to fit one man: Erich Warsitz. The He 176 would in effect be his personal rocket plane.[40]

Like the He 112, the He 176 would also receive two different rocket engines. Heinkel and the RLM decided no later than late 1937 that the first aircraft, the V1, would have a 600 kg thrust "cold" Walter motor, while the second would get the more powerful and efficient 1,000 kg, turbopump-driven, liquid-oxygen/alcohol engine similar to the one to be installed in the He 112 V4. Yet the He 176's small size was such that "the machine would already reach very high velocities in horizontal flight at a thrust of 40 to 100 kg." At an 11 January 1938 meeting, Ordnance, Heinkel, and the RLM decided to size the liquid-oxygen/alcohol engine for a thrust level of 750 kg (later reduced to 725 kg), with a capacity for the pilot to boost it to 1,000 kg for takeoff. Wernher von Braun's group also hoped to double combustion chamber pressure to 25 atm, further increasing fuel efficiency. Cooling problems, however, thwarted this plan, and the growing burdens of the army missile program kept the aircraft projects undermanned in Peenemünde-East and Kummersdorf. Ordnance promised the re-engined He 112 V4 would be ready in mid-March 1938, but technical problems postponed its return to Peenemünde-West until June 1939. The motor for the He 176 lagged even more, which must have further increased RLM skepticism about Ordnance's technology.[41]

The technical problems in fitting the liquid-oxygen/alcohol system to the little rocket plane were not confined to engine operation. From the outset, the engine mass in the tail was problematic because of its impact on the He 176's center of gravity. In early 1938 Heinkel specified a weight of only 14 kg, including the fuel circulating in the cooling jacket around the combustion chamber. Moreover, in August 1938 the Peenemünde-East engineer in charge stated: "The very difficult spatial relationships in the small machine make it necessary to divide the propellants among many tanks. For oxygen there are 3 tanks in a row one behind the other." The fuel was also divided between a fuselage tank and two in the wings—a very advanced design in which the water alcohol was contained inside the sealed wing structure. The multiple liquid oxygen tanks were particularly inopportune, because they increased warming and thus propellant evaporation loss. A small hydrogen peroxide tank was needed as well to power the steam-generator/turbopump. In truth, Ordnance's propulsion system was poorly suited to the tiny craft, which along with the He 176's marginal safety, brings into question the very design chosen by Heinkel and the Günter twins. By spring 1939 the Ordnance engine was postponed to the now projected V3 and V4 aircraft, which were to have one unified liquid oxygen tank. The He 176 V2 would receive a Walter motor.[42]

Little affected by these problems, Walter Künzel's ultrasecret "Special Development" unit at Heinkel proceeded rapidly with the construction of the V1 in 1938. In order to verify calculations of its aerodynamic qualities, the RLM paid for V1 testing from 9 to 13 July in the large windtunnel at the Aerodynamic Research Establishment in Göttingen. Meanwhile, Heinkel and Peenemünde-West began ground and air-drop tests of the separable cockpit section, which the designers had included because the He 176's anticipated high speed would make it impossible for Warsitz to make a traditional bail-out. In principle, Warsitz would fire explosive bolts and the cockpit would be separated by compressed air. The nose would be slowed by its own parachute until it reached a velocity at which he could jump out and descend on his parachute. But there were numerous problems with both the separation mechanisms and the cockpit parachute, which led to the addition of another 12 cm section behind the cockpit for a larger parachute and an inflation mechanism. The whole system was ultimately of little use, because it could only be activated above 6,000 m (20,000 ft).[43]

In late summer and fall 1938, the He 176 V1 underwent its first tow and taxi tests at Peenemünde-West.[44] It is immediately obvious that the V1 does not live up to its romantic postwar reconstructions. Most notably, it had an open cockpit and fixed landing gear, stop-gap measures likely undertaken by the Heinkel designers to accelerate the date of the first flight. (A flush canopy was available for flight tests.) The He 178 V1, the first turbojet aircraft, which was constructed in the same building, had the same features, reflecting Ernst Heinkel's desire to

Fig. 9.7. The He 176 VI at Peenemünde-West, 1938–39. Courtesy Public Record Office, London

get that airplane in the air as soon as possible in order to demonstrate the concept and establish a first. For the He 176, the plan was undoubtedly to have retractable gear and the jettisonable cockpit section on the V2. As for the V1's peculiar stance—resting on a tail skid even though it had a nose wheel—the weight distribution of the tiny craft was so sensitive that when Warsitz climbed in, he tipped it forward![45]

Because the wing design had not permitted retracting the main gear into the wings, those two wheels were only separated by the width of the fuselage: 80 cm (31.5″). The effect of this astonishingly small wheeltrack was immediately visible during the first tow tests behind a powerful car. Mole hills and other imperfections on the Peenemünde-West grass airfield caused the V1 to bang its wingtips on the ground; eventually bumpers were installed to prevent further damage. The tow test showed other problems, notably that the rudder was completely ineffective at low speeds; at some point a jet vane was installed in the rocket exhaust that activated when the rudder went hard over. Since the tow tests were not very useful, Warsitz began to make taxi tests with short bursts from the hydrogen peroxide engine in fall 1938. These revealed propulsion and stability deficiencies that led to the decision to send the aircraft back to Heinkel during the winter for modifications, ending hopes that it would fly in 1938.[46]

In March 1939, the He 176 V1 returned to Peenemünde. Warsitz soon began to take short hops of tens of meters but found that the existing runway was

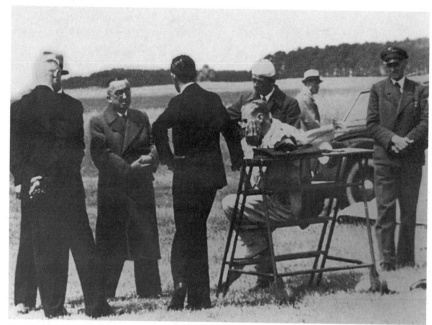

Fig. 9.8. Erich Warsitz (in white protective suit) sits with his face in his hand immediately after Gen. Ernst Udet forbade further flight tests of the He 176 V1. Third from the left is Ernst Heinkel. Courtesy Ernst-Karl Heinkel

Fig. 9.9. The only He 176 flight photo discovered so far. Whether this was a takeoff during a short hop or an actual flight is unknown. Courtesy Public Record Office

Fig. 9.10. Warsitz talks to Erhard Milch before or after a flight of the He 176 in June–July 1939. Courtesy Ernst-Karl Heinkel

too short for a full takeoff. Peenemünde-West hurriedly had to build extensions at either end. In May he was finally ready to give a demonstration to Ernst Udet and Göring's number-two man, State Secretary Erhard Milch. As soon as Udet saw the aircraft, Warsitz asserts, he exclaimed: "*Mensch*, those aren't wings, those are running boards! And you want to fly with that?" And after watching a short hop with a rather bad landing, Udet forbade Warsitz to fly the He 176 again, saying: "Every successful landing in that thing is a crash that miscarries." Warsitz allegedly flew to Berlin soon after and got Udet to lift the prohibition.[47]

After more test hops, Warsitz was finally ready on 15 June to make the first real flight. Accelerating very rapidly, Warsitz hit a new molehill and banged his aircraft's left wingtip bumper on the ground, diverting its takeoff roll to the left. Barely missing the trees, he turned and made a flight down the channel between the island and the mainland, circling back to the airfield. Warsitz claims that he exceeded 700 km/h (435 mph), but this is difficult to believe given the fixed landing gear and short flight duration. Fuel and endurance were so short, and the gliding characteristics of the airplane so doubtful, that he put the He 176 back down after only fifty seconds in the air. About 20 and 21 June, he repeated this hair-raising flight a couple more times, including once for Milch, Udet, and Heinkel.[48]

The He 176 flew for the very last time on 3 July 1939. In the hope of winning better industrial priorities for the Luftwaffe, Göring ordered that a demonstration of the latest technology be staged for Hitler at the main test center

Fig. 9.11. Adolph Hitler (third from left) witnesses the He 176 demonstration flight near Rechlin on 3 July 1939. At far left is Gen. Wilhelm Keitel, armed forces chief of staff; next to him is Field Marshal Hermann Göring, Luftwaffe commander in chief. Courtesy Ernst-Karl Heinkel

of Rechlin. Among other aircraft, the Führer saw the not-yet-flown, turbojet-powered Heinkel He 178 V1. Ernst Heinkel and the engine's inventor, Hans von Ohain, provided explanations. The climax of Hitler's visit was a flight of the He 176 from a field a few kilometers away. After a successful takeoff and quick circuit, Warsitz narrowly avoided a crash during the landing when the Walter motor quit at low altitude. He barely restarted it in time. Fortunately, this near disaster was imperceptible to nonexpert observers; an impressed Hitler ordered that Warsitz receive a prize of 20,000 marks. Not surprisingly, neither the RLM, Warsitz, nor Heinkel had any desire to see the V1 fly again. It was too risky, the attempt at record-breaking speed could only be made with the V2, and it was time to flight test the He 178.[49]

END OF THE FIRST ROCKET AIRCRAFT PROGRAM

The end for the He 176 came on 12 September 1939. In reordering priorities after Germany's unprovoked attack on Poland and the consequent, somewhat unexpected outbreak of World War II, Ernst Udet canceled the rocket plane, along with numerous other projects. Construction of the V2 through V4 airframes was abandoned. For unknown reasons, the contract with the army for the He 176's turbopump-driven, liquid-oxygen/alcohol engine continued for a few more months. Moreover, the He 112 V4 began flying again as a testbed for a similar engine in summer-fall 1939. Nonetheless, the interservice rocket-aircraft program was effectively dead. That was confirmed on 18 June 1940, when the He 112 V4 crashed at Peenemünde during its twenty-fifth flight with the redesigned engine. Another tail fire had severed the control linkages; the airplane dove into the ground, killing the pilot. Eventually the last vestige of Heinkel's rocket-aircraft work, the He 176 V1, was crated and sent to the Berlin Air Museum, where it was destroyed in an air raid in 1943 or 1944.[50]

Yet even before the He 176 and interservice programs, a transition to a second rocket-aircraft program was already underway. The RLM, and Udet in particular, were skeptical of not only the He 176's safety but also its usefulness. Ernst Heinkel and his designers, supported by Erich Warsitz, had tried to create an experimental record-breaking aircraft, the Luftwaffe's interest in a rocket interceptor notwithstanding. Heinkel's quest for fame and firsts had not been his sole motivation; he was also obsessed with protecting what was left of his autonomy against a ministry that had a monopoly on all domestic aircraft purchases, civil and military. Heinkel's decision to proceed with an aircraft that was so narrowly specialized—and so questionably designed—contributed, however, to a growing rift with the Air Ministry that would trouble him to the end of the Third Reich. Since no documents are available, it is impossible to pin down when the RLM began to disagree with Heinkel over the He 176's military impracticality, but Warsitz recalls that arguments with RLM officials caused weeks of delay. Warsitz also claims that he had to fight an order in mid-1938 not to fly the aircraft because it was unsafe. By the end of that year, the ministry had created a second rocket interceptor program at Messerschmitt.[51]

That program, which led to the Me 163 Komet, had its origin in fall 1937, when two members of the Research Division approached Alexander Lippisch, a well-known designer of unorthodox delta-wing gliders. They asked him to build an aircraft for a new, secret propulsion system, which Lippisch guessed immediately because he had put solid-fuel rockets on gliders during the late Weimar spaceflight fad. Sometime in 1938, Lippisch traveled to Rostock to discuss his project with Heinkel, the only airframe company with explicit knowledge of the rocket-aircraft program. It also possessed the special secure building for the project. As Lippisch later recalls, the meeting did not go well, because he felt that Heinkel's designers viewed him as a rival. Based in south-central Germany, Lippisch could also see potential coordination problems because of distance and different design philosophies. He had good relations with the Messerschmitt company in Bavaria, and Hans Antz, who took over responsibility in the RLM for high-speed airframes in October 1938, felt that creating a second, competing "special aircraft" group would be a good idea. Moreover, Messerschmitt had single-seater expertise. While Antz was not hostile to Heinkel, he saw that the

He 176 was purely experimental and would not lead directly to a rocket interceptor. On 2 January 1939, through Air Ministry mediation, Lippisch's group
became "Department L" at the Messerschmitt factory in Augsburg.[52]

Only after the unhappy end of Heinkel's involvement in rocket aircraft in
1939–40 did the Lippisch/Messerschmitt group become *the* Luftwaffe project
in this area. But in the meantime, the rocket interceptor concept had itself been
somewhat eclipsed by a profound transformation in aircraft reaction propulsion:
the "turbojet revolution." Knowing of Ernst Heinkel's fascination with speed,
Hans von Ohain contacted him in March 1936 through his doctoral adviser in
order to receive support for his turbojet idea. Heinkel brought him to Rostock-
Marienehe and begun funding his experiments privately, not telling the RLM.
Von Ohain, for his part, only had vague intimations of the rocket work going
on simultaneously at the plant. After he successfully demonstrated his first
primitive, bench-model turbojet in spring 1937, Ernst Heinkel and his designers saw that they indeed had a potentially revolutionary propulsion system in
their hands. But to receive priorities for materials in the tightly regulated Nazi
economy, Heinkel revealed the project to the RLM no later than December.
In spring 1938, when Uvo Pauls left Berlin to take over Peenemünde-West, he
was replaced as desk officer of "Special Engines" by an energetic, highly trained
young engineer, Hans Mauch. Mauch in turn attracted another well-trained engineer, Helmut Schelp from the Research Division, to assist him. The two immediately grasped the importance of the turbojet and set out to interest aero-
engine manufacturers in the technology.[53]

I will not repeat the details of the "turbojet revolution" in Germany here.
Suffice it to say that the RLM in the person of Mauch, Schelp, and their ally in
airframes, Antz, did not neglect turbojet technology, as Ernst Heinkel asserted
after the war. Quite the opposite, in fact, but the RLM officials were skeptical
of his airframe company's ability to mass produce engines—something Heinkel
naturally resented. They may also have been irritated by his independent streak.
After some effort, Mauch and Schelp managed to interest Junkers, BMW, and
other companies in starting turbojet programs, while Antz encouraged Messerschmitt to begin a jet fighter design in addition to its rocket plane work. But they
certainly had no intention of discouraging Heinkel—and on 27 August 1939,
five days before the German assault on Poland, Warsitz flew the He 178 V1. Two
weeks later, when Udet canceled the He 176 and many other projects, his comment on the He 178 was: "Work on single-seaters with turbojet engines must be
pushed forward with all speed, so that an operational aircraft can be created as
soon as possible." Notwithstanding Heinkel's later assertions that Udet and his
subordinates took little interest in the He 178, jets clearly had high priority
from the Luftwaffe from the beginning of the war.[54]

CONCLUSIONS

Why was the German Air Ministry so open to the turbojet idea in 1938–39, just as it was to the rocket in 1935? In both cases, personalities played important roles—in 1935, von Richthofen, in 1938–39, Mauch, Schelp, and Antz. Throughout the period one can also see the influence of general factors: notably, the absence of an entrenched establishment in the Luftwaffe, the high level of scientific and engineering competence in the German aeronautical community, and the technological and ideological enthusiasm of engineers, industrialists, and officers who wished to make Hitler's Reich quickly superior to the other powers.

Yet there is little doubt that the Luftwaffe's first foray into reaction-propulsion technology also laid the groundwork for the second. When Mauch, Schelp, and Antz came into their positions in 1938, the Air Ministry already had a considerably investment in that technology, in small part through Paul Schmidt's ongoing pulsejet research and Eugen Sänger's rocket institute, but above all through the rocket-aircraft and takeoff-assist programs increasingly dominated by Hellmuth Walter's technology. No other air force in the world had so much experience with, and interest in, rocketry and other forms of reaction propulsion. The only partial exception was the Soviet air force, but Stalin's purges derailed the USSR's rocket programs in 1938. In Britain and the United States, advocates of rocket and turbojet propulsion only began to get support from the services around that time.[55]

If the history of the Luftwaffe's quest for high-speed flight by rocket plane sheds light on the origins of the "turbojet revolution" in Germany, it also illuminates the relations between aircraft manufacturers and the Air Ministry. Heinkel's desire to protect his independence as a designer and industrialist clashed with the RLM's desire for total control over all German aviation, military and civilian. While the so-called National Socialist regime was largely capitalist in its economic base, the Nazis did not hesitate to nationalize firms or create new government-owned firms if private capital was not amenable to their aggressive aims. In the case of the aircraft industry, Hitler's regime made a frightening example of Hugo Junkers in 1933, when he was put under house arrest and forced to relinquish ownership of his firms because of his democratic and pacifist views. He died a broken man two years later. Ernst Heinkel, whose politics were certainly more congenial to the Nazis, must nevertheless have been mindful of that ultimate threat. Yet, as the He 176 and turbojet/He 178 programs show, he did try to retain as much technical and managerial control over them as was feasible—in the former case, designing the airplane for record-breaking speed rather than military use, in the latter case, attempting to finance the radical new engine technology alone. This strategy added to RLM's grow-ing irritation with him after 1938, which in turn contributed to his ultimate loss of the contracts for operational rocket and jet fighters to Willi Messerschmitt.

Finally, the history of the first German rocket-aircraft program illuminates the origins of many myths about the Luftwaffe's pioneering efforts, notably those that derive from Heinkel's memoirs. He was understandably bitter about the RLM favoring Messerschmitt, although he had pioneered both technologies. He was further embittered about his fight with the Ministry over the right to mass produce jet engines after 1939; although it eventually allowed him to buy the Stuttgart aero-engine firm of Hirth, none of his engine types got beyond the development stage. During the war, there were recriminations about the failure of the He 177 heavy bomber project as well. As a result, Heinkel unconsciously rewrote the history of the early years of rocket and jet aircraft to minimize the competence and significance of the Air Ministry. In fact, he eliminated the RLM from the origins of rocket aircraft altogether, even though it had been the driving force from the outset, and he cited Udet's dismissive comments about the He 176 V1 as evidence for the Ministry's continuing short-sightedness. As for the turbojet, after 1945 he labeled the RLM as bumbling and slow, and his views fit well with those of others, like Gen. Adolf Galland, who claimed that the Ministry and Hitler were responsible for jet aircraft allegedly appearing "too late" to alter the course of the war.[56] Although there is no doubt that the RLM's Technical Office slowly became dysfunctional after Udet took over in 1936, the reality behind these myths is an important lesson for aerospace historians, who have too often accepted memoirs and interviews uncritically, while neglecting primary research.

Despite the justified questions about Heinkel's book, and about his com-mitted service to an evil regime, there is no doubt that his imagination and energy contributed much to the achievement of the two historic firsts by the He 176 and 178. Along with Hans von Ohain, Helmuth Walther, Wernher von Braun, and many others, Heinkel played a critical role in ushering in a new era of aeropropulsion and high-speed flight. Of that place in history, at least, he can-not be deprived.

NOTES

I would like to thank Dr. Volker Koos of Rostock for his invaluable assistance during the research and writing of this article. In addition, Karlheinz Rohrwild of the Hermann-Oberth-Raumfahrt-Museum provided source materials, and Prof. William Leary of the University of Georgia made useful comments on an earlier draft. Part of this article has been reprinted from Chapter 2 of my book *The Rocket and Reich: Peenemünde and the Coming of the Ballistic Missile Era* (New York: Free Press, 1995/ Cambridge, Mass.: Harvard University Press, 1996), courtesy of the Smithsonian Institution.

1. A few Germans made flights in gliders boosted by commercial solid rockets in late Weimar; see Frank H. Winter, "1928–1929 Forerunners of the Shuttle: The 'Von Opel' Flights," *Spaceflight* 21 (Feb. 1979): 75–83, 92. The He 176 was, however, the first aircraft designed from the outset to be powered exclusively by a rocket engine. See the valuable article by Volker Koos, "Heinkel He 176—Dichtung und Wahrheit," *Jet & Prop* No. 1 (1994): 17–21, and Botho Stüwe, *Peenemünde-West* (Esslingen: Bechtle, 1995), chap. 8. For a useful overview, see C. M. Ehresman, "Liquid Rocket Propulsion Applied to Manned Aircraft—In Historical Perspective," *Journal of the British Interplanetary Society* 46 (1993): 255–68.

2. Edward W. Constant II, *The Origins of the Turbojet Revolution* (Baltimore, Md.: Johns Hopkins University Press, 1980). Constant's term effectively describes the transformation even if one does not accept his Kuhnian model of technological change.

3. Ernst Heinkel, *Stürmisches Leben*, ed. Jürgen Thorwald (pseud. for Heinz Bongartz) (Stuttgart: Mundus, 1953); translated as *Stormy Life* (New York: Dutton, 1956). See chap. 12.

4. H. Dieter Köhler, *Ernst Heinkel—Pionier der Schnellflugzeuge* (Koblenz: Bernhard & Graefe, 1983), pp. 15–16, 177.

5. William Green and Frank Ziegler, "World's First Jets," *RAF Flying Review*, July 1954, pp. 17–19; J. R. Smith and Anthony L. Kay, *German Aircraft of the Second World War* (London: Putnam, 1972), pp. 262–63, 276–79, 290–92; Heinz Nowarra, *Heinkel und seine Flugzeuge* (Munich: J. F. Lehmanns, 1975), pp. 115–16, 118; Wolfgang Wagner, *Die ersten Strahlflugzeuge der Welt* (Koblenz: Bernhard & Graefe, 1989), pp. 46–47. In *Rocket Fighter* (New York: Ballantine, 1971), pp. 18–37, William Green takes a more differentiated approach to the RLM but still is dependent on Heinkel for the rocket aircraft program. Köhler's hagiographic but fairly scholarly biography is similar: *Ernst Heinkel*, pp. 150–63.

6. Constant, *Origins of the Turbojet Revolution*, pp. 198–207; Ralf Schabel, *Die Illusionen der Wunderwaffen* (Munich: R. Oldenbourg, 1994), pp. 37–44; Heinkel, *Stürmisches Leben*, pp. 448–52. Even Schlaifer's classic study of aero-engines in Robert Schlaifer and S. D. Heron, *Development of Aircraft Engines/Development of Aviation Fuels* (Boston: Graduate School of Business Administration, Harvard University, 1950), pp. 377–78, repeats Heinkel's rocket-aircraft myth. Heinkel's stories, conveyed through Allied interrogations, obviously were influential even before they were published in memoir form.

7. The Army side was treated in the memoirs of Gen. Walter Dornberger, *V-2* (New York: Viking, 1954), and Wernher von Braun (hereinafter WvB), "Reminiscences of German Rocketry," *Journal of the British Interplanetary Society* 15 (May–June 1956): 125–145, but in both cases so superficially as to have little impact on the acceptance of Heinkel's story.

8. See Michael J. Neufeld, *The Rocket and the Reich: Peenemünde and the Coming of the Ballistic Missile Era* (New York: Free Press, 1995/Cambridge, Mass.: Harvard University Press, 1996), pp. 333–37, for a description. The FE (Fort Eustis) microfilm of Ordnance/Peenemünde records is at the National Air and Space Museum Archives Division (hereafter NASM), Garber Facility Bldg. 12. The key file on Army-Luftwaffe cooperation is FE746 on FE rolls 36–37; the original is now file RH8/v.1946 in the Bundesarchiv/Militärarchiv Freiburg (hereafter BA/MA).

9. Zanssen note, 20 May 1935, and marginal comment by "D." on von Horstig (Zanssen) to Wimmer, chief of RLM Tech. Office, 22 May 1935, in NASM, FE746; Baeumker/RLM/LC I to Becker, 10 Oct. 1934, in Imperial War Museum, MI 14/801(V). Technical Office Research Division was LC I, Development Division was LC II.

10. On the Air Ministry, see Edward L. Homze, *Arming the Luftwaffe* (Lincoln: University of Nebraska Press, 1976).

11. On German aerodynamics, see Constant, *Origins of the Turbojet Revolution*, pp. 152–60.

12. Schneider order on A-2 presentation, 15 Jan. 1935, in BA/MA, RH8/v. 1945; WvB, "Reminiscences," pp. 123–24.

13. Von Richtofen notes, 6 Feb. 1935, in National Archives (hereafter NA) microfilm publication

T-971, roll 73 (no frame numbers); von Richthofen to von Horstig, 6 Feb. 1935, Zanssen (WvB) report, 16 Feb. 1935, von Horstig (Zanssen) to von Richthofen, 19 Feb. 1935, and Junkers report of 18 Dec. 1934 in BA/MA, RH8/v. 1221; Harald Kunze, "Die Zusammenarbeit von Hugo Junkers und Johannes Winkler," NTM 24 (1987): 63–82.

14. Zanssen and WvB report, 26 Mar. 1935, on Schmidt visit, Becker (Zanssen) to RLM, 9 Apr. 1935, and WvB note to Zanssen, 30 June 1935, in Deutsches Museum Archives (hereinafter DM); P. Schmidt and F. Goslau contributions to Theodor Benecke and A. W. Quick, eds., History of German Guided Missile Development (Braunschweig: E. Appelhaus, 1957), pp. 375–418.

15. Walter to Becker, 15 Oct. 1934, in NASM, FE 724/b, and Walter to Reichswehr Ministry, 28 Oct. 1934, in NASM, FE 724/c; H. Walter article in Benecke and Quick, History, pp. 263–80. See also Hellmuth Walter, Report on Rocket Power Plants Based on T-Substance (translation of 1943 report), NACA Technical Memorandum No. 1170 (Washington: NACA, 1947); Walter, "Experience with the Application of Hydrogen Peroxide for Production of Power," Jet Propulsion 14 (May–June 1954): 166–71; Emil Kruska, "Das Walter-Verfahren, ein Verfahren zur Gewinnung von Antriebsenergie," VDI-Zeitschrift 97 (1955): 65–70, 271–77, 709–13, 823–29; and René Simard, "Hydrogen Peroxide as a Source of Power," The Engineering Journal (Canada) 31 (Apr. 1948): 219–25.

16. Walter to Becker, 15 Oct. 1934 (quote), in NASM, FE727/b; and Walter-Ordnance correspondence, 29 Nov. 1934–27 Mar. 1936, in NASM, FE727/b and /c; Walter and Irene Sänger-Bredt contributions in Benecke and Quick, History, pp. 263, 277–78, 326.

17. Constant, Origins of the Turbojet Revolution, pp. 178–204; Zanssen note, 20 May 1935, and Aktennotiz, 22 May 1935, in NASM, FE746.

18. Von Horstig (Zanssen) to Wimmer, 22 May 1935, in NASM, FE746.

19. WvB, "Stellungnahme . . . ," 27 June 1935, and von Horstig minutes of 27 June meeting in NASM, FE746.

20. Von Horstig minutes of 27 June 1935 meeting in NASM, FE746; von Richthofen notes, 27 May 1935, in NA, T-971/73.

21. Draft agreement, 2 Sep. 1935, WvB to Lorenz, 25 Oct. 1935, Kirchhoff to WvB, 10 Jan. 1936, Kirchhoff to DVL, 10 Jan. 1936, and WvB to Lorenz, 24 Apr. 1936, in NASM, FE746; WvB to von Horstig, 23 Nov. 1935, in NASM, FE727/a; Constant, Origins of the Turbojet Revolution, p. 203.

22. WvB minutes of 16 Oct. 1935 meeting, Heinkel works to WvB, 5 Oct. 1935, and WvB to Alpers/RLM/LC II, 14 Dec. 1935, in NASM, FE746. The Oct. 16 meeting must be the one that Heinkel, in Stürmisches Leben, pp. 448–50, places in November.

23. Neufeld, Rocket and the Reich, pp. 49–56; Stüwe, Peenemünde-West, p. 20.

24. Arthur Rudolph, oral history interview with Michael Neufeld, Hamburg, Germany, August 4, 1989, deposited in the NASM Department of Space History; Helmuth Trischler, Luft und Raumfahrtforschung in Deutschland (Frankfurt: Campus, 1992), pp. 208–19.

25. Heinz Gartmann, The Men Behind the Space Rockets (New York: David McKay, 1956), pp. 99–102; Irene Sänger-Bredt, "The Silver Bird Story: A Memoir," in R. Cargill Hall, ed., History of Rocketry and Astronautics (San Diego: Univelt, 1986), pp. 195–228; Eugen Sänger, Raketenflugtechnik (Munich and Berlin: R. Oldenbourg, 1933), and "Neuere Ergebnisse der Raketenflugtechnik," Flug, Sonderheft 1 (Dec. 1934): 1–22, here 19–21; Wa Prw 1 correspondence on Sänger, 16 Oct. 1934–2 Oct. 1935, in BA/MA, RH8/v. 1225.

26. Gartmann, Men, pp. 103–106; Eugen Sänger, "Arbeits-Kurzbericht der Abteilung Sänger 1936–1945," manuscript, July 1945, in American Institute of Physics, Samuel Goudsmit Papers; Sänger-Bredt, "Silver Bird," pp. 206–11; I. Sänger-Bredt and R. Engel, "The Development of Regeneratively Cooled Liquid Rocket Engines in Austria and Germany, 1926–1942," in First Steps Toward Space, ed. Frederick C. Durant III and George S. James (San Diego: Univelt, 1985), pp. 237–44; Trischler, Luft- und Raumfahrtforschung, pp. 219–20.

27. Homze, Arming, pp. 102–103, 171; James S. Corum, "The Luftwaffe and the Coalition Air War

in Spain, 1936–1939," *Journal of Strategic Studies* 18 (March 1995): 68–90, here 74–75. See also the conflict with Ordnance over how much Sänger could publish: correspondence, 19 Jan.–16 Feb. 1937, in BA/MA, RH8/v. 1225; minutes of 18 Feb. 1937 LC II-Wa Prw D meeting in NASM, FE746.

28. Wa Prw 11 to von Horstig, 27 Mar. 1936, in NASM, FE724/b.

29. W. Riedel Aktennotiz, 5 July 1936, in NASM, FE 724/b; Elektrochemische Werke München AG, "Bericht für Herrn Prof. Dr. Krauch . . . ," 17 Mar. 1942, in NA, T-73/r. 84/fr. 3396669-73; Walter, "Development," in Benecke and Quick, eds., *History*, pp. 263–80; Walter, "Experience," pp. 166–67; Simard, "Hydrogen Peroxide."

30. Kruse/RLM to von Horstig, 23 Dec. 1935, in NASM, FE724/b; William Green, *Warplanes of the Third Reich* (Garden City, NY: Doubleday, 1972), p. 594.

31. WvB to Lorenz/RLM/LC I, 24 Apr. 1936, Tschirschwitz/DVL reports, 16 June and 19 Aug. 1936, in NASM, FE746; Walter Riedel, "Raketenentwicklung . . . ," (ms., 1950), Imperial War Museum, German Misc. Doc. 148, p. 35; Dornberger, *V-2*, p. 124.

32. RLM/LC II report, 18 Feb., on monthly meeting with Wa Prw D, and RLM minutes of visits to Heinkel, 16 Jan. and 16 Feb. 1937, in NASM, FE746; Heinkel, *Stürmisches Leben*, pp. 450–51, 455; Stüwe, *Peenemünde-West*, pp. 19, 25.

33. RLM/LC II reports, 18 Feb. and 1 Mar. 1937, on monthly meetings with Wa Prw D, in NASM, FE746. The V4 was not sent to Spain, as various secondary sources report; see "Aufstellung über He112," 31 Mar. 1937, Heinkel archives, Stuttgart, kindly supplied by Volker Koos. Stüwe, based on a 1952 Warsitz interview, states that the test pilot had been involved since December 1935. This is possible, but not supported by surviving Ordnance records. Stüwe makes numerous mistakes regarding the "He 112R" due to weak archival research: *Peenemünde-West*, pp. 13–26.

34. Warsitz quoted in Bob Ward, *Wernher von Braun Anekdotisch* (Esslingen: Bechtle, 1972). pp. 7–9; Stüwe, *Peenemünde-West*, pp. 16–17.

35. RLM/LC-Wa Prw D correspondence and minutes, 18 Feb.–3 May 1937, in NASM, FE746; W. Ahlborn, "Flugmessungen an einem Stück des Flugzeugmusters FW 56 mit Walter-Rückstoßgerät," Deutsche Luftfahrtforschung Forschungsbericht Nr. 1078 (1939), NASM, German-Japanese Air Technical Documents, r. 2017; H. Walter, *Report*, p. 1, "Experience," p. 166, and "Development," pp. 264, 270; Koos, "He 176," p. 20; Stüwe, *Peenemünde-West*, pp. 31–39; Heinkel, *Stürmisches Leben*, pp. 458–59.

36. Pauls, WvB, Künzel, Warsitz report, 3 June 1937, and LC II 2e report, 7 June 1937, in NASM, FE746; Dornberger, *V-2*, p. 125.

37. RLM/LC-Wa Prw D-Heinkel correspondence, 23 June–13 July 1937, in NASM, FE746; Heinkel, *Stürmisches Leben*, p. 457; Stüwe, *Peenemünde-West*, pp. 36–37.

38. Ordnance-RLM-Heinkel correspondence and minutes, 16 Jan. 1937–3 Jan. 1938; WvB to von Horstig, 23 Nov. 1935, in NASM, FE727/a; Ordnance-Walter correspondence, 1936, in NASM, FE724/b; Stüwe, Peenemünde-West, p. 39. Footage of He 112 V3 takeoffs can be found in the 1945 Royal Air Force film "Rocket Flight," NASM.

39. Letter from Volker Koos, 17 Apr. 1996. "P 1033" is first mentioned in the 18 Feb. 1937 minutes, "He 176" in the Heinkel minutes of a 23 Oct. 1937 meeting with WvB, both in NASM, FE746.

40. Köhler, *Ernst Heinkel*, pp. 22–23, 90–91, 153–56; Koos, "He 176," pp. 19–21; Stüwe, *Peenemünde-West*, pp. 150–57; Heinkel, *Stürmisches Leben*, pp. 460–62; Antz memorandum, 14 Oct. 1938, BA/MA, RL3/780.

41. Ordnance-RLM-Heinkel correspondence and minutes, 13 Dec. 1937–15 June 1939, in NASM, FE746 (quotation from 11 Jan. 1938; see esp. Dellmeier report of 2 Aug. 1938); Stüwe, *Peenemünde-West*, p. 188; Neufeld, *Rocket and the Reich*, chap. 3.

42. Ordnance-RLM-Heinkel corr. and minutes, 8 Dec. 1937–28 Apr. 1939 (quote from Dellmeier report of 2 Aug. 1938), in NASM, FE746. The Antz memorandum, 14 Oct. 1938, in BA/MA, RL3/780, lists He 176 V3 and V4 as Walter-engine craft, but Hertel (draft by Künzel) to WvB, 6 Mar.

1939, in FE746, discusses their redesign with unitary liquid-oxygen tanks, strongly implying that V3 would be the first Ordnance-engine aircraft.

43. Koos, "Heinkel He 176," pp. 19–20; Heinkel-AVA Göttingen-RLM correspondence, May–Aug. 1938, in DLR e.V., Göttingen, copies courtesy of Volker Koos; Stüwe, *Peenemünde-West*, pp. 156–62; Smith and Kay, *German Aircraft*, pp. 276–79.

44. It was found in a 1945 British report on hydrogen peroxide, ADM 199/2434, Public Record Office, Kew. Koos first published it in his 1994 article, "Heinkel He 176."

45. On the He 178, see Hans von Ohain in Joseph J. Ermenc, ed., *Interviews with German Contributors to Aviation History* (Westport, Conn.: Meckler, 1990), p. 37; Heinkel minutes of mid-July 1938 meeting, in Wagner, *Die ersten Strahlflugzeuge*, p. 17; J. Richard Smith and Eddie Creek, *Jet Planes of the Third Reich* (Boylston, Mass.: Monogram Aviation Publications, 1982), pp. 12–17.

46. Stüwe, *Peenemünde-West*, pp. 171–75, based on a 1952 Warsitz interview and a 1963 speech by Künzel, both in Warsitz's papers.

47. Ibid., pp. 175–77.

48. Ibid., pp. 177–82. Stüwe gives reasons why the traditional first flight date of 20 June is very probably wrong. See also Warsitz's 1959 account quoted in Köhler, *Ernst Heinkel*, pp. 158–59.

49. Stüwe, *Peenemünde-West*, pp. 182–88. See also Heinkel, *Stürmisches Leben*, pp. 468–72; von Ohain in Ermenc, ed., *Interviews*, pp. 42–44; von Ohain, telephone interview with author, 21 Feb. 1996.

50. Stüwe, *Peenemünde-West*, pp. 190–94; Udet order, 12 Sep. 1939, in BA/MA, RL3/1825; Udet order, 16 Nov. 1939, in BA/MA, RL3/352; Zanssen to Dornberger, 22 June 1940, Thiel to Pauls and Thiel to Dornberger, 18 July 1940, in NASM, FE746; Schabel, *Illusionen*, p. 53.

51. Stüwe, *Peenemünde-West*, pp. 162–63, 172–73; Smith and Kay, *German Aircraft*, pp. 278–79; Köhler, *Ernst Heinkel*, pp. 21–23, 132.

52. Lippisch in Ermenc. ed., *Interviews*, pp. 166–69; Antz memorandum, 14 Oct. 1938, BA/MA, RL3/780.

53. Constant, *Origins of the Turbojet Revolution*, pp. 194–201; Schabel, *Illusionen*, pp. 38–40; Hans von Ohain, "The Evolution and Future of Aeropropulsion Systems," in Walter J. Boyne and Donald S. Lopez, eds., *The Jet Age* (Washington, D.C.: NASM, 1979), pp. 25–46, here 30–34; von Ohain telephone interview; Köhler, *Ernst Heinkel*, pp. 163–69, 176; von Ohain and Schelp in Ermerc, ed., *Interviews*, pp. 5–42, 108–10.

54. Schabel, *Illusionen*, pp. 39–42, 51–54; Constant, *Origins of the Turbojet Revolution*, pp. 200, 204–207; Udet order, 12 Sep. 1939, in BA/MA, RL3/1825; Smith and Kay, *German Aircraft*, pp. 532–33; Heinkel, *Stürmisches Leben*, pp. 474–85.

55. Frank H. Winter, *Prelude to the Space Age* (Washington, D.C.: Smithsonian Institution Press, 1983), pp. 55–71; Constant, *Origins of the Turbojet Revolution*, pp. 190–92; Sir Frank Whittle, "The Birth of the Jet Engine in Britain," in Boyne and Lopez, *The Jet Age*, pp. 3–24, here 9–10; Clayton R. Koppes, *JPL and the American Space Program* (New Haven, Conn.: Yale University Press, 1982), pp. 8–10.

56. Schabel's *Illusionen der Wunderwaffen* is the most systematic attack yet on the persistent myths about the jets.

Revolutionary Innovation and the Invisible Infrastructure

Making Royal Air Force Bomber Command Efficient, 1939–45

ROBIN HIGHAM

By the mid-1930s aviation had advanced to the point that many developments coalesced to create not only the visible signs that aviation had reached a real takeoff point but also the environment for success. These developments were not merely the visible progress in aerodynamics, engines, fuels, reliability, and economy of operation for the airlines and of range and firepower for air forces, but in the hidden infrastructure, from metallurgy to testing to operational support.

Progress to the mid-1930s could be seen in the use of all-metal construction, itself made really feasible by the development of the aluminum alloy S2024 and flush riveting, by the RAF's testing of engines to raise reliability from the meager 2 hours and 44 minutes of 1918 to some 1,700 hours by 1929, by the development of rated fuels and cast-block engines, by the appearance of the variable-pitch and constant-speed propellers, by retractable undercarriages, hydraulic brakes, flaps, and other ancillary systems, as well as by the training of fitters and riggers (mechanics) as well as pilots in rigorous schools, to mention but some of the important evidence.

But it was really the failure in 1934 of the disarmament talks, followed by rearmament and then war, that cut the purse strings and allowed air force innovation to flourish. This other side of the visible progress and revolutions that took place between 1934 and 1945 has been neglected because it has been taken for granted or overlooked. None of the revolutionary rate of innovation in this critical decade could have been possible without the invisible infrastructure that enabled innovation to be converted into functional reality. The invisible infrastructure itself was an offspring of the quiet progress of the 1918–34 period, as is demonstrated here by the long effort to make Royal Air Force Bomber Command effective.

To be successful in a period of technological change and innovation, an organization must be able to stimulate and simulate change, gamble on the future, have a vision that is multifaceted as well as clear as to objectives, and be able to allocate limited resources and make external allies. It must reward or tolerate risk-taking and expect some failures. The trouble with the RAF in the years 1919–39 was that it had little idea of the relationship of doctrine to reality. Its leadership was Western Front 1914–17 minded and colonial influenced. Air exercises showed little imagination and scant appreciation of what was happening in military thought and not much awareness of the vital role of sea power in British defense.

In late 1938, after Munich and all through 1939, the RAF was in parlous condition, though wonders were being done with increasing production. The Air Staff lacked focus (it had 59 types in production), and hand tools, spares, fitters, and riggers were in short supply, with bombs, bombsights, and navigation left over from 1918.

The British were lucky in that the German vision of war was not like theirs, of a massive air bombardment in a three-day war. Concentration on frontline strength when combined with lack of perception of the infrastructure by the RAF led to the creation of a force that, once it failed as a deterrent, could not fight effectively and efficiently. At the same time, the vast influx of hostilities-only personnel diluted the establishment.

In his 1947 *Despatches* Marshal of the Royal Air Force (MRAF) Sir Arthur "Bomber" Harris repeats the word *efficient*. As the manager of the grand-strategic bomber offensive from February 1942 to May 1945, he was responsible for converting the air weapon from hit-or-miss attacks on Germany to one that could bring the country to its knees. Harris had to harness innovation to the needs of war. His writings make plain that this was a tremendous job that took a remarkable amount of time and effort in constant battles not only simply to get an efficient airplane, the Avro Lancaster, but also to create the whole invisible infrastructure of the bamboo basket so that at the bottom throat, his airfields, the weapon emerged ready for efficient action. The story of RAF Bomber Command is by no means the only one in which the harnessing of innovation took place, but it is an example that has many lessons to teach us not complicated by mobility, overseas shipments, or outside or incoming raw and other materials, and it shows also how slow and complex the honing of innovation was, even in a highly industrialized economy overseen by the benevolent despot Winston Churchill.

REVOLUTIONARY INNOVATIONS

The years 1934 to 1945 were as revolutionary for aviation as the two decades after 1855 had been for the Royal Navy. But the eleven years that followed 1934 were both evolutionary and revolutionary. Many of the developments that were applied in the Second World War came out of the First, even if the impecuniousness of the Great Depression meant that the pace was slowed.

Between 1934 and 1945 there would be a great deal of invention and innovation, much of it interlocking. Each such advance required skilled personnel either to be switched from past skills or recruited and trained ab initio. They had not only to learn to construct everything from airfields to radar, but also to repair and service them. Thus not only did everything have to arrive at the throat of the bamboo basket on schedule and in sufficient quantities and of the required quality, but they had to be kept operational. Any lack of vital parts or personnel could render the whole organization inefficient, a reflection on command or management.

Writers have concentrated on the most obvious sides of air war: action and airplanes. But absolutely vital was the invisible infrastructure that made operations possible. This included the diplomatic, political, economic, scientific and technological, medical, social and ideological, and educational, the latter being better known as training.

The diplomatic involved the preemptive buying of the vital metallurgical ingredient, chrome, in Turkey and of ball bearings in Sweden and their transport to the United Kingdom as much as the application of the U.S. Lend-Lease legislation of March 1941. The political concerned the grand-strategic direction of the war, and it affected Bomber Command by way of decisions giving priority to overseas theaters and to the anti-U-boat campaign, which siphoned off aircraft and aircrews and sometimes dictated target selection.

The economic aspects of war were a complicated melange of materials, manpower, money, and even medicine, which limited the number of persons who could be allocated to airfield construction, to manufacturing, to building pipelines and running railways, and the use of women and older and younger persons to dilute both the civilian workforce and the armed services. Medical personnel stepped in to demand adequate rations, clothing, and rest. The scientific and technological aspects were to be seen not only in the pure science, which created radar and later the atomic bomb as well as the measures to counter these developments, but also in the use of operational research (OR) to make inventions and even ordinary weapons efficient and effective.

Medical work was very important as aircraft flew at higher altitudes and cold and anoxia became deleterious to efficiency, flights became so long that crews needed refreshments or sustenance, and the means of survival in the event of ditching became vitally important in recovering aircrew, who after six operations were priceless.

The social and ideological factors were not so obvious, but the war effort was undertaken by humans who had their own wants and needs. For example, an increase in rations preceded bad news; venereal disease was not only to be avoided, but infection could lead to a charge of self-inflicted injury to the detriment of the service. Unhealthy people on sick call or in the hospital weakened the national war effort.

Lastly, one of the most important aspects of all in the bamboo basket was training at all levels. As training of necessity had to be lengthened to meet the rising complexities not only of professionalism but also of technology, so manpower shortages impinged. One of the complaints of Bomber Command in 1944 was that essential new radar could not be maintained because there was a shortage of trained radar mechanics.

All of these things demanded more and more forethought and responsibility on the part of management and command. This in turn created an increasingly complex organizational structure. This can be seen at two levels. The wonderfully simple and straightforward Air Ministry Organization, described in the forty-five-page *List and Distribution of Duties of the Air Staff* in 1924, which had by 1944 become the four-hundred-page "telephone book."

Bomber Command itself was created in 1936 when the old Air Defense of Great Britain was compartmented. It took until June 1944, however, for the Command to arrive at a suitably functional wartime administrative organization. Parkinson's Law that complex organizations grow at a rate of 6 percent per annum was evident, but the cause in this case, as Joel Hurstfield once noted, was technology in its increasing complexity. As an example, the Handley-Page Heyford of 1934 weighed 14,500 lb and was a simple biplane with two engines and free-mounted guns. By 1937 the twin-engined Vickers Wellington medium/ heavy bomber weighed 30,000 lb and carried its defensive armament in two power-operated turrets. By 1944 the Avro Lancaster weighed 68,000 lb on take-off and, instead of the standard 250 or 500 lb bombs, could carry up to a 12,000 or even, when modified, a 22,000 lb ship-killing deep-penetration weapon. Not only did the Lancaster carry a pilot, a navigator, and a bomb aimer, but it also had aboard a flight engineer, a wireless operator, two specialist gunners, and a radar operator. Whereas the Heyford carried an observer as did the Wellington until after 1942, the Lancaster carried a navigator who could plot his position by radar and even map read up to the target on his cathode-ray tube.

The Technological or Technical Revolution of the mid-1930s replaced flapless biplanes with fixed undercarriages and perhaps fixed-pitch propellers, by a steel-tubing frame covered with canvas, with an all-metal monoplane with a monocoque structure, flaps, hydraulics, retractable undercarriage, constant-speed propellers, high-octane fueled engines, an automatic pilot to cut fatigue, and the ability to make a Standard Beam Approach on the Lorenz system for a bad-weather landing in low visibility. With their higher speeds, lower drag, endurance, and range, the aircraft of the Technological Revolution, from the Douglas DC-3 on, were way ahead of those they replaced. By making various tradeoffs, they could get high speed, long range, or great carrying capacity.

Only the De Havilland Mosquito showed that a skilled designer left on his own could produce a fast, long-ranged, hard-hitting versatile machine not made of vital materials. Moreover, this wooden wonder could penetrate enemy airspace unescorted as a high-flying photo-reconnaissance aircraft, act as a master bomber's steed at medium levels with a reasonable payload, or hedgehop and bomb accurately. At the same time, as compared to an unserviceability rate of 25 percent for the heavy bombers on the morning following a raid, the Mosquito's was generally well below 5 percent. In other words, the Mosquito, with its two engines and crew of two, was a manager's delight.

The aircraft were not the only revolutionary developments the RAF had to learn to handle in the decade from 1934 to 1945. There were a string of other interrelated improvements. All-metal construction meant a leap forward not only in metallurgy but also, as production rapidly expanded from a dozen or so to six hundred or more machines per month, in the recruiting and training of the workers to build them, including women. Whereas in the past aircraft had been constructed of steel tubing, now they were being built of crimped sheet, flush riveted and with compound shapes. Moreover, the much neglected arts of salvage and rebuild had to be understood and refined to the point where 40 percent of Bomber Command's force were factory rebuilds. The maintenance of these all-metal aircraft under wartime conditions, especially when the heavy four-engined machines came into service from 1941 onward, meant that special stands and machinery had to be developed for servicing out on the dispersed hardstands in all weathers by men and women because the hangars could only accommodate those aircraft needing one-hundred- and three-hundred-hour checks, or roughly those that had completed ten and thirty operations respectively and the necessary air tests. Because of this, Bomber Command early in the war went over to the garage system.

The third revolution came in airfields, an essential part of the invisible infrastructure. In Britain, where the climate encouraged grass, airfields were merely great fields roughly a thousand yards in diameter with a bombing circle in the center (because there were no separate bombing ranges until the late

1930s). When permanent station buildings were erected, everything was in marching distance. As the Technological Revolution produced new aircraft that weighed more and more and as rearmament led to greater frequency of operations, grass began to deteriorate, and so concrete runways had to be installed. The 444 new airfields built in Britain from 1934 to 1945 had to be designed or redesigned with three runways built to take the stress of 68,000 lb heavy bombers. Much of this work was initiated and supervised by civil engineers who had to guess soil conditions and necessary runway strengths and design taxi tracks. In the end it proved to be the latter that gave the most trouble, as the loadings caused by fully laden machines stopping along the way to the runway had not been envisaged. To create the new runways required a revolution in methods, a switch from hand and barrow work to machines to move the soil, install the drainage, mix and move concrete, and lay the runways, not to mention to erect the new standard hangars and dispersed accommodations. The latter were required both for defense against bombing and to provide personnel with quiet for medically necessary sleep.

Fourth came the revolution in electronics started by radar. At first a purely defensive apparatus for detecting incoming aircraft and when coupled with the sector system to guide defenders against the enemy intruders, by mid-1940 airborne interception (AI) sets were becoming available. Soon navigation systems were in place, and later these were combined with blind-bombing techniques (discussed at length later in this essay). Parallel to electronics came developments in not only wireless (W/T) for morse code but also radio (R/T) for voice communications. These in turn were coupled with the development of air traffic or flying control and of the Drem Mark II night landing system, and all of this was related to the operational necessity of getting as many aircraft over the enemy target as possible in the shortest span of time. When these bombers returned short of fuel with tired and wounded crews, they had to be got onto the ground as quickly as possible in good weather or bad. Thus the link between electronics and airfields was immediate.

The fifth revolution was in armaments and target marking. The standard 500 lb bombs proved to be generally ineffective, in part because they had not been tested until 1938. The switch from military targets in the open to industrial complexes and area targets came about because of poor navigation and equally bad bomb aiming. It was no good sending out a very expensive bomber force and having it fail to hit the target. After the Butt Report of 1941 made that clear, means had to be found to make hostilities-only aircrew competent and effective. The evolution of bombs went in two directions: down to the 4.5 lb incendiary, with which in the end much of the damage to German cities was done, and up to the 8,000 lb blockbuster, whose great bang kept German firefighters off the streets until after the incendiaries had taken hold.

But there was still the problem of navigating at night over a blacked-out land. This was partly solved by the introduction of the parabolic-grid "GEE" radar set, which within a limited range allowed a navigator to get a fix of within fifty yards' accuracy, avoiding giving his aircraft's position away by having to transmit for a direction-finding fix with two or three ground stations, a time-consuming process that had only limited capacity. Perhaps even more important than radar for target marking was the development of pyrotechnics for use by the new Pathfinder Force (PFF) of hand-picked highly skilled crews who marked the target with flares both on the ground and in the air, allowing for winds while navigating with the more advanced OBOE derivative of the earlier GEE radar. This was combined with the use of a Master Bomber who cruised the area during the attacks and remarked the target to correct bomb-aiming errors and also transmitted instructions to the other aircraft. Ultimately coupled with this was the introduction of the Mark XIV gyro bombsight, which replaced the old Mark IX course-setting bombsight. The former had the great advantage that the bomber could be taking evasive action, but as long as the illuminated crossed hairs were on the target at the moment of release, the bombs would land fairly accurately. To make sure how aircrews were doing and to deflate the earlier accuracy reported during debriefings, cameras synchronized with high-powered photoflashes dropped with the bombs provided black-and-white pictures of the results.

At the same time, a sixth revolution occurred in the development of oxygen apparatus to enable crews to live and function above 15,000 feet. This was essential as fighters approached 40,000 feet and bombers operated in the 20,000 foot band. And oxygen from the ground up was essential for night acuity. Long night flights required rations, hot liquids to counter the sometimes −50°F temperatures, and study of the means of keeping people awake and alert even when the aircraft were fitted with radar defenses. To help prevent fatigue, heavy bombers had the ubiquitous autopilot, universally named "George" by the pilots, and the flight engineer and sometimes other members of the crew were trained to land the aircraft—if the wounded or dead pilot could be pulled out of his seat.

Although they did not affect RAF Bomber Command, three other revolutions were in chain in the last year of the war: nuclear weapons, computers, and jet engines.

All of these evolutionary-revolutionary developments had to be focused on the throat of an hourglass, the airfield and the bombers on it. Only when everything came together could an effective strike be launched. It took well into 1944 before Bomber Command had a force of 100 squadrons of heavies, mainly Lancasters, plus a special Mosquito force for both PFF and intruder operations within the bomber stream, and Harris had a force that could break down the German defenses. This victory lessened his losses and made his force even more effective.

Many of the improvements were hidden in the invisible infrastructure and were not seen in photographs of airplanes and thus have often been missed by writers. The infrastructure in many areas of technological innovation has consistently been overlooked to such an extent that no one can now locate a standard RAF toolkit. Nor have researchers asked many of the very basic questions about the nature of operations, which can only be answered by examining group and squadron Operational Record Books (ORB). In this connection it may be noted in passing that in 1940 the serviceability or availability rate was 59 percent in Operational Training Units (OTU), 75 percent in Fighter Command, and 82 percent in Bomber Command. Well into 1943, shortage of spares and of tools were the chief culprits, as the Inspector General noted, followed by accidents and operational losses.

OPERATIONAL REALITIES

Air

Ever since July 1918 the RAF had been guided by the idea that any new war would begin with massive aerial strikes and that the way to avoid the shocking casualties of the First World War was to develop a counterstrike deterrent. Thus from 1923 the country's defense against enemy assault was a Home Defense Force, two thirds of which was to be an offensive bomber force. But during the long days of lean budgets from 1919 through 1934, the RAF did very little to work out either doctrine or suitable machines even for employment against the traditional and only enemy, France. Thus when Germany once again became the menace, the RAF was unprepared. The annual air exercises continued as before 1934 to see a future war as a repeat of the sending of the British Expeditionary Force once again to Gaul. As noted above, rearmament coincided with the revolutions in aviation. Moreover, as the Wave Theory notes, rearmamental instability lasted from 1934 well into 1943, when at last wartime equilibrium was briefly established before demobilizational instability set in.

When the war opened, Bomber Command hived off the Advanced Air Striking Force to operate from French soil. Its equipment proved hardly suitable for winter operations, and the AASF's accuracy was not great — one reason why leaflet raids got a high priority; they were not likely to injure civilians. With the

May 1940 German blitzkrieg, the RAF quickly collapsed and was evacuated to the United Kingdom. Owing to the 1936 demolition of the Air Defense of Great Britain command, Fighter Command fought the Battle of Britain with very little help from Bomber Command. The latter went off to wage its own war. Its force consisted of obsolete Whitley and Hampden squadrons gradually being re-equipped with Wellingtons, which remained operational for the rest of the war although they first flew in mid-1936, four years after design began. The availability of higher-powered engines meant higher cruising speeds, which in turn resulted in the need to replace open-cockpit gunners and Scarf-ring-mounted single guns with power-operated turrets.

Once back in Britain, Bomber Command launched raids all the way to Berlin in retaliation for German attacks on London. The trouble was that observers were not well-trained navigators and that the trickle of single aircraft operating well spaced apart had little psychological and almost no physical impact on the enemy. Thus the Germans did not take air defense very seriously for some time. These raids, which rarely exceeded one hundred aircraft, meant that the prewar amateur level of flying control, in which every command had its own instructions and peculiarities, did not show any weaknesses. However, after Air Chief Marshal (ACM) Harris became air officer commander-in-chief of Bomber Command in February 1942, things changed. Harris was a strong believer, since prewar days, in attacking the enemy's morale. In addition, his forces were gradually beginning to grow to the point that by special arrangements he was able to mount the first thousand-bomber raid in May. Putting that many aircraft into the air at once began to make some of the deficiencies in the command obvious. This was further accentuated when time over the target was changed from individual option to concentration, according to the principles of war, of the maximum effort in the shortest time so as to have the greatest impact and overwhelm the local defenses.

This had consequences at Harris's limited number of airfields. With two or more squadrons of twelve—later raised to sixteen—mediums (as Wellingtons were reclassified) and heavies (Short Stirlings from 1941, Handley-Page Halifaxes from 1942, and Lancasters from 1943) at a field, takeoffs and landings became difficult. Departure was not so much a problem as aircraft could follow one another rapidly onto the runway and climb out, but difficulties arose on the return, when all aircraft arrived within a few minutes of one another, some with fuel to spare, others low, and with wounded aboard as well as damage. In bad weather this meant that aircraft had to be stacked in orbits and fed down into a visual system for landing. On grass airfields a crash did not necessarily block the landing process, but on a runway it was critical because heavy machinery to remove wrecks was in short supply. The solution was the creation of three "crash" fields with unusually wide expanses of concrete and sufficient rescue vehicles to deal with several returns.

A second essential action was the regularizing of flying control practices so that any aircraft could be diverted to another field and accepted there. If aircraft were too valuable to lose, aircrew were even more precious. Moreover, early morning fog was a constant English problem that frequently required diversions as aircraft did not have the fuel to remain in orbit until it burned off. Thus FIDO (Fog, Intensive Dispersal Of) was born. About one dozen airfields were fitted with perforated pipes alongside the main runway, which when lit used 30,000 gallons of gasoline an hour to lift the fog while at the same time providing a massive glow that pilots could home in on as they approached to land aided by the Beam Approach System.

By 1944 the system was working smoothly enough that the time between bombers' landings was reduced from at least six minutes to less than two. This meant that the time it took to land a squadron of twelve aircraft was reduced from more than seventy-two minutes to twenty-four.

The invisible infrastructure was also employed in a wider fashion once it was realized that aircrews needed help in more ways than one after a flight over hostile territory. Thus the "Darky" net came into being. Any aircraft could call on the emergency 1240 kcs band, and "Darky" would then locate it, searchlights would be turned on, and once the aircraft had acknowledged it could see one, then these were dipped in the direction to be flown until a cone of three indicated the usable landing place. The situation was not affected if the lost bomber could not receive either R/T or W/T, but was if it could not transmit. So another method was employed that vectored a night fighter onto the lost aircraft to check identification visually if the IFF (Identification Friend or Foe) was not working and then to lead the wounded ship home.

Surprisingly, because Britain is an island, the idea that crews who came down in the North Sea might need to be rescued was slow in realization. It took several years to perfect a system under which a wounded aircraft would transmit for a bearing and then give an estimated ditching position and time. This enabled aircraft and Air-Sea Rescue (ASR) motor launches to start a search fairly close to the center of a circle of uncertainty. To enable downed aircrews to survive, they were equipped with inflatable life vests known popularly as "Mae Wests" after the buxom blonde movie queen. Aircraft dinghies were supplied as well; these inflated on being released, and crew members were equipped with shrill whistles and small red lights for location purposes. Later in the war, airborne lifeboats complete with rations, sails, and a motor were dropped to the unfortunates. Upon rescue, medical science took over with skilled treatment for wounds, warm cocoa or tea, food, and blankets. The aircraft might have been lost, but the irreplaceable personnel would live to fight another day.

For those aircraft that did make it back to their home or another field, the Drem system was an enormous help at night. The established pattern was that the aircraft let down over the upwind side of the ellipse of lights 2,000 yards from the runway, crossed over the takeoff end at 1,000 feet above ground level, turned downwind and did the usual prelanding checks, if possible, and then turned into wind for the final approach guided by the three lights of each of two vertical glide-slope indicators. All of this had by 1943 replaced the goose-neck flarepots with the standard runway electric lights. The latter had the advantage that they and the landing system could be switched off when enemy aircraft were in the vicinity. Safe recovery of aircraft was a conservation matter. So was maintenance.

Ground

Even though the heavy bombers were limited to the 100-foot width of the new Type T-2 hangar doors, under wartime conditions of dispersal of aircraft on hardstands around the perimeter track and the much more frequent inspection and overhaul necessities caused by operational and training usage, there was not enough accommodation on stations for machines to be worked on under cover. Moreover, not only was there a severe constriction of available manpower due to competing wartime demands, but also there was a shortage of steel for the larger D Type hangars with their clear span of 150 feet and a height of 25.

The whole story of spares was fortunately summarized at the end of the war by an official in the Ministry of Aircraft Production. The tale clearly indicates the difficulties associated with the introduction of complex new technology. The problem started with the failure of those responsible to switch their thinking from peacetime procurement of a dozen or so aeroplanes at a time with fair commonality of spares from type to type to new complex machines with much ancillary equipment with a quantum jump in spares needed, both because of change rather than continuity and because of greater consumption rates due to wartime use. (A bomber flew perhaps 250 hours per annum in peacetime and 960 in wartime, minimum.)

The spares difficulties started with the fact that they were not ordered when the production order was placed. Then, because the manufacturer was paid on the basis of producing completed aircraft, he was unwilling to devote floor space to spares production but in dog-in-the-manger fashion would not let spares production be subcontracted out. The result was periodic grounding of bombers because there were no spares. That, in turn, resulted in a rush aircraft-on-the-ground (AOG) order to make up the shortage, which disrupted the factory while contractors worked overtime to fill it. In the meantime it happened that the manufacturer filched spares in order to complete more aircraft and that the necessary spares arrived at the squadron from the regular pipeline because when the rush order was received at the depot, stockage clerking was behind and received spares were not yet shown as in stock. Part of this was due to the fact that maintenance, salvage, repair, and rebuilding records from World War I were destroyed as not of interest, ignored by historians who might have saved some of them, while at the same time those with the experience from 1914–18 had left the service. So there was no institutional memory in a rapidly expanding organization.

The matter of how many spares to order was also open to debate—10, 15, or 25 percent of original establishment? It was hard to know that it would take three years of wartime experience to establish a suitable spares level—by which time the type might be on the way out as obsolescent, as happened to the Stirling and the Halifax. Yet in 1936 the director of equipment had been buying spares on the basis of twenty-seven months of peacetime consumption plus four of wartime. This was in part based on the assumption that the factories would be at full wartime production rates three months after a war broke out. But as production demands swamped spares production, the director of equipment reduced the allowance to fifteen peacetime months, but this was too short a span to provide experience for reordering.

In June 1939 the RAF ordered manufacturers to supply 10 percent spares with the first aircraft and not less than that portion of the complete range with each subsequent aircraft. However, this was not effective because it applied only to new aircraft types and not to those currently being delivered, nor to engines. Then, too, once war broke out the Air Ministry found itself the unconscious victim of pipeline purdah—supplies en route were unavailable, and so even larger quantities had to be ordered to cover those in transit and losses at sea or in retreat. In ordering spares, pipeline purdah was too rarely considered.

While such problems were gradually discovered in wartime, it has been postwar historians that have made them plain. But even these historical summaries and analyses were often buried and forgotten as ministries closed, surfacing twenty-five to thirty years later, when either official histories were published or the archives opened.

In general in World War II it seems that pipeline purdah absorbed three to six months' spares with ensuing consequences. Spares quantities were based upon the initial establishment of squadrons, not on the number of aircraft being produced and their constant modification. Further, as it seemed likely that factories might be bombed, it was seen as essential that every factory, including the shadow offspring of the main factories, also produce spares. Moreover, it turned out that value theory was useless because it was not the cost but rather factory floor space that was the limiting factor, or so it was thought. Ultimately the military found that not only the failure until 1942 to make progress payments for spares but also the dislike of finance officers for large orders was hamstringing the provision of adequate parts. It was not until wartime equilibrium was reached that the humans involved could be persuaded to forgo their Depression-era training and accountability in the interest of winning the war. A further result of these failures was that spares for old types turned out to be as scarce as for new.

The situation with engines also reflected the frontline-strength, visible-deterrent mindset. Because the Air Ministry pushed for as many new engines as possible, there was a shortage in 1940. In late September 1939 there were 2,088 engines at manufacturers and another 157 in RAF Repair Depots awaiting repair, and the number was increasing daily. Not until the start of the Battle of Britain in August 1940 did the Air Ministry (AM) realize that a large capacity devoted to spares production might actually produce a larger supply of engines.

The creation in May 1940 of the Ministry of Aircraft Production (MAP) only exacerbated the problem. It was not until 28 August 1942 that the prime minister, the redoubtable Winston Churchill, a former air minister, forced his secretary of state for air to agree to the MAP proposal to get a proper balance between new aircraft and repaired ones so as to achieve a greater total. Even so, all was not solved; the Supply Board, conscious of the shortage of light alloys and steels, treated each case of grounded aircraft on its merits. That simply accentuated the rivalries for spares between the MAP's one hundred repair firms; the Civilian Repair Organization run by Morris Motors, which allocated repairs to the industry; and the seven RAF Repair Depots, which handled everything because by so doing they also trained RAF ground crews, all of whom were needed as expansion continued. This also meant training the Women's Auxiliary Air Force (WAAF) as part of the skilled workforce, a dilution, as it was called, which was part of the simplification of tasks to allow greater spreading of the workload as it got ever more complex.

Part of the RAF's problem with skilled personnel was that the combination of the Depression, the rush of innovations, and the "Expansion Schemes" resulted in only a small civilian pool with lesser skills than the service needed. In the meantime, only in September 1941 were the seven Universal Equipment Depots brought under Centralized Spares Control, and not until June 1942 was a director of aircraft spares production appointed.

Skilled Trades
The spares problem underlay the difficulties in achieving efficiency, but its solution, while certainly partly a human issue, was not the only element in keeping aircraft in the air. Manning problems had also to be addressed. The training of aircrews took about eighteen months for a pilot and lesser times for the other

members of the crew. All had to come together at an Operational Training Unit (OTU), where they were placed in a room and told to meld themselves into single crews. Self-confidence and casual connections resulted in seven young men being prepared to work as a team. At OTU the newly formed crew usually was assigned to a Wellington, a type on which they might go on operations. By the time that Bomber Command really needed large numbers of aircrews, the airfields were becoming ready along with the heavies. Thus if the crew were not siphoned off to Coastal Command or sent overseas, it either went directly to a squadron to receive instruction in its operational type or went to a new Heavy Conversion Unit (HCU) to do some ten hours on type before finally posting to a squadron. There the practice was for new pilots and navigators to do one or more trips with an experienced crew to be sure that their first flight over enemy territory as a crew would not just be throwing them to the night fighters and flak. Although the simple statistical saying was that if losses ran at 5 percent or more, no one would survive a thirty-sortie tour, in practice many of the losses came in the first five sorties. Thereafter experience bred confidence and cohesion.

Because not only the regulars but also the hostilities-only temporary wartime aircrew came from a pre-innovation background, training was all important. My personal experience of the British Commonwealth Air Training Plan in Canada in 1943–44 was that it was excellent as far as it went, but that the training establishment tended to be isolated from the rapidly changing realities of war overseas. Few instructional personnel in the Elementary Flying Training Schools (EFTS) or in the Service Flying Training Schools (SFTS), at the latter of which we got our wings, had had operational experience. Indeed, not only was the system at about the 1938 level, but when we got a flight commander who had the Canadian golden-winged O, signifying that he had completed a tour overseas, he was promptly posted to the Repair and Maintenance Unit on the other side of Currie Barracks, Calgary, because his critical comments were unwelcome to the staff. Thus when we went to an OTU we found that our navigational methods were out of date, without taking into account the new equipment. We simply had not been taught how to get from A and arrive at B at a specified time. And night navigation in crowded skies with a blackout below was very different from training in brightly lit North America.

It should be noted that the RAF's acceptance of new technology was not matched by its acceptance of new aircrew. Those who were sent to the United States to Pensacola and were thoroughly trained by the U.S. Navy, up to and including time on the Consolidated Catalina PBY, found themselves back in the United Kingdom flying Tiger Moths again, just as they had eighteen months before. The Air Ministry simply did not trust "colonials." Older prejudices overcame innovation. This was yet another weak human link in the invisible infrastructure so necessary to turn a conglomeration of innovations into an operational weapon: ground crews.

In the case of tradesmen, as they were called, the barbed-wire strand applies. Just as the facts became evidence and management made a decision, all the facts changed. In manning, perceived shortages became surpluses, which were ruthlessly pruned in the wartime manpower environment only to be faced once again with shortages. Part of this can also be related to the unpublished Bonwell-Higham thesis that facilities grow at arithmetic rates while use grows geometrically.

When the war came in September 1939, the drastic measures that the RAF had set in motion even before Munich had not yet borne fruit. Therefore, courses had to be shortened and trained personnel posted as instructors, all of which led to a decline of efficiency as units expanded — another instance of the battle of quantity versus quality. In addition, prewar financial obstruction delayed expansion, and older reservists were found no longer to have the skills needed by the new, much more technologically sophisticated fighting force. Others were even in obsolescent trades that were eventually abolished. However, it was not until 1943 that the Air Ministry realized that the postwar reserves would need to be much more sophisticated than those of the pre-1939 period. Once war broke out, it was not recruiting of the right sort of personnel, but the training of these recruits that was the insuperable problem. It was a legacy of peacetime parsimony that there were almost no training facilities, in part because graduates of No. 1 Technical Training School at Halton were then apprenticed to squadrons.

At the same time, a legacy of the 1914 War was that men in industry were placed on the Schedule of Reserved Occupations and so could not easily be recruited. Moreover, from the formation of MAP in May 1940 to the end of the war, there was a severe tension over manpower, and later womanpower, between MAP and the Air Ministry as well as the other services.

The complexity of the aircraft of the Technological Revolution made it necessary in 1938 not only to create Maintenance Command, but also to reorganize the trades it controlled and to bring in specialist officers. No longer were experts on wood and canvas aircraft needed, nor could the service tolerate the newest pilot officer on the squadron being the Engineering Officer, as there was a shortage of supervisory NCOs.

On the outbreak of war, the RAF consisted of 115,200 regular officers and men, 58,000 reservists, and 1,734 WAAFs. By 1945, excluding those wasted, the service stood at 1,186,000 officers and men and 173,000 WAAFs. There were in 1939, however, no war manning plans, except that the cabinet expected aircraft to leave the factories at the rate of 2,300 monthly. In November when the director of manning made his estimate for the first year, he cautioned the Ministry of Labour and National Service that the whole depended upon the actual rate of aircraft production. At the same time, he warned that there was no experience upon which to base wastage rates and that intake would depend upon the availability of training facilities. His later forecasts noted a need for 55,760 skilled tradesmen from September 1940 to December 1941.

By July 1943 the manpower shortage was becoming so acute that of the estimated 414,000 who would become available, the RAF would get 100,000 and MAP 212,000. If wastage was 57,000 in the year ahead, the RAF would have a deficiency of 81,000. Nor was it helped by the prime minister's ruling that fitters and riggers loaned to MAP during times of surplus in 1941 and 1942 did not have to be returned. Winston Churchill also claimed that the RAF had 200 personnel per aircraft and that this was bloated. In the end, however, the distinguished ministerial committee found in January 1944 largely in the RAF's favor. Moreover, the Air Ministry pointed out that the estimated wastage rate meant that trained personnel would have to be replaced by untrained, to the detriment of efficiency. In this climate, it was difficult to expand the frontline units.

Tradesmen were in such short supply in September 1939 that women were at once posted to the instrument trades. Massive efforts were made to expand training, including contracting it out to technical colleges and schools. But there was trouble because "skilled men" had not been defined, and those in industry were not equal to RAF tradesmen. Moreover, there were no airframe riggers in industry. Pressed as time went on to find more tradesmen, the Air Ministry developed a scheme to simplify the trades (split from 50 in 1939 to 190 by mid-1944) and bring in WAAFs, to force tradesmen to requalify for higher levels or in needed specialties. The obstacles were a shortage of accommodation for WAAFs and the need to lower the pay of skilled personnel when on course. Splitting the trades did not make for an economy of force as it took more people to do the job and they required greater supervision just when there was, as usual, a shortage of experienced NCOs. Only in 1942 was the trend reversed when it was realized that one well-trained man could do the work of more than two in the elementary trades.

The shortage of skilled radio mechanics was particularly acute in a country where "wireless" was still limited for economic reasons. Moreover, radar requirements were constantly being upgraded, and the sets were increasingly complex and thus demanded a higher educational standard. It took until February 1941 to get contracts with civilian schools to train these specialists. The deficit was largely made up by 5,000 a year trained in Canada, but this arrangement was not entirely happy because of anticolonialism in the British service.

With not only radar but also the new heavies and American aircraft now available, fifteen times the number of electricians available in 1941 were needed. So commands were combed for suitable trainees, but Balloon Command could not give up its Auxiliary Air Force personnel because of prewar contracts.

Only in June 1941 did the Air Ministry help the situation by ordering that skilled tradesmen were to be relieved of duties as guards, in working parties, and the like, and were instead to be used to the maximum extent possible in their own trades. After another political inquiry, the RAF began an internal campaign to get tradesmen to qualify at higher levels. And repair by replacement was expanded. By November 1941 RAF training facilities were able to handle both retraining and new entrants. Shortly thereafter, the Ministry of Labour began to scour the trades for "unprotected" foremen who could be directed to the RAF as NCOs. The year 1942 opened with a great surplus of skilled men, and 1943 closed with severe deficiencies due to the trickle of new men being allocated to the service. The surplus was due to gross misestimates by MAP of aircraft production, to the diversion to the USSR of both British and American aircraft, and excessive establishments caused by overestimated probable casualties. By drastic measures the surplus was gone by February 1942, but there was still a 42,000-man surplus of fitters. So cuts were made in new manpower, training capacity, and provision of refresher courses. By May the matter had been resolved and sloppy work habits and bloated establishments had been liquidated. The training system could now be devoted to improving quality, so as to be ready when expansion came, which proved to be in May. By July, as expansion once again moved forward, the RAF had released 30,000 men, whom it now wanted back. By October 17,000 were still in industry, perhaps held back by the uxorial effect.

Around the same time, in August 1942, the RAF had found that posting away of personnel was not detrimental as long as they kept key men—specialists on the aircraft equipment or location. In general, WAAFs were not a problem as they were not posted as frequently. It was found that there was a larger proportion of senior airmen overseas than at home, and this began to have an adverse effect after mid-1944, when these were due for repatriation, as there was a severe shortage of replacements.

By 1944 the key was to maintain operational and technical standards at the expense of comfort and internal security. Already by the spring of 1943 it had been laid down that no new units could be created without the approval of the Expansion and Re-Equipment Policy Committee, that there were to be no new or expanded training facilities, and a limit was placed on the W/T and communications trades, which already at 115,000 totaled some 10 percent of the RAF. More personnel had been found by reducing establishments yet again.

In May 1944 the director of manning reported that training and retraining had progressed so well that there was now a surplus in technical and other training trades so that the principle of downward employment should now be enforced to place people in closely allied, but less well-manned trades. At the same time the RAF began to have to transfer men to the army and navy, with regulars and volunteers for the RAF exempt, and surplus aircrew trainees were detailed to fill the shortages in the clerical branches. In December 1944 the cabinet ordered the RAF to transfer 20,000 persons, including officers, to the army, but this only started two months before the war ended in May 1945; some 17,000 ordered to the Royal Navy at the same time had barely started to move.

On first glance it had been expected that RAF operations would be affected by a shortage of aircrew, but in fact the truth proved to be that the vital invisible infrastructure was availability of suitable ground crew. By 1945 the RAF was getting no new allocations of manpower and was having to find 1,200 aircrew recruits a month internally, though it estimated that by September 1945 it would be 10 percent short, or roughly 75,000–90,000 personnel all told. The deficiencies risked the breakdown in clerical, medical, as well as maintenance areas and rendered postings impossible to relieve those long overseas. Since the service could not manage with a 10 percent deficiency, 37 squadrons were cut by 1 July, which provided 40,000 men, but this hazarded the need to build up for the final campaigns against Japan.

If airfields represented the throat of the hourglass, the bottom funnel of the bamboo basket, the gathering together of all pieces to make the weapon possible, then beyond the airfield still lay the necessity of a doctrine by which the innovations nurtured by the invisible infrastructure could be made an effective weapon, an efficient instrument of policy and victory.

BEYOND THE AIRFIELDS—
THE OTHER INVISIBLE INFRASTRUCTURE

In the real operational world, the constant battle of wits and weapons between the RAF's offensive bombers and German defenses both on the ground and in the air was a ping-pong on the periphery. The war required constant development, perfection, standardization, training, and practice to reach operational proficiency and save lives and aircraft. Again, the creation of innovations was not as important as their application. Having given an overview of the nonoperational side of the grand-strategic air offensive against Germany, it is necessary to pass through the throat and look at the invisible infrastructure on the operational side.

THE INVISIBLE INFRASTRUCTURE

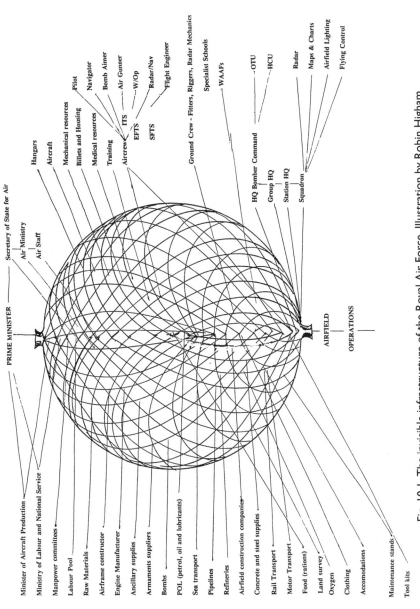

PRIME MINISTER

Secretary of State for Air

Air Ministry

Air Staff

Minister of Aircraft Production

Ministry of Labour and National Service

Manpower committees

Labour Pool

Raw Materials

Airframe constructor

Engine Manufacturer

Ancillary supplies

Armaments suppliers

Bombs

POL (petrol, oil and lubricants)

Sea transport

Pipelines

Refineries

Airfield construction companies

Concrete and steel supplies

Rail Transport

Motor Transport

Food (rations)

Land survey

Oxygen

Clothing

Accomodations

Maintenance stands

Tool kits

Hangars

Aircraft

Mechanical resources

Billets and Housing

Medical resources

Training

Aircrew

Pilot

Navigator

Bomb Aimer

Air Gunner

W/Op

Radar/Nav

Flight Engineer

ITS

EFTS

SFTS

Ground Crew - Fitters, Riggers, Radar Mechanics

Specialist Schools

WAAFs

HQ Bomber Command

Group HQ

Station HQ

Squadron

OTU

HCU

Radar

Maps & Charts

Airfield Lighting

Flying Control

AIRFIELD

OPERATIONS

Fig. 10.1. The invisible infrastructure of the Royal Air Force. Illustration by Robin Higham

As the AOC-in-C, Bomber Command, from February 1942, Harris has noted that he was influenced by many factors, including (1) the type and number of aircraft available, (2) the nature and general disposition of enemy defenses, (3) changes in the nature of the German night fighter system, (4) changes in the equipment carried by enemy fighters, (5) the development of accurate navigation and bombing aids, and (6) the introduction of radio countermeasures. We could add to these the ability to concentrate attacks in time and place and the impact of this upon landing aircraft at their home bases.

Harris divided the war into six phases, of which the most important was the last, from September 1944, after the diversions for D-Day and the invasion of France, to May 1945. During this victorious phase, feints and radio countermeasures caused the German defenses to collapse as the armies on the ground closed in.

The slow growth of Bomber Command's offensive operations was due to a combination of circumstances, including the need to phase out the older Whitleys and Hampdens, replacing them first with Wellingtons. These in turn were phased out as the three bombers of the 1936 program became available. The Stirlings were the first to arrive in 1941, but only lasted less than two years. They were followed onto operations by the Handley-Page Halifax and the Avro Manchester. The latter turned out to be unsatisfactory because of unreliable engines and resulting instability. The conversion to the four-engined Lancaster produced the ultimate mainstay of Bomber Command's forces. But the transition to modern aircraft created a heavy demand for both airfields, which were in short supply until 1944, and training.

In February 1942 the command had 37 operational squadrons and 18 nonoperational and of these only two of Stirlings and two of Halifaxes were operational with an equal number of training units. By December 1942, in spite of losses of ten squadrons to Coastal and Middle East Commands, 50 percent of the squadrons were operational even though aircraft had had to be siphoned off to create Heavy Conversion Units to which crews were posted after OTUs to learn to handle four-engined aircraft. In 1943 the Wellingtons were relegated to training roles, and Mosquitoes were added, giving an increase of tonnages in attack of 25 percent. In March the Initial Establishment (IE) of squadrons was increased from twelve to sixteen aircraft plus four spares. By the end of 1943 the command had 65 operational squadrons and 9.5 nonoperational, of which 36 were Lancasters, 17.5 Halifaxes, only 2 Stirlings, and 4 Mosquitoes. In 1944 the command could undertake great achievements with 104.5 operational squadrons, of which 56 were Lancasters, and the tonnage of bombs dropped was up 236 percent over 1943, to 500,000 tons.

The bomber stream was now protected by No. 100 Group radio countermeasures aircraft, each of whose squadrons was divided into two flights with eight aircraft and fourteen crews. By 1945 Bomber Command could not expand further due to manpower considerations in spite of the fact that there was reduced aircrew wastage as German defenses crumbled. When the war ended in May 1945 Bomber Command had at last 105 operational squadrons and only one nonoperational one, with the main force consisting of 62.5 Lancaster squadrons, 17 Halifax, and 12 Mosquito. Supporting this striking force was the invisible infrastructure below the throat.

While the four-engined aircraft revolutionized the destructive capacity of the force, Bomber Command faced additional problems, including the need for more maintenance, a shortage of suitable enlarged airfields, and the five months needed to convert aircrew and to enlarge individual crews with flight engineers and radar operators. On the ground side were several critical needs: for totally new handling equipment, to enlarge all workshops and technical accommodation, to expand bomb storage and handling equipment, and to build additional accommodations for the larger number of men and women now manning each squadron. Planning was confused by unreliable completion dates for airfields and, until the end of 1943, erratic estimates of the numbers of aircraft that would be available. The latter had to be modified on station, but all airfields were short of hangars.

The decision to develop heavy airfields was taken in October 1941, but policy making and manpower shortages delayed the redesign and reconstruction, not to mention the transfer of a number of airfields to the newly arrived USAAF 8th Air Force and the need to divert operational fields for Heavy Conversion Units. At the same time, the shortage caused squadrons to be increased in size temporarily to an IE of twenty-four aircraft with three in reserve. Even though this speeded up getting them into action, it was found that crew fatigue prevented operations on more than two nights in a row, while the press of work on ground crews working in the open all year round led to greater fatigue, and that led to a decline in serviceability, especially on the morning after a raid. Nevertheless, headquarters constantly raised planned rates of effort, and these were as often exceeded in spite of the shortages both of airfields and of ground trades.

Moreover, the practice during prewar times of devoting considerable time to establishing rates of wastage and consumption, promulgated in *SD* [*Secret Document*] 98, continued, and that manual was constantly updated so that Bomber Command could estimate wastage trends and their effect. These were interlocking considerations that involved the allocation of aircraft produced, the number of training aircraft required for the number of aircrew needed to man the operational aircraft which would be available. What was not known was the wastage on operations in terms of sorties flown. All of this then ultimately depended upon requirements for accommodation and ground personnel. So ultimately expansion depended upon there being a surplus above wastage. That it occurred was credited to the fact that wastage was less than estimates. This reflected the switch from great optimism in the fall of 1939 to much greater caution thereafter, as planners and others became experienced with war.

Operations in summer were roughly 150 percent of those in winter, with loss rates about the same. The result was that expansion generally took place in the winter, especially in October and November, and then dropped as new squadrons entered the frontline force and incurred wastage. From mid-April to mid-September 1943 and again in December 1943 through February 1944 the net increase was only ten aircraft. If the wastage rate had risen above 5 percent, Bomber Command would have contracted because losses would have exceeded production. In other words, the bamboo basket could not have disgorged sufficient aircraft even to maintain the force.

The matter of serviceability on stations was one that was tackled only slowly. After various arrangements, in November 1943 all aircraft servicing was centralized in a servicing wing composed of a servicing headquarters, a daily servicing squadron, and a repair and inspection squadron. The wing was commanded by the chief technical officer, under the station commander, assisted by specialist signals, armaments, and other officers. Squadron fitters and riggers were thus limited to daily inspections, refueling, rearming, and the like. This gave much greater flexibility, and tradesmen could be better supervised as well as transferred from one task to another as needed; thus the best possible use was made of the scarce servicing equipment.

Also in July 1944, stations centralized their administrative functions to bring them in line with practice. The assumption was that heavy squadrons could operate effectively only when backed by sufficient spares, and an adequate station, and a suitable ground-handling organization. But not until 1944 were all bomber groups "pure" on one type and not until 1945 was No. 100 (radio countermeasures) Group standardized on the Mosquito 30 and all groups otherwise reequipped with Lancasters. All in all, in the three years in which Harris commanded, 129 squadrons in effect had had to be reequipped, and this had meant a loss of effort at the rate of 10,000 tons for every week a squadron was out of action. It took forty hours per crew to convert them and four hundred man-hours to modify new aircraft to Bomber Command standards, and a lag while ground crews became familiar with new aircraft types, depending upon the kind of engines installed. Every change meant whole new categories of spares.

Another set of problems linking the bamboo basket to operational squadrons was factory rebuild and repair. It was reckoned that it took six months to get a damaged Lancaster returned to service, by which time it was out of date, and yet more labor had to be expended to bring it back to operational standards. This was part of the constant struggle between quantity and quality in war.

The other part of the invisible infrastructure of operations was the development of means of accurate delivery of bombs onto an enemy target. This started from taxiing out and taking off and ended with the safe return of the aircraft and crew. The first requirement was to get them safely airborne and on course. The Drem flying control system with its exit funnel gave the pilot immediate references for the transition from runway to instrument flying. But for a long time, navigation en route could be aided only by accurate map reading or by celestial shots as there were only a limited number of direction-finding (D/F) stations that required the aircraft to transmit a revealing signal. Map reading at night over Europe was very difficult because the only reliable landmarks were coastlines, rivers, and railways. The universal blackout meant that cities were only a pattern of dim blue lights, and areas such as the Ruhr were a mighty mess of agglomerated towns, blast furnaces, and other lights.

The first priority, then, was to get bombers somewhere near the target. Thus on 18 August 1941 the Air Ministry decided that a prewar invention, the GEE type of radar, should be fitted to all Bomber Command aircraft. By February 1942 ten GEE-equipped squadrons were ready for operations and were first used the next month. The 350-mile range of the parabolic signals enabled a skilled navigator to get a fix within fifty yards of the aircraft's actual position. This was a vast improvement over dead-reckoning, with its errant winds, lack of data, and cumulative errors. Now at last the command could bring the products of the Technological Revolution close to their targets. It also meant that it was possible to concentrate the bomber stream so that all aircraft arrived over the target within minutes rather than trickling in during the period of darkness. And while it enabled evasive routing to be introduced, it also necessitated accurate track and timekeeping. But by August the Germans were jamming GEE radar and limiting its range even though five chains had been established with six more on the Continent after D-Day.

A year after GEE, OBOE came into use. It measured distance, but not bearing, and could be used to drop bombs; its drawback was that it radiated and so could be homed upon. It was most suitable in high-flying Mosquitoes, which could get the maximum range out of it. Using OBOE, No. 109 Squadron got an accuracy of less than 300 yards over the Ruhr. The next improvement was GH, an OBOE in reverse, which became available in October 1943 to four squadrons whose aircraft carried the new 8,000 lb blockbusters. However, to maintain secrecy, GH was fitted to bombers only for specific operations. On the night of 3–4 November 1943, it was used in 10/10ths cloud during a raid on Dusseldorf with 90 percent accuracy. A year later the GH-equipped force was really into action and averaged two acres of devastation per aircraft. By the end of the war GH was a highly effective aid to precision bombing.

Another radar device, H2S, was developed early in 1942 but was kept off operations for security reasons until it was obvious that bomb aiming was so bad that in July 1942 the secretary of state for air decided that it had to be made operational to two squadrons. However, it was not used over Germany until 30 January 1943, when two PFF squadrons used it against Hamburg, where the terrain was easy to read. The raid showed that H2S was equally as valuable as a navigation aid as for blind bombing. Thereafter routes were chosen so that a solid H2S fix could be obtained from which dead-reckoning could be used to get to the target. The most successful use of H2S was when it was combined with target marking flares for the follow-on heavy bomber force.

Like most technical materiel, the effectiveness depended upon crew skills, training, knowledge of what towns would look like on the cathode-ray screen, and maintenance. Fully working sets were only obtained after Bomber Command set up a Radar School and the trained graduates reached squadrons. The ideal machines to carry the H2S Mk.II sets were PFF Mosquitoes, but there were real difficulties in fitting them into that small aircraft. In the command in general by July 1944 some 40 percent of sorties were flown by H2S-equipped aircraft. On the other hand, the German NAXOS radar could plot H2S emissions, and control could then vector night fighters onto British aircraft. Loran was not successful because of German jamming, and as it came so late in the war, its problems were not worked out.

The introduction of this invisible infrastructure into Bomber Command would not have been possible without the help of the Operational Research Section of Headquarters, assisted by the Bombing Development Unit and the Signals staff, all of whom worked to create operational techniques, accuracy, and suitable training schemes, the latter being monitored to make sure the results were solid.

In order to make sure that crews were functioning properly, medical officers kept a watching brief. Apart from problems of cold at altitudes much higher than those experienced by air personnel in peacetime, the main medical problem was not combat fatigue, but oxygen. Senior officers had not used it in peacetime, so intensive courses had to be given to all flying personnel on the dangers of anoxia, on how lack of oxygen affected night vision, on masks and economizers. By 1943 pressure chambers were being constructed on each station, crews were being issued the "G" oxygen mask, which now came in three sizes, and proper fit was emphasized as well as use of the economizer to provide greater endurance. Two problems were the freezing of moisture in the masks or in the oxygen supply tube, both being solved with a mantle over an electrically heated microphone. Additionally, new oxygen bottles had to be produced that would resist greater than a .303 bullet, and storage space had to be found for additional bottles per man. The problem was well illustrated with the Hampden, which had a ten-hour endurance, only a four-hour oxygen supply, and little space for additional bottles. Once the Wellington and the heavies were in service, the problem of space was solved, but fully loaded, the early-model Wellingtons and Stirlings could not get above 15,000 feet.

In addition to friendly radar, there was the problem of countering the enemy's. By 1941 it was obvious that the Luftwaffe controlled night fighters, and radar aids to flak were having impact on Bomber Command. But how the German apparatus worked was not known until a combination of photos and the Bruneval raid, in which a Wurzburg was captured, allowed a complete picture of the German operational system to be constructed. In July 1944 Bomber Command had a piece of luck when a lost Ju-88 complete with the latest Luftwaffe airborne interception set landed in the United Kingdom by mistake. By this time, summer 1942, losses were rising to 5.6 percent.

In the meantime, WINDOW, those little foil strips that made radar see "snow," had been invented, but it was withheld from use for fear that if the Germans got it they could turn the British defensive radar blind. So it was not until fall 1942 that radio countermeasures were permitted. Then it was a battle of wits and frequencies between the two sides, just as it was in the concurrent Battle of the Atlantic. Each side awaited fresh evidence before acting. Some measures backfired. GROUND CIGAR jammed both the RAF and the Admiralty special "Y" listening services! Later, German speakers were airborne who were able to confuse the defensive VHF all over Germany. It was also discovered that the enemy was homing on RAF IFF transmissions, and so as of 5 January 1944 the switches for these sets in the aircraft were taped off.

CONCLUSIONS

Invention and innovation can only be brought to a successful outcome if enough time elapses, enough money is supplied, and sufficient management effort is devoted to them. Problems arise when many innovations either compete or have to be brought to perfection and integrated into a complex system unused to such changes. The whole is further complicated by a wartime expansion when everything is in a state of flux, with many people in new situations, estimates of future reality are based on assumptions that may not prove to be valid, timing is off, and necessities are generated by unplanned or unanticipated enemy activities.

The difficulties of the period 1934–45 were compounded by revolutionary technical developments having to be implemented at a time when skilled labor had declined due to the Great Depression and the loss of potential middle management by the slaughter of the First World War. That conflict also cast its pall over the thinking of the RAF and ultimately over a Bomber Command that was expected to carry out the obverse of the failed deterrent without anyone's having realized how long it would take to build up an efficient destructive machine. Between 1934 and 1945 the RAF had to convert itself from a force with a cavalry-regiment mentality to a grand-strategic bomber force capable of destroying German defenses so that it could bring not just the will of the people but the industrial heartland of the Continent to its knees. Ultimately it faced the bottom line—lack of manpower in the United Kingdom.

In periods of innovation the invisible infrastructure is stressed by the need to expand its own facilities and services as well as by the constant change of tight competition or war. The personnel pool may be large and wages stabilized, but jobs have to be divided to allow less-trained and experienced talent to be efficient. Even the management and administrative structures have to be developed from old manuals to new talents and the whole invisible infrastructure made to work by foremen and noncommissioned officers.

Innovation, change, and routine activities are governed by the Chinese bamboo fish basket. Lines of activity run from top to bottom in complex patterns while feedback floats up from the bottom to the top. It is, then, a complex dynamic system of which a large part is the invisible infrastructure, too often taken for granted. One of the keys to its effectiveness and efficiency was regularization and standardization.

BIBLIOGRAPHICAL ESSAY

Background reading can be found listed in Gerald S. Jordan, *British Military History* (New York: Garland, 1988) and in Robin Higham, *Air Power: A Concise History* (Manhattan, Kans.: Sunflower University Press, 1988 and later editions). Historical and analytical background is to be found in Richard Overy's *The Air War, 1939–1945* (New York: Stein and Day, 1985) and his recent *Why the Allies Won* (London: Jonathan Cope, 1995). Owen Thetford, *Aircraft of the Royal Air Force* (London: Putnam, 1988), is the standard reference on that subject, as are Philip Moyes, *Bomber Squadrons of the RAF and Their Aircraft* (London: Macdonald and Janes, 1976) and Scott Robertson, *The Development of RAF Strategic Bombing Doctrine, 1919–1939* (Westport, Conn.: Praeger, 1995).

The official history of Bomber Command is in Air Historical Branch, *Bomber Command* (AIR 41/39) and in Sir Charles Webster and Noble Frankland, *The Strategic Air Offensive against Germany* (4 vols., London: HMSO, 1961), with more recent accounts in Max Hastings, *Bomber Command* (New York: Dial, 1979), and Denis Richards, *The Hardest Victory* (New York: Norton, 1995). An excellent modern official history is Brereton Greenhous et al., *The Official History of the Royal Canadian Air Force at War* vol. 3, *The Crucible of War* (Toronto: University of Toronto Press, 1994).

The AOC-in-C, Bomber Command, Sir Arthur Harris, wrote his controversial autobiographical *The Bomber Offensive* (London: Collins, 1947); more recently there have been biographies of Harris by Charles Messenger (London: Arms and Armour, 1984) and Dudley Saward (London: Cassell, 1989). The latter also has described operational radar in *The Bomber's Eye* (London: Cassell, 1959); see also F. J. K. Bullmore, *The Dark Haven* (London: Jonathan Cape, 1956) on flying control. This can be backed up by Ronald Clark's *The Rise of the Boffins* (London: Phoenix House, 1962); Air Ministry, *Operational Research in the Royal Air Force* (London: HMSO, 1963); and R. V. Jones, *The Wizard War: British Scientific Intelligence 1939–1945* (New York: Coward-McCann, 1978). Bruce Robertson's *Aviation Archaeology* (Cambridge: Patrick Stephens, 1977) gives some details of airfields and hangars; also see Anthony Betts, *Royal Air Force Airfield Construction Service, 1939–46* (Ware, Herts: Airfield Research Publishing, 1995).

From the Public Record Office (PRO) at Kew, London, the draft Air Historical Branch narrative histories can be obtained from the group AIR 41, as also can *Maintenance* (AP131, 1954), (AIR 10/5552) and *Works* (AP 3236, 1956) (Air 10/5559), *Signals* (AIR 10/5520), and RAF Inspectorate General (AIR 33). Even when printed, these latter two records were under the fifty-year rule, which was changed in 1972 when all the World War II records were released. Additionally, *SD 98 Data for Calculating Consumption and Wastage in War* (AIR 10/3915), *Operational Record Books* (ORB's) (AIR 27-29) and the Ministry of Aircraft Production (AVIA) papers which include AVIA 9/228, an end-of-the-war summary of the spares problem, are useful to scholars.

Recently Harris's *Despatches* (edited by Sebastian Cox; London: Frank Cass, 1996) have provided access to Bomber Command's view of how the invisible infrastructure had to be built. The matter of engine fitters and airframe riggers has been examined by a ground crewman, F. L. Adkin, in *From the Ground Up* (Shrewsbury, Eng.: AirLife, 1983). A very thorough study of RAF labor is in *Manning: Plans and Policies* (AIR 41/65); the three volumes of S. C. Rexford-Welch's *The Royal Air Force Medical Services* (London: HMSO, 1954–56) and *Physiological Disorders in Flying Personnel . . . 1939–1945* (AP.3139) (London: HMSO, 1947) should also be consulted, as should Beryl E. Escott, *Our Wartime Days—the WAAF in World War II* (Stroud, Eng.: Alan Sutton, 1995).

Testing of aircraft has been recounted by Allan Wheeler in *"that noth-*

ing failed them" (London: Foulis, 1963); Brian Johnson and Terry Hefferman, *A Most Secret Place: Boscombe Down, 1939–1945* (London: Janes, 1982); and Alex Henshaw, *Sigh for a Merlin* (London: John Murray, 1979). The Pathfinder Force is the subject of its leader D. C. T. Bennett's autobiography of the same name (London: Frederick Muller, 1958).

Air Ministry organization can be studied in the handbook from Sunflower University Press (1998). Many official history volumes from the United Kingdom and Alfred D. Chandler Jr.'s *The Visible Hand* (Cambridge, Mass.: Harvard University Press, 1977) are suggestive and substantiating.

CHAPTER 11

Riding England's Coattails

The U.S. Army Air Forces and the Turbojet Revolution

JAMES O. YOUNG

I n 1928, twenty-one-year-old RAF flight cadet Frank Whittle speculated that it would be possible to attain very high speeds — speeds in excess of 500 mph — if one could achieve stratospheric flight. He also perceived that the piston-engined, propeller-driven airplane would never do the job. To achieve the speed and altitude he envisioned, some alternate form of propulsion system uniquely suited to those conditions was absolutely essential. His deductions were prophetic.[1]

During the 1930s, the prop-driven, piston-engined airplane underwent a dramatic metamorphosis. Streamlined, all-metal, lightweight, monocoque fuselages; retractable landing gear; and a host of other airframe innovations reduced aircraft weight and drag to previously unimagined levels. And the engines? The Wright Brothers had powered their first airplane with an engine providing about twelve horsepower — or one horsepower per fifteen pounds of engine weight. By the early years of World War II, engine designers would be squeezing more than two thousand horsepower out of the churning pistons of their ever more complex, turbosupercharged combat designs (by the end of the war, the Wasp Major would be delivering up to 3,500 hp), and they had achieved a power-to-weight ratio of better than 1 : 1. To fully exploit all of this power, there had been major improvements in fuels and propeller design, as well. During the 1930s, for example, the U.S. Army Air Corps adopted 100 octane fuel, and prop designers had developed aerodynamically efficient, variable-pitch propellers that could be adjusted, in flight, for optimum performance at different speeds and altitudes.[2]

In their quest for ever greater speeds during the 1930s, designers came up with aircraft that appeared to be little more than engines with empennage and

wings. Indeed, the world speed record leaped upward throughout the decade following Whittle's original speculations. Perhaps no aircraft better epitomized this
trend than Willie Messerschmitt's Me 209V-1, which in April 1939 pushed the
record all the way to 469.22 mph (although unofficially surpassed during the
coming war, this mark would remain the official record for the next three decades). For all intents and purposes, the Me 209 defined the practical limits of
prop-driven aircraft. Its engine, the twelve-cylinder, liquid-cooled Daimler-
Benz DB 601ARJ, provided 1,800 hp—and could be boosted up to 2,300 hp for
short bursts—but it had a service life of only thirty minutes.[3] And, like so many
of its kind, the Me 209 was extremely difficult to fly; its pilot, Fritz Wendel, later
recalled that it "was a brute. Its flying characteristics still make me shudder. . . .
In retrospect, I am inclined to think that its main fuel was a highly volatile mixture of sweat from my brow and the goose pimples from the back of my neck!"[4]

Aero-engine pioneer Ernest Simpson once described the reciprocating engine as "an invention of the devil." Although a marvelous example of mechanical ingenuity and precision engineering, it was infernally complicated and tem-
peramental. Maintenance was "difficult, frequent, and often painful." Added to
this was the fact that, by the late 1930s, designers found themselves caught in
a vicious circle. Higher speeds required ever-larger engines, which consumed
greater amounts of fuel and resulted in larger and heavier airframes whose size
and weight served to negate the increased performance of the engines. And the
engines themselves—whether air- or liquid-cooled—posed monumental problems. In air-cooled engines, for example, the peak power output of an individual cylinder was something less than 175 hp and thus, to boost power, designers
were forced to add more and more pistons to a single crankshaft. The ever-
increasing mechanical complexity of such linkages became an engineering and
maintenance nightmare. Moreover, each additional row of cylinders had a detrimental impact on thermal efficiency. Instead of converting the engine's heat
into useful mechanical work (e.g., power to drive the propeller), much of it—
along with the airplane's aerodynamic efficiency, as well—had to be wasted in
the cooling of these behemoths. Propellers also created seemingly insurmountable problems. As their blade tips approached supersonic speeds, for example,
they encountered "compressibility burble"—shock waves that caused an unacceptable increase in drag—and, as the air thinned out with increasing altitude,
props lost their "bite."[5]

The field of aeronautics was approaching a crossroads by the mid-1930s.
Aerodynamicists, who had made such great strides since the mid-1920s, were
pointing in a new direction. Indeed, at the Fifth Volta Congress of High Speed
Flight, which met at Campidoglio, Italy, in 1935, the world's leading aerodynamicists began to seriously consider the theoretical possibility of flight beyond

the speed of sound.[6] It was readily apparent to those assembled that the piston engine-prop combination could never meet that challenge. It was also becoming apparent to many that, in the not too distant future, the reciprocating engine would reach a plateau beyond which only minutely small improvements in performance could be expected in return for enormous expenditures in terms of time, money, and engineering effort.[7]

Although he certainly had not considered the possibility of supersonic flight, Frank Whittle had forecast many of these developments in 1928, and while undergoing flight instructor's training the following year, he saw the solution — not in any refinements to the existing technology, but in a radically new approach. He had already rejected rocket propulsion and a gas turbine-driven prop as impractical. Next, he had examined the possibility of a ducted-fan system — a jet propulsion system in which a conventional piston engine powered a low-pressure blower. The blower and engine would both be located in the duct, and fuel would be burned in the flow stream aft of the engine to generate thrust. He had concluded, however, that this system would be far too heavy and would, in fact, offer no real advantage over the piston engine-prop combination.[8] Then, in late 1929, as he later recalled, "the penny dropped":

> [I]t suddenly occurred to me to substitute a turbine for the piston engine [in the ducted fan system]. This change meant that the compressor would have to have a much higher pressure ratio than the one I had visualized for the piston-engined scheme. In short, I was back to the gas turbine, but this time of a type which produced a propelling jet instead of driving a propeller. Once the idea had taken shape, it seemed rather odd that I had taken so long to arrive at a concept which had become very obvious and of extraordinary simplicity.[9]

Thus, after less than two years of self-directed study and speculation, he had deduced that, for very high speeds and altitudes, employing a gas turbine to produce jet propulsion was the most feasible — and, ultimately, obvious — answer. As originally conceived in his patent application of 1930, air entered the engine inlet and was initially compressed by a two-stage axial compressor and then further compressed by a single-stage, one-sided centrifugal compressor; after passing through a diffuser that transformed its kinetic energy into pressure, the highly compressed air entered a ring of combustors into which fuel was injected and then ignited; the hot, expanding gases were then expelled at high velocity through a two-stage axial-flow turbine, which drove the compressor stages by means of a shaft, and then exited through a ring of nozzles to produce forward thrust. With all of its moving parts on a single rotating shaft, Whittle believed, it would be much simpler and far lighter than piston engines.[10]

Like so many revolutionary breakthroughs, Whittle's idea was elegant in its simplicity—and, like so many such ideas, it was scorned by the "experts" as impractical. He had not been the first to speculate about the possibility of employing a gas turbine for aircraft propulsion. The idea had been studied throughout the 1920s, though usually in the context of employing a turbine to drive a propeller. Based on the generally negative findings of these studies, conventional wisdom scoffed at Whittle's proposal: compressor and turbine efficiencies would be insufficient; the temperatures and stresses imposed on a constant-pressure gas turbine would far exceed the capabilities of materials then in existence; the weight of any such engine would far exceed its thrust; and so on. They characterized his proposal as visionary, a very long-term proposition, at best. Whittle, on the other hand, believed that the application of modern aerodynamic theory would permit virtually quantum increases in compressor and turbine efficiencies and that lightweight, heat- and stress-resistant alloys could be developed that would enable him to achieve adequate thrust-to-weight ratios in the near term. Moreover, the combined effects of ram air at high speeds and low temperatures at altitude would augment the work of the compressor, making a jet engine vastly more efficient the faster and higher an aircraft flew. Scoffers there were aplenty, and in what has to rank as one of history's prime examples of official obtuseness, the British Air Ministry denied his request for a modest amount of funding to support development of the concept.[11]

By late 1935, Whittle still had not overcome official lack of interest but, after having all but given up, he had finally secured an extremely modest amount (about $10,000) of private funding to begin the design of an engine for bench tests. By March of 1937, his backers had managed to increase the total to about $30,000 and his first bench-test engine, the W.U. (Whittle Unit), was ready for its initial test run. It was an incredibly ambitious undertaking. Whittle set out to build an engine that would produce 1,200 lb of thrust at 17,500 rpm. At a time when the most efficient supercharger compressors were capable of compressing about 120 lb of air per minute to a pressure of about twice that of the atmosphere, he strove for one that could handle 1,500 lb per minute and achieve a remarkable 4:1 pressure ratio. He dispensed with the upstream axial compressor stages and employed a single-stage double-sided centrifugal compressor in order to achieve the hoped-for 4:1 compression ratio within a relatively small-diameter area. Surrounding the compressor impeller was a scroll-type volute leading into a vertical expanding diffuser pipe containing a honeycomb of divergent channels. At the top of the diffuser, the air was turned ninety degrees by a cascade of vanes in an elbow before it entered the single combustion chamber. Once ignited, the expanding gases were to exit through a nozzleless scroll-shaped turbine inlet into a single-stage axial-flow turbine, which was supposed

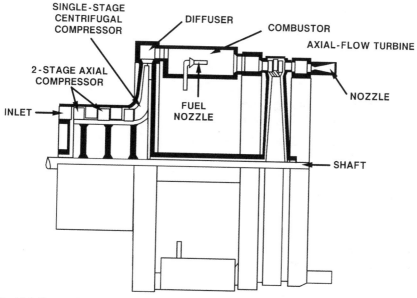

Fig. 11.1. Patent drawing for the jet engine developed by Frank Whittle. Courtesy Air Force Flight Test Center, Edwards Air Force Base, California

to provide just over 3,000 hp to drive the compressor (or more than the net power then produced by any piston engine). While he felt confident that he could achieve the targeted compressor and turbine efficiencies, Whittle was somewhat daunted when informed by experts that the combustion intensities for which he was striving were at least twenty times greater than had ever before been achieved.[12]

On 12 April 1937, Whittle ran up the W.U. for the first time—and it nearly blew apart! For the next two years, he struggled with burned-out combustors, erratic fuel pressures, turbine failures, and a host of other problems. Indeed, during that span, he had to completely rebuild the W.U. three times with leftover parts and whatever new components his meager funds would permit. The odds he faced were almost insurmountable, but Whittle was doggedly determined, and very patiently and ever so slowly, he began to overcome those odds as, with each engine reconstruction, he incorporated significant modifications. As he had intended, for example, he applied theoretical aerodynamics to the design of his turbine and, with the third version of the engine, was able to demonstrate convincingly the advantages of a "free-vortex" design. Each blade was fabricated with a twist in it to compensate for differential radial velocity and pressure across its diameter, and this produced dramatic improvements in turbine efficiency.[13]

Meanwhile, and although he was completely unaware of it, hundreds of miles to the east, a brilliant young German physicist was also developing a jet engine of his own design. Based on his study of aerodynamics, Dr. Hans von Ohain had deduced that modern streamlining and structural theory would permit speeds much higher than those possible with the piston engine-prop combination, and thus, like Whittle, he had concluded that a radical new form of propulsion — one uniquely suited for high-speed flight — would be required to exploit the full potential of airframe design. Although he had independently conceived the idea of a gas turbine-driven centrifugal-flow jet propulsion engine much later than Whittle, von Ohain had the good fortune to catch the attention of aircraft manufacturer Ernst Heinkel. And, in stark contrast to Whittle's impoverished circumstances, his efforts to build a bench-test engine were handsomely subsidized by the enthusiastic Heinkel. Employing hydrogen as fuel and providing a thrust of about 550 lb, von Ohain's engine was actually tested, for the first time, about a month before Whittle's first unit, and the success of these tests led to the development of a flight-rated engine and a small single-engined experimental airplane. Powered by von Ohain's 1,100 lb thrust He S-3b on 27 August 1939, the Heinkel He 178 became the first jet-powered aircraft ever to take to its wings.[14]

Even before this flight, however, official government interest had long since entered into the equation. For, in contrast to the situation in England, a number of other German engineers—both in industry and government—had also already perceived the virtues of the turbojet solution. Most notable among them were Herbert Wagner and Max Adolph Muller, of the Junkers Aircraft Company, and Helmut Schelp of the German Air Ministry. By mid-1937, Wagner and Muller had settled on the turbojet as "the shortest path to high aircraft speeds," and by the end of the year they had an engine under test. Unlike Whittle and von Ohain, their very meticulous studies had indicated that an axial-flow compressor was preferable because it would permit the straightest possible path for the air to flow through the engine, and it would offer the advantages of a much smaller diameter and lower drag than a centrifugal flow design.

Schelp had arrived at the same conclusion by mid-1937, and by early 1939 he had engaged all four of the major German engine manufacturers—Daimler-Benz, Junkers Motors, BMW, and Bramo—in reaction-propulsion programs. By the fall of that year, Junkers was well along in the initial development of a design that would ultimately evolve into the Jumo 004-B, an axial-flow engine producing 1,980 lb of thrust that would begin to enter mass production in the spring of 1944. Equally important, by the fall of 1939, Schelp had also already been instrumental in issuing Messerschmitt a contract to design and develop a twin-engine turbojet interceptor that, within five years, would begin to make a name for itself in the skies over western Europe.[15]

Thus, even before a turbojet-powered aircraft had yet flown, the German military had already begun to sponsor a massive effort aimed at the development of jet-powered combat airplanes. Unlike the British (and, later, the Americans), the Germans focused on the development of more efficient axial-flow engines from the outset. They were to suffer, however, from a severe shortage of skilled workers and, even more important, a near-total lack of the high-grade metals and alloys that were so essential to the development of efficient turbines and combustors. As a result, their engines were frequently inferior in terms of both materials and design. Thus, while designed for a modest service life of twenty-five to thirty-five hours, the Jumo 004B seldom exceeded ten hours of flying time in actual practice. Nevertheless, German efforts would bear fruit in a whole series of turbojet-powered aircraft that would actually enter combat service. The most notable of these was, of course, the sleek Me 262, the twin-engine, sweptwing fighter first conceived back in 1939. Capable of speeds in excess of 540 mph, the Me 262 would be unleashed with devastating effect against American bomber formations over western Europe by the fall of 1944.[16]

Whittle was completely unaware of any of these efforts when, after a successful twenty-minute demonstration of the third reconstruction of his engine to the Air Ministry in late June of 1939, he finally won official support, and with that came the go-ahead to build a flight-rated engine that would be designated the W.1. The ministry also approved the design and construction of a small single-engined experimental aircraft, the Gloster E.28/39. With its W.1 unit, weighing only 623 lb and providing almost 1,000 lb of thrust, this airplane completed its maiden flight on 15 May 1941. Curiously, and even though approval had already been granted to proceed with the development of an up-rated engine to be known as the W.2B, which would power the twin-engined Gloster Meteor, an official request to have the event filmed was inexplicably ignored. We have some poor-quality motion picture film of this milestone event only because someone violated security regulations and shot it with his own camera![17]

Among those on hand to witness the early taxi tests of the E.28/39 in April 1941, however, was an American who *was* very interested and, indeed, shocked by the enormous potential promised by the new propulsion system. Chief of the U.S. Army Air Corps Major General Henry H. "Hap" Arnold had been informed of British efforts the previous September and, prompted by alarming intelligence reports of German work in reaction propulsion, he had already launched a high-level inquiry into the subject. On 25 February 1941, he had asked Dr. Vannevar Bush, then chairman of both the National Defense Research Committee and the National Advisory Committee for Aeronautics (NACA), to establish a special committee of leading scientists to undertake this effort. Bush, in turn, had asked eighty-two-year-old Dr. William F. Durand, the "dean" of the U.S. engineering community, to head up such an effort under the auspices of the NACA and, by April, the Special Committee on Jet Propulsion had commenced its investigation with tentative inquiries into the potential of rocket-assisted takeoff, turbine-driven props, and ducted fan engines. But, by that time, Arnold had already witnessed the pure jet Whittle engine in operation on an airplane and he was absolutely stunned by how far the British had advanced. And, if the British had done it, he reasoned, there could be little doubt that the Germans were at least as far along.[18]

The fact that the United States lagged behind Great Britain and Germany and was, indeed, "taken by surprise" has been described as the "most serious inferiority in American aeronautical development which appeared during the Second World War."[19] It has inevitably raised the question, why? In his pioneering study, *Development of Aircraft Engines* (1950), Robert Schlaifer concluded that it was "simply the result of a historical accident: Whittle, von Ohain, and Wagner were not Americans."[20] In his penetrating and highly interpretive analysis, *The Origins of the Turbojet Revolution* (1980), Edward Constant considered this a "catastrophically inadequate" explanation and argued, instead, that the reason could be found in different national-cultural approaches to science and technology. The British and, particularly, the Germans were steeped in a tradition of theoretical science that encouraged fundamental research into such areas as high-speed aerodynamics and axial-turbo compressor phenomena. They were mentally and psychologically prepared to question the basic assumptions of aeronautical science, and thus England and Germany became natural spawning grounds for bold leaps into the unknown —for truly radical innovations such as the turbojet. The United States, on the other hand, "was possessed of a scientific tradition extreme in its empiricism and utilitarianism." The emphasis, Constant persuasively argued, was not on theory but on applied research leading to incremental refinements to existing technology. With a focus almost exclusively on immediately obtainable results, Americans excelled at subsonic aerodynamics, squeezing more and more horsepower out of piston engines and achieving ever greater efficiencies in propeller design. Thus, while Europeans were exploring the high-speed frontier and even looking over the horizon toward supersonic flight, Americans were focused on the here-and-now as they built the best commercial airline system in the world. Apart from a small group of immigrants, such as the Hungarian-born and German-trained Theodore von Kármán, American scientists and engineers were generally ill equipped to question the assumptions upon which the existing technology was based because their whole techno-cultural orientation was focused on palpable, here-and-now solutions to immediate problems. "The object," he concluded, "was flight, not science, practice, not theory."[21]

The whole question of why the turbojet was "not invented here" may never be answered to everyone's complete satisfaction. But, apart from national pride, it is not nearly so important as why the United States was so tardy in adopting and developing the new technology even after its revolutionary implications had become so clear to so many within the American aeronautical community. General Arnold and other Air Corps commanders may have been taken by surprise (though they should not have been), but an awareness of the potential offered by—and, indeed, the necessity for—some form of jet propulsion was fairly widespread in this country, especially after the 1935 Volta Congress on high-speed flight. During the late 1930s, for example, Ezra Kotcher was serving as the senior instructor at the Air Corps Engineering School. While specializing in aerodynamics, he was well enough versed in *all* fields to be able to teach most of the academic curriculum, and he was widely regarded as one of the few truly brilliant aeronautical engineers at Wright Field. Looking back on that period, he recalled with a certain amount of sarcasm that "it reached the point that you couldn't throw a whiskey bottle out of a hotel window at a meeting of aeronautical engineers without hitting some fellow who had ideas on jet propulsion."[22] Indeed, in August 1939, just days before the first flight of the He 178, he had submitted a report to Arnold's office (Air Corps Materiel Division Engineering Section Memorandum Report 50-461-351) recommending an extensive transonic research program and suggesting that gas-turbine or rocket-propulsion systems would have to be developed to support such an effort because of compressibility limitations on prop-driven aircraft at high speeds. His recommendations were apparently ignored by Arnold's staff.[23]

In hindsight, it may seem remarkable that Kotcher's bold recommendations should have been greeted with so little interest. However, at the time, Arnold and his staff were riveted on the immediate problem of building an air force to fight an imminent war and that meant focusing on the accelerated production of aircraft and related systems already under development. Indeed, by June 1940, Arnold informed his staff that the army was only interested in airplanes that could be delivered "within the next 6 months or a year, certainly not more than two years hence" and that all research and development activity would be curtailed in order to ensure timely production of existing designs.[24] Within this context, proposals to develop radical new technologies were relegated to the back burner. This was particularly true with regard to something as exotic as jet propulsion because the assumption in the United States—as it had been in England—was that its development would, at best, be a very long-term proposition.

Military interest in exploring the feasibility of the concept in this country actually dated back to the early 1920s. In 1922, the Air Service Engineering Division at McCook Field asked the Bureau of Standards to investigate the practicality of reaction propulsion. While conducting this study, Edward Buckingham based his calculations on a compressor driven by a reciprocating engine and did not consider any form of gas turbine. In his report, published by NACA in 1923, he concluded that "propulsion by the reaction of a simple jet cannot compete, in any respect, with airscrew propulsion at such flying speeds as are now prospect." Fuel consumption at those speeds, for example, would be about four times higher. That was true, in 1922, when the airspeeds envisioned were only about 250 mph. But he went even further, concluding that there was "no prospect whatsoever that jet propulsion . . . will ever be of practical value, even for military purposes." Unfortunately, his conclusions were based on a number of erroneous assumptions. Because he failed to consider the possibility that aircraft might someday be able to fly at speeds well in excess of 250 mph, he failed to consider the possibility that fuel efficiency might significantly improve at higher speeds. Like his counterparts elsewhere, he also assumed that compressors would necessarily have to be huge and heavy devices similar to those then used for industrial purposes. At the Langley Memorial Aeronautical Laboratory (LMAL), NACA researchers would accept Buckingham's conclusions as their own, and his erroneous assumptions would cast a pall over serious research into the subject for more than a decade. Thus, even the very few research studies that were conducted by the NACA and the Bureau of Standards during this period merely confirmed Buckingham's conclusions because they were all largely based on those same assumptions.[25]

Indeed, the piston engine-prop combination was such a given that the NACA virtually abandoned the field of propulsion research to industry and the military services and opted, instead, to commit the bulk of its resources to the study of aerodynamics. Under this circumstance, James R. Hansen has noted: "The LMAL had but one comparatively small research division devoted to engine research, but the outlook of its members was 'slaved so strongly to the piston engine because of its low fuel consumption that serious attention to jet propulsion was ruled out.'"[26]

The aero-engine industry shared this assumption and was certainly not about to shift toward any radical new concepts. Like their counterparts elsewhere, Wright Aeronautical and Pratt & Whitney poured enormous resources into progressive refinements to basically unchanging air-cooled designs. Indeed, between 1926 and 1939, the whole procurement system under which they were forced to operate actually discouraged radical innovation. There were virtually no military contracts issued exclusively for experimental research for its own sake. All such costs had to be recouped — or amortized — in subsequent production contracts. Radical innovations could well require years of trial-and-error development effort before they *might* prove worthy of mass production, and thus there was little incentive to pursue such a course.[27] The engine manufacturers had a vested interest in the status quo and seemed to be largely unaware of — or unconcerned about — the implications of the pending revolution in high-speed aerodynamics until very late in the game. Wright Aeronautical conducted no studies of its own on gas turbines, and it was only in 1941, after it had some-how obtained intelligence on the success of Whittle's experiments, that the company attempted to obtain a license for the manufacture of his engine in this country.[28] Prior to 1940, some individuals at Pratt & Whitney had briefly examined the potential of gas turbines and, indeed, by May 1941, the company was actually conducting some very preliminary tests on components for a compound engine (gas turbine wheel geared to the crankshaft of a piston engine) that had been designed by Andrew Kalitinksy of M.I.T. This was an extremely low priority effort, however, and nothing ever became of it.[29]

The major engine manufacturers' priorities were well established, and it was certainly by design that, when the NACA Special Committee on Jet Propulsion was formed in the spring of 1941, General Arnold expressly prohibited their participation. He wanted them to concentrate on the production of conventional engines to meet the crisis at hand and, backed by advice from Vannevar Bush and the chief of the navy's Bureau of Aeronautics, he also suspected that they would be resistant to any radical new departures.[30] Despite Pratt & Whitney's subsequent claim that it was late in getting into turbojet development only because of Arnold's decision, company officials apparently expressed very little interest in entering the field even after it was invited to participate. Lt. Gen. Donald L. Putt, then a project officer at Wright Field, recalled sitting in on a conference with Pratt & Whitney personnel during which Brig. Gen. Franklin O. Carroll, chief of the Engineering Division, tried to encourage them to get involved in developing turbojets. "They were very firm in their conviction that the turbine engine would never be much of a threat," he recalled. "The piston engine was going to be with us forever; it was the way to go. There might be some place for a turboprop but for a straight jet, forget it."[31]

On the military side, the Power Plant Branch at Wright Field was certainly not prepared to lead the way. First of all, in the 1920s, the NACA had very force-fully staked its claim as *the* institution responsible for fundamental aeronautical research in the United States, and it carefully guarded its monopoly throughout the 1930s. The Air Corps, by law, was to limit its activities to *applied* research, and throughout the decade officials at Wright Field were loathe to invade the NACA's turf for fear of arousing Congress's ire. As far as Air Corps leaders were concerned, it was the NACA's job to conduct fundamental research and keep up with the latest scientific developments. Always strapped for funds throughout the 1930s, they were quite willing to defer to the NACA in this regard.[32]

Thus, the fact that the NACA had abandoned propulsion research to industry and the military does not mean that anybody ever directed the Air Corps to fill the void or undertake fundamental research of any kind. The military's job was to conduct applied research, and so, as I. B. Holley has observed, the personnel of the Power Plant Branch at Wright Field "had their goals rather clearly laid out for them: they were to strive for better engines, meaning more horsepower at less weight. They were to minimize fuel consumption, to reduce frontal area in order to reduce drag, and to achieve maximum reliability and durability."[33]

Moreover, even if the military was given the job, it faced a number of other circumstances that militated against *any* kind of serious research effort. General Jimmy Doolittle once observed that research and development (R&D) is like virtue; everyone believes in it but no one wants to sacrifice for it. This was certainly true for the Army Air Corps during the interwar years. Throughout the period, its entire R&D budget generally hovered between $2 million and $4 million (and, most often, at the lower end of the scale). More tellingly, between 1926 and 1939, R&D expenditures as a percentage of the total Air Corps budget plummeted from 16 to just 5 percent.[34] Out of these paltry sums, no more than 30 percent was ever dedicated to propulsion systems and virtually none was directed toward experimental research of any kind because the emphasis at Wright Field was on the procurement of systems destined for the operational inventory. Indeed, the very structure of the Materiel Division mandated this kind of emphasis. With the establishment of the Air Corps in 1926, both R&D and procurement were brought together under the new Materiel Division at Wright Field. While the merger improved coordination between the two areas, it had a number of unintended side effects. Most important, the requirements of the procurement side of the house absorbed an ever greater percentage of the available technical manpower, facilities, and other resources in support of routine specification compliance testing of aircraft and systems submitted by manufacturers. The practical consequence of this, as I. B. Holley has noted, was that experimental research fell by the wayside.[35]

Inadequate funding also translated into serious deficiencies in both the number and the quality of technical personnel assigned. The Materiel Division suffered from a serious shortfall in engineering manpower throughout the 1930s. A single project officer assisted by a single civilian engineer, for example, was typically responsible for the development of all pursuit or bombardment or trainer aircraft. Moreover, the scientific and technical competence of the staff was well below par. Lt. Gen. Laurence C. Craigie served several tours at Wright Field during the 1930s and 1940s, and he recalled that, when he arrived in late 1934, no more than a dozen individuals, out of 1,100 personnel, could be considered as "real scientists" and that there were fewer still who, like Kotcher, could cross disciplines. Five years later, an investigating board reported "an appalling lack of qualified personnel . . . particularly in key positions." The most serious deficiency was among the officers, only a fraction of whom had any of the relevant scientific and technical training that had, by then, become so necessary to cope with the burgeoning complexity of aviation technology. A handful of the most qualified were selected each year to attend the Air Corps Engineering School. The year-long curriculum, however, provided little more than a one- or two-week orientation to the activities of each of the labs and test organizations at Wright Field. The much larger civilian staff tended to be a cut above the officers. However, low pay and limited promotion potential generally drove the best among them to higher-paying jobs in industry. Thus there were, at best, never more than a few individuals at Wright Field who were sensitive to the growing interaction between fundamental and applied research and fewer still who were capable of crossing disciplines and perceiving the sudden convergence of thermodynamic with aerodynamic principles. The upshot of all of this was not only that the Air Corps' principal R&D organization was ill equipped to conduct serious research but also that it put the Air Corps at a tremendous disadvantage in attempting to deal with the larger scientific and technical community from which it might have benefited.[36]

All of this made for an almost classic "who's minding the store?" scenario. Industry depended on the Air Corps for direction in terms of requirements, and the Air Corps, in turn, depended on NACA for fundamental research; because the piston engine appeared to be such a given, the military never called upon NACA to investigate radical new forms of propulsion, and NACA, in turn, virtually abandoned the field, leaving it up to industry and the military; but industry did not have the incentive to take on the job, and the military did not have the expertise to look in new directions or even to direct either industry or NACA to do so. By 1940, as noted above, Pratt & Whitney was doing some very limited, component-level work on a compound engine. NACA was actually conducting some useful research on compressors, and one of its most brilliant aerodynamicists, Eastman Jacobs, was preparing to demonstrate the feasibility a of ducted-fan concept first conceived by Italian Secondo Campini in 1930. If all went well, it was conceivable that this system might be ready for inflight testing by 1943. In 1936, someone in the Engineering Section at Wright Field had produced a report titled "The Gas Turbine as a Prime Mover for Aircraft," but, like Kotcher's report three years later, it did not generate enough interest to stimulate any kind of major research program. In addition to looking at jet-assisted (really rocket) takeoff, the use of piston-engine exhaust to provide supplementary jet thrust, and reviewing (and typically rejecting) proposals for all manner of reaction propulsion systems, the Power Plant Laboratory had launched a modest program in 1938 aimed at developing a successful compound engine by 1943. There was no sense of urgency in any of the above-mentioned efforts, and none of them ever evolved into successful propulsion systems.[37]

As in Europe, interestingly enough, the only projects underway that were headed in the right direction all had their genesis outside of the aero-propulsion establishment. In 1936 engineers at General Electric (GE) started publishing internal research bulletins and reports on the feasibility of employing gas turbines as a primary source of power to drive propellers, and by 1939 Dale Streid was writing optimistically about "propulsion by means of a jet reaction." These studies were ongoing right up to April 1941, when GE (Schenectady Division), Allis Chalmers, and Westinghouse were invited to join Durand's Special Committee on Jet Propulsion (each of these turbine manufacturers would ultimately commence development of its own turbojet designs).[38]

Meanwhile, Jack Northrop appeared to have stolen a march on everyone. On the basis of design studies initiated in 1939, he became convinced of the superiority of a gas turbine over the conventional piston engine for driving propellers. After commencing initial development of a turboprop engine—which he called the Turbodyne—with his own resources, he approached the U.S. Army and Navy for support. Neither showed any interest until June of 1941, when they issued a joint contract to pursue development of what was subsequently designated the XT37. Like all of the early turboprops, the project was ambitious in concept and excruciatingly slow in development. Three test engines were finally built in 1947 and, though never flight tested, one of them eventually delivered an impressive 7,500 hp during bench tests before the project was canceled in 1949. By then, Northrop's ingenious engine had been overtaken by the turbojet.[39]

By far the most interesting development was taking place at Lockheed. Since the mid-1930s, Kelly Johnson had been well aware of the theoretical implications of compressibility phenomena, and by 1939 he and Hall Hibbard had decided to do away with the prop altogether! Unlike so many others in this country, they were capable of perceiving the sudden convergence of aerodynamic with thermodynamic principles. They asked Nathan Price to design a pure turbojet that would power a truly radical interceptor at speeds never before envisioned in this country. Initial development of the engine, designated L-1000, got underway in 1940; though his initial concepts were far too complex to be practicable, Price ultimately came up with a truly remarkable design—

a high-compression-ratio, twin-spool, axial-flow turbojet promising a then extraordinary 5,000 lb of thrust at takeoff. Meanwhile, Johnson led a small design team that came up with the L-133, an equally remarkable twin-engine, stainless-steel airplane, featuring thin wings and canard surfaces and projected to attain a whopping 620 mph at 20,000 feet (and nearly that speed at 50,000 feet)! Much to Johnson's chagrin, officials at Wright Field considered the radical airplane to be a far too risky venture when he delivered the design and technical data in March 1942. The engine, however, showed enough promise for Lockheed to win a contract for further development of what became known as the XJ37. The engine never got beyond the development stage; however, Kelly Johnson's knowledgeable interest in jet-propelled airplanes had made an important impression on the Experimental Engineering Section at Wright Field.[40]

Like so many among the top Air Corps leadership, Hap Arnold had never been technically inclined, and he was probably unaware of most of these developments. But when confronted with the palpable evidence of Whittle's achievement, he immediately grasped its implications and acted quickly to expedite America's late entry into the jet age. After promising the British that he would clamp the tightest security precautions on the project, he managed to gain permission to build the Whittle engine in the United States by late summer 1941. Next, he had to decide who would produce it. For the same reasons noted above, the major engine manufactures were excluded. Brig. Gen. Oliver P. Echols, chief of the Materiel Division of the recently redesignated Army Air Forces (AAF), and his assistant, Lt. Col. Benjamin W. Chidlaw, recommended General Electric because they were well aware that the company had pioneered in turbine technology and that, over the years since World War I, it had perfected the development of turbosuperchargers that permitted piston-engined airplanes to climb to otherwise unattainable altitudes. Indeed, turbosupercharging was based on many of the same principles as jet propulsion: at high altitudes, the thin air was compressed to sea-level conditions by a centrifugal compressor and directed through a carburetor, where fuel was added, and then through an intake valve into a piston cylinder, where it was ignited; then, passing through an exhaust valve, the exhaust gases were channeled through a turbine wheel that, in turn, drove the compressor. GE's extensive work with turbosuperchargers and, most important, the high-temperature alloys necessary to build them made it the logical choice to take the next step. In a meeting in Arnold's office on 4 September 1941, GE was offered a contract to reproduce the 1,650 lb thrust Whittle W.2B engine.[41]

Arnold's choice to design and build the airframe was almost as easy. His concerns about disrupting top-priority existing development and production programs were a major factor in this decision, and, based again on advice from

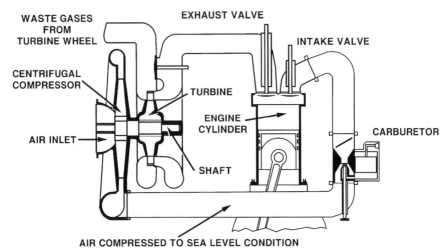

Fig. 11.2. Drawing of an early turbosupercharger. Courtesy Air Force Flight Test Center, Edwards Air Force Base, California

Echols and Chidlaw, he selected a company that certainly was not overburdened with such work. With innovative (though not very successful) designs, such as the YFM-1 "Airacuda" and the P-39 "Airacobra," the Bell Aircraft Corporation's team of designers had at least established a reputation for inventiveness, and Larry Bell's own seemingly boundless drive, Arnold and his staff believed, would guarantee that any project would be completed on time and up to expectations.[42]

Bell agreed to tackle the job on 5 September 1941. The next day, he selected a small group of six engineers and assigned them the task of creating a preliminary design for the aircraft. Working with little more than a small free-hand sketch of the engine, the "Secret Six," as they were called, prepared a design proposal and a 1/20 scale model within the span of just two weeks. Arnold gave his approval, and a fixed-fee contract for $1,644,431 was finalized on 3 October. It stipulated that the first of three "twin-engine, single-place interceptor pursuit models," with a projected combat ceiling of 46,000 feet and a top speed of nearly 500 mph, should be delivered within just eight months. A similar $630,000 contract was negotiated with General Electric for fifteen engines, with the initial pair of flight-ready engines, each providing 1,650 lb of thrust, to be available for installation on the first aircraft. Remarkably, and though Arnold doubted that it was possible, his staff was hoping that an engine-airframe combination could be designed and developed that could be rapidly transformed into a combat-worthy production fighter. This goal was remarkably ambitious, and the schedule was tight, to say the least.[43]

Chidlaw was selected by Arnold and Echols to provide overall direction for the program, and Majors Ralph Swofford, from the Experimental Aircraft Projects Section at Wright Field, and Don Keirn, from the Power Plant Lab, were assigned as airframe and engine project officers, respectively (within months Chidlaw was promoted to the rank of brigadier general and Swofford and Keirn each to the rank of full colonel). Swofford and Keirn each shouldered a tremendous amount of responsibility. In those days, a project office was responsible for all of the many functions now handled by system program offices staffed with hundreds of personnel. Due to the "Super Secret" nature of this program at its outset, no more than a dozen people at Wright Field had any knowledge of its existence. In Swofford's and Keirn's case, each was intimately involved in the design and development process on a daily basis and each had enormous authority. Every design change required their personal approval. And, indeed, during the early months of the flight test program, long before official AAF flight tests got underway, each would also find himself serving as a test pilot. After every significant modification to one of the prototype airframes, for example, Swofford would always fly the airplane before approving or disapproving it for inclusion in the production design. Small wonder that after he had retired as a two-star general years later, Don Keirn recalled that he had been entrusted with far more authority as a major during the hectic early months of this program than he would ever later enjoy as a general officer.[44]

In a fashion that would become a hallmark of the American aviation industry during the war years, a small design team hastily set to work at Bell with a profound sense of urgency and only a few rough drawings of the proposed engine in hand. Tasked with designing an entirely new type of airplane, they were further required to come up with a design that would also be suitable for combat service. Beyond the single stipulation to wrap an airframe around a pair of the new powerplants, they were free to improvise—but they had to work quickly and without the benefit of any outside advice or assistance. Because of security restrictions imposed by Arnold, for example, they were not permitted to make use of the NACA's full-scale wind tunnel facilities and were forced instead to rely on very imperfect data from the five-foot, low-speed tunnel at Wright Field. By mid-November, General Echols was already pleading with Arnold to rescind this restriction because he could already foresee boundary-layer problems with the engine inlets unless the design team could get some hard data on high-speed flow conditions. Arnold, however, was adamant, and this decision would, indeed, result in some serious miscalculations that would severely limit the performance of the airplane. Nevertheless, working in haste, the design team completed its work by early January 1942, and a small, select crew of Bell workers began to build the aircraft, literally by hand, on the closely guarded second floor of a Ford agency in Buffalo, New York. In the interests of secrecy, it had been given the designation XP-59A, a designation originally intended for a proposed Bell pusher-prop fighter that never got beyond the mock-up stage.[45]

Equally stringent security precautions were in force at GE's Lynn River facility, in Massachusetts, where another small team headed by Donald F. "Truly" Warner labored, nonstop, on a design that, again for security purposes, had been designated "Type I-A supercharger." With the benefit of Whittle's W.1X engine, which had been used in the taxi tests of the E.28/39 and on which they were able to run tests, and working from reportedly incomplete drawings of his W.2B design, they made some minor modifications to the diffuser, combustors, and bearings of the British design and built a prototype. On 18 March, just five and one-half months after taking on the job, they wheeled the engine into a test cell—aptly named "Fort Knox"—for its first test run. However, the engine stalled and this attempt was unsuccessful. But exactly one month later, on 18 April, Truly Warner once again advanced the throttle and, this time, the engine successfully roared to life. With the push of a hand, he had finally lit the flame of the turbojet revolution in America.[46]

The GE Type I-A engine was a centrifugal, reverse-flow turbojet that represented a quantum advance over Frank Whittle's original 1930 patent design. It featured inlets, configured with guide vanes, which directed air into a single-stage, double-sided impeller—a centrifugal compressor—which roughly tripled the air's pressure as it passed through the diffuser and into any of ten reverse-flow combustion chambers, where it was ignited and the intensely hot, expanding gases raced through the turbine—which drove the compressor—and exited through a single exhaust nozzle at high speed to produce thrust.[47]

The GE team proceeded with what would become a lengthy and sometimes painful development process. The thrust performance of the test unit, for example, never came close to matching the British design predictions for the W.2B (it was not until early 1943 that they would learn that the thrust curves they were using were different from those employed by the British). When Wing Commander Whittle arrived in June 1942, he found that Truly Warner and his team were struggling with excessive turbine inlet temperatures, cracked turbine blades, bearing failures, excessive carbon formation in the flame tubes due to poor combustion efficiency, and a host of other problems. Warner had found it necessary to experiment with a variety of different diffuser, combustor, and turbine bucket designs and materials, and Whittle was quick to caution that, because of the decision to locate the engine nacelles alongside the airplane's fuselage (as opposed to the wing-mounted pods that would be employed on the Meteor), boundary layer problems would severely reduce ram air efficiency. Despite all of these problems, Chidlaw reported to Arnold's office that "Bell and

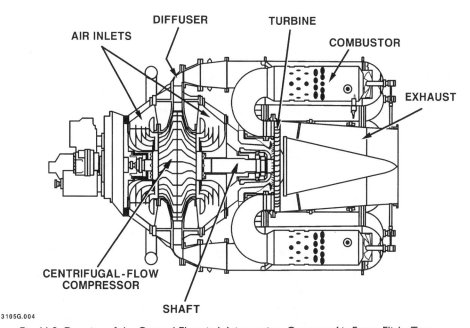

3105G.004

Fig. 11.3. Drawing of the General Electric I-A jet engine. Courtesy Air Force Flight Test Center, Edwards Air Force Base, California

G.E. have both done a bang-up job in rushing this thing through" and that the XP-59A project was "well ahead" of Britain's Meteor project which had enjoyed a one-year head start. He attributed this lead principally to the fact that General Electric's years of experience with turbosuperchargers had put the United States well ahead in the development of high-strength, heat-resistant alloys. Nevertheless, Bell's completion of the first airframe was held up by General Electric's inability to deliver flight-rated engines until early August, and it was already quite apparent that the I-A power plants would never be able to deliver more than 1,250 lb of thrust. Indeed, Warner had already proposed major modifications to the original design that would result in an I-16 unit capable of producing the desired 1,650 lb of thrust.[48]

Meanwhile, as the Bell team assembled the first airplane during the spring and summer of 1942, a continent away, the construction of a small Materiel Center test site got underway on the edge of an enormous dry lake at an out-of-the-way place called Muroc on California's high desert. Six miles to the south, Muroc Army Air Field served as a training base for fighter and bomber crews preparing for overseas deployment. The site was selected by Chidlaw and Swofford, in April of 1942, because of its extremely remote location, the excellent year-round flying weather, and the availability of the vast, forty-four-square-mile expanse of Rogers Dry Lake. It was obvious to them that the immense, concretelike lake bed would provide a natural landing field from which to explore all of the unknown characteristics of the new jet. When Bell chief test pilot Bob Stanley arrived there in August, he found what could best be described as "Spartan-like" accommodations: a water tower, an unfinished portable hangar, and a wooden military barrack. These three unimpressive structures represented the humble beginnings of what would one day become the USAF Flight Test Center.[49]

On 19 September, the engines and crated pieces of the airplane were off-loaded from box cars after a long, cross-country journey on what its weary GE escorts mockingly called the "Red Ball Express." Working, quite literally, day and night, Bell and GE personnel set about to reassemble the craft. They completed the job within a week and, on 26 September, the XP-59A rolled out from the hangar for the first time. In many regards, it appeared to be a fairly conventional design. But there were certain features that caught the eye. Fully loaded, it weighed just over 10,000 lb, and with a wing loading of 25 lbs/sq ft, its immense wings (400 sq ft) appeared to be optimized for high-altitude flight. The tail section swept upward very noticeably, and the craft rested extremely low to the ground on tricycle landing gear. And then, of course, there was no prop, and tucked beneath the wings, along the fuselage, were a pair of nacelles housing the I-A engines.[50]

Those engines roared to life on the aircraft for the first time that day and, by 30 September, just four days later, Bob Stanley and the airplane were primed for its initial taxi tests. After completing some low-speed trials, he proceeded to a series of high-speed runs in order to get a feel for the controls. On a couple of these runs, late in the day, the wheels of the aircraft actually lifted a couple of feet off the ground. Stanley, a brilliant engineer and a relentlessly hard-driving personality who seldom counted patience among his virtues, was all for making the first flight then and there. Larry Bell, however, overruled him; high-ranking official observers — such as Durand and Col. Laurence C. "Bill" Craigie, chief of the Experimental Aircraft Section at Wright Field — were not scheduled to arrive for two days. On the following day, 1 October, Stanley made four additional "high-speed taxis," during the first of which the aircraft lifted off and soared some twenty-five feet above the surface of the lake bed; on subsequent runs it climbed to as high as a hundred feet. Unofficially, the XP-59A unquestionably had flown. But the brass had not been there to witness the event, so "officially" it had not really happened.[51]

Finally, on 2 October, the brass *was* on hand. At about 1 P.M., Stanley advanced the throttles, released the brakes, and, slowly at first, the aircraft moved across the hard-baked clay. After what seemed like an unusually long takeoff roll, its wheels finally left the ground and he made what he described as a "leisurely" climb to 6,000 feet. Remarkably, just one year—almost to the day—after commencing the project, the United States had finally and officially entered the jet age.[52] GE's Ted Rogers reported what he called a "strange feeling" as he watched the flight: "dead silence as it passed directly overhead, . . . then a low rumbling roar, like a blowtorch . . . and it was gone, leaving a smell of kerosene in the air."[53] After a second flight, Stanley turned to Colonel Craigie and said: "Bill, we've only got about 45 minutes left on the engines [they had to be pulled for inspection after every three hours of running time]. How'd you like to take it up?" He didn't have to ask him twice. Although he had been on hand only to serve as the AAF's official observer, he went up for a thirty-minute flight and thus, quite by happenstance, Bill Craigie became America's first military jet pilot. As he was to recall many times: "Things were a lot less *formal* in those days."[54]

Less formal, indeed! There were no safety chase airplanes that day, and the most important instrumentation—at least during the initial flights—remained the seat of the pilot's pants. It may not have been too scientific, but by latter-day standards it was relatively inexpensive and it afforded a means of real-time data acquisition that was always certain to yield immediate analyses of any problems. There was no telemetry—indeed, the entire "mission control center" consisted of a two-way radio and an old voice recorder set up on the lake bed adjacent to the hangar—and, although the aircraft was ultimately instrumented to cover twenty to thirty different parameters, the instrumentation was often primitive, to say the least. Control stick forces, for example, were measured with a modified fish scale, and engine thrust was originally measured by means of an industrial spring scale attached to the landing gear and anchored to the ground. The lack of a satisfactory means of measuring thrust on the aircraft—especially in flight—would, in fact, hamper flight test efforts throughout the P-59 program—making it impossible, for example, to correlate airplane drag to net engine thrust.[55]

As the business of flight testing the airplane and engines proceeded, Bell and G. E. personnel encountered more than their share of headaches. Early on, for example, they had so much trouble starting one of the engines that they named the number 1 airplane "Miss Fire." Overheated bearings, malfunctioning fuel pumps and barometric controls, detached turbine blades, the three-hour inspection requirement, and countless other problems eventually forced them to remove the cowling panels so often that they later started calling it "Queenie," in honor of a much-admired exotic dancer (the designation "Airacomet" only came into use much later as a result of a contest among Bell employees). Indeed, persistent engine breakdowns and lengthy delays in the delivery of replacements, spare parts, and uprated, higher-thrust models of the engine caused the program to fall way behind schedule. Program officials in the Experimental Engineering Section at Wright Field had expected to start receiving useful performance data by January 1943, but by mid-April the airplanes had only accumulated twenty-nine flying hours. The engine problems, plus the fact that no one really knew *how* to test a jet airplane, delayed the start of the AAF's unofficial performance evaluations until late September of 1943, and the official tests were not completed until March of 1944.[56]

Although the testing proceeded at an excruciatingly slow pace, the pilots quickly became familiar with the characteristics of the jet, gaining a lot of wisdom that they would later impart in the flight manual. The throttles, for example, had to be treated very carefully. Rapid acceleration caused engine surges that could burn up the combustors and turbines. The engines' extremely slow acceleration also taught them never to go low and slow on final approach. Lacking an airstart capability, the engines also had a nasty habit of flaming out, and, as had been expected, they consumed enormous quantities of fuel. Experience with both of these problems bore out the wisdom of selecting the lake bed for the tests. In fact, attempting to get as much out of each mission as possible, the pilots eventually made it a common practice to fly until the tanks went dry and then glide in to dead-stick lake bed landings.[57]

Hoping to catch up in a hurry, the Army Air Forces had attempted to make the great leap from a proof-of-concept, experimental vehicle to a 500 mph combat fighter, all in one airplane. It was a bold hope, too bold. The performance of the XP-59A with the original I-A engines fell far short of expectations. In part, this was because the original thrust data provided by the British for the W.2B engine were misinterpreted and thus the I-A's actual performance fell about 25 percent short of what had been very optimistic projections. Even with modified I-14 engines, each providing about 1,450 lb of thrust, the maximum speed attained was only 424 mph at 25,000 feet. This speed was attained, however, only after the entire airplane's surfaces had been puttied, smoothed, and sanded and its wings polished. By comparison, in its normal "dirty" configuration, the airplane's top speed was only 404 mph at the same altitude.[58]

The performance of the slightly heavier YP-59s was even more disappointing. Some of the YPs were representative of the ultimate production version of the aircraft. For example, the wingtips were clipped and squared off, reducing the span from forty-nine feet to forty-five feet and its wing area by about fifteen square feet. The size of the vertical stabilizer was reduced and its tip squared off, as well. The hinge-mounted, side-opening canopy, which was flush with the fuselage on the XP-models, was replaced by a new sliding canopy that protruded about two inches above the fuselage surfaces, and a larger and flatter windscreen was also incorporated. Finally, the YPs were configured with the uprated I-16 models of the engine (AAF designation J31) rated at 1,650 lb of static thrust (the thrust rating for which the airframe was originally designed). To everyone's surprise and disappointment, the top speed achieved by the aircraft was only 409 mph at 35,000 feet. This poor performance, in comparison with the XP model, was primarily attributed to the substantial increase in drag caused by the new canopy and windscreen.[59]

The disappointing performance of the overall design, however, was blamed on a number of other factors. In September 1943, Bell engineer Randy Hall's plaintive cry to chief project engineer Ed Rhodes belabored the obvious: "We need thrust—thrust—and *more* thrust."[60] The low thrust-to-weight ratio and the oversized (scarcely laminar flow) wings were among the most obvious contributors. There were many other flaws, however, which conceivably could have been identified and remedied during the initial design process if the Bell team could have had access to reliable high-speed wind tunnel data. Their original calculations concerning boundary-layer effects and engine nacelle inlet area, for example, were way off the mark, and after the airplanes started flying, Bell was forced to experiment with various new configurations. The original 2.86 sq ft inlet was ultimately reduced to 2.08 sq ft, but even then it was scarcely optimized for peak performance.

The failure to completely understand the dynamics of airflow within the nacelles led to a multitude of other problems. A lot of engineering effort was expended after the flight test program got underway—for example, attempting to reduce rear compressor inlet temperatures. The aircraft also exhibited a directional "snaking" tendency that increased in severity with speed. Repeated modifications to the vertical tail and rudder were to no avail, and the aircraft was judged "unsatisfactory" as a gunnery platform during official AAF tests.[61] The real source of the problem may actually have had little to do with the rudder. It may well have stemmed, once again, from the failure to adequately understand nacelle inlet problems. At a symposium in late 1945, Benson Hamlin, one of Bell's key flight test engineers on the program, reported that the snaking "is believed to be due to the very large inlet scoops in which it is possible for the inlet ducts on either side to alternately stall and unstall, causing a fluctuating air flow in the scoops or nacelles producing an unstable directional stability of the airplane."[62]

Though it served as a useful test bed in which to explore the potential advantages—and pitfalls—of a radical new technology (and it won at least one distinction when, in February of 1944, Maj. Everett Leach climbed to an American record of 47,700 feet), the P-59 was really, for all practical purposes, a 350 mph airplane—no faster than the prop-driven fighters of its day. And, indeed, in operational suitability tests during which it was flown in mock combat engagements against P-38s and P-47s, it was outclassed in virtually every category by the conventional fighters. Ambitious plans for a major production run were canceled. In addition to the three XP- and 13 YP-59A prototypes, only fifty production models came off of Bell's assembly line. Not suited for combat, they were used to train America's first cadre of jet pilots—a role which, indeed, made them unique among the first generation of jet aircraft. More important, still, was the fact that America's aviation industry went to school with this aircraft, and those in it learned their lessons well.[63]

On 8 January 1944, just two days after the AAF first announced the existence of the P-59, another jet prototype was prepped for its maiden flight at Muroc. In contrast to the Airacomet, there was nothing conventional-looking about this airplane. Designed by Kelly Johnson and delivered by his fledgling "Skunk Works" in just 143 days, the sleek, single-engined XP-80 looked like it was made for jet power—and, indeed, it was. It was powered by yet another British import, the British DeHavilland Halford H.1B, and as he accelerated to a speed of 490 mph, Lockheed test pilot Milo Burcham put on an impressive demonstration above the lake bed that morning. Among those viewing it was Bell test pilot Tex Johnston. Immediately afterward, he fired a cable back to Bob Stanley in Buffalo: "Witnessed Lockheed XP-80 initial flight-STOP-Very impressive-STOP-Back to drawing board-STOP." Though its Halford engine was never able to deliver more than 2,460 lb of thrust, during official AAF performance tests conducted just over a month later the XP-80 became the first American aircraft to exceed 500 mph in level flight.[64]

The XP-80, however, was really only an aerodynamic test bed. Prior to the end of 1942, GE design engineers had already learned enough from their work with the original I-A engine to permit the Engineering Division at Wright Field to give the go-ahead to develop an engine that would more than triple the I-A's thrust. Development of the I-40 (J33) proceeded so rapidly that in August of 1943, Johnson was asked to design a substantially larger airframe to house an engine providing 4,000 lb of static thrust. This airplane, the XP-80A, first flew in June 1944, and it served as the prototype for America's first combat-worthy jet fighter, the P-80 Shooting Star. The first production models were accepted by the AAF in February of 1945. Capable of speeds approaching 600 mph, the P-80 demonstrated how far and how fast the United States had come in just three years. The lessons learned in the P-59/I-A engine program had paid extraordinary dividends.[65]

The turbojet airplane could have been—and, but for the delusions of Adolph Hitler, *might* have been—a decisive weapon in World War II. But it was not and, although the United States failed to put a jet aircraft into combat, with

Germany's surrender and the development of the J33-powered P-80, this country had arguably moved from the back of the pack into the forefront of the turbojet revolution within a span of just three years.

How did we do it? In large part, quite obviously because of tremendous advantages in material, skilled manpower, and industrial know-how. But also, in part and almost ironically, because of that very same focus on applied science that, Edward Constant has argued, initially put us behind. No nation in the world was more adept at — or had more impressive facilities for — transforming the fruits of pure science into superior products. In some cases, being first is not nearly so advantageous as being a really superior second, third, or even fourth. Once presented with a good idea, no nation was better prepared to run with it; a so-called weakness became an immediate strength.

Nevertheless, none of this would have been possible without the aid and ongoing assistance of the British. This lesson was certainly not lost on the man most intimately involved in the process. Returning from a trip to England in August 1943, Col. Don Keirn was exasperated by the fact "that enough emphasis has not been placed on research facilities to enable this country to keep up with developments. Our present position is largely due to the aid given us by Great Britain and our ability to sift the information and follow those lines which appear to be most immediately profitable."[66] The implications of his report extended far beyond the turbojet, and they were not lost on any of those who had been involved in importing the new technology to the United States. By the late summer of 1945, as the U.S. military was completing its inventory of Germany's massive R&D infrastructure, Brig. Gen. Laurence C. Craigie was preparing to take over as the chief of the Engineering Division. It would be his job to help build a new U.S. Air Force that could meet the challenges of the future. The recent war had taught that science and warfare had become inextricably intertwined, and in the future, he was convinced, there probably would not be time to borrow, let alone to catch up. In a speech to the International Aeronautical Society, he emphasized that the United States must "tear a page from the German book of experience and use it as a warning lest we forget that research can only rarely be hurried, that it must be continuous, and that most of it must be accomplished during years of peace." This, he further emphasized, would require the creation of a massive R&D establishment "prepared to stand on its own feet" within the Air Force, and, he concluded, "these feet can only be provided through adequate appropriations and the provision of adequate personnel and facilities."[67]

This was essentially the same message that Dr. Theodore von Kármán and the AAF Scientific Advisory Group were about to deliver to General Arnold. Indeed, he would define the establishment of a comprehensive and well-coordinated R&D capability that would be second to none—one that would not only encompass the NACA, industry, and the universities but also, for the first time, a major in-house establishment, as well—as the AAF's highest post-war priority. The turbojet was the most publicized—and, therefore, embarrassing—example of the failure of the underfunded, fragmented, and uncoordinated prewar military R&D system in this country; in that sense, it would become a useful symbol for those, like General Craigie, who were given the job of convincing an austerity-minded Congress—and, indeed, the rest of the Air Force—that being first was no longer just a matter of national pride; it was now a matter of national survival.[68]

By war's end, the turbojet revolution was still in its infancy. The AAF already had at least nineteen turbojet aircraft projects underway. Most of them, however, would be relatively crude attempts to adapt existing airframe concepts to the new propulsion technology, and even the most successful of them, such as the sweptwing F-86, could be considered as, at best, no more than transitional designs. G. Geoffrey Smith observed at the time that the turbojet revolution had precipitated a momentous turn of events: "it is only as a result of successful development of the gas turbine and jet propulsion that engine manufacturers are able, for the first time in history, to supply more powerful units than the builders of airframes can at the moment usefully employ. The relative position [of each] has been reversed."[69]

On a very basic level, the genius of Whittle and von Ohain's vision of a high-speed airplane had been based on the perception that the engine and airframe were really two components of a single system joined together in a kind of symbiotic relationship in which the capability of each was dependent on the maximum efficiency of the other. Aerodynamicists had unwittingly brought on the demise of the reciprocating engine, and now they found themselves in the position of having to catch up with the new technology that had been spawned by their efforts in order to take full advantage of its potential.

A multitude of jet engine development projects were also underway at the time, as the emphasis shifted overwhelmingly toward axial-flow designs. General Electric, Westinghouse, and the erstwhile piston-engine manufacturers poured millions of dollars into a painstaking search for lighter-weight, higher-strength, and more heat-resistant materials as they strove to achieve higher compression and thrust-to-weight ratios and reduced fuel consumption while improving the durability and acceleration capabilities of their engines. Indeed, well before the end of the war, they had made tremendous strides in aerothermodynamics (achieving combustion in high-speed airflow). They had also started looking into the advantages to be gained from various types of thrust augmentation, such as water injection and afterburning, and they were already well aware of the tremendous fuel economies that could be achieved with turbo-fan designs.[70]

The turbojet also compelled a host of developments in other fields. The tremendously high speeds and altitudes that were now within reach, for example, meant that human physiology could easily become the most critical limiting factor in the design of high-performance airplanes. Aeromedical research, a heretofore neglected field, suddenly became a top-priority endeavor, as did the development of ejection systems, G-suits, pressurized cockpits, pressure-breathing oxygen systems, and full-pressure suits. The turbojet also drove major efforts in weapon systems development. An immediate demand for dramatic improvements in lead-computing optical gun- and bombsights gave way to a massive effort to develop radar tracking systems and, among many, to the conclusion that guns and classic dogfights had become relics of a bygone age and only guided missiles could meet the requirements of future air-to-air combat. High speeds and human limitations also compelled the development of hydraulically boosted and irreversible flight controls and stability and control augmentation systems. The development of sophisticated automated fire and flight control systems, in turn, mandated the development of compact, high-speed computers. The spin-off effects of the turbojet seemed to be endless.

Like an irresistible force, the awesome potential of the turbojet also forced designers to confront the reality of transonic flight. Aerodynamicists had long speculated on the possibility of flight beyond the speed of sound, but now it was obvious that the means were at hand to actually propel a piloted airplane into that region. Speculation and theory were one thing, but no one had any valid data on high-speed stability and control and the effects of compressibility, and there was an urgent need for such information. Ezra Kotcher finally got his transonic research airplane — the Bell X-1 — and the rest, as they say, is history.[71]

The new U.S. Air Force had already made tremendous strides in all of these and many other related areas when turbojet technology finally achieved mature status in this country with the development of the Pratt & Whitney J57. On 15 April 1952, almost exactly ten years after Hap Arnold had first witnessed the E.28/39 making short hops during its high-speed taxi tests, eight prototype J57s powered the YB-52 on its maiden flight. This engine-airframe combination was an extraordinary accomplishment. Early model B-52s could outpace an F-86E at altitude, and they demonstrated an intercontinental range capability that, only a couple of years earlier, had been thought to be impossible for jet-powered aircraft. The J57 also opened the door for the development of long-range commercial airliners — and supersonic fighters. Early versions of the engine provided about 12,000 lb of dry thrust and 17,000 lb in afterburner, and it was with its burner lit that the J57-powered YF-100 became the first aircraft in history to ex-

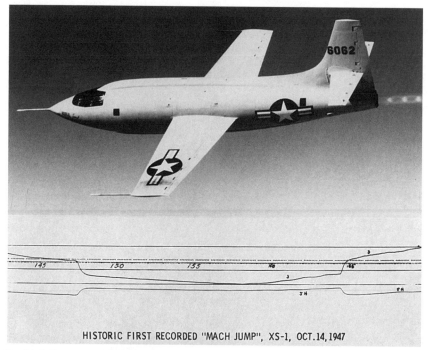

HISTORIC FIRST RECORDED "MACH JUMP", XS-1, OCT.14,1947

Fig. 11.4. Composite photograph of the Bell X-1 in operation, which first flew faster than the speed of sound on 14 October 1947 (top), with the data sheet (bottom) recording the supersonic flight. Courtesy NASA

ceed Mach 1 on its maiden flight in May of 1953. With the arrival of the YF-100 and the other first-generation supersonic fighters, the marriage of aerodynamics to thermodynamics was, at last, successfully consummated; for they were the first airplanes to achieve the kind of symbiotic harmony that, three decades before, had inspired the visions of Frank Whittle and Hans von Ohain.[72]

NOTES

1. John Golley, *Whittle: The True Story* (Washington, D.C.: Smithsonian Institution Press, 1987), pp. 23–24; Frank Whittle, "The Birth of the Jet Engine in Britain," in *The Jet Age: Forty Years of Jet Aviation*, ed. Walter J. Boyne and Donald S. Lopez (Washington, D.C.: National Air and Space Museum, 1979), p. 3; Edward W. Constant, *The Origins of the Turbojet Revolution* (Baltimore: Johns Hopkins University Press, 1980), pp. 180–82.

2. Ronald E. Miller and David Sawers, *The Technical Development of Modern Aviation* (London: Routledge & Kegan Paul Limited, 1968), pp. 47–97; Robert Schlaifer, *Development of Aircraft Engines* (Boston, Mass.: Harvard University Graduate School of Business Administration, 1950), pp. 156–320; J. S. Butz, Jr., "General Electric: Pioneer of U.S. Jet Engines," *Flying*, Feb. 1963, pp. 51, 85; Bill Gunston, *World Encyclopaedia of Aero Engines*, 3d ed. (Sparford, Nr Yeovil, Somerset: Patrick Stephens

Limited, 1995), pp. 122–23. For a useful brief history of the development of piston-driven aero engines, see Herschel Smith, *A History of Aircraft Piston Engines* (Manhattan, Kans.: Sunflower University Press, 1986).

3. Richard P. Hallion, *Designers and Test Pilots* (Alexandria, Va.: Time-Life Books, 1983), pp. 68–78; Don Berliner, *Victory over the Wind: A History of the Absolute World Air Speed Record* (New York: Van Norstrand Reinhold Co., 1983), pp. 43–48, 58–65; J. R. Smith and Anthony L. Kay, *German Aircraft of the Second World War*, 7th printing (London: Putnam & Company, 1990), pp. 520–23; Gunston, *World Encyclopaedia of Aero Engines*, p. 49.

4. As quoted in Smith and Kay, *German Aircraft of the Second World War*, p. 524.

5. James J. St. Peter, ed., *The Memoirs of Ernest C. Simpson: Aeropropulsion Pioneer* (Wright-Patterson Air Force Base, Ohio: Aero Propulsion Laboratory, Aeronautical Systems Division, 1987), pp. 9–11; Leslie E. Neville and Nathaniel F. Silsbee, *Jet Propulsion Progress: The Development of Gas Turbines* (New York: McGraw-Hill, 1948), pp. 194–95; Hallion, *Designers and Test Pilots*, p. 78; Constant, *Origins of the Turbojet Revolution*, pp. 109, 138, 152–53, 249–50.

6. Theodore von Kármán with Lee Edson, *The Wind and Beyond: Theodore von Kármán, Pioneer in Aviation and Pathfinder in Space* (Boston: Little, Brown, 1967), pp. 216–21; Richard P. Hallion, *Supersonic Flight: Breaking the Sound Barrier and Beyond* (New York: Macmillan, 1972), p. 11.

7. Clarence L. "Kelly" Johnson with Maggie Smith, *Kelly: More than My Share of It All* (Washington, D.C.: Smithsonian Institution Press, 1985), p. 95.

8. Golley, *Whittle*, pp. 24, 32; Constant, *Origins of the Turbojet Revolution*, pp. 182–83.

9. Frank Whittle, *Jet: The Story of a Pioneer* (London: Frederick Muller, 1953), pp. 24–25. See also Whittle, "Birth of the Jet Engine in Britain," p. 4.

10. Golley, *Whittle*, p. 248.

11. Ibid., pp. 34–36, 51–53; Whittle, "Birth of the Jet Engine in Britain," pp. 4–5; Constant, *Origins of the Turbojet Revolution*, pp. 138–49, 184–86; Schlaifer, *Development of Aircraft Engines*, pp. 334–35.

12. Golley, *Whittle*, pp. 64–81, 248–49; Whittle, "Birth of the Jet Engine in Britain," pp. 7–8; Constant, *Origins of the Turbojet Revolution*, pp. 186–87.

13. Golley, *Whittle*, pp. 86–91, 97–98, 101–21, 250–52; Whittle, "Birth of the Jet Engine in Britain," pp. 8–12; Constant, *Origins of the Turbojet Revolution*, pp. 191–92; Schlaifer, *Development of Aircraft Engines*, pp. 343–44, 350–51.

14. Constant, *Origins of the Turbojet Revolution*, pp. 194–200; Schlaifer, *Development of Aircraft Engines*, pp. 377–79.

15. Constant, *Origins of the Turbojet Revolution*, pp. 201–207, 210–11; Schlaifer, *Development of Aircraft Engines*, pp. 379–98, 418–28; Neville and Silsbee, *Jet Propulsion Progress*, p. 8. The Junkers Jumo 004-B had an eight-stage axial compressor that produced a pressure rise of 3.1:1 at an efficiency of 78 percent. Weighing 1,590 pounds, it produced 1,980 pounds of thrust at 8,700 rpm. The engine was 12 feet 8 inches long and 31.5 inches in diameter and had a specific fuel consumption (pounds of fuel consumed per pound of thrust produced per hour) of 1.4. Between five thousand and six thousand of the engines were produced before the end of the war.

16. Schlaifer, *Development of Aircraft Engines*, pp. 424–29; Constant, *Origins of the Turbojet Revolution*, pp. 208–13; Neville and Silsbee, *Jet Propulsion Progress*, pp. 9–10, 16, 21–33; Jeffrey Ethell and Alfred Price, *World War II Fighting Jets* (Annapolis, Md.: Naval Institute Press, 1994), pp. 42, 55. In a letter to General Arnold in early September 1944, Lt. Gen. Carl Spaatz conveyed his extreme alarm concerning the threat posed by the Me 262 and, in passing along his list of priorities for assistance, stated: "Most important of all is to put long-range jet fighters into the field at the earliest possible date," Arnold to Spaatz, 3 September 1944. His and Lt. Gen. Jimmy Doolittle's concerns only mounted as the Germans fielded increasing numbers of the airplane and employed them with greater tactical skill. See David R. Mets, *Master of Airpower: General Carl A. Spaatz* (Novato, Calif.: Presidio Press,

1988), pp. 246–47, 54; Richard G. Davis, *Carl A. Spaatz and the Air War in Europe* (Washington, D.C.: Center for Air Force History, 1993), pp. 512–13, 538–42, 574–75.

17. Golley, *Whittle*, pp. 119–20, 122–28, 165–71; Whittle, "Birth of the Jet Engine in Britain," pp. 12–15; Neville and Silsbee, *Jet Propulsion Progress*, pp. 58–63. For further details concerning the first flight and subsequent tests of the E.28/39, see Bill Gunston, "Dawn of the Jet Age," *Aeroplane Monthly*, Apr. 1977, 184–88; John Golley, "The Whittle Revolution," *Aeroplane Monthly*, June 1991, pp. 346–51. For details concerning jet engine development in England throughout the war and early postwar years, see Neville and Silsbee, *Jet Propulsion Progress*, pp. 55–97; Schlaifer, *Development of Aircraft Engines*, pp. 332–74.

18. H. H. Arnold, *Global Mission* (New York: Harper & Row, 1949), pp. 242–43; D. Roy Shoults, "Wartime Diary Tells of Exciting Days that Led to First Flight of XP-59, America's First Jet," General Electric Flight Propulsion Division *World* 1 (6 Oct. 1967): 2; Virginia P. Dawson, *Engines and Innovation: Lewis Laboratory and American Propulsion Technology* (Washington, D.C.: National Aeronautics and Space Administration, 1991), pp. 46–49; Alex Roland, *Model Research: The National Advisory Committee for Aeronautics, 1915–1958* (Washington, D.C.: National Aeronautics and Space Administration, 1985), pp. 189–91; James R. Hansen, *Engineer in Charge: A History of the Langley Aeronautical Laboratory, 1917–1958* (Washington, D.C.: National Aeronautics and Space Administration, 1987), pp. 230–32.

19. See Schlaifer, *Development of Aircraft Engines*, p. 321; Wesley Frank Craven and James Lea Cates, eds., *The Army Air Forces in World War II*, vol. 6, *Men and Planes* (Chicago: University of Chicago Press, 1953), p. 246.

20. Schlaifer, *Development of Aircraft Engines*, p. 489.

21. Constant, *Origins of the Turbojet Revolution*, pp. 151–77, 244, 271.

22. Capt. Ezra Kotcher, "Our Jet Propelled Fighter," in Bell Aircraft Corporation Technical Data Report No. 27-947-001-2: Condensed Model Specification for Twin Engine Jet Propelled Fighter Airplane, 23 Apr. 1945, p. 14. For testimony from a contemporary on Kotcher's brilliance and breadth of knowledge, see Lt. Gen. Ralph P. Swofford, Jr., USAF (Ret.), interview with Lt. Col. Arthur W. McCants, Jr., Maxwell AFB, Alabama, 24–25 Apr. 1979, Oral History No. K239.0512-1120, U.S. Air Force Historical Research Agency, Maxwell AFB, Ala., pp. 36–37. For comment on how widespread discussion of jet propulsion was, see Schlaifer, *Development of Aircraft Engines*, p. 486.

23. E. Kotcher, "Future Aeronautical Research and Development," Air Corps Material Engineering Section Memorandum Report No. 50-461-351, 18 Aug. 1939, copy on file Air Force Flight Test Center History Office (hereafter AFFTC/HO); Hallion, *Supersonic Flight*, pp. 12–13. Kotcher went on to become the primary instigator and champion of the X-1 supersonic research program. See Hallion, *Supersonic Flight*, pp. 20–26, 34–36, 40–41, 45; James O. Young, *Meeting the Challenge of Supersonic Flight* (Edwards Air Force Base, Calif.: AFFTC History Office, 1997), pp. 5–7; Hansen, *Engineer in Charge*, pp. 260, 271–73.

24. Martin P. Claussen, *Materiel Research and Development in the Army Air Arm, 1914–1945*, Army Air Forces Historical Studies No. 50 (Washington, D.C.: AAF Historical Office, 1946), pp. 98–102; Craven and Cates, *Men and Planes*, pp. 228–29; Donald C. Swain, "Organization of Military Research," in *Technology in Western Civilization: Technology in the Twentieth Century*, vol. 2, ed. Melvin Kranzberg and Carroll W. Pursell Jr. (New York: Oxford University Press, 1967), p. 540.

25. Neville and Silsbee, *Jet Propulsion Progress*, pp. 100–101; Constant, *Origins of the Turbojet Revolution*, p. 142; Hansen, *Engineer in Charge*, pp. 224–26; Roland, *Model Research*, p. 188.

26. Hansen, *Engineer in Charge*, p. 225. See also Dawson, *Engines and Innovation*, p. 43; Roland, *Model Research*, p. 186; Schlaifer, *Development of Aircraft Engines*, pp. 8, 33.

27. Irving Brinton Holley Jr., *Buying Aircraft: Materiel Procurement for the Army Air Forces* (Washington, D.C.: Center of Military History, 1989 ed.), pp. 23–25; Claussen, *Materiel Research and Development*, pp. 75–80; I. B. Holley, "Jet Lag in the Army Air Corps," in *Military Planning in the Twentieth*

Century: Proceedings of the [USAF Academy] Eleventh Military History Symposium, 10–12 October 1984 (Washington, D.C.: Office of Air Force History, 1986), pp. 135–36; Jacob Vander Meulen, *The Politics of Aircraft: Building an American Military Industry* (Lawrence: University Press of Kansas, 1991), pp. 5–7, 44–45, 53–54, 63, 77–85. It is also significant that there were practically no research contracts issued to American universities until very late in the 1930s.

28. Schlaifer, *Development of Aircraft Engines*, pp. 85, 445, 453–54; Dawson, *Engines and Innovation*, pp. 1, 47. At a 27 July 1944 meeting of the NACA Executive Committee called to consider postwar research policy and the role industry should play in fundamental and applied research, the aeroengine industry drew the most attention. Dr. Vannevar Bush concluded: "The engine people did not do a thing on that subject [jet propulsion] or on any other unusual engine." Maj. Gen. Oliver P. Echols, who had served in the Materiel Division at Wright Field throughout the 1930s and was General Arnold's wartime chief of research and development, noted a conservatism that, in fact, was not just limited to the aeroengine manufacturers: "Industry is always looking over its shoulder at its competitors. If their research is one step ahead of their competitors they are satisfied. It has always been apparent they are not interested in the general progress of the art." See "Notes on discussion at meeting of NACA, July 27, 1944," in Roland, *Model Research*, vol. 2, p. 688.

29. Schlaifer, *Development of Aircraft Engines*, pp. 451–53; Dawson, *Engines and Innovation*, p. 47; *The Pratt & Whitney Aircraft Story* (United Aircraft Corporation, 1950), pp. 154–55.

30. Roland, *Model Research*, p. 190; Dawson, *Engines and Innovation*, pp. 46–47.

31. Lt. Gen. Donald L. Putt, USAF (Ret), interview with James C. Hasdorff, Atherton, Calif., 1–3 Apr. 1974, Oral History No. K239.0512-724, U.S. Air Force Historical Research Agency, pp. 31–32. General Putt punctuated his comments by stating that Pratt & Whitney's attempt to shift responsibility from itself was "just a bunch of malarkey."

32. Holley, "Jet Lag in the Air Corps," pp. 144–45; Claussen, *Materiel Research and Development*, pp. 63, 66–67, 91–93; Roland, *Model Research*, pp. 186–87; memo, Maj. K. B. Wolfe, Chief Production Engineering Section, to Col. Oliver P. Echols, Assistant Chief, Materiel Division, 29 Apr. 1940, Records of the USAF Engineering Division, 1917–1951, Box RD 3735, Washington National Records Center, Suitland, Md. (documents from this collection have recently been transferred to the National Archives II in College Park, Md; hereafter cited as "RD" plus digits); memo, Maj. Stanley M. Umstead, Chief, Flying Branch, to Chief, Aircraft Branch, 27 June 1938, RD 3735; memo report, Maj. Carl J. Crane, Chief, Flight Research Projects, to Chief, Experimental Engineering Section, 21 Mar. 1940, RD 3735. By the late 1930s, a number of officials at Wright Field were lamenting that their dependence on the NACA to conduct fundamental flight research had become so complete. In 1938, for example, the chief of the Aircraft Laboratory proposed the reestablishment of an experimental flight research capability at Wright Field. In the memo cited above, Major Umstead, the chief of the Flying Branch, responded that, while his organization "recognizes the value of flight research and deplores the conditions which brought about its almost complete discontinuance as a [Materiel] Division activity," he did not believe such an action would be possible. "The first and most general reaction to such a request," he noted, "would be a denial on the grounds of duplication of allotment of funds and delegation of work of which the N.A.C.A. is now the responsible agency. Any deviation from the present policy would probably be interpreted as reflecting upon the results achieved by the N.A.C.A."

33. "Jet Lag in the Army Air Corps," p. 132. Though Professor Holley refers to this article as "but a modest footnote" to Edward Constant's sweeping treatise, it provides a penetrating analysis of the state of Army Air Corps R&D during the 1930s.

34. Claussen, *Materiel Research and Development*, pp. 48–52; Craven and Cates, *Men and Planes*, p. 177. Figures do not include funds appropriated for military pay and the construction of facilities.

35. Schlaifer, *Development of Aircraft Engines*, p. 267; Holley, "Jet Lag in the Army Air Corps," pp. 132–33.

36. Claussen, *Material Research and Development*, pp. 42–48; Holley, *Buying Aircraft*, pp. 97–98, 463–64; Benjamin S. Kelsey, *The Dragon's Teeth?: The Creation of United States Air Power for World War II* (Washington, D.C.: Smithsonian Institution Press, 1982), pp. 43; Lt. Gen. Laurence C. Craigie, USAF (Ret.), interview with Maj. Paul Clark and Capt. Donald Baucom, Colorado Springs, Colo., 24 Sep. 1971, USAF Historical Research Agency Oral History No. 637, 70–71; Lt. Gen. Laurence C. Craigie, USAF (Ret.), interview with author, Riverside, Calif., 14 May 1992; *Air Corps Engineering School* (Wright Field, Dayton, Ohio, 1935), Maj. Gen. Osmond J. Ritland papers, AFFTC/HO; Holley, "Jet Lag in the Army Air Corps," pp. 136–37, 139, 144; Putt interview, pp. 15, 23, 47–48; Swofford interview, pp. 34–37, 39–40.

37. Hansen, *Engineer in Charge*, pp. 222–23, 227–29, 233–44; Roland, *Model Research*, p. 191; Dawson, *Engines and Innovation*, pp. 48–49; *Eight Decades of Progress: A Heritage of Aircraft Turbine Technology* (Cincinnati, Ohio: General Electric, 1990), p. 28; Schlaifer, *Development of Aircraft Engines*, pp. 441–42; Neville and Silsbee, *Jet Propulsion Progress*, p. 101; Robert H. Goddard to General George H. Brett, Chief, Materiel Division, 27 July 1940; memo, Maj. Paul H. Kemmer, Chief, Aircraft Laboratory, to Chief, Experimental Engineering Section, 19 Aug. 1940; memo, Kemmer to Chief, Experimental Engineering Section, 14 Sep. 1940; Maj. Franklin O. Carroll, Chief, Experimental Engineering, to I. M. Laddon, 23 Nov. 1940; memo, Carroll to Chief, Power Plant Laboratory, 7 October 1940; memo, Kemmer to Chief, Experimental Engineering Section, 29 Oct. 1940; memo, Carroll to Chief, Materiel Division, 25 Mar. 1941. The Campini ducted-fan engine was employed in the Caproni-Campini C.C.2 aircraft, which first flew in Aug. 1940. Attaining a top speed of only 230 mph, the aircraft—and its propulsion system—were judged failures. See G. Geoffrey Smith, *Gas Turbines and Jet Propulsion for Aircraft* (New York: Aircraft Books, 1946), pp. 48–50.

38. *Eight Decades of Progress*, pp. 28, 38; Schlaifer, *Development of Aircraft Engines*, pp. 88, 445; Roland, *Model Research*, pp. 189–90; Dawson, *Engines and Innovation*, pp. 47–48.

39. Schlaifer, *Development of Aircraft Engines*, pp. 446–48; Fred Anderson, *Northrop: An Aeronautical History* (Los Angeles: Northrop Corporation, 1976), pp. 34–39.

40. Constant, *Origins of the Turbojet Revolution*, pp. 223–24; Schlaifer, *Development of Aircraft Engines*, pp. 448–50; Johnson, *Kelly*, pp. 72, 74–76, 79, 95; Lockheed Aircraft Corporation Report No. 2578: Manufacturer's Preliminary Brief Model Specification, Airplane, Interceptor Pursuit (Model L-133), 27 Feb. 1942; Lockheed Aircraft Corp. Report No. 2581: Performance Characteristics (Model L-133), 27 Feb. 1942; Lockheed Aircraft Corp. Report No. 2579: Manufacturer's Preliminary Brief Model Specification: Jet Propulsion Unit, 27 Feb. 1942; Lockheed Aircraft Corp. Report No. 2571: Design Model Features of the Lockheed L-133, 24 Feb. 1942. All Lockheed reports on file AFFTC/HO. Key correspondence between Lockheed and Wright Field officials throughout the development of the L-1000 may be found in *Case History of the L-1000 (XJ37-1) Jet Propulsion Engine* on file in the Aeronautical Systems Center History Office, Wright-Patterson AFB (hereafter ASC/HO). Bell had already been issued a contract to develop a single-engine XP-59B by that time. By late November of 1942, however, when it became apparent that the company was not making satisfactory progress, Col. Ralph Swofford recommended to Col. Bill Craigie, chief of the Experimental Engineering Section: "Perhaps we should consider the assignment of the project to another company, which could give us expedited delivery." See memo, Swofford to Craigie, 22 Nov. 1942.

41. Cablegram, M/A, London, to MILID, 21 July 1941 (this document, along with much of the other correspondence concerning development of the I-A series of engines cited herein, may be found in "Summary of the Whittle Jet Propulsion Engine," ASC/HO); unsigned memo to Gen. [Oliver P.] Echols, Chief, Materiel Division, subj: Summary of 4 September 1941 Meeting with G.E., 5 Sep. 1941; cablegram, Arnold to [Lt. Col. J. T. C.] Moore-Brabizon, Ministry of Aircraft Production, 4 Sep. 1941; notebook, [Maj. B. W. Chidlaw] "Notes on Conferences," 9 Sep. 1941; General Benjamin W. Chidlaw, USAF (Ret.), interview with Murray Green, Colorado Springs, Colo., 12 Dec. 1969, Murray Green Collection, Gimble Library, USAF Academy (hereafter Green Collection); General Benjamin W.

Chidlaw, USAF (Ret.), to Ronald Neal, 19 Aug. 1965, AFFTC/HO; Maj Gen Franklin O. Carroll, USAF (Ret.), interview with Murray Green, Boulder, Colo., 1 Sep. 1972, Green Collection. For more on superchargers, see Sanford A. Moss, *Superchargers for Aviation* (New York: National Aeronautics Council, Inc., 1944 ed.) and Dorothy L. Miller, "Case History of (Selected) Turbosuperchargers," Air Materiel Command Historical Office, Wright-Patterson AFB, Mar. 1951, ASC/HO. The latter is a compendium of key documents — or summaries of same — covering the period 1918 through 1950.

42. Chidlaw to Neal; Chidlaw interview with Green; "Notes on Conferences."

43. Memo, E. P. Rhodes, Chief of Engineering, Bell Aircraft Corp., to M. M. Henchan, P. A. Office, Bell, 7 Jan. 1944; Capt. D. T. Tuttle, Air Corps Technical Report No. 5234: Final Report of Development of XP-59A and YP-59A Model Airplanes, 28 June 1945, p. 3; Chidlaw to Neal; Maj. Gen. H. H. Arnold to Col. Alfred J. Lyon, Office of Special Army Observer, London, U.K., 2 Oct. 1941; David M. Carpenter, *Flame Powered: The Bell XP-59A Airacomet and the General Electric I-A Engine* (Boston: Jet Pioneers of America, 1992), pp. 13–14; Ronald D. Neal, "The Bell XP–59A Airacomet: The United States' First Jet Aircraft," *Journal of the American Aviation Historical Society* 11 (Fall 1966): 156–57; Maj. R. N. Wheat, Air Corps Cost-Plus-Fixed-Fee Contract, Contract No. W 535 ac-21931 (5748) with Bell Aircraft Corporation for Three Airplanes, Air Corps Model XP-59A, 30 Sep. 1941 (this document along with much of the other key documentation concerning development of the XP-59A may be found in "Case History of the XP-59A, YP-59A . . . [etc.]," ASC/HO); Maj. D. J. Keirn, War Department Contract No. W 535 ac-22885 (6111) with General Electric Company for 15 Air Corps Type I Superchargers & Data, 10 Sep. 1941. For XP-59A specifications, see memo, Maj. Gen. O. P. Echols, Materiel Div., to Lt. Gen. H. H. Arnold, 5 June 1942.

44. Craigie interview by author; memo, Col. R. P. Swofford to Commanding General, Materiel Command, 23 Mar. 1943; Maj. Gen. Donald J. Keirn, USAF (Ret.), interview with Murray Green, Delaplane, Va., 25 September 1970, Green Collection; D. J. Keirn, "Pilot-Engineer-Scientist," *Daedalus Flyer*, Mar. 1981, p. 19; Grover Heiman, *Jet Pioneers* (New York: Duel, Sloan and Pearce, 1963), pp. 52–64.

45. Carpenter, *Flame Powered*, pp. 19–21; Neal, "The Bell XP-59A," p. 160; Bell Aircraft Corporation, "America's First Jet-Propelled Fighter," ca. 1947, on file at National Air & Space Museum (hereafter NASM); memo, Brig. Gen. Oliver P. Echols, Materiel Division, to General Arnold, 13 Nov. 1941; Bell Aircraft Corporation Technical Data Report No. 27-943-011: Test of 1/16-Scale Bell XP-59A Interceptor Pursuit, 13 Feb. 1942, RD 813. For details concerning the design of the XP-59A, see Benson Hamlin, "Twin Aircraft Gas-Turbine Jet-Propelled Fighter," *Aircraft Gas Turbine Engineering Conference* (West Lynn, Mass.: General Electric Company, 1945), pp. 165–68. The papers in this volume were presented at the Swampscott Conference hosted by G.E., 31 May–2 June 1945.

46. Carpenter, *Flame Powered*, pp. 15–17; *Eight Decades of Progress*, p. 49; HQ AAF Routing and Record Sheet, Echols report to Arnold, 13 Dec. 1941; J. C. Miller, Aviation Division, G.E., to Lt. Col. D.J. Keirn, 16 Apr. 1942, RD 3021.

47. Neal, "The Bell XP-59A," p. 159.

48. Memo, Col. Ralph P. Swofford to Col. B. W. Chidlaw, 22 Jan. 1943; Whittle's complete reports may be found attached to a series of letters from Maj. J. N. D. Heenan, British Air Commission, to Col. D. J. Keirn, 26 June, 8 and 9 July 1942, RD 3777; memo, Col. B. W. Chidlaw, Chief, Experimental Engineering Section, Materiel Division, to Col. Beebe, 5 June 1942; memo, D. F. Warner, General Electric, to Colonel Keirn, et al., 22 June 1942; memo, Col. F. O. Carroll, Chief, Engineering Section, to Materiel Command Assistant Chief of Staff, 11 July 1942; memo, Col. D. J. Keirn to Commanding General, Materiel Command, 13 Aug. 1942; Maj. Rudolph C. Shulte, "Design Analysis of General Electric Type I-16 Jet Engine," *Aviation*, Jan. 1946, p. 44.

49. Swofford interview by McCants, pp. 44–45; memo, Col. A. E. Jones, Chief, Contract Section, Materiel Center, to Bell Aircraft Corporation, 12 May 1942; memo, R. P. Swofford for Col. F. O. Carroll, Chief, Experimental Engineering Section, to Administrative Executive, Wright Field, 27 June

1942, RD 2784; Capt. M. J. Dodd, "Origin of Desert Testing Station: Muroc Flight Test Base," 27 July 1945, on file AFFTC/HO; Robert M. Stanley, "My Thirty Years in Aviation" (unpublished manuscript), pp. 26–27; Donald J. Norton, *Larry: A Biography of Lawrence D. Bell* (Chicago: Nelson-Hall, 1981), p. 122; memorandum, Col. F. O. Carroll to Assistant Chief of Staff, Materiel Command, 11 July 1942; memorandum, Carroll to Assistant Chief of Staff, Materiel Command, 12 Aug. 1942; Craigie interview with author.

50. Carpenter, *Flame Powered*, pp. 28–30; Neal, "The Bell XP-59A," p. 162; Ted Rogers and Frank Burnham, "We Piloted the First Jet Airplane Coast-to-Coast," reprint of 1952 interview published by General Electric, ca. 1967; Jack Russell interview with author, 14 Feb. 1992 (Russell was one of the Bell employees involved in the project from the outset).

51. R. M. Stanley, Pilot's Report: XP-59A, 1 October 1942; Edgar P. Rhodes, "America's First Jet," *Rendezvous*, Sep.–Oct. 1962, p. 12; Neal, "The Bell XP-59A," p. 161; Carpenter, *Flame Powered*, pp. 30–31; Norton, *Larry*, pp. 122–23; "America's First Jet Propelled Fighter," p. 5; Russell interview with author.

52. R. M. Stanley, Pilot's Report: XP-59A, 2 Oct. 1942; E. P. Rhodes, Materiel Center Flight Test Base, to R. F. Hall, Buffalo, N.Y., 4 Oct. 1942.

53. T. J. Rogers, "The First American Jet," *Flying*, Mar. 1947, p. 74.

54. R. M. Stanley, Pilot's Report: XP-59A [2nd official flight], 2 Oct. 1942; L. C. Craigie, Pilot's Report: XP-59A, 2 Oct. 1942; Craigie interview with author. See also Lt. Gen. Laurence C. Craigie, USAF (Ret.), "P-59," *Proceedings of the XXIII Annual Symposium of the Society of Experimental Test Pilots*, 26–29 Sep. 1979, pp. 156–57.

55. Shulte, "Design Analysis of Type I-16 Jet Engine," pp. 47–48; Craigie interview with author; 1st Lt. G. J. McCaul, Materiel Center Test Base, to Col. D. J. Keirn, Power Plant Lab, 1 Aug. 1941, RD 2784; Donald Thomson interview with author, Edwards Air Force Base, Calif., 12 Feb. 1992 (Mr. Thomson worked as a Bell instrumentation technician on the XP-59A); Harry H. Clayton telecon interview with author, 14 Sep. 1992 (Mr. Clayton was the AAF's lead propulsion engineer throughout the XP-59A test program).

56. Rogers, "The First American Jet," p. 68; memo, Col. F. O. Carroll, Chief, Engineering Division, to Ass't Chief of Staff, AAF Materiel Command, 11 July 1942; memo, Carroll to Brig. Gen. B. W. Chidlaw, Chief, Materiel Division, AC/AS MM&D, 24 Apr. 1943; Capt. Wallace A. Lein, Materiel Center Flight Test Base, to Chief, Flight Test Branch, 29 Sep. 1943, RD 1061; Capt. Nathan R. Rosengarten, Materiel Center Flight Test Base, to Lt. Col. Osmond J. Ritland, Flight Test Branch, Wright Field, undated [ca. Oct. 1943], RD 1061. For details concerning all of the problems encountered with the airplanes and, especially, the engines, see AAF Materiel Center [and Command] Flight Test Base Power Plant Research Group Daily Log: XP-59A [and YP-59A], 26 Sep. 1942–13 Jan. 1944, AFFTC/HO; daily correspondence between Randolph P. Hall and Edgar P. Rhodes, 1 Mar.–29 Oct. 1943 (Hall and Rhodes took turns supervising Bell's test program at Muroc throughout this period), "Muroc Letters: Trip 1," NASM; and Bell Aircraft Corporation Special Projects Engineering Department Weekly Reports, 1 Jan.–20 Oct. 1944, "Muroc Letters," NASM. Although much of the delay in testing was caused by development problems encountered with the engines, Bell's conduct of the tests was severely criticized by AAF flight test personnel. In the letter to Lt. Col. Ozzie Ritland cited above, for example, Rosengarten complained: "The uncorrected data [from the AAF's initial "unofficial" performance tests] was turned over to Bell and, of course, when they worked up the data, they cried about us being about 25–35 miles lower in speed than what they expected. This, of course, is an old story with them and I didn't let it bother me because I knew they never ran tests on this particular airplane [I-16 powered YP-59A] and, like all their test work, it is strictly theoretical calculations." He was subsequently directed to prepare an evaluation of every contractor flight test organization. Lockheed was rated highest and Bell at the bottom of the scale. See memo, Rosengarten to Col. Ernest K. Warburton, Chief, Flight Section, 27 Mar. 1944. In a report to the Director of the Air Technical Service Com-

mand in Oct. 1944, Col. Mark Bradley, Chief of the Flying Section at Wright Field, complained that, over a nearly two-year period, Bell had yet to complete a full performance evaluation of the airplane and that the sparse results that were obtained were "erroneous and misleading." See memo, Bradley to Director, ATSC, 20 Oct. 1944.

57. USAAF AN 01-110FF-1: Pilot's Flight Operating Instructions for Army Models P-59A-1 and P-59B-1, 5 May 1945; Capt. Nathan R. Rosengarten, Engineering Division Memorandum Report Serial No. ENG-47-1739-A: Complete Performance Tests on YP-59A Airplane, AAF No. 42-108777, 15 Apr. 1944; Russell interview with author.

58. Memo, R. F. Hall, Bell Flight Test Unit, to E. P. Rhodes, Engineering, Bell Aircraft Corp., 29 Mar. 1943, NASM; Carroll to Chidlaw, 24 Apr. 1943; memo, Brig. Gen. Chidlaw, Chief, Materiel Division, AC/AS MM&D, to General Arnold, 29 Apr. 1943; B. Hamlin, Bell Aircraft Corporation Report No. 27-923-013: Performance Summary for X- and YP-59 Airplanes, 30 Nov. 1944, RD 813.

59. AAF Materiel Command Memorandum Report on YP-59A #5 Airplane, AAF No. 42-108772, 14 Dec. 1943, NASM; F. Crosby, Bell Aircraft Corporation Technical Data Report No. 27-923-008: Preliminary Speed Tests of the YP-59 Airplane with I-A Units, 12 Dec. 1943, RD 813; Capt. Wallace A. Lein, AAF Memorandum Report on YP-59A Airplane No. 42-108722: Pilot's Comments, 7 Jan. 1944, RD 813; Rosengarten, Complete Performance Tests on YP-59A Airplane.

60. Hall to Rhodes, 4 Sep. 1943, "Muroc Letters: Trips," NASM.

61. Memo, Col. H. Z. Bogert, Tech. Staff, Engineering Div., to Chief, Aircraft Laboratory, 10 July 1943; memo, Melvin Shorr to Col. R. P. Swofford, 28 Aug. 1943, RD 813; R. H. Wheelock, Bell Aircraft Corporation Technical Data Report No. 27-923-006: XP-59A Nacelle Entrance and Sealing Performance Investigation, 28 Aug. 1943, RD 813; memo, Melvin Shorr to Aircraft Laboratory, 21 Jan. 1944, RD 813; P. Largustrom, Bell Aircraft Corporation Technical Data Report No. 27-923-018: Investigation of Various Nacelle Modifications on the YP-59A Airplane, 9 Dec. 1944, RD 813; Lt. Col. O. G. Celline, Pilot's Report: YP-59A Gun Firing Tests, 16 Apr. 1944; memo, Lt. Col. Oliver G. Celline to Commanding General, III Fighter Command, 25 Apr. 1944.

62. "Twin Aircraft Gas-Turbine Jet-Propelled Fighter," p. 174. For difficulties encountered in the testing of first-generation American turbojet engines, see W. J. King, "Flight Testing of Aircraft Gas Turbines," *Aircraft Gas Turbine Engineering Conference*, pp. 241–54.

63. Rosengarten, Complete Performance Tests on YP-59A Airplane; Gen. H. H. Arnold to Maj. Gen. Howard C. Davidson, 20 Mar. 1944; AAF Proving Ground Command, Final Report on the Test of the Operational Suitability of the P-59A-1 Airplane, 17 Apr. 1944; Brig. Gen. E. L. Eubank, AAF Board Project No. (M-1) 46A: Tactical Suitability of the P-59A Airplane, 3 May 1944; memo, AC/AS OC&R to C/AS OC&R and AC/A R&S, 5 Oct. 1944; transcript of telecon, Ray Whiteman, Bell Aircraft Corp., to Brig. Gen. Orval R. Cook, 11 Oct. 1944.

64. 1st Lt. Bastian Hello, Air Corps Technical Report No. 5235: Final Report of Development, Procurement, Performance, and Acceptance [of] XP-80 Airplane, 28 June 1945, pp. 3–8, 13; C. L. Johnson et al., XP-80 Log Book, 18 June 1943–28 Jan. 1944, AFFTC/HO; Lockheed Aircraft Corporation Report No. 4592: Preliminary Flight Tests on Lockheed XP-80 Airplane, 1 Feb. 1944, AFFTC/HO; Lockheed Aircraft Corporation Report No. 4732: Performance Flight Tests of the Model XP-80— Tests 6 through 32, 5 May 1944, AFFTC/HO; A. M. "Tex" Johnston with Charles Barton, *Tex Johnston: Jet-Age Test Pilot* (Washington, D.C.: Smithsonian Institution Press, 1991), p. 69.

65. Memo, Col. H. Z. Bogert, Chief, Tech Staff, Engineering Div., to Brig. Gen. F. O. Carroll, Chief, Engineering Division, 21 Dec. 1942; Col. D. J. Keirn to R. C. Muir, G.E., 13 Mar. 1943; memo, Carroll to Commanding General, AAF, 26 July 1943; draft memo report, Col. D. J. Keirn, subj: Jet Propulsion Aircraft Engines, 13 Aug. 1943; Dale D. Streid, "Design Analysis of General Electric Type I-40 Jet Engine," reprint of article published in *Aviation*, Jan. 1946; Clarence L. Johnson, "Development of the Lockheed P-80A Jet Fighter Airplane," ca. late 1945 (unpublished manuscript); Jay Miller, *Lockheed's Skunk Works: The First Fifty Years* (Arlington, Tex.: Aerofax, Inc., 1993), pp. 22–27; E. T. Woolridge,

The P-80 Shooting Star: Evolution of a Jet Fighter (Washington, D.C.: Smithsonian Institution Press, 1979), pp. 26, 36–42, 45; Swofford interview with McCants, pp. 43–44.

66. Draft memo report: Jet Propulsion Aircraft Engines, p. 12.

67. "Research and the Army Air Forces," reprinted in *Aeronautical Engineering Review* 4 (Oct. 1945): 1, 3. For an eyewitness account of the excellence of the German R&D facilities, especially in comparison with those at Wright Field, see Col. "Toby" Tobiason, Instrument Lab, to Col. Theodore B. Holliday, Chief, Instrument Lab, 14 June 1945, attached to memo, Holliday to Brig. Gen. Laurence C. Craigie, Deputy Chief, Engineering Division, 20 July 1945, Lt. Gen. Laurence C. Craigie Papers, AFFTC/HO (hereafter Craigie Papers). Tobiason commented: "Everything is done on a big scale, nothing cheap. In other words, they have or *had* the best of facilities while we are still in the planning stage to a certain degree." He was also surprised by "the number of highly technical scientists employed by the G.A.F. [German Air Force]" in comparison with that of the AAF.

68. Theodore von Kármán, *Where We Stand* (USAAF, 1946), in Michael H. Gorn, ed., *Prophecy Fulfilled: "Toward New Horizons" and Its Legacy* (Washington, D.C.: Air Force History and Museum Program, 1994); von Kármán, "Science, the Key to Air Supremacy," in *Toward New Horizons* (USAAF: 1946); Robert Frank Futrell, *Ideas, Concepts, Doctrine: Basic Thinking in the United States Air Force, 1907–1960* (Maxwell Air Force Base, Ala.: Air University Press, 1971), pp. 275–76; Craigie interview with author; Swain, "Organization of Military Research," pp. 543–48; A. Hunter Dupree, *Science and the Federal Government: A History of Policies and Activities to 1940* (New York: Harper & Row, 1964), pp. 373–74. Craigie spoke and testified frequently on the urgent need for funding, adequately trained manpower, and state-of-the-art laboratory facilities comparable to those developed by the Germans. In particular, he pushed hard for funding ($500 million) for the development of the complex of wind tunnels and lab facilities that would be developed at Tullahoma, Tennessee (Arnold Engineering Development Center). For an example of General Craigie's dealings with Congress on these issues, see his testimony before the U.S. Senate Subcommittee of the Committee on Interstate Commerce, "To Establish a National Air Power Board," 6 June 1946, pp. 5, 7–27, Craigie Papers. For an example of a speech addressing the same issues, see "Future of Flight," delivered to the Engineer's Club, St. Louis, Mo., 8 May 1947, Craigie Papers. Old habits of mind persisted, and the battle for funding and influence within the new U.S. Air Force would be long and hard fought. In 1949, for example, Maj. Gen. Donald L. Putt, who was soon to become commander of the new Air Research and Development Command, complained: "There are those in high positions in the Air Force today who hold that research and development must be kept under rigid control by 'requirements' and 'military characteristics' promulgated by operational personnel who can only look into the past and ask for bigger and better weapons of World War II vintage. . . . They have not yet established that partnership between the strategist and the scientist which is mandatory to insure that superior strategy and technology which is essential to future success against our potential enemies." See Futrell, *Ideas, Concepts, Doctrine*, pp. 275–76.

69. *Gas Turbines and Jet Propulsion for Aircraft* (New York: Aircraft Books, 1946), p. 33. See also Neville and Silsbee, *Jet Propulsion Progress*, p. xi.

70. For the status of turbojet R&D and projections for the future, as of 1945, see Lt. Col. R. B. Clevering, Chief, Aero Equipment Section, Procurement Division, to Col. [D. J.] Keirn, Engineering Division, 25 September 1945, ASC/HO; von Kármán, *Where We Stand*, pp. 38–50; von Kármán, "Science, the Key to Air Supremacy," pp. 21–26; Frank L. Wattendorf, "Gas Turbine Propulsion," in *Toward New Horizons*, vol. 4; Maj. Langdon F. Ayers, "Present and Future Trends in the Power Plant Laboratory" (unpublished manuscript), 1 Jan. 1950, ASC/HO.

71. See, for example, memo, Brig. Gen. F. O. Carroll, Chief, Engineering Division, to Commanding General, AAF, 29 March 1944; memo, Carroll to Commanding General, AAF, 26 June 1944 (this memo was drafted by Kotcher).

72. Gunston, *World Encyclopaedia of Aero Engines*, pp. 124–25.

CHAPTER 12

Command Innovation

Lessons from the National Aerospace Plane Program

LARRY SCHWEIKART

onceived as an airplane that could fly into orbit, the National Aerospace Plane (NASP) program was started in 1986 as a project under the Defense Advanced Research Projects Agency (DARPA) and continued under the direction of the U.S. Air Force after 1988. Originally planned to "ramp up" to budgets of as much as $1 billion a year, the NASP program intended to investigate the technologies necessary for Single-Stage-to-Orbit (SSTO) flight and then, if feasible, design and build two X-30 research aircraft that would demonstrate that technology through orbital flight test missions.[1]

NASP represented a revolutionary aircraft and contractor arrangement. It required vast technology advances in at least five separate areas simultaneously: supersonic combustion jet propulsion (scramjets), active cooling with hydrogen-based fuel, computational fluid dynamics (CFD), materials, and avionics. In reality, the program demanded that technology advance in many other areas as well, including cockpit design, fuel storage and transfer, and airframe design, as well as in management structures to direct the program. Then, overlaying the other difficulties, the program sought to incorporate relatively new concepts of contractor cooperation, fused with novel government-contractor relationships. Enough hurdles existed in any one of these challenges to thwart a well-planned and well-funded program, but NASP intended to overcome all of them despite shifting mission concepts and uncertain budgets.

NASP: ORIGINS TO 1990

NASP emerged out of a recognition by the military and, to a lesser degree, the National Aeronautics and Space Administration (NASA) that the rocket-oriented technology of the 1960s and 1970s could not provide a cost-effective or reliable basis from which to conduct long-term space missions.[2] Inherently, the "user communities" tacitly admitted that rocket technology, such as the space shuttle represented, had failed to mature in such a way as to make possible either routine or short-notice capabilities. The image of the shuttle, waiting for days while weather improved, or while minor glitches were remedied, reflected the reality that rockets could not take the U.S. space program to the next level of space use, activity, or exploration.[3] Indeed, in some ways, the American space program had fallen behind that of the French, whose *Ariane* had proved superior to the space shuttle in its ability to deliver low-cost and frequent payloads into orbit.[4] From a military standpoint, there existed a need for an aircraft that could combine the operational capabilities of a spacecraft and an airplane.[5]

All of those functions demanded that any new system take off from, and return to, a traditional airplane runway. They also implied a piloted capability, as the military did not have confidence in robots to perform missions that might require rapid decision making and human evaluation. Proceeding from the assumption that the aircraft would have to operate somewhat like a traditional airplane, most experts involved in the discussions about follow-on programs to the shuttle looked to other propulsion systems, if not for a complete substitute for rockets, then as a supplemental launch system to them.[6] The most promising—if it could be made to work—was the scramjet, in which air, compressed in the inlet by supersonic speed, was combusted and expelled. Such a system required a low-speed system to build up to the higher Mach numbers; a revolutionary combustor that could perform the daunting task of igniting the fuel and air at up to 18,000 mph (likened to "lighting a match in a hurricane"); and a huge exhaust. Not only had no such system ever been built in any kind of aircraft scale, but no wind tunnel existed in the United States capable of testing such an engine above Mach 8. Much more than the aircraft itself was involved in the integrated concept, however. Any integrated program would require an entirely new generation of fuel storage and transfer facilities, flight test support structures, crew and ground support training, new ground test facilities, and, at every step of the way, environmental and safety protection studies. All of those "peripherals"—that ultimately constituted absolute necessities to demonstrating an SSTO flight—brought with them substantial costs and challenges of their own.

Fig. 12.1. Artist's conception of the National Aerospace Plane. Courtesy NASA

This led to the presumption that to test the engine, an entire integrated aircraft would be needed, in which the aircraft itself would constitute essential elements of the inlet and exhaust. The aircraft and engine would be developed simultaneously, with the aircraft providing a "flying wind tunnel." All technologies—engine, airframe, fuel system—could evolve simultaneously.[7]

The concept had a great deal of potential and tremendous appeal, but it depended on radical advances across a broad spectrum, requiring virtually all of them to mature at the same time. A scramjet-powered vehicle would have to fly a totally different trajectory than a rocket and thus would be subjected to phenomenal heat. One way to cool the vehicle was to use liquid hydrogen fuel pumped throughout the airframe and leading edges of the wings, but under any circumstances the vehicle would demand new, vastly improved materials. Nevertheless, when aerospace engineer Tony duPont, who had been working on NASA contracts for scramjet analysis, met with DARPA program manager Robert Williams in 1981 to discuss hypersonic engine work, duPont suggested that he could design an integrated scramjet-powered aircraft with existing materials of roughly 50,000 lb capable of generating speeds that could propel it into orbit without a rocket booster. Williams was intrigued, and duPont refined his concept for Williams and his superiors at DARPA.[8]

Williams, a genuine visionary capable of translating recent breakthroughs in mathematic formulations into sweeping explanations of the effects on travel or the environment, instantly was sold on duPont's approach.[9] It offered one of those rare instances of technological change that could effect a cultural upheaval, shifting transportation from fossil-fuel engines to cleaner hydrogen power.[10] Williams, therefore, looked past immediate problems or unanswered questions and maintained a faith that they would be solved with the application of focused effort and money. DuPont received further funding for engine cycle studies in 1982–83.

Still, the project might have died had not the U.S. Air Force simultaneously pursued its own investigations of hypersonic vehicles, called Trans-Atmospheric Vehicles (TAVs) at Aeronautical Systems Division (ASD), located at Wright-Patterson Air Force Base (WPAFB) in Dayton, Ohio. In 1979, Air Force General Lawrence Skantze, the commander of ASD, had ordered a study of post-shuttle vehicles that resulted in the TAV concept. Skantze, soon promoted to commander, Air Force Systems Command, in 1982 ordered the ASD planning staff to conduct further studies of advanced space vehicles. That year, the air force held a conference at WPAFB on hypersonics that demonstrated a "high level of interest," according to Col. Vince Rausch, the director of the XR section (Concepts and Innovation) at ASD.[11] In 1983, ASD awarded a contract to Batelle Columbus Laboratories in Columbus, Ohio, which involved a number of aerospace companies, including Lockheed, Boeing, Rockwell International (RI), and General Dynamics (GD).

Aware of each other's activities, DARPA and the air force held a joint TAV review at WPAFB in November 1983 when Williams briefed the participants on the first duPont studies. The participants recommended a further, more substantive study. DARPA funded such a study in 1984, led by Williams and duPont, with General Applied Science Laboratories (GASL) and other contractors evaluating duPont's claims. That phase of the program, which remained a "black" or secret program, was known by the code name Copper Canyon. DuPont produced a first-draft design of a hypersonic scramjet-powered aircraft, a 50,000 lbs vehicle that duPont's computer studies showed could attain orbital velocity of 18,500 mph, flying at a low trajectory in the atmosphere, then leaping upward for orbital insertion. Within a year, other investigators had validated duPont's claim using computer studies. But although General Electric (GE) and Marquardt were added to support the mid-range and high-speed work, only GASL ever "validated" duPont's claim that the aircraft could reach orbit.

During that early period in the history of NASP, the "validation" of the duPont studies proved critical. It loaned enough credence to duPont's claim that DARPA—which was in the business of experimenting with risky projects—

energetically embraced the integrated aircraft approach. However, even Williams appreciated the myriad of variables assumed as "givens" in duPont's concept. For example, the combustor only achieved its efficiencies at a certain size; any increase (or scaling-up, as inevitably would occur in a production aircraft) in that size would require supporting struts in the combustor, which in turn would disrupt the flow and decrease efficiencies. More obvious, duPont's design did not have landing gear; assumed new materials that had not been developed; and utilized a wing design that ran completely through the integrated, support-bearing fuel tank. Such problems directly affected scale-related development, and few expected that any research aircraft would come close to the 50,000 lb weight of the duPont design.

Williams, meanwhile, formulated a strategy for maintaining long-term funding of the research and development (R&D) program if it received a favorable Phase 1 recommendation. He understood that the nation had little patience for extended science programs and that no one service agency or civilian agency could sustain the large level of funding an integrated aircraft program would demand. He therefore won commitments from the U.S. Air Force, NASA, the U.S. Navy, and the Strategic Defense Initiative Office (SDIO) to contribute to a NASP budget directed through DARPA (with Williams as the program manager, and an on-site manager later named at Wright-Patterson Air Force Base). In late 1985, the Department of Defense (DOD) approved a five-way memorandum of agreement (MOA) that made NASP a joint program under DARPA management.[12] From Williams's perspective, the MOA ensured NASP of political support and funding, giving it time to solve the difficult technical challenges. He hoped that the relatively small commitment of each participant in the MOA would give the program an advantage, in that no one would have a great deal to gain by withdrawing.

In 1986, Phase 1 ended and the DOD gave its approval to continue into Phase 2, in which the technology would mature and the program would fabricate and test individual articles, while at the same time the contractors would continue with overall aircraft design work. DARPA gave contracts in the summer of 1986 to five airframe contractors (Boeing, Lockheed, McDonnell Douglas, General Dynamics, and Rockwell International) and two propulsion contractors (General Electric and Pratt & Whitney). Soon thereafter, Rocketdyne, a subsidiary of RI, offered to participate on its own funds, and the government admitted it to the program.

From 1986 to 1987, the contractors explored duPont's design and attempted to replicate his results, completely without success. Instead, independently, each of the five airframe contractors abandoned duPont's design—some absolutely, and some marginally.[13] By late 1987, none had an aircraft that weighed anywhere near 50,000 lbs.[14] More important, working with the propulsion contractors, they found that the scramjet efficiencies did not come close to producing the necessary thrust over drag to attain Mach 25.[15] In desperation, the airframe contractors examined ways to relocate the engines (on the sides, in Lockheed's case, or in a complete circle, in Boeing's case) or flatten the forebody (in the case of McDonnell Douglas) to increase lift. Propulsion contractors, meanwhile, explored moveable engine components. Virtually all of the contractors came to conclude that the aircraft would require a rocket for orbital insertion, and that led some (like McDonnell Douglas) to rely on the rocket to "make up the difference" at increasingly lower speeds.

During that period, the contractors operated on fixed-price contracts, meaning that they had to pour substantial amounts of their own funds into the research. They did so because they anticipated returns in two separate and distinct ways. First, the NASP Joint Program Office (JPO) planned to select the contractor with the best design in airframe and propulsion for Phase 3 of the program, which would award a contract to build two X-30 aircraft for flight tests. Second, whichever contractors received the airframe and propulsion contracts for the X-30s would have a tremendous advantage when it came time to compete for the NASP-Derived Vehicles (NDVs), or the follow-on operational aircraft. Thus, by 1989, the contractors had contributed more than $800 million to the NASP program. Much of that $800 million went to establishing a competitive base within the companies themselves—essentially "gearing up" to deal with hypersonics. But much of it also went toward a futile effort to make the duPont design work.[16]

Increasingly, program management saw that technical progress occurred more slowly than expected and consumed far more money than was planned. Funding uncertainty afflicted the budget, as the air force attempted to cut its contribution with the expectation that DOD would replace the money out of general funds. At the same time, pressures in the defense budget led SDIO and the navy to look for a way out of NASP. Indeed, the Pentagon in 1987 consolidated the DOD budgets into one NASP budget line, resulting in NASP funding coming from two sources in the budget process, DOD and NASA. Further upheaval occurred that year, when word of a deep cut in the final NASP budget by Congress prompted Williams to go outside the chain of command looking to avert the cut, and ultimately he wrote a letter that led to his removal as program manager. The reluctance of the other MOA members to fund the program, combined with the air force's desire to manage it, led the DOD to transfer management of NASP from DARPA to the air force in 1988 and to name Robert Barthelemy as the new program manager.[17]

The program also encountered—and overcame—early materials problems.

NASP management created a special program to develop critical materials and other technologies under a "Technology Maturation," or "Tech Mat," plan. In addition, the program convinced the contractors to order materials through a consortium they formed and managed. The Materials Consortium and Tech Mat proved important in pushing the development of materials that had been considered out of reach when the program first started.[18] According to then Hudson Institute researcher Bruce Abell, "in three years we've gone from materials that have potential to materials that have application. A number of materials have yielded elegantly."[19]

Cooperation in the area of materials suggested that a team approach might be applicable throughout the program. But Williams deliberately had included several different contractors in the competition for two reasons. First, he thought that the technical challenges were so great that no single company could solve them. Second, he wanted to prepare several companies for the future competition in NDVs and not leave the nation relying on a single source.[20]

Even with the progress in materials, however, NASP had too many contractors competing for the funds, which only totaled $172 million in 1987 and $249 million in 1988.[21] Consequently, in 1987 the program eliminated two airframe companies, Boeing and Lockheed, and one engine company, GE, from further competition. Williams, who made the final call on the selection, reasoned that Lockheed's design was far too heavy and that Boeing, which had abandoned its first design in favor of a radical conical shape, had lost too much ground. GE had produced the lowest power estimates of the three propulsion companies and had a design similar to Pratt & Whitney's.[22]

By 1989, the program seemed to have regained its funding momentum, with a budget of $320 million ($231 million from DOD and $89 million from NASA), and although Congress insisted on a more equitable division of burden between NASA and DOD, the program expected funding stability as it anticipated an eventual level of $1 billion per year when it came time to build the X-30 vehicles. That trend came to an abrupt halt in 1989, when the new Bush Administration came into office. The new secretary of defense, Richard Cheney, on the advice of Pentagon analyst David Chu, completely eliminated all DOD funding for NASP, essentially terminating the program.[23]

Program management went into a crisis mode and, at Barthelemy's direction, abandoned the political strategy that Williams (for two years) and Barthelemy (for six months) had followed — namely, to emphasize mission utility. In particular, the program had sought out military users, which had proved difficult as the X-30 already was overweight and mission utility required additional fuel and the addition of a bay door. But by mid-1989, no air force command had made NASP a priority. When Cheney analyzed the top priorities of each command and did not see NASP there, he ended all DOD funding. Barthelemy re-focused the program on research-oriented benefits, such as improvement in the U.S. balance of trade resulting from a more competitive aerospace sector; spin-offs of NASP technologies to other technical areas; economic growth related to low-cost access to space (and its attendant rise in employment); and other such "soft" benefits. Utilizing the contractors and NAR (the planning directorate in the JPO), Barthelemy initiated a wave of briefings to key legislators, Depart-ments of Commerce and Transportation officials, and the White House science adviser.[24]

The strategy paid off in a temporary placeholder in the budget of $100 mil-lion, pending a decision on NASP by the newly formed National Space Coun-cil. Chaired by Vice President Dan Quayle, the National Space Council was charged with planning a space strategy and determining the status of several programs teetering on the precipice. NASP advocates managed to present the program's goals and progress to Quayle's advisers, and in the summer of 1989 the Space Council restored NASP funding. However, the council extended the pro-gram's Phase 2 by two and one-half years and, while giving it more money over-all, decreased annual budgets.

Noticeable for its absence in the budget struggles—indeed, in almost any of the important decisions—was an oversight body called the Steering Group that had been established in 1986. It included representatives from DOD, NASA, the air force, and other relevant agencies and services. As conceived, the Steer-ing Group was to provide guidance, strategic direction for the success of the pro-gram, and critical assessments to keep NASP on track. But the rapid turnover in the Steering Group, its infrequent meetings, and its disappearance at crucial budget debates resulted in Williams, and later Barthelemy, exercising consider-able authority. Over time, the program managers found that they had to take initiative and then elicit support from the supervisory body. In cases in which the program had to develop innovative options to reflect technical realities, it had to prepare detailed plans that shifted resources across the board, and then work to gain approval.

APEX TO ELIMINATION: 1990–95

The 1989 budget crisis convinced program management that it needed to change more than the political strategy if NASP were to survive. With smaller annual budgets, the program no longer could support five contractors and six design combinations. Increasingly, Barthelemy and other members of NASP top management started to examine ways to push the contractors into a team in which they could exchange and share their data, arriving at a composite design.

Each company had pursued different aspects of the baseline design—each representing a substantial departure from duPont's original design—but none had come close to "closing" (i.e., developing a design that could attain orbit). By that time, Barthelemy showed less concern about NASP-Derived Vehicle contracts for aircraft in the distant future than he did about finding a way to solve NASP's technical problems.

No problems proved more difficult than the scramjet. Despite several approaches to the engine—even when combined with different body designs to improve the airflow and exhaust—the companies were stuck in the Mach 8-10 range. The integrated approach to the design continued to channel money into avionics, flight tests, fuel development, and other areas when the single most important technology, the scramjet, had yet to be demonstrated. Under more traditional approaches, the program would have attacked the most difficult technical problem first and then solved other challenges. But that was not possible with NASP because it had received its original support on the basis that it represented an integrated aircraft system. Barthelemy found that making even a marginal retreat from the single-stage-to-orbit goal, or from developing the airframe and engine in tandem, was not acceptable to his superiors.[25]

Wedded, therefore, to the integrated system, Barthelemy attempted to find a cheaper way to arrive at the optimal design without carrying five competing companies through the entire ($2\frac{1}{2}$ year) Phase 2 period. As early as June 1988 Barthelemy had received support for team formation from the chairman of the Steering Group, Robert B. Costello (also the Undersecretary of Defense for Acquisition). A series of strategy meetings in 1989–90 within the Joint Program Office convinced Barthelemy that only through the formation of a team could the program extract the best ideas of all the contractors and combine their skills in such a way as to overcome the technology challenges.[26] Since the contractors had proceeded on the basis that they were competing, however, a "pecking order" had developed in the minds of the JPO directors and, indeed, the contractors themselves. A company that perceived itself as being "in the lead" would avoid any sort of cooperative arrangement, while a company perceiving itself as trailing in the competition would welcome such relief.

Competitive strategy had led to companies emphasizing different aspects of the technology, and as a result, no company was ahead of the others across the board. McDonnell Douglas, thought by most NASP insiders to lead among the airframe companies, had a strong low-speed approach based on a lifting body design, but it trailed other airframe builders in its high-Mach-speed technical progress. GD had developed the only tested integral, structure-bearing fuel tank. Rockwell had important advantages in high-speed work. The two propulsion contractors had struggled to a rough parity, but in different areas: Pratt &

Whitney had done more advanced work in low-speed scramjets, while Rocketdyne had worked on the high-speed system.

Rockwell and GD had moved toward a two-way team in 1989. After several
meetings with the Joint Program Office, Rockwell and GD agreed to a memorandum of agreement, but, much to the JPO's consternation, McDonnell Douglas was absent.[27] Nothing official could happen until the program had the approval of the Acquisition Strategy Panel (ASP) and other superiors. In August
the ASP recommended against forming a team with the airframe contractors
but suggested teaming the propulsion companies. After further internal meetings, the Joint Program Office proposed a plan to issue a Request for Proposal
(RFP) that could be satisfied only by a team proposal. Two months later, the
Steering Group gave its endorsement to the concept of team formation proposed by the JPO. Shortly thereafter, the Joint Program Office generated its RFP
and the contractors all responded favorably. The only issue left to resolve was
the selection of the team leader, both in the corporate and the individual sense.

Barthelemy had planned for months to facilitate team formation rapidly,
and to that end he and the JPO directors had examined the options regarding
the leader of the team. Typically, in large aircraft programs the company leading the team is an airframe manufacturer, but in the case of NASP the Joint Program Office did not necessarily agree that tradition should hold. For one thing,
the most important technical element in the system was the engine. For another, the engine development lagged further behind than other technical areas. Barthelemy had admired the management style of Rocketdyne's Barry
Waldman and saw in his approach (dubbed by many "Japanese-style management" by consensus) the best opportunity to align all the contractors behind
a single design. After a series of meetings in January 1991, the chief executive
officers of the five contractors agreed that Waldman should lead the team. To
give Waldman added clout, he was transferred from Rocketdyne, a corporate
subsidiary, to the parent company, Rockwell International, and given his own
separate unit so as not to be viewed as an internal favorite.[28]

Waldman focused the top directors of each company on a single strategy; established a schedule for arriving at a composite configuration; and investigated
ways to divide work equitably. The latter proved one of his toughest tasks. Often, one company tended to dominate in a particular technical area, as with GD
and its integrated fuel tank. Waldman had to decide whether it was better to try
to bring all the companies to the same level in all areas, or foster specialization.
He compromised by encouraging specialization but placing members of different companies on every team, ensuring widespread distribution of ideas.

Actual team formation did not occur immediately, however. The secretary
of the air force, Jack Welch, had not given final approval, claiming that the air

force had needed time to examine antitrust issues. Such hardly seems the case: the air force and other agencies had anticipated team formation for at least a year and had already given their blessings at countless other reviews or meetings. Indeed, Barthelemy and other insiders had received repeated signals from the DOD hierarchy that Welch's approval was a mere formality. As matters turned out, the program did not receive Welch's blessing until late May, delaying the program—already extended in mid-1989 by two and one-half years— by another four months.[29]

Once Waldman had formal approval, however, the team moved into action fairly rapidly. In June 1990 it held data exchange, in which each company exposed its most closely held corporate secrets involving NASP. Throughout the meeting, and subsequent meetings that summer, Waldman furiously worked to prevent any dissension. At the same time, the JPO directors had to avoid any "I told you so" attitudes when discussing design flops they had spotted months or years earlier. Bill Imfeld of the JPO Engineering Directorate headed the briefings that relayed the government's data and observations. When he had finished, Waldman noted that the contractors were "pleased the government had been listening" and that the government's work during the early phases of team formation had contributed to "a great deal of leveling among the contractors."[30]

The contractor engineers, rather than take an individual company's design and refine it, sought to develop a true composite. Therefore, instead of starting with a particular design in mind, Waldman charged the teams with starting anew with trade studies. To the surprise of few in the Joint Program Office, the team found that the McDonnell airframe was the optimal vehicle design, that it needed the GD integral tank, and that it needed RI's refinements for high-end speed. Likewise, Pratt and Whitney's general philosophy of compression direction worked well with Rocketdyne's modular engine design: in October 1990, the team finalized its design, which appeared on the cover of *Aviation Week*.[31]

Managing a program that involved representatives from DOD, the air force, the navy, and NASA, as well as five major contractors and dozens of test facilities and research centers, would have been daunting under normal procurement procedures. But the mix of contractors only constituted part of the team: the government itself had to perform certain elements of work and therefore was in the unique position of being both "management" and "labor." Waldman attempted to solve this difficult management problem both strategically and structurally. Strategically, he endeavored to integrate the company members into every aspect of the operations—evenly and equitably whenever possible. He did that by placing personnel from a different contractor as the head or division chief of every important group and by mixing the teams' personnel with each other and with the government members as much as possible. Structurally, the government was integrated through a management system Waldman called "work buckets," in which tasks were arranged by relationship to each other and then placed under the direction of a contractor or government member. Although the government retained vertical control over supervision of the performance of each task, the actual management of the task devolved to the contractor or government manager.[32]

Waldman further attempted to build team unity by removing all of the participants to a neutral site. Although the contractor team office, called the National Program Office (NPO), was located first at Rockwell's Seal Beach, California, facility, eventually the NPO moved to Palmdale, California, near Edwards Air Force Base, where the NASP actually was to be fabricated and tested. But that attempt at team building did not prove as effective as hoped, largely because the contractors kept many of their personnel at their home sites.

Increasingly, though, as the contractors worked to refine the composite configuration in early 1991, they came face to face with several grim realities. First, after the early composite designs had been fleshed out, aircraft weight had grown substantially. Where once duPont had touted a 50,000 lb airplane, the contractors struggled with aircraft weights of 500,000 lb *minimum*. Operational additions, such as the payload bay doors and other features SAC had requested, drove weights to between 750,000 and 1 million pounds. Barthelemy and Waldman correctly argued that the early weights only reflected the redundancies that any unrefined design would contain. But no one had any confidence that those redundancies amounted to more than 100,000 lb, leading Waldman to call the first cut at a design "a dog" and Barthelemy to quip, "no, it's a pig."[33] The JPO and NPO finally set a design goal of a 350,000 lb vehicle — still viewed as monstrously heavy for an R&D aircraft. Waldman noted that the National Program Office had to make a "marketing judgment" about a tolerable weight, and the program, if successful in meeting that weight, could put weight back in later.

A second reality that NASP encountered in 1991 was that time was running out. NASP celebrated its fifth birthday that year — and had not yet flown a single test article. Dating back to the real origins of NASP with Copper Canyon in 1984, NASP had existed for seven years and had — in the eyes of the public — produced only fancy artwork and some computer studies. GD's work on the fuel tank, which underwent testing in 1992, represented a high point in the program's work. Many NASP participants proudly pointed to that test article in retrospect as the program's crowning achievement. Yet few in the general public or in Congress ever heard about it; and even if they had, it seemed virtually irrelevant compared with flying vehicles such as the X-15 or the space shuttle. In short, the program had made a crucial strategic error. It had failed to schedule any highly visible flight tests in such a way as to keep the program in the forefront of scientific activity. That weakness had evolved out of the commitment to the integrated program, which in essence resigned the program to flying nothing until it could fly a full-scale X-30.

Many within NASP recognized the severe disadvantage under which this placed the program. Col. Ted Wierzbanowski had worked since the late 1990s at trying to convince others in the program to adopt an incremental approach in which the first aircraft would have a far lower level of technology than the second. The first would not have SSTO capability and in fact would focus on Mach 10 flight. Nevertheless, the SSTO goal remained firmly in place, confining any planning the program made. Incrementalism made an SSTO flight before the year 2000 virtually impossible without a vastly enlarged budget.

Funding represented the third stark reality that faced the program in late 1991, moving in an inverse direction from the schedule increases. Overall funding for FY 1992 fell from a projected original level of nearly $1 billion to the 1989 compromise budget path of $303 million to actual funding of $205 million. NASA had proven unreliable in submitting strong NASP budgets. Between 1988 and 1992, the only year the actual NASA funding equaled its request was in 1990 after the Space Council stretch-out. The trend, however, was ominous: in FY 1992, NASA requested only $72 million for NASP (when Congress had insisted that the NASA contribution equal that of the air force) and received only $5 million. Thus, NASP had started on a funding descent, overall and especially in the NASA component.

The fourth, and most serious, difficulty facing NASP came in the scramjet technology, which had not matured as hoped. While some technical progress had been spectacular (materials, fuel, CFD), the area that counted most showed steady but slow improvement. The lack of progress in scramjet performance sharply interacted with the other realities. It affected weight negatively because the lower the scramjet performance, the lighter the aircraft had to be. With early NASP designs weighing 500,000 lbs, the aircraft would demand an exceptionally efficient scramjet. Slow progress in the scramjet affected funding and schedule by requiring more money to be diverted to the scramjet and by requiring more time to improve the technology. An inverse relationship between money and time existed: the longer the program took, the costlier it became. On the other hand, each time the program pushed the single-stage-to-orbit flight further into the future, it lost political support and public interest.

By 1992 NASP found itself in a box. It could not redirect funding and technical energy toward perfecting the scramjet at the expense of other technologies because that would appear to abandon the SSTO goal. It could not continue on its downward glide path because the money and interest would disappear before the engineers solved the scramjet. It could not push scramjet development any further by improving the airframe because the heavy airframe already had emerged as a disadvantage—another problem that had to be solved. And it could not change the schedule by pushing flight dates further into the future out of concern that it would destroy what little political support that remained. In many ways, NASP resembled a giant army moving across a desert at a slow pace, unable to discard heavy equipment to speed up and using water at a deadly rate because of the effort involved in carrying the equipment.

Prudence dictated that the program restructure dramatically around the single technical challenge of the scramjet and temporarily abandon all other technical activities. As of 1992, it still had the opportunity to refocus on a series of subscale scramjet tests. Suggestions to that nature surfaced within the Joint Program Office, which first looked for a "bridge" subscale vehicle that would stop short of Mach 15 but would provide crucial scramjet data for the engineers. Such a vehicle, called an "X-30X," was conceived as a one-third scale, 50,000 lb Mach 10-15 aircraft that would cost $3-5 billion (the original cost of the entire "real" X-30 two-aircraft program). That projection concealed internal program estimates of a NASP two-vehicle X-30 program that would carry a price tag of $12–15 billion. Even then, realists admitted that the two-vehicle X-30 program would exceed $20 billion.[34] The X-30X required a carrier aircraft, such as a B-52 or Boeing 747, which would transport the vehicle to various altitudes then drop it, allowing the vehicle to turn on its engines and gain about two minutes worth of data.

Perhaps not surprisingly, the NASP Washington office killed the X-30X, contending that it would represent abandonment of the single-stage-to-orbit goal. The NASP Information Office (NIO), the Washington NASP office that was to serve as the "information" arm of the program, had steadily assumed greater authority and power over the program in the absence of a viable Steering Group presence. It claimed to represent DOD and air force views and "spoke" for the air force when it came to the program. Thus, by late 1992, rather than Barthelemy making policy and "informing" the air force for its approval, NIO gained a sense of what the air force wanted and instructed the JPO and NPO as to what policies to present.

Matters were made worse by a leak from the program to a Los Angeles newspaper that NASP no longer had a goal of SSTO. The Steering Group had scheduled a meeting on 12 December 1992 when word of these comments circulated, reaching the ears of Vice President Quayle. On 11 December 1992, Secretary of the Air Force Donald Rice asserted that "the Air Force will not walk away from the goal of reaching orbit with the National Aero-space Plane," contrary to published reports.[35] NASA's Ming Tang, who headed the NASP Information

Office, firmly instructed the Joint Program Office that it had to delete any mention of the X-30X from its briefings.

NASP had made another attempt to develop a bridge between the SSTO X-30 and the technology as it stood in 1992 through a project called HYFLITE. HYFLITE (for Hypersonic Flight Test Experiments) was comprised of two, and possibly three, subscale scramjet tests to be conducted by launching scramjet test articles from Minuteman II missiles. HYFLITE I would focus on boundary layer transition/shock boundary layer interaction to verify linear stability and high-speed inlet operability. HYFLITE II would conduct scramjet integrated flowpath tests. Col. Wierzbanowski, of the JPO's Detachment 5 at the National Program Office, headed the effort. Wierzbanowski's group presented the concept to the Quarterly Technical Review in November 1992, where it received approval from the air force and NASA officials.

While sensible and appropriate in most respects—indeed, long overdue as a technical approach—the HYFLITE program had the perverse effect of further expanding a program that advocates had hoped would shrink to a "skunk works" size. Instead, the new effort involved yet another agency, the Ballistic Missile Program Office, as well as additional contractors. Increasing size had characterized NASP as it had expanded between 1989 to 1992 to enter the Phase 3 fabrication process. Yet during those years, the expansion process had cost the program much of its revolutionary zeal, replacing high-ranking research-oriented visionaries and risk takers with conservative, production-oriented lower-grade officers. Moreover, the program continually expanded in government and contractor personnel, becoming more unwieldy with each additional person. Williams, Barthelemy, and Wierzbanowski had hoped at one time that NASP could escape much of the procurement bureaucracy that slowed so many other programs. By late 1992, it was clear that that had not happened.

Planning and preparations for HYFLITE I and II continued, based on early estimates of $200 million total (with $25 million for HYFLITE I). Many inside the program realized that even those estimates were low—especially if any delays at all occurred—and that they still did not address the crucial shortcoming that NASP faced in bridging the article tests and the SSTO orbital flight. In particular, engineers desperately wanted some way to obtain actual flight data in the Mach 10-15 range, even if it came from a subscale vehicle.[36] To that end, Ming Tang's office developed a HYFLITE III concept utilizing an accelerator scramjet tested in two or three launches from a Minuteman. The accelerator would not be reusable, and, according to most engineers, would provide only a few extra data points. Worse, it would carry a price tag of $1.5 billion. Even when completed, the program still probably would require a scaled X-30.

Some proponents of the subscale X-30X and the HYFLITE III hoped that they could build enough of a database in the tests that it might be possible to eliminate the orbital test altogether and leap directly to a prototype "S-30" NASP-Derived Vehicle. But most observers thought that fanciful and expressed concern that the program was squandering what few resources it had on a few, expensive tests. Meanwhile, HYFLITE I and II tests were scheduled to begin in 1995.

The long delay in producing anything capable of flying that would attract public attention had opened the door for competitor systems. In January 1993, McDonnell Douglas prepared to flight test a rocket single-stage-to-orbit system called the Delta Clipper or DC-X that used a vertical takeoff with a moon-type "soft" landing.[37] Members of Congress, meanwhile, had held discussions with Tony duPont and others left out of the NASP program for the purpose of reviving the "five-year-to-flight, 50,000-lb., $5 billion aircraft" duPont had promised almost a decade earlier. Hearings held in 1993 did not result in a new program as duPont hoped, but they did embarrass NASP by the testimony, mostly from critics bitter about being eliminated from the NASP program or ignored entirely.

Budget problems continued, mostly from NASA allocations. In FY 1993, the DOD request had been $183 million—an amount Congress two years earlier had anticipated NASA would match. Instead, NASA only requested $80 million. Congressional cuts reduced the actual DOD funding of NASP to $150 million, which still would have provided a solid base on which to continue work if NASA had received its full funding for NASP. Instead, NASA received no money for NASP. Insiders expressed dismay at the routine low funding from NASA, and most concluded that it reflected the pressures from the huge amounts then eaten up by the space station project (totaling more than $8 billion). More than a few suspected that NASA leadership simply had made little real effort to fund NASP over the years, and under NASA Administrator Dan Goldin the effort grew even weaker. Even DOD's trough had started to run dry: the Gulf War in 1990–91 had forced the Pentagon to levy internal "taxes" on all units to pay for the conflict. Although NASP was spared in the first round of those cuts, the program nevertheless felt the upheaval associated with still lower anticipated funding levels.

The unrelenting budget decline had led Barthelemy, already planning a reassignment to the Training System Program Office at Wright-Patterson Air Force Base, to explore virtually any funding avenue that he could find. One source—team arrangements with foreign governments—had gained momentum as France, Germany, Great Britain, and Japan all had seen their hypersonic programs slashed even further than NASP. The keynote address at the hypersonic community's annual meeting, the Fourth Annual Advanced International Aerospace Planes Conference, proposed international cooperation to build a scramjet-powered orbital aircraft, and papers were presented supporting such an idea.[38] Ultimately such a notion was unacceptable to the program and certainly to Washington. NASP advocates, especially Barthelemy after 1989, had sold the program by touting its contributions to America's competitiveness, employment, and research base. Certainly no one planned to give away the advantages that had rescued NASP in 1989 and sustained the program for years.[39]

Barthelemy left NASP for his new position in February 1993. Although it was part of a normal military rotation, to outsiders it looked like the captain deserting the ship. In fact, Barthelemy (and Wierzbanowski as well) had stayed with the program much longer than was normal in hopes of finally making NASP a reality. Even so, the final demise of the program lurked in the near future.[40]

A briefing of updated costs for the HYFLITE I and II projects — Barthelemy's last briefing for the program — went to ASD in February 1993, and the numbers had grown substantially. Program officials put the cost of HYFLITE I and II only at $600 million, an amount triple that first projected. HYFLITE I and II and an X-30X vehicle (which suddenly the program was permitted to discuss) would cost between $3 billion and $5 billion. An option with HYFLITE I and II and a full-size X-30 had a price tag of $15 billion at minimum. Even that option was designated as a high-risk option. To lower the risk for a full-size X-30 involved at least an additional $3 billion. That summer, the program received an FY 1994 budget of $95 million to support the technical activity of five major contractors.

As the program struggled along with weak funding, management held out hope that it could present a clear strategy, using HYFLITE tests and a "bridge," such as HYFLITE III, to reduce the risk to a full-scale vehicle. HYFLITE III still proved the stickler: no one could say with confidence how much it would cost or, more important, what data it could guarantee. In May and June 1993, JPO and NIO working groups arrived at a HYFLITE III cost estimate of $1.4 billion. Program management members, especially in Washington, were in a panic. If such a number escaped, and the earlier HYFLITE III costs of $3–5 billion reached the public, no one would take the program's numbers seriously again. In historical perspective, though, the $1.5 billion figure looked even worse. Accounting for inflation, the HYFLITE III cost of three test aircraft articles that would not reach orbital velocity and could not be reused had grown to the same dollar amount as the original 1986 two-vehicle NASP program. For several years, program management had labored to keep the annual budget request under $1 billion, including those years in which the program had planned on actually fabricating aircraft. By 1993, virtually every option that flew a self-powered vehicle, either the X-30X or HYFLITE III, bumped the price tag above the magic number. NIO made clear that the program had to complete HYFLITE in a six- to seven-year window at a total cost of no more than $2 billion.

NIO's role in creating HYFLITE III virtually marked the final transition of power from the Joint Program Office to Washington. Over the preceding two years, more than a dozen "old-timers" had left the program, taking with them years of experience and rank. Colonels were replaced by majors, and majors by captains. The effect was deeper, however, in that the new personnel came from procurement programs, not R&D programs. Waldman, seeing its effect on management from the JPO to the contractor, called the changes "profound."

Indeed, the NASP Information Office refused to plan a strategy until it had consensus at the top; yet the program could not allocate resources, plan tests, or move forward in any way without a strategy. Worse, the lack of strategy left Congress looking for ways to cut the program further. According to Waldman, there "was a concern that such expenditures without proper direction from above would be wasted money."

Concluding that HYFLITE, in almost any manifestation, would be too expensive, the Joint Program Office looked for an even smaller, less costly alternative that in some way would continue the hypersonic research. In late 1993 and early 1994, program management desperately sought to fly a scramjet on a booster. The replacement program was called HySTP (for Hypersonic Scramjet Test Project), funded at $300 million and concentrating on testing a 25 percent scale scramjet in the Mach 12 to 15 range using a Peacekeeper or Minuteman missile. The scramjet test would release a scramjet test article at Mach 12, which would be turned on, but which would not generate enough thrust to overcome its drag. Rather, it would only show that it could take in air, mix it with fuel, combust it, and expel it. Congress allowed $45 million to start the new HySTP program, a sum that represented full funding. But it released only $10 million, pending testimony of the secretary of the air force that the air force would commit to full funding through FY 2000.

NASP—which originally had been slated for budgets exceeding $1 billion—by that time had shrunk to a tiny research program whose sole hope for survival was that it could fly a one-quarter scale scramjet test article that would not even generate thrust over drag. That simple fact testified to the end of NASP. In reality, the final "de-funding" of NASP came when the secretary of defense levied an internal tax on all programs to pay for operations in Haiti and Somalia. DOD could not find other funds to pay for the proposed HySTP part of the tax, and on 3 January 1995, the air force terminated the contract for HySTP and allowed NASP until May 1994 to close most programs. The NPO closed in January 1995, at which time Waldman left for other Rockwell assignments. Early in 1995, former JPO and contractor personnel held a wake for NASP, with Barthelemy returning to deliver the eulogy.

What did NASP accomplish? It saw improvement in technology in materials, computational fluid dynamics predictions, hydrogen fuel manufacturing and operations, and an overall understanding of the integrated airframe/propulsion design. Tremendous advances had taken place in the ground-test infrastructure essential to the development of hypersonic vehicles. The government learned a great deal about forming contractor teams and about government/contractor joint programs. But had the program gotten close to flying an X-30? No. It did not do so for a number of reasons. Among the "lessons learned" from NASP:

The commitment to an integrated aircraft system approach resulted in political weakness. By attempting to develop dozens of technologies—many of them radical or revolutionary—simultaneously, the program accepted the strategy of deferring near-term demonstrations of flying hardware in favor of a distant goal of the orbital flight by a full-scale integrated aircraft. NASP had no high-profile tests, flights, or demonstrations (some called these "stunts") that maintained interest and support. With the exception of the integrated fuel tank, the NASP program never produced the kind of hardware that supported an actual flight—hardware that could provide evidence of progress upon which lawmakers could base their votes for funding.

The Steering Group, which was intended as both an advocacy body and a source of direction for the program, proved to be neither. The Steering Group never seemed to determine its proper role, and certainly never had enough continuity to have any influence over the program. By 1991 the Steering Group was a nonplayer. NASP needed just the opposite—a person or agency that would serve as a "champion" and shepherd the program through budget battles and maintain user support. Vice President Dan Quayle proved the strongest of all NASP's political allies, but the 1992 election ended any role he could have played in the program.

Without a source of direction, NASP program managers had to walk a fine line between meeting the SSTO mission statement and operating in the reality of the technology and budget. Barthelemy found that the budget and technology at the time would not support the integrated aircraft or the single-stage-to-orbit mission without major incremental steps. Yet he was not permitted to pursue those incremental steps by the NASP Washington office out of concern that it might appear that the program was "abandoning" SSTO.

The attempt to insulate NASP from the budget cycle through an interservice/ interagency team failed to provide the program with either a stable constituency or a budget. Indeed, it may even have weakened support for NASP by diluting "ownership" of the program among many participants. Robert Williams thought he had established an ironclad agreement between NASA, the air force, the navy, SDIO, and DARPA that would "lock" each organization into financial and institutional support of NASP. It had just the opposite effect: with so many participants, each had an incentive to become a "free rider" on the budgets and efforts of the other. NASA, in particular, which was expected by Congress to become a full equal partner to the air force, consistently backed off of its commitments. In retrospect, Col. Wierzbanowski suggested that future programs like NASP needed an independent budget line, making their existence and growth directly the responsibility of Congress.

Decisions that shape program strategy, such as that to proceed with an integrated aircraft design that entails a wide array of facilities, efforts, environmental studies, and so on, should be undertaken only when a substantial number of independent or clearly validated studies support the strategy. In the case of NASP, the decision to proceed with a full aircraft development program before validating the scramjet technology cost the program dearly. It appears that if the program had started with scramjet tests, such as those embodied in the HySTP project, it might have arrived at the point where further work required the fabrication of a research aircraft. But by starting with the assumption that the program had to fly to orbit, under a certain budget, and within a certain schedule, to claim success, NASP was doomed. Once the numerous peripheral projects, test facilities, studies, and support services started to absorb resources, they diluted money from the scramjet effort.

Moreover, the weaknesses of the duPont study should have been more apparent. Every one of the airframe and propulsion contractors, including those eliminated in the 1987 downselection, abandoned the duPont design within a year after the program let contracts. Perhaps duPont should have been given a budget and free reign to test his design. But no other contractor except GASL ever reproduced the key duPont data.

Other lessons arose from the NASP experience, but in the "bigger picture," the United States needs to reconsider how it undertakes highly risky and innovative science and technological problems. One approach, but one routinely rejected by the modern U.S. government, is to establish a prize. In the nineteenth and early twentieth centuries, prizes were offered routinely as ways to encourage development of technology or to attain great achievements. The government must ask itself, "If in 1980 the United States had established the goal of attaining SSTO in a piloted aircraft by 1995, and offered a prize of [say] $1 billion to the first individual or company to accomplish that feat, would that feat have occurred by 1995?" History suggests that it would have been accomplished even sooner. The government argues that such a prize would be a stunt and would not result in real technical progress. That is unlikely.[41]

Another approach—long admired by some within the military—is the "skunk works" strategy, in which a small group of engineers and managers seclude themselves and, freed from standard government reporting procedures or policies, develop unique systems such as the XR-71. But such an approach demands that the government relinquish its control, a feat seldom accomplished in modern bureaucracies. Moreover, the government must be willing to accept the fact that "no is an answer, too." Indeed, the research from the NASP program may have shown quite clearly that in the case of a scramjet-powered aircraft to orbit, "no" was a perfectly acceptable answer—for now.

NOTES

1. Material for this paper comes from the author's forthcoming book, *The National Aerospace Plane and the Quest for an Orbital Jet* (Washington, D.C.: Office of Air Force History), as well as from a number of articles, including "From Team to Team: Revolutionary Management Structures in the National Aero-Space Plane Program, 1982–1990," *Proceedings of the 1991 Acquisition Research Symposium*, vol. 2 (Washington, D.C.: Defense Systems Management Association, 1991); "Aerospace Asia," *Journal of East Asian Affairs* 6 (Summer 1992): 504–28; "Managing a Revolutionary Technology, American Style: The National Aerospace Plane," *Essays in Business and Economic History* 12 (1994): 118–32; "Hypersonic Hopes: Planning for NASP, 1982–1990," *Air Power History* 41 (Spring 1994): 36–48; "Space Plane Challenges Full Spectrum," *National Defense*, December 1993, pp. 32–33; and the predecessor to this article, "The National Aerospace Plane: Origins to Apex, 1982–1992," in Jacob Neufeld, ed., *Proceedings of "Technology and the Air Force: A Retrospective Assessment"* (Washington, D.C.: Office of Air Force History, forthcoming). All program documents cited are in the possession of the U.S. Air Force, National Aerospace Plane Program. A fuller discussion of the issues appears in a document prepared for the program by the author for Science Applications International Corporation, "National Aero-Space Plane (NASP) Advanced Technology Impacts, Final Report: Program Management Document," 31 Mar. 1995. It is unlikely, however, that many of the internal documents remain in program files. Col. Ted Wierzbanowski (Ret.) donated his personal files, which contained many of these documents, to the Edwards Air Force Base History Office. Other material was taken from more general studies of defense contracting and procurement, including Jacques S. Gansler, *The Defense Industry* (Cambridge, Mass.: MIT Press, 1980) and his follow-up book, *Affording Defense* (Cambridge, Mass.: MIT Press, 1989), as well as Michael Porter, *The Competitive Advantage of Nations* (New York: Free Press, 1990).

2. An excellent history of these developments appears in Richard P. Hallion, ed., *The Hypersonic Revolution: Eight Case Studies in the History of Hypersonic Technologies: From Max Valier to Project Prime*, vol. 1, *1924–1967* (Dayton, Ohio: Special Staff Office, Aeronautical Systems Division, 1987), and *The Hypersonic Revolution: Eight Case Studies in the History of Hypersonic Technologies: From the Scramjet to the National Aero-Space Plane*, vol. 2, *1964–1986* (Dayton, Ohio: Special Staff Office, Aeronautical Systems Division, 1987). The Schweikart manuscript cited in note 1 was commissioned as vol. 3 in this series.

3. Several excellent works have discussed the space shuttle program, including Roger D. Launius, "NASA and the Decision to Build the Space Shuttle, 1969–72," *The Historian* 57 (Autumn 1994): 17–34; Joseph Trento, *Prescription for Disaster: From the Glory of Apollo to the Betrayal of the Shuttle* (New York: Crown, 1987); John Logsdon, "The Space Shuttle Program: A Policy Failure?" *Science*, 30 May 1986, pp. 1099–1105, and his "The Space Shuttle Decision: Technology and Political Choice," *Journal of Contemporary Business* 7 (1978): 13–30.

4. It is hardly accurate, however, to suggest (as NASP advocates often did) that the United States

had lost the competitive edge in space-related activities. For example, despite the downsizing of the air force, the number of satellite and other orbital payload launches had grown dramatically in the 1980s. By 1990, the U.S. military space budget had increased almost 550 percent, far outstripping Japan's growth and eclipsed over a four-year period (in rate of growth *only*) by France. The twelve European Community nations *combined* only spent one-twelfth the U.S. level. Moreover, U.S. satellite manufacturing contractors dominated worldwide satellite markets. American manufacturers held 72 percent of the market, with two U.S. manufacturers—GE and Hughes—each having three times more market value in satellites projected for the period 1990–96 than their nearest competitor. The Europeans commissioned their own study, which concluded that Hughes and GE "have pulled away from the competition and appear likely to pace the market in the 1990s" (Peter deSelding, "Study Finds U.S. Builders Are at Top of Market," *Space News*, 25–31 Jan. 1993, p. 7). America's space industry, according to the study, remained "clearly dominant." In Sep. 1993, European governments expressed similar sentiments when they allied with industry officials to block "a threat of American domination of the future market for mobile satellite communications" (deSelding, "Europeans Fear U.S. Monopoly in New Market," ibid., 20–26 Sep. 1993, p. 1). Government officials at that time feared "a risk of monopoly by U.S.-led consortia in the provision of (satellite communications) services. We want to make sure that our industry is not left out in the cold," a spokesman said of the new telecommunications satellites (ibid., p. 20).

The U.S. market share of all launches had declined, but the world launch market had expanded to more than fifteen a year. American decline in the share of the world launch market represented both the appearance of several new competitors, including *Ariane*, Japan's N-1 and H-1, and China's *Long March*. But it also reflected a two-year grounding of the space shuttle fleet following the *Challenger* disaster. Nevertheless, becoming preoccupied with the share of the launch market in the face of overwhelming dominance in the satellite market is akin to Hollywood worrying about who makes compact disc players when it controls the world market in the music that goes on the CDs.

5. Donald Johnson, Angel Espinosa, and Jeffrey Althuis, "NASP Derived Vehicles: Not Just to Space," paper presented to the AIAA Fourth Annual Aerospace Planes Conference, 1–4 Dec. 1992, #AIAA-92-5052.

6. The official documentation appears on the surface to provide little support for the notion that NASP was viewed widely as a replacement for traditional launch systems that used rockets. For example, the Office of Technology Assessment (OTA) produced two separate reports in which it dealt with NASP. The first, *Launch Options for the Future: Special Report* (1988) (Washington, D.C.: Office of Technology Assessment, 1988) treated NASP as an "emerging technology" and did not assess the costs or potential benefits of a scramjet-powered aircraft system on space launch capability. But by 1990 when the OTA produced its *Access to Space: The Future of U.S. Space Transportation Systems* (1990) (Washington, D.C.: Office of Technology Assessment, 1990), a different attitude was evident. NASP was compared with other launch systems, which were evaluated higher than NASP in their potential to reduce launch costs and meet demand. NASP played a prominent role only in the "expanded demand scenario." Industry studies, however, proved far more optimistic about the returns from NASP-derived vehicles. Several contractor-commissioned studies—which the government maintained were biased—estimated extremely substantial gains by NASP-derived vehicles over traditional rocket-powered launch systems. See A. Totan, J. Fong, R. Murphy, and W. Powell, "NASP Derived Vehicle (NDV) Space Launch Operating Costs and Program Cost Recovery Options," paper presented to AIAA Third International Aerospace Planes Conference, Dec. 1991, #AIAA-91-5080; Y. Ohkami, T. Yamanaka, and M. Maita, "Space Activities in the 21st Century—Expectation for [the] Space Plane," ibid., #AIAA-91-5085; General Dynamics, *Future Roles for Hyper-Velocity Vehicles* (Ft. Worth: General Dynamics [now Lockheed Ft. Worth], 1990).

7. The difficulties of the task were well recognized, even at the time. See William Piland, "Technology Challenge for the National Aero-Space Plane," paper presented to the 38th International As-

tronautical Congress, 14 Oct. 1989, Brighton, Eng.); Ted Wierzbanowski, "The Challenge of the X-30 Flight Test," paper presented to the AIAA First National Aero-Space Plane Conference, 20–21 July 1989, Dayton, Ohio); and Carl Sypniewski, "The NASP Challenge: Technical Breakthrough," ibid.

8. Trish Gilmartin, "Bob Williams: Aggressive Nature Sets Him Apart from Government Managers," *Defense News*, Oct. 1989; T. A. Heppenheimer, "The Hypersonic World of Robert Williams," *Air and Space*, Feb./Mar. 1988, pp. 52–55; Tony duPont, interview with author, Cleveland, Ohio, 24 Oct. 1989; Robert Williams, interviews with author, Washington, D.C., various dates, 1989–94.

9. An indication of Williams's vision appears in an address he made to the First International Conference on Hypersonic Flight in the 21st Century, entitled "Forces for Change and the Future of Hypersonic Flight in the 21st Century," (20–23 Sep., Grand Forks, North Dakota), copy in author's possession and available through DARPA [now Advanced Research Projects Agency, or ARPA].

10. A few publications appreciated the enormity of the change SSTO and/or scramjet flight offered. See William Welling, "Spaceplane," *International Combat Arms*, Jan. 1989, pp. 66–73, 92; Malcolm W. Browne, "Clean Hydrogen Beckons Aviation Engineers," *New York Times*, 24 May 1988; and "Faster Than the Speed of Sound? You Bet," *Washington Times*, 12 Oct. 1988. Of course, *Aviation Week & Space Technology* [henceforth called *Aviation Week*] maintained steady reporting on the project. See Craig Couvalt, "Aero-Space Plane Leading U.S. Hypersonic Research," *Aviation Week*, 27 Feb. 1989, pp. 18–19.

11. Col. Vince Rausch, interview with author, Washington, D.C., July 18, 1989.

12. "Memorandum of Understanding Between the DOD and NASA for the Conduct of the National Aero-Space Plane Program," 18 June 1986, in Robert Barthelemy's files, NASP office, WPAFB.

13. Author interviews with the NASP directors who oversaw the contractors' work support the material for this section, including interviews with Lt. Col. Rodney Earehart, Maj. Dennis Minor, Lt. Col. Rick Roach, Lt. Col. Ken Griffen, Lt. Col. Scott Parks, Maj. Tim Roberts, Tom Richmond, Frank Boensch, and Col. Tad Wierzbanowski, all interviewed in Dayton, Ohio, 1989–94.

14. Material on the airframe contractors was derived from numerous author interviews with program managers, including Larry Winslow and Frank Rafchiek, Boeing, Seattle, Wash., July 14, 1989; Tom Cornell, Boeing, telephone interview, 29 Aug. 1989; Frank Capuccio, Bob Sheldon, and other anonymous Lockheed officials, Burbank, Calif., 12 July 1989; Hershel Sams, John Steurer, and Ed Will, McDonnell Douglas, 10 July 1989; Fred Kelly, General Dynamics, 6 July 1989; and Curt Wiler, Rockwell International, Downey, Calif., 11 July 1989.

15. Author interviews with Tom Donahue, General Electric, Cincinnati, Ohio, 5 July 1989; Carl Sypniewski, Pratt & Whitney, West Palm Beach, Fla., 9 Oct. 1989; and Fred Pienemann and Barry Waldman, Rocketdyne, 12 July 1989, as well as extensive interviews with Waldman between 1989 and 1994.

16. On these issues, also see Brenda Forman, "The Political Process in Systems Architecture Design," notes for course at the University of Southern California, fall 1992, in author's files.

17. Craig Couvalt, "X-30 Technology Advancing Despite Management Rift," *Aviation Week*, 7 Mar. 1988, pp. 36–43.

18. Material for this section comes from author interviews with Terry Ronald, Dayton, Ohio, 10 Apr. 1990; Howard Wright, Dayton, Ohio, 31 May 1989; Richard Culpepper, Dayton, Ohio, 20 June 1991; Tom Gregory, telephone interview, 12 June 1990; Chuck Anderson, Dayton, Ohio, 27 Feb. 1990; Robert Gulcher, Downey, Calif., and telephone interview, 11 July 1989, as well as "National Aero-Space Plane Program Technology Maturation Plan, Version A," Dec. 1986, in NASP JPO files; "Report of the Defense Science Board, 1988," in NASP JPO files; and S.C. Dixon, Darryl Tenney, Donald Rumler, Allen Wieting, and R. M. Bader, "Structures and Materials Technology Issues for Reusable Launch Vehicles," *NASA Technical Memorandum 87626* (Hampton, Va.: NASA Langley Research Center, 1985).

19. Bruce Abell, telephone interview with author, 13 Mar. 1990.

20. Williams telephone interviews, various dates.

21. On NASP budget issues, see John D. Moteff, "National Aero-Space Plane," *Congressional Research Service Issue Brief*, IB89128, 2 Jan. 1991.

22. Author interviews with NASP program directors cited in note 11, as well as interviews with Barthelemy, Williams, and Gen. Kenneth Staten, Dayton, Ohio, 17 July 1989.

23. Some NASP insiders took umbrage at the notion that Cheney ended the program, citing the $89 million contribution from NASA. But NASA had no intention of serving as the sole source of funds for the X-30, and had the Cheney cut stood, NASA would have ended its NASP participation.

24. One of the most effective briefings created by the contractors during this time was "Pioneering New Frontiers: Developing National Assets, Supporting National Interests," summer 1989, NAR files, and in author's possession. Some directors had favored such an approach all along, especially NASA's Howard Wright, who gave out copies of Ira Magaziner and Mark Patinkin's book, *The Silent War: Inside the Global Battles Shaping America's Future* (New York: Random House, 1989), to all JPO directors.

25. Author interviews with Barthelemy and Col. Ted Wierzbanowski, Dayton, Ohio, and Palmdale, Calif., various dates, 1988–94.

26. Whether or not there were advantages to team formation versus traditional competition in military procurement remains in dispute. See the discussion in "American Aerospace in the 21st Century: The Role of the National Aerospace Plane," 17 Apr. 1992, copies available from U.S. Space Foundation, Boulder, Colo. (esp. the comments of Adam Jaffe and Warren Brookes); Donald Pilling, *Competition in Defense Procurement* (Washington, D.C.: Brookings Institution, 1989); Michael L. Beltrano, "A Case Study of the Sparrow AIM-7F," *Program Manager*, Sep.–Oct. 1985, pp. 28–35; Frank Swofford, "U.S. Must Breathe Life into Shipyards," *Defense News*, 8–14 June 1992, pp. 27–28; Robert Drewes, *The Air Force and the Great Engine War* (Washington, D.C.: Defense University Press, 1987); Jacques Gansler, "International Arms Collaboration," unpublished paper presented at Harvard University, in author's possession; Thomas McNaugher, *New Weapons, Old Politics: America's Military Procurement Muddle* (Washington, D.C.: Brookings Institution, 1989); Fen Olser Hampson, *Unguided Missiles: How America Buys Its Weapons* (New York: W.W. Norton, 1989); A. Ernest Fitzgerald, *The Pentagonists: An Insider's View of Waste Mismanagement and Fraud in Defense Spending* (Boston: Houghton Mifflin, 1989); Frank Gertcher, *The Political Economy of National Defense* (Boulder, Colo,: Westview Press, 1987); and D. Douglas Dalgleish and Larry Schweikart, *Trident* (Carbondale, Ill.: Southern Illinois University Press, 1984).

27. Fred Kelly Jr. to National Aero-Space Plane, "Memorandum of Understanding, March 23, 1989," and C. O. Wiler to Air Force Systems Command National Aero-Space Plane Office, 25 May 1989, in NAK (Contracting), JPO files.

28. Material on Waldman's selection comes from author interviews with Barthelemy, Dayton, Ohio, 12 Apr. 1990; Waldman, Seal Beach and Palmdale, Calif., 9–14 Aug. 1990; and Wierzbanowski, Dayton, Ohio, various dates, 1990–91, as well as dozens of internal NASP documents in contracting and planning.

29. "Five Firms Form Unique Partnership on AeroSpace Plane," *Washington Times*, 25 May 1990.

30. Author interviews with Waldman, Seal Beach and Palmdale, Calif., various dates; Bill Imfeld, Dayton, Ohio, 9 Apr. 1991; Tom Harsha, Seal Beach and Palmdale, Calif., 9–14 Aug. 1991.

31. Stanley W. Kandebo, "Lifting Body Design Is Key to Single-Stage-to-Orbit," *Aviation Week*, 29 Oct. 1990, pp. 36–37; "Teaming Agreement Stresses Equality among Five NASP Prime Contractors," ibid., pp. 38–39; "NASP Researchers Forge Ahead with Propulsion and Technical Advances," ibid., pp. 40–41; "JPO Studying Flight Test Issues in Early Phases of X-30 Program," ibid., pp. 46–47.

32. "Teaming Agreement Stresses Equality," *Aviation Week*, 29 Oct. 1989, pp. 38–39.

33. Author interviews with Waldman and Barthelemy, Washington, D.C., Dayton, Ohio, and Palmdale, Calif., various dates, 1991.

34. Suggestions for the X-30X came from the "X-30X Concept Evaluation Study, 17 Dec. 1992, Detachment 5 files, Palmdale, Calif.

35. Printout of e-mail from Col. Phil Bruce to the JPO, 11 Dec. 1992.

36. The issue of scale at one point had been seen as critical. In late 1989, the program solicited from the contractors responses to the following questions: (1) What speed must the research vehicle attain to have confidence that it can achieve orbit? and (2) What scale must the research vehicle be to have confidence that it would achieve orbit? The contractors responded to the first question with speeds of Mach 15 (McDonnell Douglas) to 25 (Rockwell) as necessary to adequately predict scramjet performance, materials, and aerothermal survivability necessary for orbital insertion; and they all agreed that the vehicle had to be at least 70 percent (Rockwell) to full scale (McDonnell Douglas) for reliable prediction of performance. Based on those study results, the JPO concluded that nothing short of a full-scale, Mach 25 aircraft would provide useful data. See "X-30 Options Study Results," in "National Aero-Space Plane (NASP) Advance Technology Impacts: FINAL REPORT, Program Management Document," 3:26, in author's possession.

37. Leonard David, "Unorthodox New DC-X Rocket Ready for First Tests," *Space News*, 11–17 Jan. 1993, p. 10; Maj. Jess Sponable, "Single Stage Rocket Technology," *Program Review*, Mar. 1993, NAR files, NASP Program, WPAFB.

38. John Swihart, "Keynote Address: Advanced Technology Demonstrators, Prototypes, and Hypersonic Flight," AIAA Fourth Annual International Aerospace Planes Conference, 1–4 Dec. 1992; J. Gabrynowicz, John Graham, Matthew Bille, and Deborah Bille, "The Case for International Cooperation on Hypersonic Technology Development," paper presented to the AIAA Fourth Annual International Aerospace Planes Conference, 1–4 Dec. 1992, #AIAA92-5000.

39. Indeed, in the late 1980s and early 1990s, a sudden burst of books warned the United States against losing its technological advantage to foreigners by "selling our security." See Alfred Eckes, "Trading American Interests," *Foreign Affairs*, Fall 1992, pp. 135–52; Martin and Susan Tolchin, *Selling Our Security: The Erosion of America's Assets* (New York: Knopf, 1992); Marc Levinson, "The Hand Wringers," *Newsweek*, 26 Oct. 1992, pp. 44–46.

40. Waldman, interview with author, Palmdale, Calif., and telephone interview, 13 Dec. 1993.

41. Even if unsuccessful, such an approach has been taken repeatedly in history, as in the case of the British government's offer of ten thousand pounds for a reliable method of establishing longitude. See Dava Sobel, *Longitude* (New York: Walker and Co., 1995).

About the Authors

Janet R. Daly Bednarek is associate professor of history at the University of Dayton. She is the author of several publications, including "Lost Opportunities and False Beacons: The Failure of Planning in Dayton, Ohio," in *Proceedings of the Sixth National Conference on American Planning History* (1995); "From the Baydorfers to the Strategic Air Command: Aviation Dreams in Omaha, Nebraska, 1908–1948," *Journal of the West* (1997); and a United States Air Force history of the enlisted force. She is presently working on a history of airfield establishment in the interwar years.

Louis Brown is emeritus member of the Department of Terrestrial Magnetism, Carnegie Institution of Washington, D.C. A career physicist, he has turned to history as a discipline and is completing a study of radar in World War II.

Tom D. Crouch is senior curator in the Aeronautics Department at the National Air and Space Museum, Smithsonian Institution. A well-known historian of aviation, he is the author of the *The Bishop's Boys* (1989), a prize-winning biography of the Wright brothers, and several other books.

Deborah G. Douglas, a recent Ph.D. graduate from the University of Pennsylvania's history of science and technology program, is currently working on a history of aviation research in the National Advisory Committee for Aeronautics at the NASA Langley Research Center, Hampton, Virginia. Her publications include *U.S. Women in Aviation: 1940–1985* (1990). She is completing a history of airfield development.

Norriss S. Hetherington teaches the history of science at the University of California, Berkeley. He is the author of numerous books and articles and is presently working on a history of the National Advisory Committee for Aeronautics.

Robin Higham, a pilot in the Royal Air Force from 1943 to 1947, is professor of history at Kansas State University, Manhattan. He is the author of numerous studies of aviation, including *Britain's Imperial Air Routes, 1918–1939* (1960), and *Air Power: A Concise History* (1988). He is also the editor of the *Journal of the West* and president of Sunflower University Press.

Roger D. Launius is chief historian of the National Aeronautics and Space Administration. He is the author and editor of several books and articles on aerospace history, including *NASA: A History of the U.S. Civil Space Program* (1994), *Spaceflight and the Myth of Presidential Leadership* (1997), and *Frontiers of Space Exploration* (1998). He is presently completing a study of the development of aviation in the American West.

William M. Leary, a former flight operations officer for KLM Royal Dutch Airlines at Gander, Newfoundland, is professor of history at the University of Georgia, Athens. He has written numerous books and articles, including a history of the China National Aviation Corporation, Civil Air Transport, and the U.S. Air Mail Service, 1918–27. He was the 1996–97 Guggenheim Fellow at the National Air and Space Museum, Smithsonian Institution, where he completed a history of the first undersea polar mission.

Stephen L. McFarland is a member of the history faculty of Auburn University. He is the author of numerous books and articles relating to aviation technology and air power, including *To Command the Sky: The Battle for Air Superiority over Germany, 1942–1944* (1991), with Wesley Phillips Newton.

Michael J. Neufeld is a curator of aeronautics at the National Air and Space Museum, Smithsonian Institution, Washington, D.C. He is the author of the prize-winning *The Rocket and the Reich* (1995).

Larry Schweikart is professor of history at the University of Dayton, Ohio. He has written several books and articles, including *Trident* (1984), and a history of the NASP program.

Bayla Singer is an independent scholar in Palm Beach Gardens, Florida.

James O. Young is historian of the United States Air Force Flight Test Center, Edwards Air Force Base, California. He is a specialist in the history of high-speed flight and has written numerous articles and monographs on the subject.

Index